BANKING AND ECONOMIC DEVELOPMENT

BANKING

AND

ECONOMIC DEVELOPMENT

Some Lessons of History

EDITED BY

RONDO CAMERON

New York
OXFORD UNIVERSITY PRESS
London 1972 Toronto

We have need of history in its entirety,
not to fall back into it,
but to see if we can escape from it.

José Ortega y Gasset

Those who cannot remember the past
are condemned to repeat it.

George Santayana

Preface

Some years ago I published, in collaboration with others, a volume entitled *Banking in the Early Stages of Industrialization*.[1] The primary purpose of that book was to discover what, if anything, could be learned from historical experience that would be relevant to the problem of financing economic development in contemporary underdeveloped and developing countries. It was my intention to follow up with a study of recent and contemporary banking experience in Latin America. Unfortunately for that purpose, my attentions were deflected elsewhere before the project could be completed, although some of my collaborators and students persevered and produced valuable contributions.[2] Meanwhile I encouraged my students to undertake research on similar topics, and other young scholars likewise discovered the fascination and importance of the relationship between banking and economic development. The present volume may, therefore, be regarded as a report on work in progress. Before a definitive synthesis can be achieved many more case studies, both historical and contemporary, must be made, criticized, and

1. Rondo Cameron, with the collaboration of Olga Crisp, Hugh T. Patrick, and Richard Tilly, *Banking in the Early Stages of Industrialization: A Study in Comparative Economic History* (New York, 1967).

2. Robert L. Bennett, *The Financial Sector and Economic Development: The Mexican Case* (Baltimore, 1965); Carlos M. Pelaez, "The Economic Consequences of Monetary, Exchange and Fiscal Orthodoxy in Brazil, 1889–1945," and other articles by the same author in a special issue of the *Revista Brasileira de Economia*, June 1971. Dr. Pelaez is currently collaborating with Sergio Ramos da Silva and Wilson Suzigan on "A Monetary History of Brazil, 1822–1970." Two of my former students at the Instituto de Economía in Santiago, Chile, Jorge Arrate and Francisco Mezzadri, prepared *memorias* dealing with the financial systems of Chile and Argentina, respectively; although not carried far enough to merit publication, they clearly showed the applicability to Latin America of the methodology developed for *Banking in the Early Stages of Industrialization*.

revised; it is a task that will require many years and an international collaboration. Happily, such collaboration is already under way on an informal
basis.[3]

Although the substantive chapters here are in part a report on work in
progress, they can stand on their own as valuable contributions to the
economic history of the countries with which they deal. Those concerned with
economies that have heretofore been unduly neglected, especially by English-
speaking scholars, can justly be termed pioneering.

Needless to say, my collaborators in this volume have exercised complete
freedom of expression, but it should be pointed out that they do not adhere
to any one school or doctrine. I myself disagree with some of their interpretations in particular instances; in the introductory chapter I point out some
of the more important alternative interpretations. By this I do not in any
way mean to detract from the value of the chapters themselves, for I believe
that anyone interested in the relationship between the banking system and
economic development, or in the economic history of the countries treated,
can learn much from them.

Numerous individuals and institutions have contributed to the preparation
of this volume. My collaborators have incurred a number of obligations that
it would be inappropriate for me to comment on here. Personally, I wish
to acknowledge especially the support, primarily for research on other topics,
but which enabled me to put the finishing touches on my contribution to
this volume, of the John Simon Guggenheim Memorial Foundation, the
Rockefeller Foundation, and Emory University. As editor, I wish to acknowledge the cheerful and efficient aid of my secretary and research assistant,
Mrs. Millicent Lambert.

Bellagio, Italy   RONDO CAMERON
July 1971

3. The Fifth International Congress of Economic History (Leningrad, 1970) devoted a
session to "Banking and Credit as Factors in Economic Growth," with contributions on
Great Britain, France, socialist Poland, and the recently liberated countries of Asia, as well
as my general report. These will be published in the proceedings of the congress. The
Institute of Economic History of the University of Copenhagen has undertaken a compre-
hensive study of Danish industrialization employing the methodology of *Banking in the
Early Stages of Industrialization*; see Svend Aage Hansen, *Early Industrialisation in Denmark*
(Copenhagen, 1970).

Notes on Contributors

RONDO CAMERON is William Rand Kenan University Professor, Emory University. He served as founder and director (1959–69) of the Graduate Program in Economic History in the University of Wisconsin. He has also taught at the University of Chicago, Yale University, the University of Glasgow, and the University of Chile.

JON S. COHEN is Assistant Professor of Economics in Yale University. He received his Ph.D. in 1966 from the University of California (Berkeley), where he studied with Henry Rosovsky.

GEORGE D. GREEN is Assistant Professor of Economics and History in the University of Minnesota. He received his Ph.D. in 1968 from Stanford University, where he studied with David Potter and John G. Gurley. During 1969–70 he was a Research Fellow at Harvard's Charles Warren Center for Studies in American History.

JOHN R. LAMPE, Assistant Professor of History at California State College, Hayward, received his Ph.D. from the University of Wisconsin in 1971. He was a Foreign Service Officer in the Department of State from 1964 to 1967 and served as Economics Officer in the United States Embassies in Belgrade and Sofia.

RICHARD L. RUDOLPH is Assistant Professor of History in the University of Minnesota. He has done research in Vienna and Prague both before and since receiving his Ph.D. from the University of Wisconsin in 1968.

RICHARD SYLLA is Associate Professor of Economics in North Carolina State University. He received his Ph.D. from Harvard University, where he studied with Alexander Gerschenkron, in 1968.

GABRIEL TORTELLA is Assistant Professor of History in the University of Pittsburgh. A native of Spain, he received his Ph.D. from the University of Wisconsin in 1971. He helped found and headed the Economic History Group in the Bank of Spain Research Department (1967–68).

KOZO YAMAMURA is Professor of Economics and Asian Studies in the University of Washington. He is author of *Economic Policy in Postwar Japan: Growth vs. Economic Democracy*, and numerous articles on Japanese economic development and economic history.

Contents

BANKING AND ECONOMIC DEVELOPMENT

CHAPTER I

Introduction

The great differences in methods of production, levels of living, and quality of life that currently exist between rich and poor nations emerged for the most part within the last two centuries—even, one might argue, within the past century. Although one can detect obvious differences in these matters in the eighteenth century and earlier, perhaps as early as the fifteenth century for Eurasia, the width of the gap increased enormously in the course of the nineteenth century as a result of the phenomenon of industrialization, which, beginning in Great Britain, spread with greater or lesser rapidity to some— but by no means all—of the nations of Europe and North America, and established beachheads in a few other areas. In the first half of the nineteenth century Belgium and France followed Britain's lead; by the middle of the century Germany was on the eve of its great industrial expansion. After about 1850, and especially after 1870, nations that were beginning to industrialize could imitate or borrow from the accumulation of skills, techniques, experience, liquid capital, and institutional innovations of these more advanced nations.

If one views economic development in global perspective, the half-century or so preceding World War I acquires special significance. It was a period of rapid improvement of transportation and communication facilities, of relatively free trade, and of large-scale migration of both capital and people. In short, it was an exceptionally favorable period for the diffusion of industrialism, and the period in which today's pattern of development and underdevelopment took shape. In addition to those European countries that had already experienced substantial industrialization, Switzerland, the Netherlands, and Scandinavia—especially Sweden—industrialized rapidly. In contrast, the lands of the Habsburg Monarchy adopted modern industry much more slowly and incompletely, whereas the Mediterranean countries

3

experienced only weak and largely ineffectual attempts to acquire modern industry. Throughout eastern Europe, despite Russia's state-prodded great "spurt" of the 1890's, modern industries were rarities on the prewar landscape. Outside Europe, the United States, notwithstanding a population/resources ratio that seemed to indicate that the nation would have to specialize in agriculture and extractive industries, emerged as the industrial colossus of the world. Even more surprisingly, densely populated Japan, after centuries of self-imposed isolation, moved rapidly toward industrialization; Japan was far from a major industrial nation on the eve of World War I, but it had already laid the foundations for its subsequent impressive performance. The British dominions attained high living standards by specializing in primary production while remaining receptive to both technical and financial innovations. Elsewhere in the world, modern methods in industry, agriculture, or finance were exceptions to the rule; they were spotty and superficial.

Since 1914, except for the rise of the Soviet Union as a military-industrial giant and the easily explicable case of Israel, the relative rank of rich and poor nations has not changed greatly. In spite of wars and depressions, the nations of western Europe, North America, and Japan have not only held their lead but have increased it. There have been scattered instances of the beginnings of industrialization and agricultural modernization in Latin America, eastern Europe, and both the People's Republic of China and the Republic of China (Taiwan), but on the whole the pattern of development and underdevelopment is much the same as it was in 1914. Thus it is to the latter half of the nineteenth century that one should look to discover why some nations were able to modernize and become wealthy, whereas others, with essentially the same opportunity, remained wedded to traditional methods of production and ways of life.

A THEORETICAL FRAMEWORK

Why are some nations rich and others poor? Conventional economic analysis is of limited direct usefulness in answering this question. It can, to be sure, point to key differences between rich and poor nations: in the former more capital is applied in production than in the latter; in rich nations there is greater specialization and division of labor than in the poor, with the consequence, among others, of greater "skill, dexterity and judgement" in the application of labor, as Adam Smith pointed out two hundred years ago. But these statements are essentially tautological. They are not operationally useful either in explaining how the present inequalities came about or in advising policy-makers in poor countries what they should do in order to overcome their countries' poverty. The reason for this is not difficult to discover: conventional economic theory, whether micro or macro, static or dynamic, assumes that certain parameters of the economic system are "given and fixed." Prominent among these parameters are tastes, technology, and institutions, both economic and noneconomic. Now, in the historical process of the economic development of rich nations it was precisely in those categories that some of the most significant changes occurred. In short, in moving from conventional economic analysis of developed countries to the study of actual economic development, the parameters become the variables, and conventional methods, although not wholly useless, are of much more limited applicability.

What is required for the study of concrete cases of development (and failure of development) is a broader framework of analysis. This can be supplied by economic history. Historically, the process of development involves interactions among four broad categories or classes of factors, or variables: population, resources, technology, and social institutions. Unfortunately for the purposes of precise analysis, these bundles or clusters of variables are not single-valued, nor, except for population, can they be easily quantified. Nevertheless, it is useful and even necessary to take them into account in order to arrive at a clear understanding of the process of development. For example, when a society has unchanging technology and social institutions—the situation in most societies for much of human history—the resources available to that society set the effective upper limits to its economic achievements in terms of the number and well-being of its members.[1] But of course the essence of economic development is change in both technology and social institutions, change that permits those upper limits to be expanded. In the last two centuries in particular, technological change has been the driving force behind industrialization and its concomitants, urbanization and the modernization of agriculture. Social institutions may either hinder or facilitate technological innovation. In general, institutions tend to be stable and to resist change; but the possibility of institutional innovation does exist. One such innovation of considerable importance in the history of industrialization was the invention of modern banking systems.

THE ROLE OF BANKING

Economists have expressed a wide variety of opinions on the effectiveness of banking systems in promoting or facilitating economic development.

---

1. This statement ignores the role of capital; but capital equipment, including buildings, is itself embodied technology, and the amount or value so embodied is a function of total output, individual and social choice, and efficiency of financial intermediation. Much the same can be said for human capital. In other words, in the long run, the amount or value of capital in a society is a result, not a cause, of development or the lack thereof.

Schumpeter, the first modern economist to study the relationship, regarded the banking system as one of the two key agents (the other being entrepreneurship) in the whole process of development.[2] John G. Gurley, on the other hand, has written that "recent experience strongly suggests that banking systems as intermediaries are not highly essential to the growth process."[3] It is probably safe to say that the true importance of the banking function lies somewhere between these two extremes. Stanley Engerman has recently estimated that the cost to the American economy of the failure to renew the charter of the Second Bank of the United States in 1834 was on the order of 0.1 to 0.15 of one per cent of the gross national product.[4] The percentage figure seems small, but the dollar value ... ? In any case, that was one bank; moreover, the main office of the bank in Philadelphia continued to operate for several years under a charter from the state of Pennsylvania, and the branches in other states were immediately replaced by dozens of state-chartered institutions. It would be interesting if an econometric historian would undertake to estimate the social saving attributable to the banking system as a whole. But could a modern, industrial, market-oriented economy function at all without a banking system? Perhaps the "axiom of indispensability," with which Robert Fogel belabored the railway buffs,[5] should be laid at the door of the banking enthusiasts.

This book is not econometric history, and we make no claim of indispensability for the banking system.[6] In terms of the theoretical framework sketched above, the banking system is one of many institutions that impinge on the economy and affect its performance for better or worse. (Others are government, religious institutions, the educational system, ethics and esthetics, etc.; the list is almost infinitely extensible and divisible, depending

2. J. A. Schumpeter, *The Theory of Economic Development* (Cambridge, Mass., 1933); see also Schumpeter, *Business Cycles: A Theoretical, Historical, and Statistical Analysis of the Capitalist Process* (New York, 1939).

3. *American Economic Review*, LVII (1967), 953. Gurley gives as examples "many socialist countries" and Taiwan, Israel, and Venezuela. He might also have mentioned Kuwait and Libya.

4. Stanley L. Engerman, "A Note on the Economic Consequences of the Second Bank of the United States," *Journal of Political Economy*, 78 (July/August 1970), pp. 727–28. Engerman also estimates the social saving attributable to paper currency (banknotes) at from 0.35 to 0.58 of one per cent in the period 1825–1858.

5. Robert W. Fogel, *Railroads and American Economic Growth: Essays in Econometric History* (Baltimore, 1964).

6. In the anti-banking hysteria following the panics of 1837 and 1839 some American states *did* try to dispense with a banking system. The consequences are highly illuminating. See, *inter alia*, Alice E. Smith, *George Smith's Money: A Scottish Investor in America* (Madison, Wis., 1966) for the story of the Milwaukee Fire and Marine Insurance Co., and Bray Hammond, "Banking in the Early West: Monopoly, Prohibition, and Laissez-faire," *Journal of Economic History*, 8 (May 1948), pp. 1–25.

upon the nature and scope of the analysis.) As an economic institution (unlike ethics or esthetics), the banking system might be expected to be more directly and more positively related to the performance of the economy than most noneconomic institutions; but such cannot be taken for granted. Religious institutions, for example, including both the resources they control and the values they espouse, may have a more powerful influence on the economy, either positive or negative, than the banking system. Certainly that is true of the institution of government, which has the power to shape and control the banking system. A banking system may make a positive contribution to economic growth and development, but its effect may be offset or counteracted by other factors, such as an unfavorable resource endowment, a population that grows either too slowly or too rapidly, or inept government policies. Conversely, if other factors are sufficiently favorable, even a bad or indifferent banking system may not absolutely hinder growth. What can be asserted without fear of contradiction is that any given banking system might, with different policies, have been made more or less effective in its contribution to economic development.

At the risk of appearing pedantic, it may be worthwhile to review briefly the functions of a banking system. The first and essential function of any banking system is to act as an intermediary between savers (or holders of idle money balances) and persons able and willing to borrow. (The relationship is sometimes stated as one between "savers and investors," but there is no necessity for the borrower to invest, in the sense of acquiring or producing a new capital good.) This function is shared, however, with a number of other financial institutions, including insurance companies, savings and loan associations, and ordinary moneylenders or pawnbrokers.

What distinguishes banks from other financial intermediaries—this is the second function, and the one that makes them of special importance in market economies—is that they alone, of all private (i.e. non-government) institutions, furnish part or all of the means of payment, or money supply.[7] They may do this either by issuing their own promises to pay (that is, banknotes); or by holding and transferring the monetary deposits of the public. In either case they are in a position not merely to serve as the custodians of the stock of money, but also to increase or decrease that stock. The consequences of this power for society at large can be considerable—and either favorable or unfavorable.

A third possible function, although it is not inherent in the definition of a banking system, is the provision of entrepreneurial talent and guidance for the economy as a whole. That is, instead of restricting themselves to a purely intermediary function, bankers may actively seek out and exploit profitable

---

7. Cf. R. S. Sayers, *Modern Banking* (5th ed., Oxford, 1960), p. 1.

undertakings in manufacturing, commerce, or any other productive activity. In modern, highly industrialized economies this function is rarely directly performed by banks; indeed, the very idea meets with the disapproval of the authorities, both legal and theoretical. But historically, in underdeveloped and especially in developing economies, this banking function has been of great importance.

The way in which banks perform these functions in underdeveloped and developing economies may well determine the degree of success of the development effort. As intermediaries, they may vigorously seek out and attract reservoirs of idle funds which will be allocated to entrepreneurs for investment in projects with a high rate of social return; or they may listlessly exploit their quasi-monopolistic position and fritter away investment possibilities with unproductive loans. As creators and providers of the means of payment, they may redirect real resources into more productive activities; or, as a result of government pressure or private corruption, they may swamp the economy with a flood of inflationary paper issues. Finally, as potential entrepreneurs, they may set their country on the road to continuing growth, or they may waste its resources in uneconomical or fraudulent activities.

In *Banking in the Early Stages of Industrialization* my collaborators and I made a comparative study of the role of banking in the economic development of the first five European nations to achieve substantial industrialization —namely England, Scotland, France, Belgium, and Germany—as well as its role in two important cases of "latecomers" to industrialization, Imperial Russia and Meiji Japan. In that book we adopted what might be called, without any specific biological, sociological, or architectural implications, a "structural–functional" theory of the role of banking in economic development. Whether or not the banking system makes a positive and substantial contribution to economic development does not depend primarily upon the personal qualities of the bankers, although those qualities are not a negligible consideration. The structural characteristics of the system, and the laws, regulations, and customs that govern its behavior, will normally be far more important determinants of its effectiveness. This was perceived as early as 1913 by officials of J. P. Morgan and Company, who declared that the concentration of financial power in the United States was "not due to the purposes and activities of men, but primarily to the operation of our antiquated banking system."[8]

But what is meant by "banking structure"? There are a number of quantitative measures: density, measured as a ratio of the number of bank offices to either population or area; size of the banking system relative to the total

8. See below, p. 262.

economy (e.g. total bank assets as a proportion of national product or wealth); size distribution of banks within the system (indicating degree of oligopolistic or monopolistic power); geographical concentration or dispersion of bank offices; and so on. In addition, there are some nonquantifiable aspects of banking structure, such as the legal status of banking, which may range from absolute prohibition to "free banking," with many gradations in between. In short, by "banking structure" we mean the ensemble of ratios and relationships, quantitative and other, that characterize the components of the system and tie it into the economy of which it is a part.

Of the many possible determinants of banking structure, two are of overwhelming importance: the strength and character of the demand for financial services, and the attitude (or official policy) of the authorities toward banking. The banking system is an integral, interdependent part of the total economy, and without a demand for its services it would not, of course, exist. But granted that it does exist, its structure will be shaped very largely by the actions of the political authorities in the form of laws, decrees, regulations, and by more direct participation, such as government ownership. In no other sector of the economy, with the possible exception of foreign trade, have governments intervened so broadly, so consistently, and with such telling effect—usually bad.

Is there such a thing as an "optimum banking structure"? Probably not— at least not one that is universally valid, although one can imagine that for any given economy there is one structure that would produce the "best" results. Nevertheless, it seems likely that, with due allowance for the peculiarities of time and place, some types of structures produce better results than others. Historical research can discover both favorable and unfavorable structural features, as well as identifying the unique aspects of each economy's success or failure.

THE GERSCHENKRON HYPOTHESIS

One of the most widely discussed recent explanations of the role of banking in the historical process of industrialization—the industrialization of once-backward countries in particular—is that of Alexander Gerschenkron.[9] Although the banking system is by no means the only element in Gerschenkron's explanation of the distinctive patterns of industrialization in various European countries, he considers that it does play a key role at certain stages

9. See Alexander Gerschenkron, *Economic Backwardness in Historical Perspective: A Book of Essays* (Cambridge, Mass., 1962), esp. chap. 1 and the "Postscript"; *idem.*, *Continuity in History and Other Essays* (Cambridge, Mass., 1968).

of the industrialization process. The "Gerschenkron hypothesis," therefore, has been given careful attention and analysis in this volume.[10]

Gerschenkron views industrialization as a process that spread from its birthplace in England to "more backward" countries. In general, "backwardness" varies directly with the distance from England, as do the dates for the inception of industrialization. The "degree of backwardness" thus becomes an organizing principle according to which Gerschenkron classifies a number of features of the development process. "Depending on a given country's degree of economic backwardness on the eve of its industrialization, the course and character of the latter tended to vary in a number of important respects."[11] Gerschenkron names six ways in which a country's variation from the English pattern is greatest according to its degree of backwardness: (1) the country experiences a discontinuous sudden spurt and high rate of growth of manufacturing output; (2) its emphasis is upon large scale of both industrial plant and enterprise; (3) its emphasis is upon producers' rather than consumers' goods; (4) it puts greater pressure upon levels of consumption; (5) the more backward the economy is, "the greater . . . [is] the part played by special institutional factors designed to increase supply of capital to the nascent industries and, in addition, to provide them with less decentralized and better informed entrepreneurial guidance"; and (6) it leaves a smaller role for agriculture.[12]

From the viewpoint of this volume the fifth characteristic is the most important, although the first three also merit attention. Gerschenkron distinguishes three "typical" cases with respect to capital and entrepreneurship: England, the pioneer; Germany, an area of "moderate backwardness"; and imperial Russia, an area of "extreme backwardness."

England, according to Gerschenkron, began to industrialize with relatively small-scale enterprises, requiring little capital or specialized entrepreneurship. Initial capital requirements were supplied from the entrepreneur's own savings or those of his relatives, friends, customers, and suppliers; growth took place by means of the reinvestment of profits. No outside agency was needed to supply either capital or entrepreneurship, because the enterprise itself was the source of both.

But when Germany began to industrialize, technology and markets were more complex; the optimum scale of plant was larger, requiring larger blocs

10. Earlier versions of the chapters by Professors Rudolph, Cohen, and Yamamura were prepared for a session of the American Historical Association's annual meeting in December 1968, devoted to "Banking and Industrialization among the Late Comers: An Examination of the Gerschenkron Hypothesis." This accounts for the difference in the number of references to Gerschenkron's work in the various chapters.

11. Gerschenkron, *Backwardness*, p. 353.

12. *Ibid.* pp. 353f.

of investment; and Germany, as a "moderately backward" area, had fewer potential entrepreneurs and less liquid capital. As a result, the banking system became the prime source of both capital and entrepreneurship:

> The inadequacy in the numbers of available entrepreneurs could be remedied or substituted for by increasing the size of plant and enterprise above what otherwise would have been an optimal size. In Germany, the various incompetencies of the individual entrepreneurs were offset by the device of splitting the entrepreneurial function: the German investment banks—a powerful invention, comparable in economic effect to that of the steam engine—were in their capital-supplying functions a substitute for the insufficiency of the previously created wealth willingly placed at the disposal of the entrepreneurs. But they were also a substitute for entrepreneurial deficiencies. From their central vantage points of control, the banks participated actively in shaping the major—and sometimes even not so major—decisions of individual enterprises. It was they who very often mapped out a firm's paths of growth, conceived far-sighted plans, decided on major technological and locational innovations, and arranged for mergers and capital increases.[13]

In Russia, which was even more backward than Germany, not even the banking system was adequate to the task of providing capital and entrepreneurship for industrialization. There the imperial government played the major role in initiating large-scale, capital-intensive industries in the late 1880's and 1890's. At the same time it nurtured a banking system which, by about 1900, after Russian industry had made its first great spurt, was able to take over more of the functions of entrepreneur and capital supplier, in a manner analogous to the German banks a half-century earlier. (Meanwhile, German industry had come of age and had become more independent of the banking system, in much the same way that English industry had.)

This is an attractive and plausible thesis. Stated and restated with variations in numerous essays and in Gerschenkron's inimitable literary style (to which this brief summary has not done justice), it has already almost acquired the status of Revealed Truth. In many respects it is compatible with the results of my own and my collaborators' research. Yet doubts remain. Is this explanation applicable to other European countries? (Gerschenkron has applied it to Italy and Bulgaria with inconclusive results; he refers in passing, without giving details, to its applicability to Austria-Hungary, France, etc.) But more particularly, is it accurate for and does it explain the true situation in the three countries for which it seems most appropriate?

In the first place, Gerschenkron has apparently misunderstood the nature of the English banking system. The relatively small scale of English country

13. Gerschenkron, *Continuity*, p. 137.

banks during the classical Industrial Revolution, and their normal (though not universal) reluctance to make long-term investments in industrial enterprises, was due to legislation, and not to the choice of either bankers or industrialists. Laws that limited banking partnerships to six persons and forbade them limited liability determined the structure of the English banking system and thus to some extent limited its functions. Even so, there were numerous instances in which banks made long-term commitments to industrial enterprises;[14] indeed, banks were often founded by industrialists for precisely that purpose. Moreover, although English manufacturing firms grew largely through the reinvestment of profits, country banks played a vital role in the process of reinvestment by enabling the manufacturers to economize on working capital and thus allowing them to plow back earnings into fixed capital. It would be impossible to explain the rapid proliferation of the banks in the last two decades of the eighteenth century and the first quarter of the nineteenth without reference to the demand for their services, which in turn resulted from the growth of industry and trade.

Gerschenkron's characterization of the German banking system is more nearly correct than is his description of the English system. Yet it, too, is debatable. On the one hand, he exaggerates the shortage of entrepreneurship and capital in Germany;[15] on the other, he overemphasizes the ubiquity of the *Kreditbanken*. Paraphrasing Riesser, he says that German banks accompanied their clients "from the cradle to the grave, from establishment to liquidation,"[16] forgetting that many of the most notable German industrial enterprises antedated the joint-stock banks by several years or decades. The most misleading feature of the Gerschenkron hypothesis here, however, is the notion that the German joint-stock banks were somehow a "substitute" for "missing prerequisites" (i.e. England's reserves of capital and her many entrepreneurs).[17] Gerschenkron has shown the fallacy of W. W. Rostow's concept of "necessary prerequisites," or preconditions for industrialization; but by replacing prerequisites with "substitutes" he comes dangerously close to falling into the trap of "historical inevitability" which he has elsewhere

---

14. See Cameron *et al.*, *Banking*, chap. II *passim*.

15. Knut Borchardt, "Zur Frage des Kapitalmangels in der ersten Hälfte des 19. Jahrhunderts," *Jahrbucher für Nationalökonomie und Statistik*, 173 (1963); Udo E. G. Heyn, *Private Banking and Industrialization: The Case of Frankfurt am Main, 1825–1875* (unpublished doctoral dissertation, University of Wisconsin, 1969). In the 1840's, when Frenchmen were investing in the German mining industry, many German private bankers and rentiers in Frankfurt and elsewhere were purchasing American railway bonds. It is surprising that Gerschenkron, with his thorough knowledge of German history, could believe that there was a serious shortage of potential entrepreneurs in nineteenth-century Germany.

16. Gerschenkron, *Backwardness*, p. 14.

17. *Ibid.* p. 358 *et passim*.

criticized so eloquently.[18] Was it "inevitable" that Germany would become a great industrial power? And if Germany did, why did not Austria? Gerschenkron's error arises partly from an anachronism: the "heroic age" of modern German industry lasted roughly from the founding of the *Zollverein* in 1834 to the outbreak of the Franco-Prussian War in 1870 (Rostow dates the German take-off from 1850 to 1873); but the first German joint-stock bank was not founded until 1848 (the Schaaffhausen'scher Bankverein, erected on the ruins of an illiquid private bank as an emergency measure), and there were fewer than a dozen such banks as late as 1869. Not until 1870 and afterward were the vast majority of the great joint-stock banks established. In fact, as Krueger and Tilly have shown,[19] it was the German, especially the Rhenish, private bankers in the 1830's, 1840's, and 1850's who worked out the techniques of "mixed" or "universal" banking that the joint-stock banks subsequently applied on a large scale. The creation of the French Crédit Mobilier in 1852 and its participation in the founding of the Bank of Darmstadt in 1853[20] served to popularize the idea of joint-stock investment banking, although the techniques had already been used in Belgium by the Société Générale and the Banque de Belgique in the 1830's, as well as by French and German private bankers.[21]

Russia experienced her first great industrial spurt at the end of the nineteenth century. Granted that governmental initiative played an important role in stimulating that spurt, one should not lose sight of the means that the government employed to encourage industrialization. Apart from railway construction (which at no time accounted for more than 5 per cent of government expenditures) and high tariff protection, the government's major promotional effort was "a vast public relations campaign to enlist support for industrialization at home and abroad."[22] The actual agents of industrialization were profit-oriented private entrepreneurs, engineers and investors, many of them foreign, as McKay has so ably demonstrated. The banking system, too, although supported in emergencies by the State Bank, was likewise privately owned and for a time was dominated by foreign capital and foreign entrepreneurs. In any case, was it inevitable that Russian industrialization, with or without government encouragement, should have

18. *Ibid.* esp. pp. 31–51; for Gerschenkron's strictures on Rostow, see also pp. 355–56.

19. Alfred Krueger, *Das Kölner Bankiergerwerbe vom Ende des 18. Jahrhunderts bis 1875* (Essen, 1925); Richard Tilly, *Financial Institutions and Industrialization in the Rhineland, 1815–1870* (Madison, Wis., 1966).

20. R. Cameron, "Founding the Bank of Darmstadt," *Explorations in Entrepreneurial History*, VIII (1956).

21. Cameron *et al.*, *Banking*, chap. V; R. Cameron, *France and the Economic Development of Europe, 1800–1914* (Princeton, 1961), pp. 119–25.

22. John P. McKay, *Pioneers for Profit: Foreign Entrepreneurship and Russian Industrialization, 1885–1913* (Chicago, 1970), p. 7.

begun when it did—or at all? After all, the Russian government had played a prominent role in the economy from at least the reign of Peter the Great, but with few beneficial consequences. The policy shift favoring economic modernization that occurred after the Crimean War did not really begin to show notable effects until the 1880's; that is, until the banking system, which had been completely reorganized to permit a greater element of private initiative and enterprise, foreign as well as Russian, was already in a vigorous phase of development. The Russian financial expert who declared that Russia's economic evolution was due to its banking system no doubt exaggerated, but he cannot have been wholly wrong.[23] The mere fact that a government decides that industrialization is a necessity and takes steps to obtain it does not ensure the success of its policies: witness the many abortive schemes of recent years. If industrialization is to take place the policies themselves must be realistically formulated and efficiently executed. With respect to the Russian experience, Olga Crisp has written that "both the State Bank and the Imperial Government acted with wisdom and restraint. . . . The large foreign debt and the government's intense concern for its financial reputation abroad . . . had a very salutary restraining effect upon government action and upon officials responsible for financial policy."[24]

As illuminating as Gerschenkron's explanation of the unique features of German and Russian development is, it is difficult to see how a similar explanation can be applied to other nations. Precisely because it has been employed to explain the peculiarities or uniqueness of particular cases, it forfeits claim to generality. Moreover, Gerschenkron's organizing principle, "the degree of backwardness," cannot be measured, and thus it is not an operational concept. Was Sweden an area of "extreme" or only "moderate" backwardness in the 1870's? How about Italy or Spain? Spain in the 1850's undertook a vigorous program of railway construction and financial promotion not unlike the later Russian program; Italy did the same in the 1860's. But in both cases the result was a fiasco which set back the progress of industrialization and economic development by at least a generation. It is also difficult to see how a hypothesis devised to explain the unique features of development of a large country such as Russia can be usefully applied to a small country such as Bulgaria, in spite of their cultural affinities. For such cases the structural–functional approach appears to be more promising.

These criticisms are not made with intention to denigrate. The most fruitful scientific hypotheses are those that stimulate the greatest amount of original research and critical reflection, regardless of the ultimate judgment as to their validity, and in that respect the Gerschenkron hypothesis has

23. E. Epstein, *Les banques de commerce russe* (Paris, 1925), p. 50, cited by O. Crisp in Cameron *et al.*, *Banking*, p. 233.
24. *Ibid.* p. 238.

already established a permanent place for itself in the literature of economic history. This volume is, in itself, a part of the evidence.

THE CASES AT HAND

Although the chapters that follow serve as a test of the Gerschenkron hypothesis, they also have a broader and more general purpose. In the cases of the European countries, the purpose is, to put it bluntly, to find out what went wrong. All four European case studies deal with countries that either failed to achieve significant industrialization before 1914 (Serbia, Spain), or whose industrialization was tardy and incomplete (Austria, Italy). On the other hand, Japan and the United States were extraordinarily successful—both achieved high rates of industrial growth.

In studying the European countries, we find that there are various possible answers to the question: What went wrong? Perhaps the countries were so poorly endowed with resources, natural and/or human, that industrialization was simply out of the question. On the other hand, although not every country has a Ruhr Valley, there are other possibilities for industrialization, as the case of Japan shows. In the countries that failed to industrialize was the banking system at fault? Or did their governments' economic policies stifle the natural possibilities for growth? In each of the cases under consideration it is likely that so many factors were at work hamstringing the economy that even a drastic restructuring of the banking system would have resulted in only a slightly better over-all performance. One can hope, nevertheless, that just as a pathologist learns from diseased as well as healthy tissue, these case studies will better inform us about the interplay of banking and economic development.

Austria—that is, the Cisleithanian provinces of the Habsburg Monarchy (see below, p. 26n.)—had, in the mid-nineteenth century, a population and territory slightly larger than that of Prussia. It was the nucleus of a formidable land empire whose area was greater than that of the future Second Reich, and in 1850 it had forced Prussia to back down on an important political issue without so much as firing a shot or even mobilizing an army. Its capital, Vienna, was one of the great cultural centers of Europe and was an important financial market as well. Its universities and technical schools ranked with the best in Europe. Its wealth and economic resources were, so far as anyone knew at the time, as good or better than those of any other German state.

Fifty or sixty years later, although Austria was still the senior partner in the Austro-Hungarian Empire, the Empire itself was the junior partner of the Dual Alliance. The German Empire had outstripped the Habsburg Monarchy in wealth and population, as well as in military strength. In industrial output Prussia alone produced far more than the entire Monarchy. The German banking system was probably the most powerful in Europe; in comparison with it the Austrian system was little more than a poor relation.

It may be true, as Professor Rudolph suggests, that the development of the Austrian economy did more to shape the banking system than the banking system did to shape the development of the economy. And if that is true, then the same might be said of the German economy and banking system. But as yet we do not know enough to make either statement with certainty.

Joint-stock investment or promotional banking began almost simultaneously in Austria and Germany (preceded in both by two or three decades of increasingly active private investment banking), but with the exception of two or three brief periods, it rarely showed the dynamism and success in Austria that it did in Germany. Moreover, according to Rudolph's index of Austrian industrial production—a signal contribution to our knowledge of Austrian economic history—there was no Gerschenkronian great "spurt" in Austria. Instead, there was a gradual *dec*eleration of the growth rate between 1880 and 1913, in spite of a brief (small?) spurt in the last few prewar years. (See Table II.3, p. 33.) Nor did the Austrian bankers behave as we are told the German bankers did. They had no "cradle to the grave" philosophy of industrial promotion and guidance; instead, they preferred the "plump, juicy firms with favorable prospects, with the difficulties and risks of their early years already completed," and with these they settled into a quiet current account and commission business relationship. Apparently they were more willing to underwrite issues of government securities than to float new joint-stock companies. In spite of all this, Rudolph does not find any evidence of a notable lack of entrepreneurial talent in Austria, while Gerschenkron insists that there was such a lack in Germany. (Without quite saying so, Rudolph suggests that there was no stringent capital shortage in Austria either; but that idea is difficult to reconcile with the large foreign investments that were made in both the public and the private sectors of the economy.)

Metaphorically, what it adds up to is a puzzle in which some of the pieces are missing and some of the others may be counterfeit. We begin with two economies of similar size and structure, add two banking systems, also similar in structure—but observe very different bank behavior as well as a different industrial outcome. A part of the solution is simple, of course: Austria has no Ruhr Valley. That in itself goes a long way toward explaining the differences in outcome; it may explain in part the difference in bank behavior as well. Given different objective economic opportunities (which bankers should be able to see, if anyone can), one would expect different responses on the part of profit-motivated bankers. Perhaps that is why the Austrian bankers preferred to serve the "plump, juicy firms" that had left their difficult years behind them. But there are other possible reasons for both the different behavior and the different outcome, and these are rooted mainly in public policy. Whereas Prussia, the *Zollverein*, and the Reich followed liberal trade policies until 1878, and only moderately protective ones thereafter, throughout the same period Austrian policy was consistently protectionist. That, together with a limited domestic market (low incomes, high transport costs), might well have engendered less aggressive behavior on the part of both bankers and industrial entrepreneurs. Whereas the cartels created and serviced by the German bankers might have limited competition on the domestic market, they could nevertheless be aggressive and expansionist in foreign markets. The Austrian cartels, on the other hand, apparently remained content with a quieter, more sluggish domestic market.

Austrian public policy hindered the economy and the banking system in other ways as well. The North German Confederation provided for free incorporation in 1870, and even before that time charters for joint-stock companies had been relatively easy to obtain in one or another of the German states. Austria, on the other hand, did not allow free incorporation until 1899, and at the same time the government *increased* discriminatory taxation on joint-stock companies. Finally, the perennial deficits of the Austrian Treasury and the privileged position of government securities in the Bourse surely affected both bank behavior and capital formation. The late T. S. Ashton used to insist that capital formation in England in the eighteenth century was inhibited by the government's privileged position in the financial market—and yet the yield on consols rarely went above 5 per cent! The size and inefficiency of the Austrian bureaucracy gobbled up much private saving at the same time that the attractive yields on government securities (as much as 8 per cent on long-term issues, and even higher on short-term ones)—and the lucrative underwriting business—deflected both the capital and the attention of the bankers from riskier industrial investments.

What of Italy? Professor Cohen concludes (as Professor Gerschenkron did before him) that Italian bank behavior and industrial growth conform to the Gerschenkron hypothesis. He points to the simultaneous beginning of effective tariff protection, other government encouragements, and the founding of new industrial credit banks in 1894 (foremost among these was the Banca Commerciale Italiana, with German capital and leadership), followed in 1898 by Italian industry's big "spurt" (identified by Gerschenkron), which continued (with fluctuations) until 1913. Statistical quibbles apart, there is little question about the facts, but the interpretation one places upon them is another matter. For example, was Italy an area of "moderate" or "extreme" backwardness? One cannot answer that question without implicitly granting greater weight either to the intervention of the government or to that of the banks. Gerschenkron opted for the banks, calling the new tariff policy "inept" and "one of the obstacles in the road of Italian industrialization." Cohen is more equivocal; while not "defending" the tariff policy, he does credit it with contributing to industrial growth.

More fundamentally, however, Cohen and Gerschenkron in my view both miss the mark by failing to account for the more than three decades of stagnation—or even retrogression—between the achievement of Italian unification and the first faint stirring of industrial growth. Political unification occurred after a decade or more of economic progress, at least in northern Italy, and especially in Piedmont.[25] All indicators in 1861 pointed toward a continuation of that progress: a unified national market, a vigorous program of railway construction with both direct and indirect benefits, a lively inflow of foreign capital and entrepreneurship, including a newly created Credito Mobiliare under the aegis of the famed French Crédit Mobilier. All of the elements of a Gerschenkronian big "spurt" were present. Yet the anticipated growth failed to occur.

From the point of view of the general relationships between the banking system and economic development, a detailed study of Italian economic history from 1861 to 1893 would be as interesting as one of the period between 1894 and 1914. The structure of the banking system was actually quite similar in the two periods, the chief difference being the greater control by government over the note-issuing system and the greater powers of the Bank of Italy after 1894. In both periods there was a multiplicity of small local credit institutions, but, more importantly, in both periods the banking system was dominated by a small group of large banks that operated throughout the nation as industrial credit banks. (Cohen's vague reference to the earlier banks' investments in "highly speculative real estate and urban construction activities" scarcely does justice to the variety and extent of their involvement in industrial, commercial, and transportation enterprises.) The Credito Mobiliare occupied the same position of prominence in the system between 1863 and 1893 that the Banca Commerciale Italiana did thereafter. In the absence of any detailed studies of the two periods, the following comments are offered as a tentative explanation of the failure of the banking system to lead a more vigorous industrial growth before 1893, as compared with the limited success in growth that was achieved subsequently.[26]

25. See K. R. Greenfield, *Economics and Liberalism in the Risorgimento: A Study of Nationalism in Lombardy, 1814–48* (Baltimore, 1934; reissue, 1966); also R. Cameron, "French Finance and Italian Unity: The Cavourian Decade," *American Historical Review*, LXII (1957), 552–69.

26. For supporting details see Cameron, *France and the Economic Development of Europe*, pp. 448–57; and Gino Luzzatto, "The Italian Economy in the First Decade after Unification" in F. Crouzet, W. Chaloner, and W. Stern (eds.), *Essays in European Economic History* (New York, 1969), pp. 203–25.

In spite of the favorable conditions mentioned above, the obstacles in the way of Italian economic development were enormous. Poverty of natural resources, primitive techniques employed in industry and especially in agriculture, and widespread illiteracy and ignorance were handicaps that could scarcely be dealt with through conscious policy, at least in the short run, even if the policy-makers had been inclined to do so. More susceptible to control, and more immediately related to the urgent problem of capital accumulation, was the financial administration of the state. Assumption of the public debts of the pre-unification governments was, perhaps, a political necessity; but it constituted an enormous burden for the already fragile system of public finance, especially since almost 50 per cent of the debts were held abroad. On top of this dead-weight obligation, the government was quite unable to balance current receipts and expenditures, and, as a result, the national debt quadrupled in the first twenty years after unification. The war of 1866 against Austria and the consequent suspension of currency convertibility was the most disastrous episode in this unhappy sequence of deficits, but time and again the fickle behavior of the Italian Parliament upset responsible measures intended to secure financial reform. Given the financial instability of the government and its privileged competition with private enterprise in the capital market, private domestic capital accumulation on any significant scale was virtually impossible. Foreign capital was available (the Credito Mobiliare and all other important banks had sizable amounts of foreign funds), but the government—or, more exactly, the Parliament— systematically discriminated against and penalized foreign capital and entrepreneurs. This discriminatory policy was especially notable in the case of railways, and it helps to account for the disappointing contribution of the railway system to Italian economic growth; but it also affected other sectors of the economy, including banking.

The provisional conclusion to be drawn from these observations is that if a banking system is to be effective in contributing to industrial capital forma- tion, the government must assure minimal conditions of both financial and political order and refrain from random *ad hoc* interference that increases uncertainty for long-range investment planning. This conclusion is reinforced by the experience of Spain in the middle decades of the nineteenth century.

Professor Tortella's account of the origins of the modern Spanish banking system shows clearly why that system did not contribute significantly to industrialization. Preoccupation with public finance and railway construction, both objectives dictated by the political authorities, deflected the bankers from a more balanced view of the needs and opportunities of the economy. This suggests that, contrary to the implications of the Gerschenkron hypoth- esis, Spain would have benefited more from a larger number of relatively

small local banks catering to local commerce and industry than from the few
large banks operating from Madrid. (Incidentally, Tortella's comparison of
paid-in capital of railways and of manufacturing corporations may be misleading, since most manufacturing enterprises at that time had not adopted
the joint-stock form of organization.) On the other hand, the predominance
of foreign entrepreneurs in both the large banking enterprises and the railways is indicative of another weakness in the Spanish economy for which
the banking system can scarcely be blamed. It is a fair presumption that the
foreign entrepreneurs were more interested in quick promotional profits
than in the long-term development of the economy, especially in view of
their behavior. They were drawn to those activities that promised quick
profits. But where were the native Spanish entrepreneurs? On the evidence
available, it would appear that they were very few in number, and that their
motives did not differ greatly from those of the foreigners. This raises
questions about the Spanish economy, society, and value system that far
surpass our limited enquiry, but that urgently call for investigation. It is of
more than passing interest that Tortella's analysis of the banking system
provides material for a major reinterpretation of Spanish political
history.

The Serbian example, discussed by Dr. Lampe, appears to approximate
most closely the situation of contemporary underdeveloped economies. Here
was a genuinely "new nation," recently liberated from the domination of a
foreign power and culture, with a predominantly agrarian and imperfectly
monetized economy, striving consciously to acquire both the appearance and
the substance of modernization. Serbia's history demonstrates even more
clearly than Spain's or Italy's the limitations on, as well as the possibilities
open to, banking policy and the banking system in an underdeveloped
nation. Within a relatively few years after achieving full independence
Serbia had acquired a surprisingly well-developed banking structure, with a
central bank of issue, several joint-stock banks, and a ratio of financial
assets to national product comparable to that in far more industrially
advanced nations. In spite of the modern appearance of this financial super-
structure, however, the progress of industrialization was limited, to say the
least. Dr. Lampe has, it seems to me, correctly identified the principal
weakness of the Serbian economy, which the banking system, or economic
policy in general, was almost powerless to counteract: namely, the shortage
of human capital at the managerial or entrepreneurial level as well as throughout the labor force. Similar shortages can be observed in the Spanish,
Italian, and even Austrian cases (as contrasted with, for example, those of
Germany, Scotland, or Japan); but the Serbian case, less complicated by
other potentially retarding factors, is unusually clear. Nevertheless, the
privileged position of the government in the capital market, and its penchant

for unproductive expenditures—just as that of Austria, Italy, and Spain—made it difficult for the banking system to contribute to industrial development.

The other chapters in this volume do not deal with economies that failed to develop; on the contrary, they consider two of the most outstanding examples of rapid economic growth. The main outlines of Japanese economic growth in the half-century or so following the Meiji Restoration are now well known. Although it is possible to quibble over the exact percentages, it is clear that Japan experienced very high growth rates of both industrial production and per capita income—possibly the highest of any country for a sustained period prior to World War II. (The fact that Japan started from a very low statistical base imparts an upward bias to the growth rates, but that does not alter the unique character of Japanese development.) A number of observers and analysts have credited the Japanese banking system with making vital contributions to that growth. One of these was my collaborator in a previous work, Professor Hugh Patrick.[27] Professor Yamamura does not dispute the importance of the banking system, but he does suggest that it acted somewhat differently than is generally believed. Specifically, he rejects the idea that the Japanese experience fits the Gerschenkron schema of the economics of backwardness.

Professor Patrick synthesized the existing literature as well as supplying new empirical evidence of his own. In his view (and in his terminology), the Japanese banking system until about the time of World War I was "supply-leading" rather than "demand-following." "That is to say, the banks did not concentrate on short-term, self-liquidating commercial loans. Instead, because of their close ties with industry and industrialists, banks and bankers until late in this period increasingly served the function of industrial banks, providing funds for fixed investment as well as for working capital."[28] Although Professor Patrick did not say so explicitly, this interpretation fits very neatly into Gerschenkron's scheme, in which the banking system and/or the government in backward economies must take the initiative in industrial promotion and finance. It is precisely this view that Professor Yamamura challenges. In his view the sequence was just the reverse: in the early period (until about World War I) the banks followed the English practice of short-term commercial lending to established enterprises; it was only in the 1920's that a few of the great zaibatsu began to engage in the German type of "universal" banking. He presents evidence, moreover, that in a number of important instances industrial entrepreneurs struggled through the first difficult years of establishment with little or no assistance from the banks;

27. Cameron et al., Banking, chap. VIII.
28. Ibid. p. 288.

only after they began to show sizable and sustained profits were they able to interest bankers in assisting their expansion.[29]

In view of the incomplete and partially contradictory nature of much of the empirical evidence, it would be unwise for one who is not well versed in the Japanese language and who is not familiar with the Japanese sources to attempt to resolve this difference of opinion. It is clear that there is some evidence to support both views, and the seemingly diametric opposition may turn out to be more a matter of emphasis than of fundamental reality. Methods of finance undoubtedly differed from firm to firm as well as from industry to industry, and whether there were clear-cut patterns either for various industrial groupings or for the industrial sector as a whole can only be determined on the basis of further research. There is also the matter of chronology: were there real, detectable shifts in methods of industrial finance and the behavior of banks over time, and if so, in which direction?

In spite of these problems it is possible to draw two firm conclusions about the role of banking in Japanese economic development: that role was an important one, and much more research needs to be done to determine its modalities and mechanisms.

Professor Green's contribution, on banking and economic development in the United States, specifically in Louisiana prior to the Civil War, deals with an entirely different type of situation. Here the focus is not on an entire national economy, but on a limited regional economy, and on a "frontier" area at that. Moreover, there is no question of economic development *qua* industrialization, but economic growth through the expansion of market-oriented agriculture and commerce. These different circumstances allow us to obtain a new perspective on the question of the relationship of banking to economic development. To be sure, the relatively high levels of per capita income and the high proportion of the urban population in Louisiana were mainly the result of its favorable geographical location in an age that depended heavily on water transport; but Professor Green finds that the banks in Louisiana made a positive contribution to the economic welfare of the state's citizens. Bank finance was not merely a passive or permissive factor in the growth of New Orleans and its hinterland; instead, "financial growth was an

29. This observation corresponds to Rudolph's, that Austrian bankers preferred to deal with established profitable enterprises, and both Yamamura and Rudolph seem to regard the bankers as somehow shirking their duty. There is nothing surprising in this behavior, however. As I have remarked previously, "There is a widespread impression . . . that banks lend only to already established, successful firms. . . . By and large, the impression is correct. For any given bank the majority of its borrowers must be both established and profitable, otherwise both the bank and its customers would soon go out of business. While the impression is correct in a general sense, the inference it suggests—that banks do not finance innovation—is wrong, or at least grossly oversimplified." (*Ibid.* pp. 12–13.)

independent cause, an active contributor to more rapid real economic growth."

My earlier comparative study of banking and industrialization contained no chapters on the United States. I explained the omission by stating that "the enormous variety and complexity of the American financial system . . . merits a separate comparative study of its own components." [30] In fact, there was not *one* American banking system, but *n* plus 1 systems, where *n* equals the number of states and organized territories at any given date. Professor Green has provided one element for such a comparative study; readers familiar with the contributions of Redlich and Hammond, [31] among others, will appreciate the diversity of the American system. Nevertheless, in the concluding chapter of my earlier work I included some quantitative data on the United States banking system for comparative purposes, and ventured the following generalization: "It seems likely that in the cases of England and the United States the banking systems were essentially passive or permissive, responding fully to the demand for financial services but not inducing growth directly." [32] I did, however, add the following *caveat*: "This generalization should be accepted very tentatively for the United States pending further study. Certainly there were periods in American history—the 1830's and possibly the period from about 1885 to 1929—when the banks played a more positive, active role." [33] Green's data show that the banks did indeed play an active, growth-inducing role in Louisiana in the 1830's, and to a lesser extent in other decades as well; and there is no reason to believe the situation was different in other states. As for "the period from about 1885 to 1929," Professor Sylla, in his chapter on the American system as a whole, has demonstrated conclusively that in the entire period from the Civil War until World War I (at least), the National Banking System was consistently biased in favor of the industrial sector of the economy, although not in ways that the authorities intended.

Professor Sylla's chapter is remarkable for several reasons. Its economic analysis is clear and incisive. He has shown not only that the banking system promoted industrialization and thus encouraged the growth of the northeastern states generally, but that this growth took place, in part, at the expense (in terms of slower growth than might otherwise have occurred) of agriculture, and of the South and West generally. Thus the complaints of the Populists and other agrarian interests were not without foundation, although

30. *Ibid.* p. 5.

31. Fritz Redlich, *The Molding of American Banking: Men and Ideas*, 2 vols. (New York, 1947–51; reissue, 1968); Bray Hammond, *Banks and Politics in America from the Revolution to the Civil War* (Princeton, 1957).

32. Cameron *et al.*, *Banking*, p. 304.

33. *Ibid.*

their arguments were misdirected. True, the East benefited at the expense of the South and West, but the "monopolistic bankers" were not the Eastern bankers—they themselves were subject to intense competition—but the local rural and small town bankers of the South and West! This ironic conclusion assures that Sylla's chapter, like Tortella's, will be of interest to political as well as economic historians.

Professor Sylla merits further commendation for placing his subject in a comparative context, a rarity among American historians. As a result, he is able to confirm the importance of freedom of note issue as an inducement to enter the banking industry; more importantly, he demonstrates that *all* of the institutional mechanisms for the mobilization of industrial capital, described by Gerschenkron as "substitutes" for one another, were simultaneously operative in the United States. This can scarcely be explained by the "relative backwardness" of the American economy; instead, it was due in part to deliberate governmental policy (railway subsidies, protective tariffs, etc.) and in part to historical accident: a tragic civil war which resulted in the emergency creation of a badly designed banking system that accidentally favored the growth of a powerful capital market. The superimposition of these various devices that mobilized capital for employment in industry must be credited with a large share of the impressive growth rates of American manufacturing when, on grounds of comparative advantage, one would have expected more rapid growth in agriculture and the extractive industries.

IN LIEU OF A CONCLUSION

The Conclusion usually comes at the end of a book. The individual chapters in this volume speak for themselves; but a few general remarks are in order, and should be considered in connection with the findings of both this and the volume that preceded it.

Banking systems are not "neutral" with respect to economic development. Where they exist, they do so because there is a demand for their services, and such a demand is usually evidence of a growing, developing economy. But it is frequently said that banking systems are "passive" or "permissive" agents, merely responding to the demand for their services. On the evidence assembled here it becomes increasingly difficult to sustain this notion. This is not to say that banking systems invariably make a positive, growth-inducing contribution. Clearly, they do not. If, as Professor Tortella points out, the banking system is "tilted" by unwise legislation and policy, it can distort and even thwart the growth of the economy. Although the fundamental dynamics of economic development lie outside the banking system, the way the system is structured can either significantly hasten or retard development. It is thus a matter of some importance for policy-makers to know what structural characteristics are especially favorable or unfavorable.

In the conclusion to my previous volume on this subject I pointed out that there is "no single model of a banking system [that] is appropriate for all economies." [34] At the same time I indicated that where banking was left most free to develop in response to the demand for its services, it produced the best results. Restrictions on freedom of entry almost always reduce the quantity and quality of financial services available to the economy, and thus hinder or distort economic growth. Competition in banking, on the other hand, acts as a spur to the mobilization of idle financial resources and to their efficient utilization in commerce and industry. These conclusions do not arise from any doctrinaire attitude, but solely from examination of and reflection on historical experience. The cases reported on here have reinforced those conclusions for me—but I invite the reader to decide for himself.

34. *Ibid.* p. 318.

CHAPTER II

Austria 1800–1914

RICHARD L. RUDOLPH

A number of economists have stated that financial intermediaries had a major role in the industrialization of central Europe. The view that their role was greater in this region than elsewhere has been expressed so often that it has come to be taken almost for granted in most of the literature. The present chapter is written with the intention of partially countering this view and placing the role of the banks in a better perspective within the over-all process of economic development. This discussion is written in the context of an examination of the views of Alexander Gerschenkron, the most sophisticated and articulate exponent of this view of the major role of the banks. Professor Gerschenkron has focused attention on what he sees as the vital role of investment banking in large parts of Europe, and he has evoked a number of studies on the subject. The question here is whether or not Gerschenkron's schema is an appropriate one for banking and industrialization in Austria in the nineteenth and early twentieth centuries.[1]

In my view, Gerschenkron's generalizations concerning the role of investment banking have two distinct and not necessarily complementary parts. In the first place, Gerschenkron argues that in a "relatively backward economy," the bloc of investment required to get industrialization under way will be particularly great. In his view, a "relatively backward country" will have a poorly developed capital market and a scarcity of entrepreneurial talent, and it will need a larger average size of plant and concentration on branches with relatively high capital-output ratios. Reliance upon the banks in such a country will be much greater than in a country like England, where

1. The term "Austria" is used here in an arbitrary manner to describe the western part of the Austro-Hungarian Monarchy, i.e. the seventeen provinces known as "Cisleithania," which is officially named "*die im Reichsrate vertretene Königreiche und Länder.*" This excludes "Transleithania"—i.e. Hungary, Croatia, and Slovenia.

industrialization was able to proceed more gradually, and where, consequently, capital accumulation on a smaller scale (flowing directly from trade, modernized agriculture, and from industry itself) was sufficient.[2] The second part of his argument goes a bit further. Gerschenkron develops the idea that the industrialization ideology embodied in the Pereire brothers' Crédit Mobilier was carried over and institutionalized in other Continental banks, particularly in Germany and in Austria. In the latter countries, the weaknesses of the Crédit Mobilier were compensated for by the establishment of banks that combined investment banking and regular commercial banking activities. Thus Gerschenkron speaks of "a truly momentous role of investment banking of the period for the economic history of France and of large portions of Europe."[3] He contends that "the continental practices in the field of industrial banking must be conceived as specific instruments of industrialization in a backward country."[4] And he accepts, with several qualifications, the saying that a German bank "accompanied an industrial enterprise from the cradle to the grave, from establishment to liquidation throughout all the vicissitudes of its existence."[5] In a further extension of his argument, Gerschenkron holds that where neither private entrepreneurial activities nor banking activities are sufficient, the state must move in to provide the impetus for industrialization.

If this brief account does not do justice to the nuances and corollaries of the argument, it does serve to outline the basic schema.

With the first part of the argument, there is little ground for disagreement, *if* the conditions Gerschenkron lists are present in the backward country. If there is a poorly developed capital market, a lack of entrepreneurial talent, and a need for large blocs of investment, then it is reasonable to assume, *a priori*, that banks may have a much broader function than would otherwise be the case. In considering Austria, there are serious questions concerning all of these assumptions, particularly the degree to which entrepreneurs were lacking, the degree to which industrialization was not gradual, and the degree to which large blocs of investment were required. Several of these questions will be touched upon later. The second part of the argument is a different matter. It is one thing to speak of an expanded role for the banks, but it is quite another to see them as engines of industrialization or as leaders in economic development. To begin with, one must ask why bankers, often

---

2. Gerschenkron's views are to be found throughout his works; the basic argument is put forth in his essay "Economic Backwardness in Historical Perspective," in Alexander Gerschenkron, *Economic Backwardness in Historical Perspective* (Cambridge, Mass., 1962).

3. *Ibid.* p. 12.

4. *Ibid.* p. 14.

5. *Ibid.* p. 14.

characterized as a cautious breed, and wary of industrial investment to this day, should have been the initiators of industrialization in the mid-nineteenth century? It might, in fact, be more advisable to examine the activities of the banks not so much as being guided by St. Simonian ideas as by criteria of relative profitability, risk on various investments, and the like, as these were framed by the real non-monetary sector of the economy and by the institutional setting within which the banks operated.[6]

It is not at all clear whether the concept of the bank *qua* entrepreneur or *qua* industrial promoter carried over fully from the Crédit Mobilier to the central European banks. German banks are the prototype of the Gerschenkron schema, and the degree to which these banks initiated industrial development and were tied to industry has been questioned by some writers.[7] Richard Tilly is probably correct in stressing the "adaptive and facilitating" role of financial institutions, rather than the initiative role, and in placing vital emphasis upon the non-monetary sector. Tilly points out that "promotional banking required an adequate demand for its services. Where other ingredients of industrialization were in short supply, such institutions could produce few results of significance."[8] This is particularly true of the Austrian case.

The distinction made here between the two parts of the Gerschenkron schema is important. The function of banks in industrialization as mobilizers of capital may be extensive, as the first part of the hypothesis states, but the second part suggests that the banks operate the levers of industrialization, when, in fact, the general condition of economic opportunity may be the real formative agent influencing the activities of the banks. Further, the Gerschenkron typology of the industrial process in various countries— private entrepreneurs, then banks, then the state—may serve to obscure both the degree of gradual change taking place within the economy and the possibly conjunctive or alternating role played by each of these three elements. In viewing the Austrian experience, the evidence suggests that the Gerschenkron hypothesis and typology may not be appropriate, and that in Austria, while the role of the banks in industrialization was an extensive one, it was not a leading one, nor was it possibly as extensive as some have held.

6. Gerschenkron makes an important contribution in emphasizing the degree to which the given structural pattern of industry and of the economy in general at the onset of large-scale industrialization establishes "basic tendencies" or priorities for the banks' participation in industrialization (*ibid.*, p. 15). This concept flows more from the first part of his argument, and it tends to underscore the adjunctive rather than initiative role of the banks.

7. See P. Barrett Whale, *Joint Stock Banking in Germany* (London, 1930), chap. 2; and Richard Tilly's discussion of Germany in Rondo Cameron *et al.*, *Banking in the Early Stages of Industrialization* (New York, 1967), chap. 5.

8. Richard Tilly, *Financial Institutions and Industrialization in the Rhineland 1815–1870* (Madison, 1966), 114f.

In fact, the view could be advanced that the very weakness, or backwardness, of the economy, and not entrepreneurial fervor, was the dominant factor in shaping banking activities.

INDUSTRIAL GROWTH

Research concerning the character of industrial growth in Austria is just beginning, but it is possible to delineate the main outlines of that growth. It is generally held that little economic progress occurred in the period before the Revolution of 1848. The several decades following, however, have come to be known as the great period of industrial promotion (*Gründerzeit*) in Austria; the upswings in the economy of 1850–57 and 1867–73 were years of extensive industrial promotion and investment in railroads. The Bourse Crash of 1873 then initiated a long crisis; recovery from it began only in 1880. From 1880 onward industrial output increased, but growth was sporadic until 1896. In that year there began a significant upswing in the economy, but it was ended by the European depression of 1900. In 1903 the upswing was again renewed and, with one short period of recession, continued until the eve of World War I. If one were to attempt to identify a "spurt," or industrial leap, the period after 1896 would most clearly fit the description. Eduard März has spoken of the 1850's and 1860's as "false starts" in the economy and has contended that the post-1895 period, the "second *Gründerzeit*," marked the actual "take-off" of the Austrian economy.[9]

While März is basically correct, in that a period in which one may speak of the onset of "self-sustained" growth did not appear until after 1903, it could also be argued that the process of capital formation took place on a much more gradual and extensive basis than that posited by advocates—including Gerschenkron—of industrial "spurts" or "take-offs." Nachum Gross's recent pioneering work on Austria indicates that there was considerable growth; he estimates that the annual percentage per capita rates of growth of industrial product were around 2.2 per cent from 1841 to 1865, 4.09 per cent from 1865 to 1885, and 3.42 per cent from 1880 to 1911.[10] Gross's estimates are limited to years for which census data are available. I have opted for more limited sectoral coverage and have constructed an index of industrial output for Austria in the years 1880 to 1913, which provides a

9. Eduard März, "Zur Genesis der Schumpeterschen Theorie der wirtschaftlichen Entwicklung," in *On Political Economy and Econometrics* (Warsaw, 1965), 371. The post-1880 upswings occurred in 1880–83, 1888–91, 1896–99, and 1903–13 (with a recession in 1908–9).

10. Nachum Gross, "Austrian Industrial Statistics 1880/85 and 1911/13," *Zeitschrift für die Gesamte Staatswissenschaft*, 124 (1968), 67.

TABLE II.1

Austrian Industrial Production, 1880–1913

Year	Index (1900 = 100)
1880	44
1881	49
1882	51
1883	57
1884	59
1885	56
1886	60
1887	62
1888	61
1889	66
1890	72
1891	77
1892	78
1893	80
1894	86
1895	89
1896	90
1897	91
1898	98
1899	99
1900	100
1901	105
1902	105
1903	106
1904	107
1905	113
1906	118
1907	135
1908	132
1909	129
1910	130
1911	137
1912	150
1913	144

Source: Richard L. Rudolph, "The Role of Financial Institutions in the Industrialization of the Czech Crownlands, 1880–1914," Ph.D. dissertation, University of Wisconsin, Department of History, 1968, Appendix I.

TABLE II.2
Austrian Industrial Production, 1880–1913

Index (1900 = 100)

Year	Mining	Metal-making	Engineering	Foodstuffs	Textiles
1880	46	20	10	48	58
1881	49	22	7	53	66
1882	51	25	8	57	65
1883	56	29	5	58	85
1884	56	38	21	61	78
1885	58	34	23	63	65
1886	58	32	18	63	80
1887	61	36	23	64	81
1888	67	44	30	62	75
1889	71	46	36	66	82
1890	76	51	41	72	88
1891	79	48	40	76	92
1892	78	49	44	79	94
1893	81	54	48	84	94
1894	82	62	57	87	105
1895	86	68	63	89	106
1896	88	75	71	92	97
1897	94	80	75	91	100
1898	98	89	82	94	112
1899	102	94	90	97	105
1900	100	100	100	100	100
1901	105	99	98	104	110
1902	101	99	100	101	118
1903	103	98	98	101	118
1904	104	104	108	100	121
1905	110	117	121	104	124
1906	118	128	133	111	121
1907	125	140	143	117	160
1908	126	153	156	118	139
1909	123	146	150	109	148
1910	122	160	171	113	136
1911	126	171	179	113	152
1912	135	195	208	120	164
1913	140	189	196	116	153

Source: Rudolph, "The Role of Financial Institutions," Appendix I.

CHART II.1

Growth of Austrian Industrial Production, 1880–1913
(By Industrial Sector, Constant Prices)

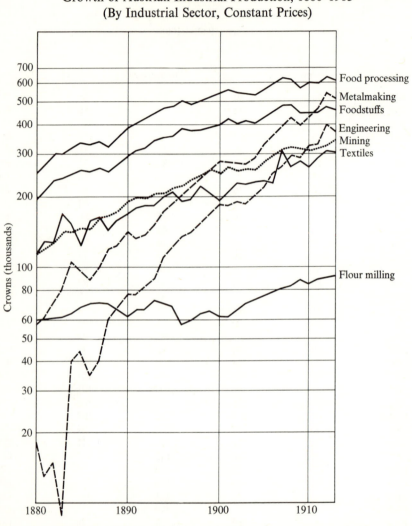

Source: Rudolph, "The Role of Financial Institutions," Appendix I. This chart is intended to show rates of growth and consists of series for representative branches used in the construction of the index, rather than the production of each branch in its entirety.

somewhat more dynamic view of the economy (see Tables II.1 and II.2).[11] The results substantiate and extend those of Gross. My own estimates show an annual average growth rate for industrial output in the years 1880–1913 of 3.6 per cent (compound), with a rate as high as 7.8 per cent per annum reached in the boom years of 1904–07 (see Table II.3). Generally speaking,

TABLE II.3

Austrian Annual Average Rates of Growth (%) (compound)

Period	Total Output	Mining	Metals	Engineering	Food-stuffs	Textiles
1851–1913	—	4.0	3.8	—	—	3.4
1880–1913	3.6	3.4	7.0	9.5	2.7	3.1
1851–1872	—	4.8	0.1	—	—	4.8
1880–1890	4.9	5.1	9.8	15.3	4.1	4.1
1890–1900	3.4	2.8	6.8	9.3	3.4	1.3
1900–1913	2.8	2.6	5.0	5.3	1.1	3.6
1895–1912	3.2	2.7	6.4	7.3	1.8	2.6
1902–1912	3.6	2.9	7.0	7.6	1.8	3.4
1903–1907	6.3	5.0	9.3	9.8	3.7	7.9

then, while growth was not remarkable, a fairly gradual and extensive increase in the industrial sector did take place after the Bourse Crash of 1873. There was rapid growth in several branches, particularly mining and metallurgy, machine-building, and food processing, and very extensive growth in most branches of the economy in the early years of the twentieth century.

THE ORIGINS OF MODERN INDUSTRY, 1800–1848

There was considerable growth in Austrian banking in the nineteenth and early twentieth centuries. In the first half of the nineteenth century, financial

11. A more extended analysis of the Austrian economy and details concerning the construction of the index are in my doctoral dissertation, "The Role of Financial Institutions in the Industrialization of the Czech Crownlands, 1880–1914," University of Wisconsin, 1968. In this index I have attempted to overcome the data limitations faced by Gross by opting for more limited sectoral coverage.

intermediation was dominated by the National Bank, founded in 1816, and the great private mercantile banking houses. The National Bank, which after 1877 became the Österreichisch-ungarische Bank, served as a central bank and held a monopoly of note issue. Like the Bank of France, it rarely altered its interest rates, it dealt primarily with high-grade paper, and its lending and discount operations were based upon criteria which excluded all but the most reliable and wealthy clients. In effect, the bank served only the government and several of the large private banking houses,[12] among them the great private banks of the Rothschilds, Geymüllers, Sina, Stametz-Mayer, and Arnstein-Eskeles. These houses were involved primarily in government loans and loans to the nobility. They apparently devoted only a small part of their funds to dealings in short-term credit and had little traffic with industry. Small industrialists, who had no commerce with the National Bank, were forced to get credit at second or third hand at high rates,[13] and attempts to expand the number of credit institutions were resisted by both the National Bank and the private banks.[14] In brief, the capital market was poorly developed in the early 1800's. Even in Reichenberg, a major center of the textile industry, until the 1850's at least one manufacturer had to take his bills to Prague or Zwittau, and, in most cases, he was forced to rely on unofficial brokers.[15] In several cases the government attempted to persuade the private banks to tender individual loans to industrial firms, but it had little success. For example, the government sought in vain to procure assistance from the banks for a projected joint-stock steam engine company, and finally was itself forced to intercede with financial aid.[16] Prior to the 1850's there was little industrial promotion; the few joint-stock firms of this period were usually formed by families, or by small groups of business associates, rather than through shares placed upon the market.[17]

12. As late as 1855, *Die Presse* reported that it was "an open secret" that of the 65 million gulden worth of bills of exchange in the portfolio of the bank, one-third came from three major houses, another third from the Escomptebank, and the remaining third from other clients. (*Die Presse*, July 6, 1855, cited in Eduard März, "Die historischen Voraussetzungen des Credit-Mobilier-Bankwesens in Österreich," *Schmollers Jahrbuch*, LXXIX [1959], 71n.)

13. Ludwig Vidéky, "Das Geld- und Creditwesen Österreichs und die Industrie," in *Die Gross-Industrie Österreichs*, VI (Vienna, 1898), 166 *et passim*; März, "Besonderheiten in der Entwicklung des österreichischen Bankwesens," *Schmollers Jahrbuch*, LXXVII (1957), 61–65.

14. Alois Brusatti, "Unternehmensfinanzierung und Privatkredit im österreichischen Vormärz," *Mitteilungen des Österreichischen Staatsarchivs*, XIII (1960), 336f.

15. *Die Gross-Industrie Österreichs*, IV, 74.

16. Brusatti, "Unternehmensfinanzierung . . . ," p. 350. The government did, after much effort, persuade the Stametz House to finance a cotton spinning joint stock company in Trumau (*ibid.* p. 350).

17. Vidéky, "Das Geld- und Creditwesen Österreichs," p. 165.

In spite of the weakness of the capital market, there was gradual development of an industrial structure. As early as the latter part of the eighteenth century, strong textile, metallurgical, and glass industries were already developing. These were often begun under the auspices of the government, which provided tariff protection and generous subsidies to large land holders to aid them in industrial ventures.[18] It must be emphasized that this gradual development of industry most often had its beginnings upon the estates of such large landowners, and it was these men who later, after the 1850's, often had the greatest access to bank credit. During the early nineteenth century there were only a few ironworks that were not in the hands of the landlords or the crown.[19] Although a movement away from the large-estate enterprise began in the 1830's, with the transition from charcoal to coal fuel, a large number of the nobility remained tied to various firms throughout the latter half of the century. In some cases, an enterprise begun by one of the nobility was taken over by others, as was the Witkowitz iron works, which was founded by the Archbishop of Olmütz in 1829. It was purchased by the Rothschild and Geymüller houses, who had an interest in the building of the Northern Railway (Nordbahn). In other cases members of the nobility maintained ownership, particularly in the coal mining industry. Even before 1848 there were a number of free-style entrepreneurs. Alois Brusatti notes that a surprisingly large number of such entrepreneurs were estate agents (*Gutsverwalter*);[20] merchants accounted for another sizable portion; and in the textile industry there was a small influx of Germans and Englishmen.

It is particularly difficult to specify the precise nature of financing in the period before the 1850's, but it is clear that the initial capital for a number of firms came from mercantile profits, loans from family or friends, or from marriages into wealthy families. Furthermore, the relatively low initial capital requirements and the gradual expansion of such industries as textiles leads one to believe that re-investment of profits played a part in financing

18. Alois Brusatti, *Österreichische Wirtschaftspolitik vom Josephinismus zum Ständestaat* (Vienna, 1965), p. 17. The extensive activity of the nobility in economic activities is discussed in a number of studies: Johann Slokar, *Geschichte der österreichischen Industrie und ihrer Förderung unter Kaiser Franz I* (Vienna, 1914); Arnošt Klíma, "Industrial Development in Bohemia, 1648–1781," *Past and Present*, XI (1957), 87–99; idem, *Manufakturní obdobi v Čechach* (Prague, 1955); and Herman Freudenberger, "Industrialization in Bohemia and Moravia in the Eighteenth Century," *Journal of Central European Affairs*, XIX (1960), 347–56. For a discussion of the development of metallurgy on the large estates, see Arthur Salz, *Geschichte der böhmischen Industrie in der Neuzeit* (Leipzig and Munich, 1913), pp. 5–29 *et passim*.

19. Otakar Mrázek, *Vývoj průmyslů v českých zemích a na Slovensku od manufaktury do roku 1918* (Prague, 1964), p. 116.

20. Brusatti, *Österreichische Wirtschaftspolitik*, p. 31f.

expansion in many more firms than those for which data are available.[21] It is especially interesting that a number of entrepreneurs in this period tended either to diversify their interests or to build factories in the same industry in other localities. This would appear to reflect not a lack of capital or entrepreneurship—at least not for some branches of industry and some men—but restrictions imposed by small regional markets.[22]

Some of the smaller private banking houses were also involved in a limited number of industrial enterprises. At the close of the eighteenth century Johann Reichsgraf von Fries, who was active in high government circles, established brass and silk factories and built up his own banking house, Fries u. Co. After his death, his widow, the daughter of a factory owner in Lyons, personally took over her husband's interests, and in the early nineteenth century she took the initiative in founding a number of industrial projects, including cotton printing factories and several sugar refineries in various parts of the Monarchy.[23] Herman Todesco of Pressburg also moved into banking from industry; Todesco began with a machine cotton spinning mill, then went on to become active in banking. He financed several factories, as well as the Austrian Southern Railway (Sudbahn).[24] For the most part, however, only the smaller banking houses had dealings with industry.[25] Undoubtedly the loans that the larger houses made to the nobility did serve to promote industry, particularly in timber,[26] but the main opening into industry for these banks came with the development of the railroads. Here again it must be noted that the banks held back from risk at every step. The building of the Austrian rail network took place either through operations by the state with additional private financing or through private firms aided by state guarantees of their investments. From the mid-1830's on, the Rothschilds became involved in transport; they stood ready to finance the Danube Steamship Company (Donaudampfschiffahrtsgesellschaft), but only with a

21. A number of examples may be found in Josef Mentschl and Gustav Otruba, *Österreichische Industrielle und Bankiers* (Vienna, 1965) and in Bundesministerium für Handel und Wiederaufbau, *100 Jahre im Dienste der Wirtschaft* (Vienna, 1961); in the latter, see, esp., the description of the growth of the Moravian cloth industry, I, 26ff.

22. For example, Lorenz Rohmberg established a mechanical linen spinning firm with a small loan from a cousin and then went on to establish diverse enterprises in several parts of the Monarchy. (Mentschl and Otruba, *Österreichische Industrielle*, p. 83f.) Also, there were several major sugar factories established in Moravia which were financed by the profits made by cloth manufacturers. (Cf. *100 Jahre im Dienste der Wirtschaft*, I, 28f.)

23. Mentschl and Otruba, *Österreichische Industrielle*, pp. 39–46.

24. Max Grunwald, *History of Jews in Vienna* (Philadephia, 1936), p. 497f. Todesco also became the director of the railroad.

25. *Die Gross-Industrie Österreichs*, VI, 164; Brusatti, "Unternehmensfinanzierung . . . ," p. 373.

26. *Ibid.* p. 351f.

government guarantee of repayment on the loan.[27] In late 1838 Salomon Rothschild utilized his personal contact with Metternich, who had received several private loans, to obtain the concession for building the 600-km. Kaiser-Ferdinands-Nordbahn. Rothschild kept a substantial portion of the shares himself, but when the price of the stock fell by nearly half, he sold his interests and held back from further participation and the government had to intervene. In connection with the building of the railroad, Rothschild joined with the Geymüller House to purchase the Witkowitz iron works and the anthracite mines in the area.[28]

It must be stressed that there were, in the early nineteenth century, a significant number of industrial enterprises established, albeit on a relatively small scale, and these largely without bank assistance. A large number of firms in textiles, mining, metallurgy, and other industries were in operation long before the appearance of the first investment banks in 1855. The number of firms and of entrepreneurs involved in industrial activities belies both the theory that there was entrepreneurial weakness as well as the theory that there was a sudden spurt of industry at the time when the great banks were established. It is quite true that industrial activities were often limited to the confines of regional markets by the poor system of transportation, but it is important to differentiate between the Austrian case, where gradual capital accumulation was taking place in industry, and that of the "theoretical" underdeveloped country, which must build its industry *ab ova*, or which is tied to extractive industry or agriculture. And it is the "theoretical" case that most closely resembles that of the Gerschenkron hypothesis.

To a large degree, the firms with which the banks came to have connections after 1855 were either firms which were already fairly successful enterprises or else groups of existing firms which were consolidated either by banks or by individuals. To cite one example, the Österreichisch-Alpine Montangesellschaft, one of the largest metallurgical complexes in the Monarchy, was formed through the consolidation of a large number of smaller firms. These firms, many of which were small mines and mills formed as early as the seventeenth and eighteenth centuries, were gradually combined by merger or purchase. By these means their number had decreased to thirty-eight by 1848; these thirty-eight firms were then consolidated into eleven firms in about 1868; and they were again combined in 1881–82 into the Alpine-Montangesellschaft.[29] When the individual firms involved had first been

27. *Ibid.* p. 348f.

28. The first coke-blast furnace in the Monarchy was installed in the works, which became one of the leading metallurgical firms in the Monarchy.

29. *Die Gross-Industrie Österreichs*, I, 186. Generally speaking, most mergers and attempts to build cartels which occurred prior to 1900 were primarily begun as defensive measures in the face of declining markets.

established, members of the nobility had often owned or headed them, and various merchants and individual entrepreneurs had participated in them.

INDUSTRY AND FINANCE, 1848–73

Following the Revolution of 1848, the government's interest in the completion of the railroads, as well as the increased commercial demand for short-term credit, brought into being three important joint-stock credit institutions. Two of these, the Niederösterreichische Escomptegesellschaft (Vienna, 1853) and the Banca Commerciale Triestina (Trieste, 1854) were designed to meet short-term credit needs. A third institution, the famous k. k. priv. öst. Creditanstalt für Handel und Gewerbe (1855), was intended to satisfy a wide range of financial needs.

At first glance, when one examines the nature of the Creditanstalt and the number of great banks which followed in its wake, the picture of banks serving as a motive force in industrialization seems quite plausible. When the Rothschilds won out over the brothers Pereire in competition for the favor of the government, they did so by emulating the Pereire concept of a crédit mobilier bank—an institution combining the investment banking of the Pereire bank with regular commercial banking, in the style of the subsequent German "universal" banks. They did this on a grand scale with the founding of the Creditanstalt in 1855 with the then enormous sum of 60 million gulden in share capital. The bank set out with the intention of participating in the building of railroads, the promotion of industry, and the provision of short-term credit. Other banks of a similar nature followed soon thereafter; by 1883 an Austrian authority designated 13 of the 58 major Austrian banks as "Crédit-Mobilier" banks.[30]

Professor Gerschenkron has recognized that the Rothschilds were for many years the chief antagonists of the Crédit Mobilier and of the concepts upon which it was based, and that the Creditanstalt was formed for the most part as a defensive measure to stay the penetration of the French bankers into Austria. Nevertheless, Gerschenkron maintains that in spite of themselves

> [the Rothschilds] succeeded only because they became willing to establish the bank themselves and to conduct it not as an old-fashioned banking enterprise but as a crédit mobilier, that is, as a bank devoted to railroadization and industrialization of the country.[31]

30. Heinrich Rauchberg, "Österreichs Bank- und Credit-Institut in den Jahren 1872–1883," *Statistische Monatsschrift* (Vienna, 1885), p. 8f.

31. Gerschenkron, *Economic Backwardness*, p. 13. Gerschenkron also writes that "in Austria proper the banks could successfully devote themselves to the promotion of industrial activities" (*Ibid.* p. 20).

Here again, the primary difference between the approach presented here and that of Gerschenkron is one of emphasis. In a number of ways the activities of the new universal banks were crucial to the development of industry, but a devotion to the promotion of industrial activities does not seem to have been widely in evidence. In 1854 the government promulgated a new railroad concession law which called for private investment in railroads and offered a guarantee for such investment. It was in the battle for this lucrative business that the Pereires and Rothschilds joined issue and the Creditanstalt was born. Thereafter, until the crash of 1873, railroad construction was far and away the prime "industrial" interest of the large Vienna banks. The banks were generally much more cautious about becoming involved in other industrial activities. The important distinction between railroads and other industrial ventures has been drawn quite clearly in a fairly recent contribution by Professor Gerschenkron himself: he noted that European railroads had little difficulty in attracting both foreign and domestic capital, even in relatively backward countries, whereas "capital for industrial investment was timid and reluctant." [32]

In the period between 1855 and 1873 the character of Austrian banking clearly changed. As late as 1855 a leading industrialist was forced to pay 15 per cent interest to have his bills discounted by a Viennese bank.[33] After 1855 the new commercial banks greatly extended the possibilities for short-term credit. Further, the period of railroad building brought with it a general expansion of many branches of industry. It was in this period that major financial institutions became involved in industrial activities: a few large firms were purchased outright by the banks, others were changed into joint-stock companies (*Aktiengesellschaften*), while still others obtained substantial long-term financing. In the late 1860's, and up to the Bourse Crash of 1873, the number of joint-stock banks and the quantity of their promotional activities rapidly increased. From 1868 to 1873 there took place the great "fever" of speculation in all types of promotion. Whereas earlier few industrial shares had been sold on the Bourse, now the public at large was eager to speculate on almost any prospect. In actuality, most of the promoted firms existed only on paper, and few survived when the 1873 depression came. Economic historians concerned with Austrian finance maintain that one major result of the Bourse Crash was a lasting aversion to joint-stock companies and industrial shares on the part of the government, the banks, and the public, and that this came to be part of the fact and folklore of the post-depression period.

32. Gerschenkron, *Continuity in History and Other Essays* (Cambridge, Mass., 1968), p. 103.

33. See [Creditanstalt-Bankverein], *Ein Jahrhundert Creditanstalt-Bankverein* (Vienna, 1957), p. 28.

FINANCE AND INDUSTRY, 1873–1913

Although most of the speculative activities were carried out by independent promoters, it was in the period preceding 1873 that many of the banks lived up to their roles as crédit mobilier institutions. For a number of these banks, dealing in the securities of various enterprises had comprised the main part of their business.[34] After 1873, however, the investment banks made a sharp transformation in their policies. As one contemporary author expressed it: "In the epoch following 1873 the *Mobil-Bank* developed into a new type, which is characteristic of Austrian banking: regular bank business was to be the underlying basis of the bank's existence."[35] This concentration on current business became the predominant feature of Austrian banking for many years, and it strongly affected the relationship between financial intermediaries and industrial enterprises. In 1907, Dr. Eugen Lopuszanski, secretary to the Finance Minister and one of the best informed men in financial affairs, suggested that the concentration on current business predominated in banking until the economic upswing of 1904. Lopuszanski held that after 1873 this concern was intensified with every downswing in the economy, and reached its peak in the depression of 1901–03, when there was almost a complete standstill in business with securities and few or no new corporations or new firms were established by the banks.[36]

Part of the reason for the lack of promotional activity lay in the public's reluctance to invest in industrial securities, but it also lay in the Austrian tax structure. From the 1870's on, various laws and taxes discriminated against the joint-stock form of organization, and a new tax law of 1898 increased the burden. A more liberal incorporation law, passed in 1899, eased restrictions upon the formation of such companies, but an industrial inquiry of 1904 still showed that the joint-stock companies were taxed two times, and often three to four times, as much as unincorporated enterprises. Thus a company which became incorporated paid a large penalty. As a result, incorporation proceeded at a very slow pace. While from 1867 to 1873 concessions were granted for 1,005 new joint-stock companies, in the entire

34. Several of the large banks, such as the Creditanstalt and the Anglo-österreichische Bank, stayed generally aloof from the period of speculation. See Mentschl and Otruba, *Österreichische Industrielle*, p. 71; Carl Morawitz, "Fünfzig Jahre Geschichte einer Wiener Bank," in Gesellschaft österreichischer Volkswirte, *Jahrbuch 1914* (Vienna, 1914), p. 13f.

35. Fritz G. Steiner, *Die Entwicklung des Mobilbankwesens in Österreich* (Vienna, 1913), p. 265.

36. Lopuszanski, *Das Bankwesen Österreichs* (Vienna, 1907), p. 7. A knowledgeable contemporary, speaking of the attitude of financial institutions in Bohemia from 1873 to the 1890's, noted that "insofar as promotional activity, initiative in establishing new enterprises [was concerned], not a thought was given to it during this time" (Josef Horák, *Přehled vývoje českých obchodních bank* [Prague, 1913], p. 92).

period from 1874 to 1880 only 43 such concessions were recorded.[37] It was not until the turn of the century that this form of organization began to show any serious growth (see Table II.4). The relatively backward develop-

TABLE II.4

Joint-stock companies in Austria, 1880–1912

Year	Number	Share Capital (million crowns)	Assets (million crowns)
1880	406	1,255	3,954
1885	380	1,269	4,180
1890	385	1,316	4,864
1895	433	1,489	6,429
1900	529	2,010	8,371
1905	587	2,411	10,787
1910	709	3,304	16,595
1912	780	4,171	19,946

Source: Compiled from data in *Österreichische statistisches Handbuch* (hereafter cited as *ÖSH*), given years.

ment of the joint-stock companies can be seen from the fact that as late as 1907 Germany had eight times as many joint-stock companies as Austria, and even Russia had almost three times as many.[38] Further, although there was fairly rapid growth of joint-stock companies after 1903, industrial securities still held a minor place in the capital market. As late as 1910 industrial and railroad securities accounted for only 2.3 per cent of all issues in Austria-Hungary, as compared with 63 per cent for Great Britain and the United States, 29 per cent for Germany, 16 per cent for France, and more than 20 per cent for both Italy and Rumania.[39] In 1913 Carl Morawitz, president of the Anglo-österreichische Bank, characterized the role of the banks: "If one can find fault with the banks in the period before 1873 for carrying through too much promotion, one can also criticize them for holding back new enterprises in the period 1878–1895."[40]

37. *Creditanstalt-Bankverein*, p. 65. Taxes on shares (*Aktiensteuer*) were also imposed on shareholders, and reached one-fourth of the returns to the owners. See Friedrich Hertz, *Die Produktionsgrundlagen der österreichischen Industrie vor und nach dem Krieg* (Vienna, 1917), p. 182f.

38. Zdeněk Jindra, "Průmyslové monopoly v Rakousko-Uhersku," *Československý časopis historický*, IV (1956), 238.

39. *Compass, Finanzielles Jahrbuch für Österreich-Ungarn* (1913), I. Bd., 13. Bank stocks equaled 18 per cent of all Austro-Hungarian issues, while government, provincial, and municipal issues accounted for approximately 80 per cent (*Ibid.* p. 13).

40. Morawitz, "Fünfzig Jahre Geschichte einer Wiener Bank," p. 18.

The picture drawn here, of a weak market for industrial securities and a penchant by the banks to avoid industrial promotion, does not in itself constitute an argument against the importance of financial intermediaries. Theoretically, an industrial enterprise that lacked the opportunity to float shares on the market was faced with two alternatives: it could either press on hopefully through the reinvestment of profits or it could lean even more heavily on external financing, primarily by the banks, for both short- and long-term credit.

When one attempts to define the role of financial intermediaries in this period, however, it must be stated at the outset that any conclusive answers to the question of the degree to which firms relied upon external (or indirect) as opposed to internal (or direct) financing must await more detailed research. In the interim, however, it is still possible to sketch the broad outlines of the bank–industry relationship. By the beginning of the 1880's most sectors of the Austrian economy were recovering from the 1873 depression, and thereafter they showed significant, if at times erratic, growth. In the 1880's there was extensive rationalization, mechanization, and expansion in mining, metallurgy, sugar manufacture, Galician petroleum, and several other industries, all of which contributed to unprecedented growth in engineering. In the early 1890's the new electro-technical industry was established and grew rapidly. It is clear, however, that there was relatively little industrial promotion by the banks during this period, and Morawitz maintained that "the expansion of large firms took place primarily through private [non-bank] capital and the reinvestment of profits." [41]

Like their German counterparts, which they closely resembled, the main link between the Austrian banks and industry lay in the short-term credit on current account, which in a number of cases became in reality long-term financing (line credit). Such large-scale or long-term credit as was granted by the banks was generally given in this guise, but the practice apparently began only around the 1890's. A second substantial link developed from the widespread practice of the banks in undertaking commission sales of a number of products for industrial enterprises. In the 1860's the banks began taking over part or all of the output of given firms on a commission basis, at first in the coal and sugar industries. This practice continued through the 1880's, and in later years such items as petroleum, agricultural products, lumber, and the like were added to the list of commodities sold by banks and special bank sales bureaus.

A fairly typical case of the development of bank–industry ties would be the following: A current account connection was made by an agreement between the bank and its industrial client, possibly on condition that the bank conduct commission sales for the firm or that it have exclusive rights to

41. *Ibid.* p. 19.

conduct the client firm's general banking business. In the late 1880's the practice developed whereby, if the bank was quite sanguine as to the firm's prospects, the bank would grant it credit up to a given amount, nominally on a short-term basis, but actually with terms providing for repayment over a much longer period. Here it must be emphasized that the Viennese banks were not the venturesome substitutes for entrepreneurs that the brothers Pereire envisioned. Rather, the great banks appear to have selected plump, juicy firms with favorable prospects, with the difficulties and risks of their early years already completed. It was with such firms that the banks built up expanded credit dealings, in many cases granting unsecured bank credit in fairly large, and possibly increasingly large, sums, for a period of several years. Toward the end of the century, if the bank was particularly interested in a firm and if the firm required capital of more than ordinary magnitude, steps would be taken to turn it into a joint-stock company. The bank would take upon itself the underwriting and promotion of the stocks issued, or enter into a consortium with other financial intermediaries to this end. In many cases the bank could not find a ready market for the shares and would be forced to hold them for months and even years before placing them. In the meantime, the bank would continue its ties with the firm through the current account connection and would often seek to obtain as much control over the firm as possible, through command over various aspects of business or by means of interlocking directorates. In very few cases would the bank seek to hold onto the shares of the companies concerned indefinitely. In the economic upswing at the beginning of the twentieth century, the problem of placing industrial securities and extending credit on current account led to the practice on the part of the banks of vastly extending their own share capital.[42] In the 1880's and 1890's the implication of the weighty role of the current accounts was, in fact, that large-scale or long-term credit was given on a highly selective basis, and generally only to firms which were already doing quite well. New venturesome enterprises in new branches, or new firms in old branches, were obviously limited in the amount of aid they could receive from the banks by this means.

The keynote of banking was, above all, caution. This becomes clear when one examines both the timing of the banks' interest in given branches of industry and the type of firm with which the banks dealt. Between the depression of 1873 and 1888 the banks played almost no part in promotional activities or in providing long-term credit to industrial firms. For the most part, the banks drew closer only to those firms with whom they had dealt before the crash. The areas of involvement were almost exclusively firms in coal mining, metallurgy, and the sugar industry.

42. See Table II.5. The discussion above and in the following pages is based to a large degree on my own research in the archives of the Creditanstalt.

In the coal mining industry a distinction must be made between the mining of lignite and anthracite. Lignite production was closely linked with the German market, and therefore it was a growth industry, even during most of the depression years. This branch was already fairly concentrated by the middle of the nineteenth century, and it appears to have been financed by the Böhmische Escompte-Bank, a subsidiary of the Niederösterreichische-Escomptebank which came to be known as the "House Bank" of the lignite industry. The mines were often located on large estates, and the recipients of credit were often men such as Prince Salm—men of stature, whose names had been linked with the private banks of earlier times and were to be found in the lists of the boards of directors of the new investment banks.[43] As late as 1898, however, a newspaper article maintained that while the Bohemian lignite industry took its bills of exchange to the banks, the banks evinced little other interest in the mines.[44]

This lack of interest in mining can be seen in the relationship of the major Prague bank, the Živnostenská banka, with the "Moldava" lignite mine in Loma. During the depression the firm had defaulted on its credit and had been taken over by the bank. After 1882 the bank attempted to form a joint-stock company to work the mines, but it found no support for this venture. The bank then attempted to sell the firm and only succeeded in doing so after 1888. It is significant both that the mines were located in what proved to be one of the best areas in the important northern Bohemian lignite districts and that the bank encountered such great difficulty in locating purchasers for the promising firm.[45]

Anthracite, on the other hand, was largely consumed domestically, and most anthracite mines were vertically integrated with the primary metal-lurgical firms, which purchased the mines from the large landholders.

A high degree of concentration had already been reached in the production of iron and steel by the early 1880's, with three major firms dominating the industry. The largest company, the Alpine Montangesellschaft in Styria, was formed in 1880 from a host of smaller companies on the initiative of Eugene Bontoux, with his establishment of the Austrian Länderbank backed by the French Union Générale.[46] From its earliest days financial backing for the

43. The firms which received the attention of the investment banks before the 1880's appear to have been largely those whose leaders were either aristocrats (Prince Salm, Fürstenburg, Schwarzenberg) or industrialists who were themselves on the boards of directors of the great banks (Schöller, Lanna, Hornbostel, etc.).

44. *Neue Freie Presse*, November 27, 1898.

45. See Horák, *Přehled vývoje*, p. 96, and *Živnostenska banka v Praze 1869–1918* (Prague, 1919), p. 34.

46. Concerning Bontoux's role in the founding of the Länderbank, his plan to form a metallurgical complex in Austria, and the nature of other French activities in Austria, see Jean Bouvier, *Le Krach de l'Union Générale (1878–1885)* (Paris, 1960), pp. 58–70, and Rondo Cameron, *France and the Economic Development of Europe* (Princeton, 1961), pp. 198, 220, *et passim*.

large company appears to have come from a variety of sources, including stocks and bonds floated internationally, internal financing, and various short- and long-term credit arrangements with individual financial intermediaries who represented the different enterprises making up the larger company.

The second largest company, the Prager Eisenindustrie-Gesellschaft, was similarly a composite of three smaller companies consolidated in 1857 by Adalbert Lanna, a Prague industrialist and member of the board of directors of the Creditanstalt. The Creditanstalt furnished 3.5 million gulden to the new *commandite* company as a mortage loan, while the remainder of the eight million gulden capital was represented primarily by shares given to the previous owners in exchange for their properties. In supplying the loan, the Creditanstalt stipulated that it should have the right to participate in the affairs of the company and to hold preferred shares; from then on several directors of the Creditanstalt were active in the leadership of the firm.[47] In the railroad boom of the late 1850's and 1860's the company could not obtain enough funds from the Creditanstalt, and it sought additional credit from the German Darmstädter Bank. The directors of the firm attempted to get the Creditanstalt to agree to turn the company into a joint-stock company, but the bank put them off. In 1862, however, the Creditanstalt and the Darmstädter banks joined in underwriting the company as a joint-stock company.[48] By the late 1870's the firm had come under the control of one of the great entrepreneurs of the Monarchy, Carl Wittgenstein. Wittgenstein had dealings with several major banks; his relatives were directors of the Niederösterreichische Escomptegesellschaft, and for a short period Wittgenstein himself sat on the board of directors of the Creditanstalt. Throughout the life of the firm, however, Wittgenstein and his group appear to have remained independent agents, and in later years the firm seems to have required little aid from the banks.[49]

The third major firm, the Witkowitz iron works, remained the possession of the Rothschild House and the Brothers Guttmann.

The commission sales of sugar, and loans made to the sugar producers for tax payments, brought a number of banks close to the sugar industry before 1873. In the course of the depression the banks continued their commission sales and in some instances took over firms that were deeply in debt. Most of the banks had some dealings with major sugar-producing firms.[50] The commission sales contracts, which lasted from one to three years, were at times

47. *Creditanstalt-Bankverein*, 39; *Sto let kladenských železáren* (Prague, 1959), p. 30f.

48. *Ibid.* pp. 50–53.

49. Jan Kořan, "Z dějin českého železářstvi v počátcích kapitalismu," *Sborník pro hospodářské a sociální dějiny*, II (1947), 164f.; *Obzor národohospodářský*, XIV (1909), 389; Archives of the Creditanstalt Bankverein, Verwaltungsrats-Protokoll, December 13, 1898. Wittgenstein was the leader in the formation of metallurgical cartels in Austria, beginning with a rail cartel in 1878.

50. See *Compass* (1905), II. Bd., 770.

a source of considerable profit to the banks, but the close ties thus engendered also served, in this unstable industry, as a source of illiquidity for the banks, particularly during the crisis in the industry in the mid-1880's. Consequently, it led them to avoid making commitments to other weak firms in this branch of industry, or even to develop ties with other branches.

At the end of the 1880's there appeared a renewal of bank interest in industry, culminating in the so-called second *Gründerzeit* following 1895. The extension of bank ties with industry subsequent to 1888, however, took place in a manner which makes the description of it as a new promotional period somewhat misleading. The long-run interest of banks in industry is more realistically seen as a process that ebbed and flowed with the changing fortunes of industry. Thus one sees an intensification of interest after the economic upturn from 1888 to 1891, another following the recovery from the Bourse Crisis of 1895, and the greatest of all during the upswing from 1904 to 1908. In each case, the increased interest of the banks in industry followed, rather than preceded, the economic upturn. In 1888 there were a number of discussions in government circles concerning the inability of the Monarchy to emulate the healthy upswing in the German economy, which had been taking place since 1886, and Finance Minister Steibach publicly criticized the banks' neglect of industry as contrasted with the activities of German banks.[51] The Austrian upswing of 1888, and the increasing competition among the banks for regular bank business, led to greater involvement in industry. This involvement took the form of the development of closer banking ties with a number of select firms, with the banks' ties being deepened gradually over the years with *these* firms, rather than widening into a more general promotional activity. The Austrian bankers were hesitant; they discussed a number of wide-ranging plans for industrial promotion in various branches, but the feeling that the boom might not last pervaded their thoughts, and little came of the plans.[52] While the banks were involved to some degree in newer branches of industry, such as rubber and electricity, and they showed an increasing interest in petroleum, from 1888 to 1895 a series of large international loan operations took much of their attention.[53]

One of the basic factors that diverted capital from industry was the relatively high yield on government bonds. In the mid-1890's, however, the consolidation of Austrian state credit and the decreasing profitability of state and municipal loans led to increasing competition among the banks for current business; this in turn provided an incentive for banks to strengthen their ties with individual firms and to develop promotional activities in

---

51. Cited in Eduard März, *Österreichische Industrie- und Bankpolitik in der Zeit Franz Josephs I* (Vienna, 1968), p. 254.

52. See *Creditanstalt-Bankverein*, p. 96.

53. *Ibid.* p. 97.

industry.[54] This renewed interest in industry was evidenced by a sharp increase in the number of industrial joint-stock companies, which took place despite the many complaints of prohibitive taxes on this form of organization. After 1895 the Viennese great banks not only increased their activities with the firms with which they had formerly done business, but they also began to increase their involvement in new branches of industry and with new firms. "New firms," however, must again be qualified, the *new* firms in this instance being firms that had grown without the aid of the banks and that had come to maturity and profitability on their own. With the economic growth of the late 1890's, and even more, in the boom after 1904, the banks entered into long-term credit financing, involvement in business affairs, and promotion of joint-stock companies on an entirely new level. In discussing this period one is justified in saying that there was a deep involvement of banks in industry as that phrase is commonly understood. But once again, in actuality, the banks dealt *only* with the most profitable firms. When one examines three of the major branches with which the banks came to be involved—the electro-technical, machine-building, and petroleum industries—it is clear in case after case, and branch after branch, that the financial intermediaries took an interest only in those firms which had already proved themselves to be exceptionally well off. The electro-technical branch provides a typical illustration of this process. The impetus for the establishment of this branch came to Austria from Germany as early as 1887, and the growth of electro-technical firms into the early 1890's also was supported primarily from Germany.[55] It was not until the mid-1890's, however, that the Austrian banks began to be seriously involved in this branch. A case in point is the decision of the Creditanstalt to form ties with this type of enterprise. According to a discussion which took place among the directors of the Creditanstalt in 1895, the bank had been considering the idea of getting into the field for some time. Nevertheless, it had held back, because the majority of propositions which came its way were either foreign or would have required large amounts of capital to install.[56] In 1895, however, the bank decided to begin a credit relationship with a "most solid" firm in Brünn. This firm had been established in 1887 under private auspices, and had become a leading producer in the Monarchy by the time the bank entered into a creditor relationship with it. The firm had sought for a number of years to be transformed into a joint-stock company, but the bank, while tendering it substantial credit, held back from this step. In subsequent years the bank transferred its interest from this firm to the Berliner Allgemeine Elektrizitäts-Gesellschaft, and joined forces with another bank, the Boden-Creditanstalt,

54. See März, "Besonderheiten . . . ," pp. 66f.
55. *Die Gross-Industrie Österreichs*, III, 181.
56. Creditanstalt Archive, Verwaltungsrats Protokoll, February 5, 1895.

to finance that firm's project for strengthening and reorganizing the Vienna A.E.G.-Union Elektrizitäts-Gesellschaft, which had originally been a German enterprise.[57] The experience of the Živnostenská banka in Prague was similar. In 1894 this bank extended credit to an electro-technical firm owned by František Křižik, which had been built up on a gradual basis by Křižik since the 1870's, and it was on the basis of this firm that the bank established a joint-stock company. In the following year the bank purchased a firm, Kolben Co., which in several years had become one of the leading producers of electric motors and dynamos in Austria. The bank turned the enterprise into a joint-stock company and entered into close managerial and credit relations with it.[58]

In other branches of engineering the story was strikingly similar. A number of major firms, Škoda, Ringhoffer, and the Wiener Neustädter Locomotiv-fabrik among them, were formed on a family or business partnership basis, gradually overcame the uncertainties of the market, and at a relatively late stage applied to the banks for large credits. Emil Škoda, for example, had built up his extensive factory from an initial loan made by relatives, who had enabled him to open a machine shop. Thereafter he assiduously avoided close ties with banks until just before his death in 1900. At that time, and in the years following, when the firm was run by his son, the increased scale of investment led the firm to seek increased bank credit and to convert into a joint-stock company.[59] In the petroleum industry, as well, the initial growth was based upon private, non-bank initiative.[60] In the case of petroleum, however, the picture is somewhat mixed. In the early 1880's the Galizsche Creditbank acquired large blocs of land and began to take over the production facilities of numerous small producers.[61] Nevertheless, in most cases private entrepreneurs of the nobility, or outsiders, such as Simeon Bergheim of England and William Henry MacGarvey of Canada, who built up large petroleum enterprises on the basis of re-invested profits, were more typical.[62]

When the banks took more and more of an interest in prospering firms

57. Creditanstalt Archive, Verwaltungsrats Protokoll, February 5, 1895, March 7, 1899, October 17, 1899, November 25, 1902, December 18, 1902, December 20, 1904; *Die Gross-Industrie Österreichs*, III, 183.

58. Cf. *Die Gross-Industrie Österreichs*, III, 206–211; Pavla Vrbová, *Hlavní otázky vzniku a vývoje českého strojírenství do roku 1918* [Prague, 1959], p. 194.

59. Václav Jísá, *Škodovy zavody, 1859/1919* (Prague, 1965), pp. 36, 85f., 97; Creditanstalt Archive, Verwaltungsrats-Protokoll, January 20, March 24, December 22, 1891, January 5, 1892, December 18, 1902, and December 16, 1903.

60. See *Die Gross-Industrie Österreichs*, I, 330–33.

61. *Ibid.* p. 330.

62. *Ibid.* pp. 332–35; see also Johann Zaránski, "Über die Petroleumindustrie in Galizien," in Freie Vereinigung für staatswissenschaftliche Fortbildung in Wien, *Wirtschaftliche Zustände Galiziens in der Gegenwart* (Vienna and Leipzig, 1913).

TABLE II.6 (cont.)

F. MORTGAGE LOANS (million crowns) (cont.)

1900	32	58	d	11
1905	32	n.a.	d	n.a.
1910	25	n.a.	d	3
1912	n.a.	n.a.	d	n.a.

a 1881.

b Includes only the six major Viennese great banks which were involved with the financing and founding of industrial firms: Anglo-österreichische Bank, Creditanstalt, Österreichische Landerbank, Union-Bank, Niederösterreichische Escomptegesellschaft, and Wiener-Bank-Verein.

c Total short-term credit is represented by debtors on current account, bills of exchange, and advances on goods and securities.

d Insignificant quantities.

Sources: All Austrian banks, including Austro-Hungarian Bank, *Österreichische Statistik* (1903), 6. Bd., 3. Hft. xliii and *ÖSH*, given years. All Czech banks, *ÖSH*, given years. Austrian joint-stock banks and Bohemian Lands' joint-stock banks, 1880, *Statistisches Jahrbuch der Österreichisch-Ungarischen Monarchie*, 1880, VIII. Hft.; 1885, *Österreichische Statistik*, 16. Bd., 3. Hft.; 1890, *Ibid.*, 37. Bd., 3. Hft.; 1895, *Ibid.*, 48. Bd., 2. Hft.; 1900, *Ibid.*, 67. Bd., 3. Hft.; 1905, *Ibid.*, 80. Bd., 2. Hft.; 1910, "Die österreichischen Banken im Jahre 1910," *Mitteilungen des k.k. Finanzministeriums*, XX. Jhrg., 2. Hft. (1914); 1912, *Österreichische Statistik*, N.F., 15. Bd., 2. Hft.

TABLE II.7

Selected Liabilities of Banks in Austria and the Bohemian Crownlands

A. NOTES AND TIME DEPOSITS (million crowns)

Year	All Banks		Joint-stock Banks	
	Austria	Bohemian Lands	Austria[b]	Bohemian Lands
1880	197.9	76.1[a]	76.3	65.7
1885	160.5	52.9	64.1	48.9
1890	170.9	66.2	63.6	64.3
1895	220.6	104.8	60.1	97.7
1900	281.3	n.a.	80.5	109.0
1905	329.1	134.8	105.3	111.2
1910	n.a.	n.a.	302.2	328.9
1912	1,105.2	439.9	410.0	373.0

As Percentage of Total Liabilities

Year	Austria	Bohemian Lands	Austria[b]	Bohemian Lands
1880	6	20[a]	13	44
1885	5	15	8	41
1890	4	14	7	43
1895	4	14	4	39
1900	3	n.a.	5	25
1905	3	7	4	17
1910	n.a.	n.a.	8	22
1912	9	11	· 10	19

TABLE II.7 (cont.)

B. PAYABLES[e] (million crowns)

| | All Banks | | Joint-stock Banks | |
Year	Austria	Bohemian Lands	Austria[b]	Bohemian Lands
1880	363.0	42.0[a]	218.0	26.3
1885	412.1	28.7	291.0	23.0
1890	651.3	64.2	426.8	35.2
1895	1,075.0	122.7	724.8	78.2
1900	1,524.0	133.9	809.1	197.4
1905	2,481.5[f]	482.6	1.367.4[f]	355.2[f]
1910	3,755.6[f]	n.a.	1,971.0[f]	653.0[f]
1912	4,535.0[f]	988.3	2,401.9[f]	696.4[f]

As Percentage of Total Liabilities

Year	Austria	Bohemian Lands	Austria	Bohemian Lands
1880	12	11[a]	38	18
1885	13	8	35	19
1890	17	13	44	24
1895	20	17	53	31
1900	21	10	50	45
1905	26	23	58	55
1910	26	n.a.	56	44
1912	27	26	57	43

C. *PFANDBRIEFE*, i.e. INTEREST-BEARING MORTGAGE BONDS
(million crowns)

| | All Banks | | Joint-stock Banks | |
Year	Austria	Bohemian Lands	Austria	Bohemian Lands
1880	974.2	195.6[a]	—	10
1885	961.8	221.3	—	—
1890	1,206.0	311.7	0.6	—
1895	1,592.2	403.7	0.2	—
1900	2,327.4	n.a.	0.7	2
1905	n.a.	n.a.	—	9
1910	n.a.	n.a.	—	—
1912	n.a.	n.a.	—	51

As Percentage of Total Liabilities

Year	Austria	Bohemian Lands	Austria	Bohemian Lands
1880	32	53	0	7
1885	29	61	0	0
1890	30	64	d	0
1895	29	55	d	0

TABLE II.7 (cont.)

C. *PFANDBRIEFE*, i.e. INTEREST-BEARING MORTGAGE BONDS
(million crowns) (cont.)

1900	32	n.a.	d	0.5
1905	n.a.	n.a.	0	1
1910	n.a.	n.a.	0	0
1912	n.a.	n.a.	0	3

ᵃ ᵗᵒ ᵈ See notes a to d in Table II.6.
ᵉ Payables consist primarily of items on current account.
ᶠ Includes *Giro* accounts, which are not significant quantities in preceding years.

Source: See Table II.6.

TABLE II.8

Annual Rates of Growth (Compound) of Selected Assets and Liabilities of Banks in Austria and the Bohemian Crownlands (percentage)

Period	All Banks		Joint-stock Banks	
	Austria	Bohemian Lands	Austriaᵉ	Bohemian Lands
Total Short-term Credit				
1880–1912	6.1	8.6ᵃ	6.6	8.3
1880–1890	3.2	1.4ᵇ	5.1	2.1
1890–1900	4.9	14.5	6.0	12.0
1900–1912	9.6	11.2	8.3	10.7
Debtors on Current Account				
1880–1912	7.1	11.0ᵃ	7.9	10.4
1880–1890	5.3	5.7ᵇ	8.8	6.3
1890–1900	5.3	13.6	6.3	12.0
1900–1912	10.0	13.4	8.5	12.6
Bills of Exchange				
1880–1912	5.3	6.2ᵃ	4.9	6.0
1880–1890	0.8	−0.6ᵇ	−1.5	0.2
1890–1900	5.8	11.6	7.5	10.1
1900–1912	8.9	7.7	8.2	7.6
Advances on Goods and Securities				
1880–1912	4.8	7.7ᵃ	3.8	8.9
1880–1890	3.4	−6.1ᵇ	3.3	−34.6
1890–1900	1.0	17.2	1.2	55.0
1900–1912	9.4	12.0	6.4	11.5

Period	All Banks		Joint-stock Banks	
	Austria	Bohemian Lands	Austria[c]	Bohemian Lands
		Notes and Time Deposits		
1880–1912	5.8	5.6[a]	5.4	5.6
1880–1890	−1.5	−1.4[b]	−1.8	−0.2
1890–1900	5.1	n.a.	2.4	5.4
1900–1912	12.1	n.a.	14.5	10.8
		Payables		
1800–1912	8.2	10.4[a]	7.8	10.8
1880–1890	6.0	4.3[b]	6.7	2.9
1890–1900	8.9	7.6	6.6	18.8
1900–1912	9.5	18.1	9.5	10.8

[a] 1881–1912. [b] 1881–1890. [c] Six major Viennese great banks. See Table II.6, note b.
Sources: Calculated from data in Tables II.6 and II.7.

fervor and with the express purpose of establishing new industrial enterprise and engaging in industrial promotion, in each case the ink was barely dry upon the bank's statutes when the bank turned away from industrial activities.[63] The Czech banks came to follow precisely the same pattern as the larger Viennese banks; they gave extensive long-term credit to and made close ties with only those firms that were already prospering. By 1908 the leading Czech banks had turned away from industrial promotion at home and had become engaged in extensive financial activities in banking and even in industry in the Balkans.[64]

In retrospect, it is fairly clear that the particular character of the bank–industry relationship in Austria was less a cause than a consequence of the pattern of industrial growth. Subsequent to the railway investments in the 1850's and 1860's there was little industrial promotion or large-scale credit extended by the banks to industry until the late 1890's. Thereafter, banks established strong ties with industry, but only with the most substantial firms. It is also clear that the broad extension of a network of branch banks played an important role in the mobilization and provision of short-term credit for

63. For a description of the growth of banking in the Bohemian Crownlands, see Horák, *Přehled vývoje.*

64. See Karel Herman, "K vývoji českého kapitálu," in Ustav dějin, Komunistické strany Československa, *Otázky vývoje kapitalismu v českých zemích a v Rakousku-Uhersku do roku 1918* (Prague, 1957); *idem,* "Novoslovanství a česká buržoasie," in Československá akademie věd, *Kapitoly z dějin vzájemných vztahu národu ČSR a SSSR,* Vol. I (Prague, 1958); Stanislav Kukla, *Srbské peněžnictví a český kapitál* (Prague and Belgrade, 1912).

a number of industrial firms. In addition, in the great "spurt" after 1903 the banks were a substitute for a strong market for securities: they raised their own share capital to provide funds for industrial expansion. If the role of the Austrian banks was not greater, the bankers' caution is not difficult to understand, given the fluctuations in the conditions for economic growth in the economy.

The preliminary exploration tendered here has not been so much an attempt to evaluate the economic role of the banks in its entirety as it has been directed toward demonstrating the potentially deceptive nature of a schematization which depicts the banks as the holders of the levers of industrialization, ready at what Gerschenkron calls the "moment" of industrialization to furnish entrepreneurship for and guidance to a backward country. A sharp distinction must be made between a non-industrialized economy and one in which industry and capital accumulation gradually develop to the point where it may become profitable for the banks to invest in industry. The evidence suggests that in Austria the process of industrialization was much more gradual than has been generally assumed, and that, while financial intermediaries played an important role, that role was far less significant, particularly with respect to the banks' role in guiding industrial development, than scholars have heretofore maintained.

CHAPTER III

Italy 1861–1914[*]

JON S. COHEN

Italy first experienced rapid industrial growth on a broad front during the twenty years prior to World War I.[1] Its industrial expansion coincided with an upswing of the international business cycle, a rise in world prices (which reversed a decline that had begun in the 1870's), and a general increase in the level of world trade. Not only did Italy's industrial production, national income, and total foreign trade grow absolutely, they also rose relative to those of the other countries of western Europe and those of the United States.[2] Although Italian growth statistics for the period had an upward bias caused by the low base from which measurement began, these years were the first during which comparisons of this sort had any meaning.

These observations concerning Italian economic expansion after 1894 must be tempered. As was the case in most countries, industrial expansion was not impervious to international economic crises, nor did individuals, geographic groups, and regions in the Italian economy benefit equally from the upswing. While the expansion was unaffected by the 1900 world recession,

[*] I am especially grateful to my colleagues, Luigi Tomasini and Edwin Truman, for their helpful criticism and suggestions.

Although this discussion deals with the period 1861–1914, that is, from the unification of Italy to World War I, lack of adequate data for early years forces me to concentrate on the period after 1870.

1. See, *inter alia*, Luciano Cafagna, "La formazione di una 'Base Industriale' fra il 1896 ed il 1914," in A. Caracciolo, *La formazione dell'Italia industriale* (Bari, 1963), 138; and R. Romeo, *Breve storia della grande industria in Italia* (Rocca San Casciano, 1963), 66.

2. See V. Paretti and G. Block, "La production industrielle en Europe occidentale et aux Etats Unis de 1901 à 1955," in *Moneta e Credito*, IX (Dec. 1956), 269 for comparisons of income and production. For trade data see Bonaldo Stringher, "Gli scambi con l'estero e la politica commerciale italiana dal 1860 al 1910," in *Cinquanta anni di storia italiana* (Milano, 1914), III, 94.

it was drastically slowed by that of 1907–8.[3] Most of the new industry was established in northern Italy, so that the disparity between the north and south grew in terms of product per capita and the flow of labor and savings out of the south was accelerated.[4] A rise in the degree of industrial concentration through holding companies, trusts, and cartel agreements accompanied industrial growth. This not only involved a reduction in competition; it also caused an increase in the economic and political power of a small group of industrialists, financiers, and landowners. While the data indicate a rise in real per capita income from 1865 lire in 1894 to 2359 in 1913 (in 1913 prices), income distribution remained highly unequal both among classes and among regions.

In an analysis of the Italian economy, Alexander Gerschenkron identified 1898–1913 as the period of Italy's "big spurt," and he provided the first sound statistical foundation to support this position.[5] His article was an attempt to test the specific applicability of his general hypothesis, which is concerned with the relationship between the timing and speed of industrial growth, the nature of the institutions which provided industrial capital, and the degree of economic backwardness. He concluded that the hypothesis successfully explained Italy's industrial expansion between 1881 and 1914; he particularly emphasized the crucial role played by the industrial credit banks as sources of funds, entrepreneurship, and technical assistance.

In an earlier article on banking and industrialization between 1894 and 1914 in Italy, I argued that Gerschenkron's interpretation of Italian industrial growth was well-founded.[6] In that article I discussed the industrial credit banks, which were established in Italy after 1894, and I attempted to provide a detailed account of the role those banks played in the country's industrial expansion.[7] The one shortcoming of Gerschenkron's study of Italian industrialization was its failure to examine in detail essential aspects of the supply of industrial capital, particularly the processes of forced saving, the reallocation of financial capital, and the reorganization of portfolios held by savers.[8] Given the poor quality of the data available and the broad sweep of Gerschenkron's approach, this omission is understandable.

3. R. Bachi, "L'evoluzione della economia italiana alla vigilia della prima guerra mondiale," in L. Cafagna, *Il Nord nella storia d'Italia* (Bari, 1962), 435, 449.

4. S. Clough and C. Livi, "Economic Growth in Italy: An Analysis of the Uneven Development of the North and South," *Journal of Economic History*, XVI (Sept. 1956), 334–49.

5. A. Gerschenkron, "Notes on the Rate of Industrial Growth in Italy, 1881–1913," *Journal of Economic History* (Dec. 1955), reprinted in A. Gerschenkron, *Economic Backwardness in Historical Perspective* (Cambridge, 1962).

6. See Jon S. Cohen, "Financing Industrialization in Italy," *Journal of Economic History*, XXVII (Sept. 1967), 363–382.

7. *Ibid.*

8. A. Gerschenkron, *Economic Backwardness*, ch. 4.

In this chapter the analysis of the previous article and the work of Gerschenkron will be expanded and I will examine, in a broader context, and
for the years 1861–1914, the supply of capital to industry. The purpose of
this discussion is to explain the influence which financial institutions had on
the timing and composition of Italian industrialization. Since the process of
industrialization both influences and is affected by the existing structure of
the economy, I will discuss industrial change in its historical context. Because
a complex network of interdependencies compose this economic structure, I
will examine these relationships in terms of a general theoretical framework.
These preliminary sections will permit me to isolate the causal links which
made industrial growth possible in Italy. In the remaining parts I will treat
industrial growth in relation to the expansion of the market and the supply
of capital, not as independent but as closely interrelated phenomena.

The Setting

Italy's industrial growth was constrained by both natural and historical
factors. The country lacked rich deposits of coal, iron ore, and other natural
industrial resources. It imported most of its coal and, as late as 1914, industry
imported as much pig iron as it produced domestically. Because of this,
imports of raw materials rose when industrial production expanded, and, to
avoid a severe balance of payments crisis, either commodity exports or
capital imports had to rise.

Two-thirds of the arable land in Italy is either mountainous or hilly, and
in 1861 many of the plains were marshy and malarial and were therefore
unusable. Yields per acre and per man-hour in agriculture were low compared with those recorded by other countries of western Europe. Surpluses
created in this sector, if any, were small and incomes remained close to
subsistence. In 1914 agriculture was still the largest sector in terms of employment and value, and its poor performance was one of the main reasons
that Italy's domestic market for manufactured goods remained small.

These conditions contributed to the high risks associated with industrial
investment. Financial institutions in Italy were poorly developed; they were
limited geographically to the northern and central parts of the country and
were conservative in policy. Financial markets were in general inefficient
allocators of funds and financial capital was scarce. The cost of capital to
borrowers, especially to industrial firms, was very high, while the return to
savers was low.

That Italy managed even to begin to industrialize under these adverse
conditions suggests that the capital distributing mechanism became more
efficient, making better use of limited resources, and that, in general, savers
and institutional investors became more willing to purchase industrial

securities. These changes were related to the increased reliability of the financial system as an intermediary between savers and investors and to a reduction in the risks associated with industrial investment. These, in turn, depended on the economic policies of the government. It is this dependence and these changes which I wish to examine in the theoretical framework.

The Theoretical Context

We can divide an economic system into four sectors: agriculture, industry, commerce, and government. Changes occur within and between these sectors as an economy undergoes modern economic growth. These changes include population shifts from the countryside to the cities; a relative increase in the urban labor force; a relative decline in the value added by agriculture to gross domestic product, accompanied by both a relative and an absolute increase in value added by industry; a rapid rise in the value of capital equipment in industry; an expansion of the domestic market for manufactured goods; improvements in the allocative efficiency of the financial system; and greater concern for and emphasis on economic growth by the government.[9] The causal role (if any) played in economic development by any one of these changes depends on the economy under consideration and the alternatives open to it.

Consider the particular characteristics of the economic relationships that existed within the Italian economy before 1914. These are shown in Diagram III.1. This diagram portrays possible, though not necessarily actual, inter-relations. It is useful for clarifying the main elements of industrial expansion, especially as they change over time. The boxes represent different groups associated with one of the four sectors, the circles enclose commodity production, and the arrows show the direction of flows of goods, expenditures, funds, and non-quantifiable items between these groups. While members of each group do not necessarily have identical objectives, they display similar attitudes toward other groups. The purpose of this exercise is to determine how changes in the flows between groups will cause the industrial production circle to expand and how these changes will affect relative income positions and political power of the various groups within the system.

The diagram suggests that two conditions were necessary for industrial growth. First, the market for manufactured goods had to grow (either through domestic or foreign demand), and second, the size of the capital stock had to increase through investments in new plant and equipment. We can now

9. These characteristics are taken from a variety of sources including S. Kuznets, *Modern Economic Growth, Rate, Structure and Spread* (New Haven: 1966), 1; and H. Chenery, "Patterns of Industrial Growth," *American Economic Review*, 50 (Sept. 1960), 624–654.

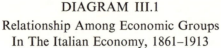

DIAGRAM III.1
Relationship Among Economic Groups
In The Italian Economy, 1861–1913

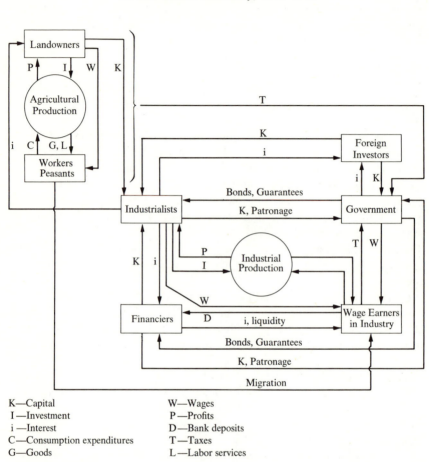

K—Capital	W—Wages
I —Investment	P —Profits
i —Interest	D—Bank deposits
C—Consumption expenditures	T—Taxes
G—Goods	L—Labor services

consider possible means of realizing these two conditions in more detail.

The potential quantity of funds available for domestic industrial investment varies with the rates of personal and business saving and the inflows of capital from abroad. The funds can come from agriculture by means of a direct transfer of any surplus by landowners or through a forced reallocation of the surplus by taxes. The success of either of these two expedients depends on the existence of a surplus. If there *is* a surplus, its size fluctuates with productivity, prices, and tenure systems. Higher yields per acre and per man-hour result in a greater surplus. In general, surpluses are larger in periods of rising prices for agricultural commodities than in times of stable or falling prices, since factor costs tend to be stable. The tenure system determines who gets the surplus, and consequently it determines the use to which the surplus is put. Thus, systems which concentrate the surplus in the hands of a few will probably generate greater potential investment funds than those in which the distribution is more equitable. If the government taxes most of the surplus away, then the tenure system is relevant only in terms of its effect on productivity.

The rate of business profits will determine the quantity of funds available for reinvestment by industry, although whether or not these funds will satisfy demand depends on the rate of growth of real investment in this sector. The international movement of long-term capital depends on a variety of complex national and international factors, not the least of which are political considerations. Foreign lending to Italy (both direct and portfolio), however, which came primarily from France, Belgium, and Germany before 1914, seems to have varied positively with swings in the Italian business cycle.[10]

A banking system cannot create savings; it is unable to influence the net worth of the economy, since any increase in the quantity of inside money is offset by debt. Improved efficiency of the intermediation process, however, can reduce the cost of borrowing for investors and raise the return on funds for savers.[11] The existence and development of a banking system that provides a reasonably safe means to earn a return on savings may encourage more widespread postponement of consumption by the population and certainly will facilitate the inflow of foreign portfolio investments.[12] The financial system is in a position to affect the flow of funds between sectors, and it can, therefore, direct a greater quantity to industry. Its willingness to reallocate funds in this fashion depends on the discounted value of returns on various investment alternatives and the risks associated with these investments. Since banks are essentially passive instruments in the saving-investment process, their impact on the flow of funds within an economy will depend on their ability to attract depositors and investors.

The government can use a number of policy instruments (taxes, tariffs, subsidies, direct expenditures, and the money supply) to influence domestic saving, investment, and demand for manufactured products. These instruments normally work indirectly, by altering the relative rates of return on

10. Both Feis and Cameron emphasize equally political and economic factors in explaining fluctuations in foreign lending to Italy. See H. Feis, *Europe the World's Banker, 1870–1914* (New York, 1956), 235–242, and R. Cameron, *France and the Economic Development of Europe, 1800–1914* (Princeton, 1961), 284–302.

11. See M. Abramowitz, "Economics of Growth," in B. Haley (ed.), *Survey of Contemporary Economics*, Vol. II (Homewood, Ill., 1952), 164.

12. See, for example, W. A. Lewis, *The Theory of Economic Growth* (London, 1965), 229.

various uses of funds, by changing relative prices, or by affecting the distribution of income. Direct expenditures affect the level of domestic demand for
consumption and investment goods both directly and indirectly through the
multiplier. The impact of any policy on domestic consumption, investment,
or saving depends on the specific conditions of the system, but the direction
is predictable.[13] Finally, and this is particularly relevant for understanding
the causes and effects of these policies, the government's decisions are
influenced by its objectives, and these depend on the relative political power
of groups within the system and on their goals.[14]

In terms of Diagram III.1, industrial production in Italy grew rapidly after
1894, partly as a result of the increased investment by industrialists in
productive plant and equipment. While it is difficult to determine the actual
value of direct transfer of capital out of agriculture before 1880, it dwindled
rapidly after that date. Although agricultural production expanded after
1896, the capital-intensive nature of this expansion between 1896 and 1914
did not permit a flow of capital out of the sector. Direct foreign investment
in Italian industry fell in the 1880's, especially after 1887, when the tariff
wars began and a depression set in. When foreign investment was renewed
after 1894, it was made primarily through the financial system. Since re-
invested profits could not match investment demand by industry, the
financiers (in this case, the banks) assumed a major role as a source of capital
to promote industrial expansion. This was made possible largely by the
economic policies of the government, in the form of guarantees of solvency
for the banks and guarantees of markets for industrial products. The former
encouraged savers to hold deposits with the banks, while the latter reduced
the risks of industrial investment. Neither the policies of the government nor
capital-intensive production techniques adopted by Italian industry encouraged the development of a large and expanding national market. In
fact, it appears that the relative income position of the workers and peasants
at best remained unchanged, while the political power of the financiers and
industrialists was enhanced.

INDUSTRIAL PRODUCTION AND GROWTH OF THE MARKET

Industrial production expanded at an unprecedented rate between 1894 and
1914. Gerschenkron estimates a 6 per cent average annual growth rate of

13. For example, a tariff on pig iron will cause a fall in the quantity demanded of foreign
pig and a rise in demand for domestic production, although actual values depend on
elasticities of demand and supply.

14. Political scientists seem much more aware of these relationships than economists;
see, for example, A. F. K. Organski, *The Stages of Political Development* (New York,
1967), especially 56–79.

industrial production for the years 1896–1908: the rates by sectors are given in Table III.1.[15] The main thrust was in the producers' goods sectors: electric power, chemicals, engineering, and iron and steel. Large investment expenditures on new plants and equipment provided the productive capacity to raise output in these branches of manufacturing. A recent estimate of investment in industry and services reveals an almost fourfold increase between 1892–96

TABLE III.1

Average Annual Growth Rates of Industrial
Production, by Sectors, 1894–1913

Sector	1894–1913	1896–1908	1908–1913
Electricity	+15.0	+17.0	+10.5
Chemicals	+12.9	+12.9	+3.5
Iron and Steel	+10.7	+13.8	+5.0
Engineering	+7.5	+12.2	+2.0
Wool	+5.3	+5.3	+4.9
Cotton	+3.5	+4.7	−0.2
Silk	−0.4	+1.0	−2.5

Source: Jon Cohen, "Financing Industrialization in Italy," *Journal of Economic History*, Vol. XXVII (Sept. 1967), 364.

and 1910–14 (3.6 billion lire to 11.5 billion lire), an average annual rate of growth of 6 per cent. No other period of equal length in Italian history before 1894 showed a comparable rise of investment in industry and services; the maximum achieved was 3.3 per cent between 1870–74 and 1885–89.[16] The rapid expansion of industrial production could be sustained only through an expanding market. At the same time, financial capital was needed to support capital formation in heavy industry.

15. The growth rates in this table are, for the most part, based on the work done by Gerschenkron (A. Gerschenkron, *Economic Development in Historical Perspective*, Appendix 1). Shortly after the publication of these results, the Istituto Centrale di Statistica came out with a nine-volume work which reconstructed the growth of national income in Italy between 1861 and 1956; Istituto Centrale di Statistica (*ISTAT*), "Indagine statistica sullo sviluppo del reddito nazionale d'Italia dal 1861 al 1956," *Annali di Statistica* (Roma, 1957, Serie VIII, Vols. 1–9). These results substantiated Gerschenkron's finding with the exception that between 1881 and 1887 they discovered a lower growth rate for industry than his average annual of 4 per cent a year. The conclusions of *ISTAT* emphasize even more than those of Gerschenkron the revolutionary nature of the industrial expansion between 1894 and 1914.
16. Ornello Vitali, "Nuova stima disaggregata dello stock di capitale in Italia," *Rassegna dei lavori dell'Istituto Nazionale per lo studio della congiuntura*, No. 12 (1968), Table 9.

Italy's traditional trading partners, led by France until the late 1880's, were the countries of northern and central Europe and the United States. Throughout the latter part of the nineteenth century Italy sent its processed food products (wine, olive oil, *pasta*), citrus fruit, nuts, milk products, raw and semi-worked silk, marble, and sulfur to those countries, and from them purchased almost all of its coal and coke, raw cotton and wool, dyes, a variety of finished and semi-finished manufactured products, and large, though fluctuating, quantities of cereal crops and other agricultural products.[17]

There was a marked decline in international trade between 1887 and 1891, but Italy's foreign trade remained at a relatively low level until 1897. The sharp upswing which began in that year was sustained almost without interruption until 1914. The fall in trade coincided with the introduction of a tariff on goods imported into Italy, the subsequent tariff war with France, and the general economic depression that hit Italy between 1890 and 1894. The renewed trading activity was linked to a general rise in world prices and the upswing in the business cycle experienced by most European countries. Italy's imports rose threefold between 1892 and 1910, while its exports more than doubled. The resulting imbalance on current account was offset by immigrant remittances and foreign investment.[18]

Certain distinct changes differentiate the period between 1894 and 1914 from that between 1870 and 1886 in the composition and pattern of Italy's foreign trade. While imports of industrial raw materials such as coal and cotton continued to dominate imports (they quadrupled between 1892 and 1910), Italians began to import greater numbers of machines and scientific instruments than they had in the past. Of more importance, exports of manufactured goods, led by cotton and silk cloth, rose more rapidly than any other item in the trade accounts. Between 1892 and 1910 Italian exports of manufactures rose from 122.4 million lire to 600.2 million lire—an annual average rate of increase of 7.2 per cent.[19] Italy managed to expand its trade by locating new markets in southeastern Europe, the Near East, and South America. Although over half of Italy's imports came from and 60 per cent of its exports went to its traditional partners in 1910, exports to Argentina rose from 2.8 per cent of the total in 1892 to 7.3 per cent in 1910 and, on a smaller scale, exports to Egypt and Turkey also increased.[20]

While these changes reflected Italy's industrial expansion at home and the ability of its textile industry to compete with other European countries abroad, it was still unable to secure foreign markets for heavy industrial products such as iron and steel, industrial chemicals, and machinery. In

17. Stringher, "Gli scambi con l'estero," especially pp. 97, 101, 102.
18. *Ibid.*, pp. 97, 120–136.
19. *Ibid.*, p. 97.
20. *Ibid.*, pp. 58, 108.

addition, the old staples—processed food products, semi-finished silk, and selected agricultural products—continued to account for over half the total value of exports, while manufactured items represented only a quarter.[21] The sustained growth of industrial production depended, therefore, on the ability of domestic demand to absorb rising output.

Table III.2 contains data on national per capita income and consumption for the years 1871–1914. These data indicate that average per capita con-

TABLE III.2

National Per Capita Income and Consumption in Italy,
1871–1914 (1938 lire, five-year averages)

Period	(1) National Income	(2) Total Private Consumption	(3) Consumption of Food and Shelter	(4) (2)/(1)	(5) Conversion Values (%) (3)/(2)	(6) (3)/(1)
1871–1875	1,895	1,762	1,144	90.3	64.9	60.4
1876–1880	1,919	1,791	1,132	93.3	63.2	59.0
1881–1885	1,884	1,743	1,135	92.5	65.1	60.2
1886–1890	1,885	1,742	1,158	92.4	66.5	61.4
1891–1895	1,888	1,737	1,081	92.0	62.2	57.2
1896–1900	1,938	1,745	1,144	90.0	65.6	59.0
1901–1905	2,169	1,872	1,210	86.3	64.6	55.8
1906–1910	2,365	2,043	1,295	86.4	63.4	54.8
1911–1915	2,478	2,132	1,472	86.0	69.0	59.4

Sources: National income and consumption: Istituto Centrale di Statistica, *Annali di Statistica*, Serie 8, Vol. 9, Table 37.

Consumption of food and shelter was given neither on a per capita basis nor in 1938 lire. Population estimates were taken from *Annali di Statistica*, Table 37, and conversion values from Istituto Centrale di Statistica, *Il valore della lira dal 1861 al 1965*, p. 42.

sumption remained constant through 1895, and, of greater importance, that a relatively constant percentage of this consumption was devoted to food and shelter. After 1896 average per capita of saving rose, although the data show no real decline in expenditures on food and shelter. Given the poor quality of the data, the conclusions based on these observations must be tentative; it is hardly worthwhile trying to manipulate them with more sophisticated techniques.[22] In fact, the most accurate estimates of consumption of food and shelter are those for the years 1871–75 and 1911–15

21. Based on data presented in Stringher, "Gli scambi con l'estero," p. 102.

22. For example, it would be useful to derive an Engels curve to get some idea of the elasticity of demand for food and shelter with respect to income, but the results would remain open to serious doubts.

(particularly the latter period), and these estimates suggest that there was a high and perhaps rising percentage of consumption of these items.[23]

We can make some observations based on indirect evidence. The low levels of real income per capita in Italy through 1896 restricted the size of the domestic market and the ability of the population to create a surplus for investment. While the rise in per capita income after 1896 did permit some increase in saving, most of new consumption was devoted to food, drink, and housing. This is not surprising in the light of the observations made by Bolton King and Thomas Okey in 1901:

> One is bound to conclude that in spite of his large consumption of vegetables and fruit, including a good deal of pulse of high nutritive value, the typical Italian is underfed. Cases of death from starvation are very rare, but there is a terrible, permanent lack of food. Recent inquiries into the food of school children have proved that in Perugia one-third have little or no dinner, that at Pavia one in ten, at Milan one in twenty-eight, have no dinner at all. The case of the adults is probably worse.[24]

This indicates that even after 1896 the domestic market for manufactured goods remained small and did not expand at a rate proportionate to the growth in per capita income. Furthermore, since most of the population still lived in rural areas, it is likely that much consumption of clothing and other non-food items took place outside of the market and was not recorded in national income statistics. Given proper incentives, non-market activities would have declined in favor of market-oriented consumption and production, but this was not the method chosen by Italian industry or the government.[25]

For example, the high rate of direct and indirect taxation in Italy worked against expansion of the domestic market: not only did Italians pay income tax rates which were high relative to those in the rest of Europe, but they also paid taxes on flour, bread, and *pasta* until 1902. Taxes were paid on cattle, death duties were assessed at a fixed rate, and property taxes were imposed on even the smallest pieces of land.[26] While every new government that came

23. For a discussion of the data see Istituto Centrale di Statistica, *Annali di Statistica*, Serie 8, Vol. 9, 179–183.

24. B. King and Thomas Okey, *Italy Today* (London, 1901), 131.

25. One aspect of economic development in a pure decentralized, capitalist economy is greater reliance on the market by the population to allocate goods and resources. Such use of the market leads to more interdependence within the economy, increased specialization of economic activities, and frequently a reorganization of production such that non-market output is reduced while marketable output rises. The success of this aspect of development depends partly on the existence or creation of incentives which encourage interdependence and reorganization of productive activities. Italy did not rely on the expansion of the domestic market to foster industrial expansion; industry was too impatient and the government was willing to support it.

26. King and Okey, *Italy Today*, pp. 138–140.

to power between 1891 and 1914 promised a reform of the tax structure, only a few minor changes were introduced.[27]

The heavy tax burden did reduce the autonomous expansion of the domestic market, but it also guaranteed that increased income would not be spent on consumption goods. The government in effect redistributed income in a way that permitted a higher rate of saving out of income, favored a larger market for industrial goods, and stimulated greater investment in industrial capital. Seen in this light, the tax policies were in accord with other policies pursued by the government, especially after 1894.[28]

Economic Policies of the Government and Domestic Demand

The government, viewed as a sector of the economic system with its own objectives, had an interest in economic growth only insofar as that growth furthered its own objectives—the maintenance of power and stability. By 1871, when the unification of Italy was complete, a small group of industrialists, financiers, and landowners, who controlled most of the nation's reproducible wealth, came to exert a decisive influence on the policies of the government. Even as late as 1914 Italy lacked a large middle class, and, as in many developing nations today, wealth and income were unequally distributed. The tariff of 1887 favored this group, as did most of the government's industrial policies, and furthermore, the process of industrialization helped to maintain its position. The capital-intensive production techniques used by industry yielded high profits which were used for further investment in plant and equipment and left income distribution much as it was in the past.

The government increased the demand for Italian manufactures through a variety of policies. In 1878 the Cairoli government broke with the free trade position established by Cavour and introduced a tariff. Some scholars argued that this tariff was not yet protectionist; it was not yet ". . . the instrument of decided intervention by the state in the direction of economic activity."[29] While support for the tariff was in fact largely reformist and concerned with government revenue, the new duties did provide some protection, especially

27. See Paolo Carcano, "Finanze e tesoro," *Cinquanta anni storia italiana* (Roma, 1911), Vol. II, for a history of public finance and taxation in Italy. It should be noted that it was less difficult for the governments of Giolitti and Sonnino to introduce reforms between 1900 and 1914 since the increase in domestic economic activity yielded greater tax revenue and thus made it possible to remove some of the exceptionally regressive taxes.

28. This was similar to the tax policies followed by the Meiji government in Japan. See H. Rosovsky, *Capital Formation in Japan* (Glencoe, 1961), ch. 4.

29. E. Corbino, *Annali dell'economia italiana* (Città di Castello, 1931), Vol. II (1871–1880), 204.

for domestic textile producers. This decision by Italy to move away from free trade coincided with similar steps taken by Germany in 1879 and by France in 1881, which, taken together, marked the end of the relatively short era of free trade.

After 1885 the Italian government's economic policies clearly revealed a new attitude toward its role in the economy. In December of that year the Depretis government introduced legislation that resembled in intent the Navigation Acts which Great Britain had discarded in the 1850's, after two centuries. The law attempted to reserve much of the carrying trade to and from Italy for Italian lines, using Italian ships. In this way the government not only supported the domestic merchant marine, it also worked at revitalizing shipbuilding in Italy.[30] This law did not represent the first attempt by government to subsidize the Italian merchant marine; such policies had a long history. But unlike previous policies, which had been adopted for reasons of national security, this one was consciously designed to promote domestic industrial growth at the expense of foreign competitors and domestic consumers.

In 1886 the government, along with the Banca Generale and a group of northern industrialists, and with the active support of the military, set up Italy's first modern steel mill, at Terni. Since all raw materials had to be shipped in and all finished products transported out, the location was chosen largely for strategic, not economic, reasons. Nevertheless, the government was beginning to make clear its support of domestic industry. This step indirectly established a market for the new firm, since the government made an agreement to order its military equipment from Terni. In fact, the government was able to persuade private industry and the bank to participate in the development of Terni mainly because it placed some orders before production began.[31]

On July 14, 1887, the Parliament passed a new general tariff act, which went into effect in January 1888. The new duties were unequivocally protectionist, intended to "... second the evolution of Italian industry [and] to provide major protection for production held most in need of it ... and not as an ultimate goal to procure a major relief for the treasury."[32] It accorded increased protection to textile manufactures, to iron and steel production, and to wheat production. Most raw materials were allowed to enter duty free; in some instances, existing duties on certain industrial raw materials were removed. Thus, within a period of three years, the Italian government made apparent its decision to foster industrial expansion.

30. On this see Corbino, *Annali* Vol. III (1881–1890), 282 and G. Roncagli, "L'industria dei trasporti marittimi," *Cinquanta Anni di Storia Italiana*, Vol. I, 28–29.
31. Corbino, *Annali*, Vol. III (1881–90), fns. 126–27.
32. Stringher, "Gli scambi con l'estero," p. 23.

These commitments on the part of the government were not followed by immediate results; a number of factors combined to cause a severe economic depression in Italy which lasted from 1890 through 1895. The policies of support for domestic production were maintained and in some cases expanded after 1894. For example, the subsidies given to the merchant marine were expanded in 1896 to contain even greater monetary inducements to use domestically produced equipment, including Italian iron and steel. While various changes in the provisions governing support in this area occurred up to 1914, the principle of assistance remained unaltered.

Once the government committed itself to an active role in the domestic economy it was forced to move on various fronts. In 1905 the government assumed control of the railroads. They had been run by private firms, which had leased the rolling stock from the state twenty years earlier. These companies had neglected the equipment, so the government was compelled to undertake an extensive renovation program. It gave most of its orders for new rolling stock to domestic industry. Between 1905–6 and 1908–9 the state ordered over 1000 locomotives, 3000 baggage and passenger cars, and 25,000 freight cars, most from domestic manufacturers.[33] While these orders encouraged an expansion out of line with the normal state of demand, they allowed many engineering firms to invest in new capital equipment and to develop techniques which made them more competitive on world markets after 1910.

Italy's new power source, electricity, derived an enormous impetus from the industrial expansion occurring elsewhere in the economy. In the same fashion, chemicals, as an input in the production of other manufactured goods and as a fertilizer in agriculture, grew prosperous on the strength of growth in industrial production. Thus, both directly and indirectly, the economic policies of the government created a demand for the products of Italian industry and fostered the rapid expansion of domestic production.

It is true that the tariff of 1887 raised the cost of iron and steel products required by engineering firms and thereby slowed expansion in that sector. The government could have given more direct support to chemicals, although that industry grew rapidly even without it. Gerschenkron, in fact, contends that the government's tariff policies were misguided and did not exploit Italy's real comparative advantages.[34] My discussion is not intended as a defense of the economic policies of the government; it merely indicates the probable impact they had on Italian industrial growth. The forced reallocation of expenditures and consequent impact on saving, however, were necessary conditions for industrial growth. The economic policies of the government,

33. Corbino, *Annali*, Vol. V (1901–14), 135.
34. A. Gerschenkron, *Economic Development*, Chapter 4.

which created a secure market for certain industrial products, not only made industrial expansion possible, it also encouraged a flow of capital to industry.

THE SUPPLY OF CAPITAL AND THE FINANCIAL SYSTEM

Although the funds to finance industrial investment could have been internally generated, after 1894 such sources were inadequate to satisfy the industrial concerns' immense demand for capital. In most cases these firms were forced to seek external financial assistance.[35] Table III.3 shows the

TABLE III.3

Nominal Capital of Joint-stock Companies in Italy by Industry
and Net Changes in Nominal Capital, 1900–1913
(millions of 1938 lire)

Industry	1900–1902	1911–1913	Average Annual Increase (%)
Transport	842.3	1,124.6	2.0
Textiles	165.3	511.0	7.3
Engineering	61.0	308.3	9.3
Metallurgy	70.7	308.6	9.0
Electricity	116.0	466.0	8.5
Chemicals	102.0	271.6	7.8
Mining	71.3	178.3	3.1
Total	2,070.3	3,114.3	6.7

Total Number of Joint-stock Companies
  (all industries), 1900–1902 = 903;   1911–1913 = 2,952
Annual Average Net Increase in
  Nominal Capital (all industries), 1900–1913 = 5.9%

Source: Nominal capital, by industries, E. Corbino, *Annali dell'Economia Italiana*, Vol. V (1901–1914), 433.

expansion of joint-stock companies in Italy between 1900 and 1913, and it provides some measure of the extent to which Italian industry resorted to external financing to expand investment and output.[36] Between 1900–1903 and 1911–13 the average annual rate of increase in the nominal value of equity capital in selected industries was 6.7 per cent, with engineering, electricity, chemicals, metallurgy, and textiles above the average. The number

35. See Jon S. Cohen, "Financing Industrialization in Italy," pp. 364–65.
36. A more meaningful measure would require good balance sheet and income statement data, both of which are incomplete and unreliable for Italian industry during this period.

of joint-stock companies more than tripled and net increases in their nominal capital exceeded 200 million lire per year. These figures indicate how much the growing sectors relied on external financing.

This growth in external financing was supported at least partly by foreign investments in Italian industry. Although Italian exports increased throughout the period from 1896 to 1914, imports grew even more rapidly. Consequently, Italy had a continuing and rising trade deficit. It was financed in part through immigrant remittances, but primarily through direct and indirect foreign investment in Italian firms by means of security purchases, through direct investment in capital equipment, and through the creation of foreign subsidiaries in Italy.[37] Stringher estimated the value of each of these categories, but his results represent at best a crude approximation. Nevertheless, it appears that the bulk of increased foreign investment occurred in and through the banking system.[38] In fact, the most striking feature of the years between 1894 and 1914 was the expansion of the intermediary activities of the financial system on both a national and an international level.

As Table III.4 indicates, the financial sector as a whole grew steadily

TABLE III.4

Financial Assets and Net Reproducible Capital in Italy,
1880–1914, Five-Year Averages
(billions of 1938 lire)

Period	Total Financial Assets (FA)	Net Reproducible Capital (K)	$\dfrac{FA}{K}$
1880–1884	25.7	152.0	16.9
1885–1889	39.5	168.2	23.4
1890–1894	47.4	180.5	26.2
1895–1899	51.0	187.8	27.1
1900–1904	57.8	198.2	29.1
1905–1909	73.1	223.7	32.7
1910–1914	83.0	264.3	31.4

Sources: Total Financial Assets: Banca d'Italia, *I bilanci degli istituti di emissione* (Roma, 1967), Table 2, for assets of note issuing banks (excluding accounts between banks). Banca d'Italia, *I bilanci degli istituti di emissione*, Table 23, for assets of other financial institutions. Figures converted to 1938 values using wholesale price coefficients in Istituto Centrale di Statistica, *Il Valore della lira*, p. 42.

Net reproducible Capital: Ornello Vitali, "Nuova stima disaggregata dello stock di capitale in Italia," *Rassegna dei lavori dell 'Istituto Nazionale per lo Studio della Congiuntura*, No. 12 (January 1968), Table 17 (beginning with 1881).

37. Stringher, "Gli scambi con l'estero," pp. 123–131.

38. Both Stringher (see previous footnote) and Feis (*Europe: The World's Banker*, p. 242) agree that foreign ownership of Italian government debt decreased rapidly after 1894; total investment did not, it was merely rechanneled.

relative to the economy between 1880–84 and 1910–14. The assets of this
sector continued to expand relative to the real capital stock of the economy
even after 1894, when the economy's growth accelerated. In Table III.5 I

TABLE III.5

Primary Securities, Financial Assets, and an Estimate
of Intermediation, 1880–1884 to 1900–1914
(billions of 1938 lire)

Period	(1) Government Debt[a]	(2) Private Securities	(3) (1) + (2) Primary Securities	(4) Total Financial Assets	(5) (4)/(3) Intermediation Ratio
1880–1884	58.8	8.2	67.0	25.7	0.38
1885–1889	67.2	10.4	77.6	39.5	0.51
1890–1894	73.8	11.4	85.2	47.4	0.56
1894–1899	77.5	10.3	87.8	51.0	0.58
1900–1904	78.6	14.4	93.0	57.8	0.62
1905–1909	73.4	25.2	98.6	73.1	0.74
1910–1914[b]	67.5	27.0	94.5	83.0	0.88

Sources:
    Government Debt 1880–1903: Ministero di Agricoltura, Industria e Commercio, *Annuario Statistico Italiano 1904* (Roma, 1904), 609.
    Government Debt 1906–1910: Direttore Generale della Statistica e del Lavoro, *Annuario Statistico Italiano 1911*, 2da Serie (Vol. I), 314.
    Government Debt 1911–1914: *Annuario Statistico Italiano 1915*, 2da Serie (Vol. 5), 340.
    Private Securities represent nominal value of equity capital outstanding.
1880–1890: E. Corbino, *Annali dell'Economia Italiana*, Vol. III (1881–1890), 446.
1890–1900: Corbino, *Annali*, Vol. IV (1891–1900), 389.
1901–1914: Corbino, *Annali*, Vol. V (1901–1914), 433.
    Total Financial Assets: See Table III.4.

    [a] 1904 and 1905 were unavailable. In addition, up to 1884, government debt outstanding represents a year end figure; from 1884, the figures are for June 30.
    [b] 1914, unavailable.

have attempted to measure the change in financial intermediation within the
economy. This table shows that the ratio of total financial assets to primary
securities increased throughout the period, with a sharp rise in the period
between 1899–1900 and 1909–10. Although the evidence is limited and not
wholly reliable, these two tables indicate a similar phenomenon: the financial
sector expanded rapidly, especially after 1894, and at the same time it assumed
a larger role in the intermediation process.

By 1914 the scope of the financial system had radically altered its position
in the economy. This change in scale and relative size can be measured in
two ways. As Table III.6 shows, the system was able to attract a growing
percentage of national income; in fact, in the years between 1895–99 and

TABLE III.6

Debt Held by Non-note-issuing Financial Institutions Toward
Private Sector and as a Percentage of National
Income, 1880–1914, five-year Averages
(millions of 1938 lire)

Period	Total Debt Toward Private Sector (DPS)	National Income (Y)	$\dfrac{DPS}{Y}$
1880–1884	8,915	56,783	15.7
1885–1889	14,193	58,011	24.4
1890–1894	15,132	60,429	25.0
1895–1899	16,932	62,910	26.9
1900–1904	23,199	72,678	31.9
1905–1909	33,113	83,463	39.6
1910–1914	39,995	90,433	44.2

Sources:

Total debt toward private sector taken from Banca d'Italia, *I bilanci degli istituti di emissione*, Table 23, converted to 1938 values using wholesale price coefficients of Istituto Centrale di Statistica, *Il Valore della lira*, p. 42.

National income taken from Istituto Centrale di Statistica, *Annali di Statistica*, Serie VIII, Vol. 9, Table 37.

1910–14, there was a sharp rise in the ratio of debt held by the financial sector relative to national income. With more capital available, the system could and did claim a return on a greater portion of real assets; Table III.7 reveals this and, following the trend noted in other data, shows a noticeable increase after 1895–99. When all of this evidence is brought together, it becomes clear that the role of the financial system in the economic activities of the nation grew constantly after 1880 and seems to have spurted toward the end of the nineteenth century. In particular, the system assumed an expanding position in the intermediation process, attracting funds from savers and directing them toward ultimate investors. While the distance between the two groups grew, the real cost of funds to investors fell and return to savers rose. The cost-reducing aspects of the banks' operations frequently meant that capital was available where it had not been in the past.

The Financial System Analyzed[39]

The aggregate data provide an idea of the changes which occurred in the financial system relative to the economy as a whole. Changes which took

39. Part of this section is based on Jon S. Cohen, "Financing Industrialization in Italy."

TABLE III.7

Credit from Commercial and Investment Banks and from Total
Non-note-issuing Banks to Private Sector:
Totals and Percentages, five-year Averages
(billions of 1938 lire)

Period	(1) Total Credit Toward Private Sector	(2) Commercial & Investment Bank Credit to Private Sector	(3) Net Reproducible Capital	(4) (1)/(2)	(5) (1)/(3)
1880–1884	9.2	3.3	130.4	35.9	7.1
1885–1889	15.3	5.7	143.5	37.5	10.7
1890–1894	15.4	4.3	152.7	27.8	10.2
1895–1899	13.5	3.3	158.9	24.4	8.5
1900–1904	16.9	5.9	168.7	34.7	10.2
1905–1909	23.8	9.7	193.6	40.7	12.3
1910–1914	28.5	11.2	232.5	39.4	12.3

Sources:
For data in columns 1 and 2; see Table III.6, source for total deposits toward private sector.
For data in column 3, see Table III.4 source for net reproducible capital. This estimate of capital stock,
however, excludes government capital in highways, ports, etc.—public works in the strict sense.

place within the system itself were equally important, especially in regard to
the relationship between finance and industrialization.

In the Middle Ages Italy had been the source of new banking technique,
and its illustrious banking families had financed much of the commercial
and state building activities of merchants and monarchs in the fifteenth and
sixteenth centuries. By the beginning of the nineteenth century, however,
Italy had lost its leadership in financial matters, and at unification it possessed
only a few modern banks. Moreover, the banks were not distributed evenly
throughout the country, nor were their services available to all levels of the
population. Northern and central Italy, especially Piedmont and Tuscany,
had the most well-developed financial systems, but even in these areas the
major houses were located in cities such as Turin and Florence, and they
provided services for speculators and large merchants. Thus, in Italian
banking after unification there were a number of interrelated but separable
developments: one was the rise of institutions adapted to the needs of the
growing urban labor force and the peasantry; a second was the growth of
banks designed to finance the small-scale manufacturers, farmers, and
merchants; and a third was the creation and expansion of banks established
to assist the large-scale industrialists.

The working classes, both urban and rural, needed a safe place to deposit their savings. There were two main groups of institutions which met this need, the savings banks (*casse di risparmio*), and the postal savings banks (*casse di risparmio postali*). The former were among the oldest and largest financial institutions (in terms of assets) in Italy up through 1914, and savings deposits accounted for over two-thirds of their liabilities.[40] An individual savings bank normally confined its operations and branches to one province, or at most to a single region, although all cities and most small towns had at least one of these institutions.

The savings banks were restricted by their charters from undertaking extensive commercial and industrial credit activities; between 1870 and 1914, land credit and mortgage loans, holdings of government securities, and loans to municipal and other local public institutions annually accounted for over half of their assets. As Tables III.8A and III.8B indicate, however, a high proportion of their assets were in the form of commercial and industrial credit during the 1870's, although this category exhibits a steady decline from the high of 1870–74 through 1910–14. Although industrialists frequently made use of the credit services provided by some of the larger savings banks, it seems clear that they were not a major source of industrial credit.[41]

In 1876, Parliament established the postal savings banks. They held only savings deposits and, while they paid a smaller yearly interest on deposits than the regular savings banks did, their customers (mostly peasants and workers) regarded them, correctly, as the least risky means to gain some return on their savings. The postal savings banks held only government securities as assets. While this apparently was not one of the major considerations when the creation of these banks was proposed to Parliament, they did provide an efficient means to fund the government's debt. It must be noted that the increasingly active role which the government came to play in the industrialization process meant that these funds were indirectly channeled into productive economic activity. Thus, these institutions contributed, in a minor way, to the flow of savings to private domestic investment.

In 1864, under the guidance of Luigi Luzzatti, the first cooperative bank (*banca popolare*) was established in Montelupo, in the province of Florence. From then until 1914 more and more of these cooperative banks were established, especially in rural areas in the northern and central regions of the country. They were designed to provide credit facilities for workers, artisans, small-scale manufacturers, and farmers, all of whom were unable to get financial assistance from the major commercial and investment banks. Most users of the banks' funds also deposited their savings with them, in either

40. Banca d'Italia, *I bilanci degli istituti di emissione italiani 1845–1936* (Roma, 1967), Table 22.
41. See Jon S. Cohen, "Financing Industrialization in Italy," p. 372.

TABLE III.8A

Total Assets, Commercial and Industrial Assets, and Deposits of Ordinary Credit Banks, Savings Banks, and Cooperative Banks 1880–1914 (millions of 1938 lire)

ORDINARY CREDIT BANKS

Period	No. of Banks	Total Assets	Commercial and Industrial Assets		Deposits[a]	
			Total	% of Total Assets	Total	% of all Banks Deposits
1880–1884	115	5,187	2,244.0	43	2,544.5	30.4
1885–1889	150	9,015	3,563.6	39	3,574.1	29.4
1890–1894	144	7,080	2,290.8	32	2,661.6	20.8
1895–1899	140	5,977	2,058.4	34	2,109.0	16.3
1900–1904	138	8,590	3,073.9	36	2,258.5	16.1
1905–1909	151	13,048	5,774.2	44	3,912.7	19.1
1910–1914	126	15,285	7,205.0	47	4,743.0	21.0

SAVINGS BANKS

Period	No. of Banks	Total Assets	Commercial and Industrial Assets		Deposits[a]	
			Total	% of Total Assets	Total	% of all Bank Deposits
1880–1884	190	5,213.8	1,324.9	25	4,527.5	54.1
1885–1889	212	7,422.0	1,717.0	23	6,458.5	53.2
1890–1894	214	9,060.0	1,381.8	15	7,655.4	59.7
1895–1899	193	10,528.0	1,234.0	12	8,681.5	67.0
1900–1904	182	11,755.2	1,421.9	12	9,644.7	64.1
1905–1909	182	14,434.6	2,021.6	14	11,893.8	58.0
1910–1914	186	16,325.0	3,145.0	19	13,287.6	58.9

TABLE III.8A (cont.)

COOPERATIVE BANKS

Period	No. of Banks	Total Assets	Commercial and Industrial Assets		Deposits[a]	
			Total	% of Total Assets	Total	% of all Bank Deposits
1880–1884	217	1,818.3	1,015.3	56	1,289.9	15.5
1885–1889	602	3,392.0	2,105.0	62	2,116.9	17.4
1890–1894	639	3,547.2	1,663.8	47	2,400.0	18.7
1895–1899	598	3,652.0	1,723.0	47	2,162.0	16.7
1900–1904	643	4,658.6	2,372.3	51	3,117.6	20.7
1905–1909	653	6,930.0	3,506.7	51	4,643.0	22.6
1910–1914	377	8,355.0	3,835.0	46	4,509.6	20.0

Source: Banca d'Italia, *I bilanci degli istituti di emissione italiani 1845–1936*, Table 22.

The number of banks included in the observations for the years 1913 and 1914 represents a small sample of the existing number of banks, although more than three-fourths of the total assets. For all years for each class of bank, the number of banks represents the number used for estimating the data in the table and in every year these account for at least 80% of the existing banks.

Commercial and industrial assets include discounted commercial paper, advances, overdrafts, securities of joint-stock companies, and short- and long-term loans to industry and commerce.

a Deposits include both demand and savings deposits.

savings or demand accounts. In fact, although regulations varied among banks and regions, the normal practice was to limit credit to those who were members of the cooperative and who held deposits with the bank.

The cooperative banks reproduced on a small scale the activities of the major credit institutions. Over two-thirds of their liabilities were in the form of savings or demand deposits during the entire period from 1870–74 through 1910–14.[42] Furthermore, as Tables III.8A and III.8B reveal, their deposits rose throughout this period, matching the expansion of other banks in the system.

These banks were committed to support the industrial and commercial credit needs of their members and, as Tables III.8A and III.8B show, they devoted a consistently large percentage of their assets to these uses. Their total number far exceeded that of the other banks included in Table III.8A, but their average size was small. By 1914 they provided approximately one-third of the amount of industrial and commercial credit that was given by the investment and commercial banks. These cooperative banks tended to restrict their activities to single communes or provinces and were a means of mobilizing local savings to finance local economic activities. For example, in the period after 1896, when agriculture began to recover from its long depression, the cooperative banks came to play a major role in financing the agricultural investments on which the increases in output per hectare were based. The activities of these banks complemented those of the major industrial credit houses, but, unlike the latter, they did not mobilize credit on a large scale nor did they have a major impact on the flow of savings between sectors and regions of the country.

The large-scale industrialists used the private and joint-stock commercial and investment banks (*banche di credito ordinario*) to meet their capital requirements. As Tables III.8A and III.8B indicate, the assets of these banks grew swiftly, both absolutely and relative to other groups in the financial system. Furthermore, the data reveal that an average of 40 per cent of their assets were used for industrial or commercial purposes; thus these institutions represented the main source of external financing for industry. The sharp decline in assets and liabilities held by the banks between 1885–89 and 1890–94 was caused by a severe depression and financial crisis, which brought down many of the major banks then in existence. Following this crisis, these banks expanded more rapidly than others in terms of assets, and they devoted a rising percentage of these assets to industrial uses. Their share of total deposits held by the financial system also grew, so that they were able to transfer a growing proportion of domestic savings to industrial uses.

These observations on changes in the flow of funds within the economy must be combined with our knowledge of the activities of these investment

42. Banca d'Italia, *I bilanci degli istituti di emissione*, Table 22.

TABLE III.8B

Average Annual Rate of Change in Total Assets, Commercial and
Industrial Assets, and Deposits of Ordinary Credit Banks,
Savings Banks, and Cooperative Banks, 1880–1914

ORDINARY CREDIT BANKS

Period	Total Assets	Commercial Industrial Assets	Deposits
1880–84—1890–94	+0.6	—	—
1895–99—1910–14	+7.8	+12.5	+6.2
1880–84—1910–14	+5.7	+6.5	+2.5

SAVINGS BANKS

Period	Total Assets	Commercial Industrial Assets	Deposits
1880–84—1890–94	+4.9	—	+4.6
1895–99—1910–14	+2.7	+7.7	+2.6
1880–84—1910–14	+6.3	+4.1	+5.7

COOPERATIVE BANKS

Period	Total Assets	Commercial Industrial Assets	Deposits
1880–84—1890–94	+6.3	+4.3	+5.7
1895–99—1910–14	+6.4	+6.5	+5.4
1880–84—1910–14	+10.6	+8.2	+7.3

Source: based on data in Table III.8A.

banks to appreciate the full impact of those banks' policies on industrial
growth. Industrial credit banks acted as the prime source of external financing
for industry. They provided credit through loans, security purchases, or
advances on unissued equity. Almost all firms that expanded between 1894
and 1914, and all the major ones founded during these years, relied on one
of these financial institutions for capital and other credit services. Many of
the banks' activities do not appear in their balance sheet data: they were
major underwriters of new security issues; they assisted firms in transforming
themselves into joint-stock companies; they provided technical advice on new
technology and frequently played an entrepreneurial role in organizing a
group to form a new company under their auspices and with their assistance.
For example, the electric power industry developed almost exclusively under
the tutelage of one of these banks, the Banca Commerciale Italiana, and a

similar case, with perhaps a different bank, can be made for developments in chemicals, engineering, and iron and steel.[43]

The substantial increase in the flow of financial capital and services to industry marked a break with the past. Although the industrial and commercial credit banks expanded in the period before 1890 and directed a large percentage of their funds to industry and commerce,[44] the scale of their investments in industry was far smaller than that of the banks which came after 1894. For example, as Tables III.8A and III.8B show, the banks after 1894 devoted a greater percentage of their expanded assets to industry; and Table III.7 reveals that these credit activities represented a larger portion of net reproducible capital in the economy than they had previously. In addition, the banks before 1894 committed a large share of their assets to investments in speculative real estate activities and urban renewal, especially in the 1880's. As an example of this, a profit and loss statement on securities held by the Credito Mobiliare indicated that of the 30 million lire in losses sustained after 1887, over half came on holdings of real estate or related investments.[45] Similarly, Gino Luzzatto noted:

> With the economic recovery which began in 1879 . . . the activity of the Banca Generale took a new slant, its capital was doubled, and then its participation in the building speculation in Rome and then in Naples began and grew rapidly. . .[46]

If we consider the Italian industrial experience between 1861 and 1894, it becomes clear why these banks pursued such investment policies. The crisis of 1874–77 demonstrated the great risks associated with industrial investment in Italy; between 1873 and 1879 the number of joint-stock companies in Italy declined by almost 20 per cent and their equity capital declined by over 50 per cent.[47] Since there were high risks associated with all types of economic activity, investment in highly speculative real estate and urban construction activities had the positive feature that the pay-off was quick—much faster than returns on investments in industry—and no more risky than other alternatives. After 1894 the major industrial credit banks held portfolios that were composed primarily of illiquid industrial assets. This position made them vulnerable to even short-run cyclical fluctuations.

43. Jon S. Cohen, "Financing Industrialization in Italy," pp. 377–79.
44. M. Pantaleoni, *Scritti Varii di Economia* (Roma, 1910), 325. Pantaleoni's remark that the two major industrial credit banks before 1894 (the Credito Mobiliare and the Banca Generale) owned in some measure almost all Italian manufacturing firms corroborates this evidence.
45. M. Pantaleoni, *Scritti Varii*, p. 447.
46. G. Luzzatto, *L'Economia Italiana dal 1861 al 1914* (Milano, 1963), p. 250.
47. I. Sachs, *L'Italie, ses finances et son développement économique, 1859–1884* (Paris, 1885), 656.

The Government and the Financial System

The government's economic policies after 1886, which it pursued with vigor after 1894, reduced the risks associated with industrial investment and thus encouraged the industrial credit banks to make funds available to industry. These policies included not only those which provided a market for domestically manufactured consumer and producer goods, but also one which established the Bank of Italy, in 1894. With this latter act the government supplied the banking system with a true lender of last resort and the country with a well-regulated, sound money supply. The government also thus created a new policy instrument to control national economic activity.

The Bank of Italy acted as a lender of last resort on a number of occasions between 1894 and 1914. Given the tendency of the major investment banks to hold portfolios with a high percentage of industrial assets, they were unable to withstand even the minor panics that frequently accompanied economic crises. For example, in 1907, the Società Bancaria Italiana was under severe pressure, and it was saved from bankruptcy by a 43 million lire loan, made by the Bank of Italy.[48] In 1911 the Bank of Italy organized and directed a group of banks which financed the restructuring of the iron and steel industry, at that time on the verge of bankruptcy which threatened not only that industry but the industrial credit banks with imminent disaster. The existence of such potential support reduced the risks of holding portfolios containing a large percentage of illiquid industrial assets, and thus permitted the banks to pursue ambitious industrial credit policies. These actions by the Bank of Italy had the salutary side effect of bolstering public confidence in the banking system and thereby encouraging the flow of personal savings into deposits with the banks of ordinary credit; as Table III.8A shows, these deposits rose sixfold between 1894 and 1910.

Up through the 1880's the main concern of the government was the financing of its enormous deficits, which had been caused initially by the costs of unification and which were continued thereafter by the extravagant policies it followed in nation-building. During the period 1861–90 the government's budget was in deficit every year, and the public debt grew from 2.4 billion lire in 1861 to 12.1 billion lire in 1890.[49] The government's success in funding its debt depended partly on its ability to float bonds on foreign markets, at very high premiums, and partly on the cooperation of the domestic note-issuing banks.[50] In the latter case between 1866 and 1883 the

48. C. Supino, *Storia della circolazione cartacea in Italia dal 1860 al 1928* (Milano, 1929), 180–181.

49. 1861 to 1880 from I. Sachs, *L'Italie*, p. 486; 1881 to 1890 from Ministero dell'Agricoltura, l'Industria e Commercio, *Annuario Statistico Italiano 1904*, p. 609.

50. In 1861, five banks in Italy had the right to issue bank notes: the National Bank (Banca Nazionale nel Regno), the largest of these institutions, with branches throughout

government gave these note-issuing banks the right to issue inconvertible currency (*corso forzoso*) in exchange for a series of large, low interest loans. While the *corso forzoso* was not necessarily a bad policy (it acted as a devaluation of the lire), the banks abused their privilege and consequently raised the public's suspicion of the banking system and reduced its confidence in the banks' notes.

The technique of domestic deficit financing by the government further contributed to the chronic instability of the domestic money supply. The notes that the banks loaned the government were inconvertible, while those issued to finance their own activities were fully convertible. The clearing problem was formidable, and notes of a particular bank were frequently unacceptable outside of the areas in which branches of the bank were located. In addition, coins and notes issued prior to unification still circulated within the country. The situation resembled that in Japan following the Meiji Restoration. Hugh Patrick observed that two major tasks of the Japanese government at that time were to establish a national currency and to return to convertibility.[51] His observation holds equally well for the Italian government.

Italy's solution to these two problems also resembled that of Japan. While Italy managed to return to convertibility without the severe deflation that Japan had experienced, the financial crisis of 1890–94 gave the government the opportunity it needed to reorganize the note-issuing banks. Like Japan, Italy created a central bank, and through this institution the government managed to establish a national currency.[52] While a central bank that issues notes is not the only means of creating a sound currency, it is the technique which most countries adopt. Furthermore, while a well-regulated national currency is neither a necessary nor a sufficient condition for economic growth, a mismanaged currency and one which is unacceptable between regions within a single country may constrain interregional trade and reduce labor and capital mobility, thus slowing the pace of economic change. While

---

the country; the Tuscan National Bank (Banca Nazionale Toscana) and the Tuscan Bank of Credit and Industry (Banca Toscana di Credito e d'Industria) with offices only in Tuscany; and two southern banks, the Bank of Naples and the Bank of Sicily, the former servicing the southern regions of the mainland, the latter with branches in Sicily. The Pontifical States became a part of Italy in 1870 and its bank, the Roman Bank (Banca Romana), was allowed to retain the right of note issue within the area of the old Pontifical States. While numerous moves were made to reduce the number of note issuing banks to one, regional opposition and vested interests in the existing system successfully thwarted such attempts.

51. See H. Patrick, "Japan, 1868–1914," in R. Cameron et al., *Banking in the Early Stages of Industrialization* (New York, 1967), 252.

52. In law, the Bank of Naples and the Bank of Sicily retained the right of note issue but, in fact, the Bank of Italy controlled the money supply and was a central bank.

such statements are difficult to document, the rapid increase in economic growth after 1894 in Italy appears to have been facilitated by the Bank of Italy both in its capacity as a lender of last resort and as a regulator of the national currency.

Certain patterns traced by the money supply in relation to other variables illustrate the Bank of Italy's impact after 1894. (See Table III.9.) In the years prior to the creation of the Bank, the government was unable to control the

TABLE III.9

Money Supply, Income Velocity, and
Reserve/Deposit Ratio, 1880–1914
(millions of 1938 lire)

Year	Money Supply[a]	Income Velocity	Reserves/Deposits[b] %
1880	18,213.9	3.2	44.2
1881	19,397.6	2.8	43.9
1882	18,928.6	3.0	46.3
1883	20,541.8	2.8	45.8
1884	22,158.3	2.6	47.3
1885	23,030.5	2.5	44.8
1886	24,964.5	2.4	42.1
1887	25,686.7	2.2	41.7
1888	25,594.7	2.3	42.7
1889	25,635.2	2.2	45.6
1890	24,509.9	2.4	48.4
1891	24,302.7	2.5	51.5
1892	25,228.0	2.3	51.8
1893	25,710.3	2.4	53.9
1894	25,463.2	2.4	56.7
1895	25,974.7	2.4	54.7
1896	25,617.9	2.4	58.2
1897	26,463.2	2.3	55.4
1898	27,044.6	2.4	60.9
1899	29,484.8	2.2	56.7
1900	29,995.2	2.3	54.8
1901	31,137.8	2.4	52.6
1902	32,362.8	2.2	51.7
1903	33,421.3	2.2	48.9
1904	35,382.0	2.1	46.4
1905	38,561.5	2.0	43.3
1906	38,757.9	2.0	43.7
1907	40,680.9	2.1	42.9
1908	43,277.4	1.9	41.4

TABLE III.9 (*cont.*)

Year	Money Supply[a]	Income Velocity	Reserves/Deposits[b] %
1909	47,141.7	1.9	40.2
1910	51,950.7	1.6	39.2
1911	49,894.6	1.8	38.6
1912	50,423.4	1.8	39.4
1913	52,528.2	1.8	38.5
1914	56,445.9	1.6	41.5

a Beginning with 1898, Monte dei Pieta banks are included in the sample.

b It was impossible to separate those government securities held as reserves from those held for other purposes. Consequently reserve/deposit ratio is higher than one would expect and probably higher than that which the banks themselves would calculate. Nevertheless, it does change in the proper direction and is an acceptable first approximation.

Sources:
   Money Supply: (1) Paper money in the hands of the public, Banca d'Italia, *I bilanci degli istituti di emissione*, Table 5.
      (2) Coins in circulation, *ibid*. Table 14.
      (3) Deposits with non-note-issuing banks, *ibid*. Table 23.
      (4) Deposits with note-issuing banks (excluding interbank deposits) *ibid*. Table 2.
   Income Velocity (income/money supply) based on national income estimates from Istituto Centrale di Statistica, *Annali di Statistica*, Ser. VIII, Vol. 9, Table 37, and money supply as calculated above.
      Reserves: Reserves of all non-note-issuing banks. Includes, in addition to deposits with note-issuing banks, cash on hand and cash deposited with other financial institutions, treasury bills, other government securities, deposits with the Casse Postali, and deposits made to guarantee circulation of checks. (See note *a* for further discussion.) Taken from Banca d'Italia, *I bilanci degli istituti di emissione*, Table 23.
      Deposits: Deposits of all non-note-issuing banks. Includes both savings and demand deposits. Same source as reserves.

stock of money; its main concern was funding its debt. The money supply varied with the inflow of specie, government borrowing, bills of the note-issuing banks in circulation, and the reserve-deposit ratio. The steady rate of increase of the money supply before 1894 was due, therefore, to the enormous requirements of the government and the uncontrolled licence of the note-issuing banks (reflected in their direct issues and the violent fluctuations in the reserve/deposit ratio), both of which tended to neutralize fluctuations in the specie flows. As it did in most developed and developing nations, velocity declined, which suggests that there was a rising demand for money balances on the part of the public.[53] Given the mild price decline, it seems likely that the money supply could have grown even faster in the years before 1897. The more rapid rise in the money supply after 1894 and the mild inflation, however, were due as much to gold discoveries in South Africa and Russia as to a conscious expansionary policy on the part of the Bank of Italy. Nevertheless, the deposit/currency ratio rose throughout the period 1861–1914, and much more steadily after 1894 than before that date. As Milton Friedman and Anna Schwartz point out, fluctuations in this ratio indicate

53. The results of simple regression of the per capita demand for real money balances on per capita real income substantiates this observation.

variations in the confidence which the public has in the banking system.[54] In Italy, financial panics were endemic before the creation of the Bank of Italy.

Agriculture and the Supply of Capital

Agriculture deserves special attention because it was the major sector in terms of output and employment of resources up through 1914 and was, therefore, a potential source of capital for industry. It is debatable whether a growing surplus was created in this sector and, if so, whether that surplus was transferred to non-agricultural activities or was reinvested in agriculture. The creation of a surplus depended on the ability of producers to raise output per acre and per man-hour with relatively minor increases in capital equipment. To transfer the surplus to another sector, producers had to prevent its dissipation. In Japan, the government provided farmers with information on new materials and techniques and captured through taxation the surplus thus created.[55] While the Italian government could have played the same role, it did not.

Rosario Romeo has argued that the expansion in agricultural production between 1861 and 1879 led to the creation of a surplus. The funds were transferred out of agriculture through personal savings or taxes and were used to finance a portion of the investment made in building an infrastructure in Italy.[56] Gerschenkron took issue with Romeo on methodological grounds, while Luzzatto indirectly questioned the empirical validity of Romeo's observations. In particular, Luzzatto stated:

> ... one can estimate that wheat yields remained a little greater than six quintals per hectare [in the 1860's and early 1870's in Italy]. This is very far from the kind of progress in agriculture which is sometimes noted during these years, and a comparison not only with the wheat yields per hectare in Germany, in France, and in England at that time, but also with yields achieved later in Italy, is enough to give an impression of the extremely backward situation in which grain production took place. ...
>
> [Furthermore,] there are other indirect indications, such as the negligible use of chemical fertilizers, the continued reliance on traditional rotation methods, and the absence in most areas of advanced farm machinery, which suggest that little or no progress occurred in Italian agriculture in the decade 1860–1870 and, in fact, probably not until 1874.[57]

54. M. Friedman and A. Schwartz, *A Monetary History of the United States, 1867–1960* (Princeton, 1963), 684.

55. On Japan, K. Ohkawa and H. Rosovsky, "The Role of Agriculture in Modern Japanese Economic Development," *Economic Development and Cultural Change*, IX, 1, Part 2 (October 1960), 43–67.

56. See R. Romeo, *Risorgimento e Capitalismo* (Bari, 1963), 111–130.

57. G. Luzzatto, *L'Economia Italiana*, p. 124.

While it is impossible to resolve the controversy here, Luzzatto's work represents a more careful appraisal of the data than does Romeo's and, on the whole, appears to be more reliable.

Whatever the situation was prior to 1880, from that date until 1897 agriculture was in a period of depression, and, consequently, the sector's surplus was limited. Beginning in 1896 and continuing through 1914, agricultural output rose rapidly. For example, production of the major grain crops—wheat, corn, and oats—jumped one and one-half times between 1895–99 and 1910–14, and there were similar increases in wine and citrus fruit production.[58]

These increases, particularly in cereal crops, resulted from more intensive working of the land and greater use of farm machinery and chemical fertilizers. The evidence to support this contention, while indirect, is persuasive. Between 1887 and 1908–10, the importation of fertilizers rose in value from 4 to 60 million lire, and the domestic production of fertilizers rose almost tenfold.[59] The value of imported farm machinery jumped from less than one million lire in 1888 to over 21 million lire in 1910.[60] Furthermore, the amount of land devoted to agricultural activity remained relatively constant after 1887 and, what was most significant, the amount of land used for cereal crops remained practically unchanged. Finally, the labor force employed in agriculture declined steadily from the early 1890's through 1914 as families left the land for the cities or emigrated to the United States or to Latin America. Thus, increased agricultural production was a consequence of more capital-intensive farming techniques.[61]

Improved yields per hectare which accompanied the greater use of capital were concentrated in the northern plains area, in the regions of Piedmont, Lombardy, the Veneto, and Emilia-Romagna. For example, in 1909 the output per hectare in these four regions averaged 14 quintals of wheat, compared with 9.6 in Sicily, 10.2 in Basilicata, 9.8 in Campania, and 8.5 in Calabria. Only one southern region, Puglia, was even close to the northern average.[62] Most of the rural immigration occurred in the south, so there is

58. Istituto Centrale di Statistica, *Sommario di Statistiche Storiche Italiane, 1865–1955* (Roma, 1958), 106–113.

59. On imports of fertilizers, see G. Valenti, "L'Italia agricola dal 1861 al 1911," *Cinquanta Anni di Storia Italiana*, vol. II, 53. On domestic production see Istituto Centrale di Statistica, *Sommario di Statistiche*, p. 131.

60. G. Valenti, "L'Italia agricola," p. 53.

61. It is possible that the new production techniques were not labor-saving. It may have required more man-hours or man-days per year to produce the increased output, and the ability of workers to leave the farm without affecting production may merely disguise a reorganization of rural activities and a reduction in non-agricultural production. Without any estimates of production functions, it is impossible to say what happened and, given the quality of the data, it is unlikely that production functions would be of much value.

62. G. Valenti, "L'Italia agricola," p. 63.

reason to believe that it was in these regions that any reorganization of rural activities took place. Farming in the south was carried out on large estates (*latifundi*) by day laborers (*braccianti*) or peasants (*contadini*) seeking to supplement their earnings from their very small plots. Production was directed by stewards (*fattori*) who represented absentee landlords. Therefore, any surpluses which resulted from the combination of tariffs and the world price rise after 1896 were captured by the landlords and transferred out of agriculture through personal consumption and saving. In addition, because of the tax structure in Italy, the relative burden of taxation was much greater on the southern peasant than on his northern counterpart, which suggests that the state transferred a larger share of available funds from agriculture to other sectors in the south than it did in the north.

In the two decades prior to World War I, northern farmers tended to reinvest much of their surplus in agriculture, and they made increased use of the financial institutions, especially the cooperative banks, to finance these activities.[63] In the south, on the other hand, the landlords continued to transfer what surpluses were created out of agriculture, and the southern peasantry continued to pay a relatively greater share of their income in taxes than the northerners did.[64]

CONCLUSIONS

The role of finance in the industrialization process must be viewed in the context of the economic system as a whole. Financial intermediaries are essentially passive institutions that transfer surplus funds of savers to debtors. The financial system's ability to attract funds depends on the services it can offer savers, while its ability to influence industrialization depends on the demand for funds by industrialists. Thus, the role banks and other credit institutions will play in industrialization depends on the availability of funds, the demand for these funds by industry, and the willingness of the financial system to meet this demand.

In this essay I have focused attention on certain aspects of the supply of capital to industry, in particular the process of forced saving, the reallocation of financial capital, and the reorganization of portfolios held by savers. Such changes in the flow of funds in the Italian economy affected both the composition and timing of industrialization. Since internally generated funds

63. It should be recalled that the growth of these banks occurred primarily in the rural areas of the northern and central regions of the peninsula.

64. This conclusion confirms the observation made by Antonio Gramsci that it was impossible for capital accumulation to occur in the south. (See Massimo L. Salvadori, *Il mito del Buongoverno* (Turin, 1963), 504–512.)

were inadequate to satisfy the investment needs of industry, firms were forced to seek external financial assistance. To encourage savers and institutional investors (the industrial credit banks in particular) to hold large quantities of secondary and primary industrial assets, the government pursued policies that guaranteed both industrial investments and the solvency of the financial intermediaries in temporary crises. These policies included tariffs that protected the domestic market, subsidies that encouraged the use of domestic products, and central bank policies that provided lender of last resort services.

CHAPTER IV

Spain 1829–1874

GABRIEL TORTELLA

This study covers the development of the Spanish banking system from the year the Bank of Saint Ferdinand (whose name was later changed to the Bank of Spain) was founded to the year the Bank of Spain was granted the national monopoly of note-issue. From the standpoint of Spanish economic and political history, this is a well-defined period, with certain unique characteristics.

The literature of the period is scanty, and the statistical material has been little explored. Yet a survey can be made of it. The first conclusion that emerges from such a survey is that the pace of industrialization was very deficient, although by no means stagnant. The description which most adequately fits the evolution of the Spanish economy during these years is that of an effort to industrialize that failed rather than that of a general stagnation. The economic gap between Spain and its northwest European neighbors was probably wider at the end of the period than at the beginning.

The disappointing performance of the Spanish economy in the nineteenth century is surprising on two counts: first, because it represents a discontinuity with the hopeful signs of economic progress shown in the eighteenth century; and second, because it contrasts sharply with the experience of its west European neighbors, where industrialization and economic progress, within a wide spectrum of patterns and in quite varied time sequences, took place decisively during the nineteenth century.

Spain's underdevelopment is thus more exceptional than is generally realized. Even a comparison with the other southern European peninsulas turns clearly into Spain's disfavor since, unlike Italy and Greece, Spain was both politically independent and unified, and was not subject to foreign rule, which might have constituted an obstacle to economic development. Spain's backwardness is, so to speak, its own doing. Its politics, its social framework, its resource endowment may be blamed for it, but not outside imposition. Only its Iberian neighbor, Portugal, offers a close parallel.

That the failure to industrialize was so much a domestic affair is what makes nineteenth-century Spanish history so fascinating. One has the conviction that a study of the Spanish experience should yield certain clues to the causes of today's underdevelopment in large areas of the world at a time when industrialization has made such strides in other areas. (The coexistence of lunar exploration and mass hunger on Earth in the last third of the twentieth century is no more surprising than, and probably closely related to, say, the coexistence of telegraphic communication and mass illiteracy in Europe a century earlier.) It might also suggest some ideas about what policy-makers should *not* do in a country striving for industrialization.

This is the standpoint from which this study has been conceived. Hirschman has remarked that "present-day interest in economic development has led economic historians to re-examine the early stages of the industrialization process in Western Europe" with the purpose of "identifying key factors responsible for this unique instance of successful development."[1] But failure is often a better teacher than success; development, after all, is a problem of removing obstacles as much as it is one of moving along already cleared paths. Moreover, the situation of the "third world" today is very different from that of Europe in the eighteenth and nineteenth centuries. In Landes's words, "Western Europe . . . was already rich before the Industrial Revolution."[2] Using Deane's figures, one can see that British per capita income in the mid-eighteenth century was roughly similar not to that of today's poor countries, but to that of today's semi-industrialized countries.[3] Given the enlarged scope of communications and the metaphoric shrinking of our planet, the economic situation of today's poor countries is similar to that of Europe's poor countries one century ago rather than to that of the industrial pioneers. This is why, going back to Hirschman, "historical studies of the conditions under which efforts at industrialization have turned out be abortive may yield more valuable lessons"[4] than those analyzing successful case histories.

When surveying Spanish banks in the nineteenth century one becomes increasingly aware of being confronted with one such "abortive effort." To start with, Table IV.1 offers a striking spectacle of growth and contraction in the third quarter of the century.

The number of banking corporations started to increase during the 1840's,

1. Albert O. Hirschman, *The Strategy of Economic Development* (New Haven, 1965), p. 134, n. 2.
2. David S. Landes, *The Unbound Prometheus* (Cambridge, Eng., 1969), p. 13.
3. Phyllis Deane, *The First Industrial Revolution* (Cambridge, Eng., 1965), pp. 6–7.
4. Hirschman, *Strategy.*

TABLE IV.1

Joint-stock Banks in Spain, 1829–1874

(December of each year, savings banks excluded)

Year	(1) Banks of Issue	(2) Credit Companies	(3) Other	(4) Total
1829–43	1	0	0	1
1844	3	0	0	3
1845	3	0	1	4
1846	4	0	3	7
1847	3	0	3	6
1848–54	3	0	1	4
1855	3	0	2	5
1856	4	6	3	13
1857	10	6	3	19
1858	10	7	3	20
1859	10	7	3	20
1860	11	8	3	22
1861	11	12	3	26
1862	12	17	3	32
1863	14	20	3	37
1864	21[a]	34[a]	2	57
1865	21	35	2	58
1866	21	32	1	54
1867	21	26	0	47
1868	20	21	0	41
1869	19	14	0	33
1870	16	14	0	30
1871	16	14	2	32
1872	16	14	4	34
1873	16	13	4	33
1874	1	13	8	22

[a] From 1864 on (and especially after 1867) these figures may be somewhat inflated since it is likely that some banks and credit companies went out of business without having been officially dissolved (like the Banco de Valladolid, out of business since 1864 but not officially dissolved until 1870).

Sources: Biblioteca Nacional, Madrid: Collection of banking pamphlets (hereafter cited as BNM); *Colección Legislativa de España* (CLE); *Anuario Estadístico de España* (AEE); *Gaceta de Madrid* (GdeM); Archivo del Banco de España (ABE), Secretaría, Leg. 647; Shareholders reports of the leading banks: Collection of the Bank of Spain.

and then jumped spectacularly in the late 1850's and early 1860's, reaching a maximum figure of 58 (of which 21 were banks of issue) by 1865. Then a reverse process set in: ten years later the total figure of banking corporations was 22, and a monopoly of issue had been vested in the Bank of Spain. This reduction in numbers cannot be attributed to a merger movement. There were no bank mergers between 1865 and 1874 except during the latter year, when 11 out of 15 provincial banks of issue merged with the Bank of Spain under government auspices.

Other banking and monetary variables show comparable fluctuations. The fully paid-in capital of issuing banks more than doubled between 1856 and 1866 (taking 1856 = 100, the index was 215.7) and then it went down almost continuously until 1873, the last year before the Bank of Spain assumed its monopoly of issue (the index for 1873 was 193.8). If the Bank of Spain is excluded from the picture, the fluctuation is much wider: the index goes up to 354.1 in 1866 (also a maximum year for provincial banks *alone*) and then down to 270.3 in 1873. Fiduciary circulation reached a peak in 1864 and fluctuated downward thereafter.[5]

My evidence shows that the fluctuations in banking activity are closely related to the failure of industrialization. Nevertheless (insofar as this kind of statement is permissible), it is not with the banking system that the ultimate responsibility lies for the failure of Spain to industrialize successfully. A series of social and institutional obstacles discouraged investment in industry, and the banking system only adapted itself to this distorted market.

It seems fairly clear that the government was largely responsible for Spain's failure to achieve industrialization. It is not that governmental indifference kept industry in a lethargic state; rather, the government actively discouraged industry, partly deliberately, partly through misguided action. Three main lines of policy implemented by the government during these years were devastating for industrialization. They can be summarized as follows:

(1) The government established a disentailment and enclosure program, by which it auctioned large tracts of land previously owned by the Church, the nobility, and the villages. Given the increase in population during these years, disentailment was an absolute necessity. But the way in which lands were redistributed (and many other aspects of the operation) had disastrous short- and long-term consequences. Among its many negative effects, disentailment diverted large sums of capital away from industrial endeavors. I have not been able to analyze in detail the agrarian policies of the Spanish government in the nineteenth century, and a satisfactory over-all study is unfortunately missing, but some quantitative data are available which may give an idea of the magnitudes involved. From 1836 to 1856 the government sold real estate worth some 481 million pesetas (at that time, 1 franc = 0.95 peseta) under the disentailing program. In 1856 the authorized capital of all manufacturing corporations combined was 73 million. Between 1856 and 1865 disentailed lands worth 816 million were sold, and in 1865 the total

---

5. The pertinent series are compiled in my forthcoming work on Spanish banking in the nineteenth century.

authorized capital of all manufacturing corporations was 98 million.[6] The disentailing program transferred large amounts of funds from private investors to the government chests, whence a fraction was distributed in indemnities to the land's original owners (who had a low propensity to invest in industry) and the rest was devoted to basically unproductive government expenses,[7] thus diverting a sizable share of domestic savings away from industry. Since the economic mentality of the Spanish wealthy classes was backward, and the political outlook unstable, landholding was preferred to industry; little attention was given to marginal rates of return. (It is also possible that most wealthy people considered land to be a prestigious asset, but conclusive data are not available.)

(2) In spite of the additional receipts that disentailment brought in, there was a budget deficit practically every year. The volume of public debt outstanding increased continually, yet Spain was a country where loanable funds were far from abundant. The government, furthermore, was a privileged competitor in the scramble for loans. The Bank of Spain, whose assets were about half those of all issuing banks, was almost entirely devoted to short- and long-term loans to the government, and the private sector only received residual amounts from it. To substantiate this statement I have sectorized and consolidated the Bank of Spain's end-of-year balance sheets from 1852 (there are no earlier balance sheets available) to 1873. According to my calculations, the average end-of-year government indebtness to the Bank was 82.1 million pesetas. The corresponding figure for the private sector was 20.0 million. The Caja de Depósitos, a government agency which enjoyed the largest volume of deposits of all credit institutions, devoted its entire resources to supplying the government with funds. The Bank of Barcelona, the second largest issuing institution, and located in the country's main industrial center, loaned an average of 378,000 pesetas a year on industrial equity from 1858 to 1866, and an average of 2.3 million pesetas on public debt securities. It is no wonder that in 1859 the combined capital of all manufacturing corporations (100 million pesetas) was less than the capital of one single railway company (Madrid-Saragossa-Alicante, 114 million).

(3) Industrial enterprise was actively discouraged by a law passed in 1848, which submitted all corporations to government approval under a very long administrative procedure. This law was amended in 1855, 1856, and 1859 to give more freedom for the formation of railroad, banking, and mining corporations, with obvious detriment to manufactures. The result was

6. *Anuario Estadístico de España* [*AEE*], *1859*, and *AEE*, *1862–1865*.

7. Unfortunately, there is no satisfactory study of government expenditure in nineteenth-century Spain, but examination of official data totally supports this statement. Cf. *Estadística de los presupuestos generales del Estado y de los resultados que ha ofrecido su liquidación, años 1850 a 1890–1* (Madrid, 1891), pp. 80–81, *et passim.*

overcapitalization in railways, which attracted a large share of bank assets. Railway-building lost a considerable amount of its stimulative effects due to the fact that most of the equipment and skills (and even a share of the manpower) were imported from abroad. Furthermore, railways were built ahead of demand, since the goods to be moved by them were not being produced in sufficient quantities; in 1866, when the railway companies defaulted on their bonds, the banking system collapsed and many of the mobilier-type societies went bankrupt.

Let us try to give a more formal expression to the statements contained in point (3), since they are central to the theses of this chapter. This can be done with the help of concepts developed in Chapter 5 of Hirschman's *Strategy of Economic Development*. (The case of Spanish railways, by the way, is an excellent illustration of the principles and conclusions developed by Hirschman in that chapter). Spain in the mid-1850's can be regarded as an underdeveloped country which had the ability to mobilize a limited amount of resources and which had a choice between alternative fields of investment. Following Hirschman, I divide these fields into two main categories, Social Overhead Capital (SOC) and Directly Productive Activities (DPA). In this case, the range is rather narrow, since the main SOC item is the railroad system and DPA is restricted to manufacturing. Projects such as roads, canals, power stations, and agriculture and services are excluded from both SOC and DPA.

Naturally, the final objective of the Spanish "planners" was to "promote public wealth" in a very general sense. Nevertheless, however general, the growth envisaged had to imply an increase in the levels of consumption and, therefore, an expansion of the directly productive activities. This could have been done by direct investment in DPA or by stimulating DPA by means of SOC investment. The first possibility is what Hirschman calls "development via shortage" of SOC. In the Spanish case, growth of the manufacturing sector would have increased the demand for transportation services, putting a strain on those that were available and creating a bottleneck. The second possibility is called "development via excess capacity" of SOC. In this case, the railroad network was built in the hope that the manufacturing sector would be stimulated by the availability of transportation services.

Obviously, the second alternative was chosen in Spain. But development via excess capacity poses some problems. The chief one is that it is permissive rather than stimulative. The railroad network was a great help to manufactures, but it did not remove the other roadblocks that were opposed to the growth of manufactures. It might be compared to a cheap money policy in times of depression: if the stimulus to invest is not there, easy terms for loans are largely irrelevant. In a parallel way, if the pressures for industrialization are not there, transportation facilities are redundant. The railway system was built ahead of demand and, when the main lines were ready, the companies discovered that traffic barely covered variable costs. They were unable to pay interests and dividends, let alone the principal of the debts incurred in the actual construction of the system.

What about the stimulative effects of SOC investment? In other words, what about multiplier and backward linkage effects? The multiplier model applies to an economy with excess capacity, where a positive shift in aggregate demand sets off a chain reaction among closely knit, interdependent sectors; that is to say, it is effective in a fairly industrialized community. In an underdeveloped country where a near-subsistence economy is still widespread, the markets are scattered, most industrial branches are missing, and the leaks are too numerous to put any faith on the multiplier as a stimulus to growth. Backward linkages could have been more effective; backward linkage effects of railroad building are generally taken to have been a powerful stimulus to economic growth in the United States and Europe, although recent research has cast some doubts about their role in the United States. In the case of Spain the linkage effects, as will be seen in greater detail later, might have been felt in France, Belgium, and England, but certainly not in Spain itself, since virtually all the manufactured equipment was imported during the period of intense construction.

For all these reasons, the words of Hirschman apply totally to the Spanish industrialization effort of the 1850's and 1860's: "In situations where motivations are deficient, it . . . seems safer to rely on development via shortage than on development via excess capacity." [8]

There are still other reasons why the policy of development via excess capacity may fail. When investible funds are scarce, SOC may turn out to be competing for funds with the DPA it is supposed to be helping. It is not only that the existence of a railway line may not be sufficient in itself to foster investment in manufactures. It may very well be that it prevents such investment because it is using up the funds that could otherwise have been devoted to building a manufacturing plant. This again seems to have been the case in Spain, as I will try to show later.

Finally, development via excess capacity may not only be self-defeating in its developmental purposes; it may, under certain conditions, be self-destructive; built ahead of demand, under-utilized because of the absence of the customers it has itself helped keep in abeyance, it is likely to disappoint whatever efficiency or profitability criteria laid down for it, and thereby discourage future public or private investors. Again, this may have been the case with Spanish railroads. After a decade of accelerated construction in

8. *Strategy*, p. 93.

1856–65, when almost 5,000 kilometers of rail lines were installed, it took another 35 years to build the next 5,000 kilometers. Spain has remained, to this day, among the countries with lowest railway densities (per capita and per square mile) in Europe.

To sum up, the railways were built at the expense of the manufacturing sector they were supposed to help. While mileage increased year by year, the number of joint-stock manufacturing companies and the capital invested in them stagnated. By the mid-1860's the railway companies started to suspend payments and to clamor for government support, while the banking system, whose portfolios were filled with railway bonds and shares, found itself in a desperate state of illiquidity and a large proportion of banks were forced to dissolve.

The role of the banks in this unfortunate operation was central, but they by no means determined it. Insofar as it can be ascertained, it was the government that created the mechanisms which tilted the financial system toward railway construction. The banks only grew and developed within this framework, and they seized the investment opportunities offered them. They were effective in the creation and mobilization of instruments of credit, but they lacked creativity and originality in that they blindly followed the directives from above and did not strive to find other fields of investment or spread their assets. Some bankers finally realized the danger of their exclusive concentration in railway finance and started talking about diversifying their assets, but by that time it was too late. The inflated banking system, born in special circumstances, was shattered and reduced to pieces when these circumstances changed. The banking structure which emerged after 1874, when the social and economic turmoil precipitated by the 1866 crisis subsided, was very different and extremely conservative.

The manufacturing sector never really took off during this period. It was largely based in Catalonia, more specifically in Barcelona, around a cotton textile industry which chronically lagged in modern equipment and which, furthermore, was gripped in 1862 by the cotton shortage caused by the American Civil War. The obstacles mentioned earlier, plus others, legal, social, and institutional, kept textiles and metallurgy in a very backward state.

EVOLUTION OF THE FINANCIAL STRUCTURE: THE EARLY YEARS

The history of modern banking corporations in Spain starts with the Spanish Bank of Saint Ferdinand (Banco Español de San Fernando), established

9. On the Bank of Saint Charles see Earl J. Hamilton, "The Foundation of the Bank of Spain," *The Journal of Political Economy*, LIII, no. 2 (June 1945), and "The First Twenty Years of the Bank of Spain," *ibid.*, LIV, nos. 1 and 2 (February and April 1946).

in 1829 to replace the old and ailing Bank of Saint Charles.[9] The main reason for chartering the Saint Ferdinand was, from the government's standpoint, to reach an arrangement with the creditors of the Bank of Saint Charles. This opinion was shared by the staff and managers of the Saint Ferdinand. Few viewed it as a lever of economic progress, and those who did probably did not know how this vision could actually be implemented. It is not surprising, therefore, that the first years of the Saint Ferdinand were inauspicious; the first meeting of shareholders took place in 1833, and the complaint of the Bank's managers was that they could find no employment for its funds, so that about half of the paid-in capital (10 million pesetas)[10] remained inactive.[11]

To the lack of positive initiative and the conservative spirit of the royally appointed bank managers one must add the final history of the Bank of Saint Charles as a factor contributing to the Saint Ferdinand's lethargy. It was generally agreed in the financial circles of Madrid at the time that Saint Charles's temerity in handling the public debt (*vales reales*) had brought about its ruin. The Saint Ferdinand's managers, consequently, preferred to keep on the safe side on all policy matters. Parsimonious, the Bank limited itself to discounting bills with three reliable signatures and to the transfer of funds for merchants and landowners between ports and provincial capitals and Madrid, and vice versa.

After 1833 the Bank felt the pressure of an increasingly important but by no means new customer: the state. With the Carlist war raging in the countryside, the Madrid government, already indebted to national and foreign bankers for the Napoleonic wars, the 1820 revolution, and the wars of independence of Spanish America (1808–24), turned to the Saint Ferdinand for the ready cash it needed to keep the army going. By 1834 the government was pressuring the Bank for help. It asked the Bank to increase its capital by 50 per cent but the Bank successfully resisted this and other exhortations to engage in operations it considered hazardous.

In 1836 the government started to expropriate (with indemnity) and sell Church lands as a way to meet its increasing deficit, with the Bank of Saint Ferdinand advancing money against the promissory notes of the land buyers. The Bank's help to the finances of the government did not stop until the Carlist civil war (1833–39) ended. From 1833 onwards the main function of the Bank was to advance money to the government for current budgetary

10. For purposes of convenience, the *peseta* is used as unit of account throughout this paper, although the *real* was the legal monetary unit until 1864 and the *escudo* from 1864 to 1868. The peseta, which became the official unit in September 1868, was equivalent to 4 reales and to 0.4 escudos.

11. *Primera Junta General del Banco Español de San Fernando, de los años 1830, 1831 y 1832, celebrada en su propio establecimiento en 1° de Febrero de 1833* (Madrid).

payments, with tax receipts as its main guarantee. On occasion the Bank was charged with the collection of taxes, as happened during the fiscal year 1836–37, and eventually this function of collecting taxes and advancing money to the state became the object of long-term contracts between both partners. Helping the government solve its most pressing budgetary problems was the principal economic function of the Bank during the nineteenth century. The extent to which this was so in the years 1829–44 can be gauged from the profit figures published by the Bank. From 1830 to 1844, interest from direct loans and other services to the government averaged 48.1 per cent of gross profits.[12] Figures of Treasury bills discounted were not separated from bills discounted for private individuals, so we can only vaguely guess here, but it would be fair to estimate that, when Treasury bills and all other credit to the government is added, at least three-quarters of the profits came from services to the government. This provides us with a very rough idea of the distribution of the Bank's assets between the public and the private sectors. This proportion (between 3 and 4 to 1 in favor of the public sector) is very similar to the one that emerges for a later period (1852–73) from the sectorization of the Bank of Spain balance sheets, a much more reliable source.

There are some indications of industrial activity in Spain during the 1830's, especially in Barcelona, where a series of cotton factories were created, and where a textile machinery shop was opened in 1832. Credit to commerce and industry was supplied by unspecialized merchant bankers for whom financial activities were one way to give employment to idle funds. The most notable of these merchant banking houses was Girona Hermanos, Clavé y Compañía, a partnership whose main component, the Girona family, would provide a large share of Spain's banking entrepreneurship during the nineteenth century. The bulk of the textile investments during the 1830's, however, seem to have been made with capital brought back from the former Spanish American colonies by Spaniards expelled or fleeing from the new nations.[13]

The 1840's witnessed a first wave of business euphoria in Spain. It was probably brought about by the removal of a series of political obstacles which stood in the way of economic progress, the main one undoubtedly being the Carlist civil war, which was ended by an armistice in 1839. The European recovery after the 1838 international crisis undoubtedly con-

---

12. As presented in Ramón Santillán, *Memoria histórica sobre los Bancos Nacional de San Carlos, Español de San Fernando, Isabel II, Nuevo de San Fernando y de España* (2 vols.; Madrid, 1865), I, pp. 234–35. The figure above is undoubtedly an underestimate, since total gross profits are unduly inflated in Santillán's figures.

13. Jorge Nadal Oller, "La economía española, 1829–1931" in *El Banco de España. Una historia económico* (Bank of Spain, Madrid, 1970).

tributed, and so also did the earliest plans for a national railroad network, which began to be discussed around this time. But probably the most immediately decisive factor were the rumors that, the war finished, the government was preparing to resume fair payment of the public debt. These insistent rumors, not totally unfounded as far as intentions were concerned, revitalized the sleepy Madrid stock exchange and stimulated the quotation of government bonds. Prices went up and capital became more easily available.[14]

A series of joint-stock banks were created during this period, three of them enjoying the right to issue banknotes. These issuing banks were the Bank of Isabel II (of Madrid), the Bank of Barcelona, and the Bank of Cadiz. The non-issuing joint-stock banks were the Union Bank (Banco de la Unión) and the Overseas and Development Bank (Banco de Fomento y Ultramar), both of Madrid, and the Valenciana de Fomento, of Valencia. Other incorporated banking houses, of which very little is known, were also founded during these years, such as the Caja de Descuentos Zaragozana (Saragossa Discount House).

The Bank of Isabel II[15] was a project by a group of Madrid businessmen who had grown impatient with Saint Ferdinand's caution and lack of initiative. The need for a joint-stock bank which would actively support business ventures and which would stimulate economic activity by means of a brisk fiduciary circulation was widely felt among this group. The government agreed, probably figuring that it could get more loans from two banks than from one only. The Isabel II opened its doors in 1844 and there immediately ensued a silent war between the two institutions, a war whose main results were a tremendous increase in banknote circulation in Madrid (from 6 million pesetas in January, 1844, to 28 million in September, 1845), frantic speculative activity in the Madrid stock exchange, and the eventual merger of the two rivals in 1847 to prevent the impending bankruptcy of the Isabel II.

In spite of its short and unsuccessful career, the Bank of Isabel II made a number of contributions, the main one probably being that it shook the Bank of Saint Ferdinand out of its monopolistic conservatism, forcing it to enlarge its bank note circulation, to pay more attention to the private sector, and to attempt to make credit more accessible to a wider range of people. The Isabel II also introduced several innovations which were sooner or later adapted by the Saint Ferdinand or by other later banks: banknotes of relatively small denominations (200 reales, or 50 pesetas, instead of the

14. See the speech of Luis M. Pastor in Sociedad Libre de Economía Política, "Sesiones celebradas en 7, 18 y 27 de Mayo y 2 de Junio de 1863 para discutir y examinar los obstáculos que se oponen a la reapertura de las Bolsas extranjeras para los valores de crédito en España, y los medios más a propósito para conseguirla" (pamphlet; Madrid, 1863).

15. For the next two paragraphs, Gabriel Tortella, "El Banco de España entre 1829 y 1929" in El Banco de España, and sources and works cited there.

500 reales which were the smallest banknotes previously issued by Saint Ferdinand); lending to industrial and railroad enterprises on their own shares as collateral; lending on a current account basis; and initiating branch banking. This last point is connected with the creation of the Bank of Cadiz, which was established in 1846 as a branch of Isabel II and, after the merger of the two Madrid banks, became an independent bank of issue.

The Bank of Barcelona was founded in 1844 and had a monopoly of issue in that city. The charter for the bank was given to the private banking house Girona Hermanos, Clavé y Compañía. The Bank of Barcelona really was the representative of the largest and most solid business interests in the city, so it could establish as a policy principle that in ordinary times only a fraction (usually 25 per cent) of the authorized (nominal) capital would be paid in, with the understanding that the unpaid capital could be called in times of crisis. According to some writers, this policy was very effective in weathering the 1848 crisis.[16] The Bank of Barcelona soon became the first real commercial bank in Spain, discounting bills for merchants and industrialists, and carefully expanding its means of payment. After the 1848 crisis it was inclined to restrict its fiduciary circulation, and its current account deposits became its largest contribution to the money supply until 1856.

The 1848 crisis shattered this incipient banking system in Madrid, but not in the provinces. The Union Bank, which was a financial springboard for the activities of its directors,[17] and the Overseas and Development Bank, organized to finance a transatlantic navigation company which never actually started operations,[18] did not survive 1848. The Bank of Isabel II, after three years of bold, or rather, reckless, operations, was merged with the Saint Ferdinand by government fiat in 1847, at which time one of its directors, José Salamanca, was finance minister. Because of the fact that most of the assets in the Isabel II portfolio were worth next to nothing due to the crash in the stock exchange, but were valued at par in the merger, the new bank resulting from the merger (called the New Spanish Bank of Saint Ferdinand) was in severe financial embarrassment and had to suspend convertibility in 1848. Not until 1851 could it resume its normal activities.

The 1848 panic had an effect on the Spanish financial community and government authorities not unlike the early eighteenth-century "bubbles" in France and England. Joint-stock companies and banks of issue were

16. Ramón Canosa, *Un siglo de Banca privada (1845–1945)* (Madrid, 1945), p. 30; Jose María Tallada Pauli, *Historia de las finanzas españolas en el siglo XIX* (Madrid, 1946), p. 231; Banco de Barcelona, *Memoria que la Junta de Gobierno presenta a la General Extraordinaria de Accionistas en 20 de Mayo de 1894. Quincuagésimo aniversario de su creación* (Barcelona, 1894).

17. Banco de la Unión, *Memoria, 1847*, Biblioteca Nacional, Madrid [*BNM*].

18. Banco de Fomento y Ultramar, *Memoria de la Junta Liquidadora*, BNM.

regarded as dangerous institutions to be used very sparingly, if at all, and always under the watchful eye of the government. Accordingly, in 1848 a very stringent law was issued which prohibited *all* joint-stock companies, with two exceptions: (1) Banks of issue, public transportation companies, and companies enjoying a legal privilege, which could be chartered by the Cortes (Parliament); and (2) "Companies whose object is the general welfare," which could be chartered by the government after a long procedure intended to prove that "general welfare" was indeed the object of the prospective company. All other companies were excluded from organizing, not only under the ordinary corporate form (*sociedad anónima*, the equivalent of the French *société anonyme*), but also under the *commandite par actions* form (*comanditaria por acciones*). The 1848 Corporation Law was very effective during the depressed years of 1848–51, when few people would have dreamed of founding a corporation even if all kind of encouragements were given by the government. After 1851 the economic outlook appeared brighter, and the restrictive character of the 1848 law, plus the inspection and control powers it gave to government officials, were increasingly resented by the business community.[19]

In 1852 a new element was added to the skeletal Spanish credit system, the Caja General de Depósitos (General Deposits Office). This was a government agency whose original purpose was to provide custody for judicial deposits by the public. Service was also provided, however, to handle ordinary deposits, and these immediately became its most important item. In fact the Caja de Depósitos soon became one of the main sources of government finance. It paid high interest rates for long-term deposits, especially after 1860, and its net specie balances reached very high levels by Spanish standards. The employment given to these funds was the acquisition of public debt in its various forms. A fraction was devoted to government railway bonds, and the rest (over four-fifths) was devoted to other forms of public debt of which the ordinary 3 per cent type (quoted at less than half its nominal value) constituted the largest part.[20]

YEARS OF EXPANSION

The restrictive legislation of 1848 remained in force for over twenty years. It was, however, substantially modified immediately after the Revolution of 1854, which swept the Progressive party into power for two years. During

19. This is expanded in Gabriel Tortella, "El principio de responsabilidad limitada y el desarrollo industrial de España, 1829–1869," *Moneda y Crédito* (March 1968).

20. Nicolás Sánchez-Albornoz, "La crisis de 1866 en Madrid: la Caja de Depósitos, las sociedades de crédito y la Bolsa," *Moneda y Crédito* (March 1967).

that time several "liberal" laws were issued on economic matters. Among these were the railway law of 1855 and the banking laws of 1856. The railway law was intended as a stimulus to railroad construction: it relaxed considerably the legal requirements for the establishment of railway corporations, in addition to giving special facilities to foreign investment in railways, tariff exemptions for importation of railway equipment, government subsidies, and other favorable measures. The banking laws of 1856 (one on banks of issue, the other on investment banks) similarly eased the creation of banking corporations.

The main features of the Banks of Issue Law may be summarized as follows: (1) It established a system which may be concisely described as "plurality of issue": "in each town only one issuing institution will be permitted, whether a private [i.e. non-official] Bank, or a branch of the Bank of Spain." (2) The Bank of Saint Ferdinand was definitely rebaptized as the Bank of Spain. (3) Banknote issue could not exceed three times the paid-in capital or specie reserve, whichever was smaller. Except for the Banks of Barcelona and Cadiz, the capital of all issuing banks had to be fully paid in before they started operations. (4) Government control was to be exercised through the governor of the Bank of Spain and through a royal commissary for each of the other banks of issue.

TABLE IV.2

Caja de Depósitos: Net Specie Balances, 1852–1868

Year (end of month)	million pesetas	Year (end of month)	million pesetas
1852 (Dec.)	7.4	1860 (Dec.)	259.5
1853 (Dec.)	23.0	1861 (Dec.)	224.2
1854 (Dec.)	15.7	1862 (Dec.)	381.2
1855 (Dec.)	12.0	1863 (June)	414.3
1856 (Dec.)	20.0	1864 (June)	420.4
1857 (Dec.)	34.2	1865 (June)	365.8
1858 (Dec.)	51.5	1866 (Jan.)	353.5
1859 (Dec.)	86.7	1867 (Feb.)	329.4

Sources: *AEE, 1862-5*, pp. 556-7; *Gaceta de los Caminos de Hierro* (hereafter cited as *GCH*), XI, p. 119; and XIII, p. 212.

Investment banks were regulated by a separate law, which called them credit companies (*sociedades de crédito*). The Credit Companies Law of 1856 was undoubtedly modeled on the charter of the French Crédit Mobilier, which was then at the apex of its success. Credit companies were allowed a wide range of activities, from government loans and tax collecting to industrial promotion and commercial banking. They could start business with a minimum paid-in capital of 10 per cent of the total nominal figure. They could also issue their own bonds up to ten times the capital if it were totally paid in; five times the paid-in capital otherwise. Authorization to establish a credit company could be obtained from the government or from the Cortes. The companies were required to send a monthly balance sheet to the Finance Ministry to be published in the *Gaceta de Madrid* (the government's daily bulletin), and the government had a right to inspect them at any time.

Through the door opened by the banking and credit laws of January 28, 1856, entered a number of new financial institutions into Spanish economic life. The demand for credit facilities (stimulated by the agricultural boom of 1852–56, and reinforced by the unusual demands due to the Crimean war) was finally met by a new supply after the rigors of the 1848 Corporations Law were at last partially eased. Six credit companies, seven banks of issue, and a discount bank company were founded during the two years that followed the publication of the new laws. By the end of 1858 there were four times as many joint-stock banks in Spain as there had been at the time the banking laws were enacted.

Let us examine these new banks and their main activities. We will look first at the three large French credit companies founded in Madrid and having, quantitatively and qualitatively, distinct personalities of their own; we will later examine the credit companies in the rest of Spain; and then we will turn our attention to the banks of issue.

The three French credit companies in Madrid were the Crédito Mobiliario Español, the Sociedad Española Mercantil e Industrial, and the Compañía General de Crédito en España. The Crédito Mobiliario Español was a creation of the men who had launched the French Crédit Mobilier, i.e. the brothers Émile and Isaac Pereire and their collaborators. The Spanish Mobiliario had a nominal capital of 114 million pesetas (456 million reales, or 120 million francs), which was fully paid in by 1864.

This was a huge capital accumulation for Spain. The Bank of Spain, by far the largest in the country up to 1856, had a capital of 30 million pesetas until 1865, when it increased it to 50 million. Total government receipts for the fiscal year 1863–64 amounted to 577 million pesetas, or slightly more than five times the paid-in capital of the Crédito Mobiliario. The pattern of the Mobiliario's activities was already clearly discernible by the end of 1856. Its first published balance sheet shows that 63.5 per cent of its assets consisted of investments in the Spanish Northern railway (a line from Madrid to the French border at the western end of the Pyrenees, whose concession it had recently secured), coal mines in northern Castile, and the Madrid gas company. The largest share of this (13.6 million pesetas) was invested in the railroad. Most of its remaining assets (30.2 per cent of the total) were held in the form of government debt.[21] The following year the Mobiliario's assets were distributed as shown in Table IV.3.

TABLE IV.3

Crédito Mobiliario Español: Percentage Distribution of Assets, December 31, 1857

1. Government bonds	8.4
2. Shares	16.1
3. Advances to the Madrid Gas Company	20.3
4. Advances to the Norte	43.3
5. Advances to mining and other companies	4.2
6. Other advances	6.5
7. Furniture and cash	1.1
8. Other	0.1
9. Total (million pesetas)	26.1

Source: Calculated from Crédito Mobiliario, Shareholders report, May 31, 1858.

The Pereires wanted to secure a railway concession from Madrid to Cadiz, but they were able to secure only a part of it, the Córdoba–Seville line. When they realized they could not secure the southern half of their planned Bayonne–Madrid–Cadiz railway, they created a separate company to build and manage the Bayonne–Madrid system, and called it Compañía de los Caminos de Hierro del Norte de España (North of Spain Railway Company; hereafter called Norte) in December 1858. In addition to the Norte, the Crédito Mobiliario also took an interest in the Córdoba–Seville railway, a company organized by the Pereires and the banker Charles Laffitte, together with some English and Spanish entrepreneurs.[22]

The Sociedad Española Mercántil e Industrial (Spanish Mercantile and Industrial Company) was organized by James de Rothschild, head of the French Rothschilds, and his representatives in Spain, Daniel Weisweiller and Ignacio Bauer. Its total authorized capital was 76 million pesetas, but that figure was never actually paid in; the highest figure of paid-in capital, 22.8 million, was reached in 1857, but in 1862 paid-in capital was reduced to

21. Crédito Mobiliario Español, Shareholders report, 30 May 1857.
22. Rondo Cameron, *France and the Economic Development of Europe* (Princeton, N.J., 1961), pp. 250, 252; Crédito Mobiliario Español, Shareholders report, 30 May 1857.

15.2 million, and there it stayed until the company was dissolved in 1868. The Sociedad Española's main and almost exclusive area of concern was railways. It promoted, and was a sizable stockholder of, the MZA (Madrid–Saragossa [Zaragoza]–Alicante) Railway company, whose network was based on two main lines: the Madrid–Alicante, which was inaugurated in May 1858, and the Madrid–Saragossa, which was completed in 1863. Almost three-fourths of the Madrid–Alicante line was already in service when MZA was founded, but the Madrid–Saragossa line was only beginning to be built. The Sociedad Española acted as the building contractor of the MZA for this line.

The general attitude of the Rothschild company can be usefully contrasted with that of the Crédito Mobiliario. Their respective capital policies already supply an index of their divergence. While the Mobiliario invested heavily in Spain, the Sociedad Español was quietly disinvesting part of its paid-in capital and, as we will see later on, preparing to decrease its direct involvement in the Spanish economy. It can generally be said that the Pereire bank was much more ambitiously conceived than that of Rothschild. In the annual reports, there is evidence suggesting that the Pereires envisioned a vertically integrated economic empire in Spain whose spinal cord would be the Norte railway, which (among other tasks) would take coal extracted from the Old Castile mines acquired by the Mobiliario and deliver it to the gasworks and "large metallurgical factories" that were to be built along the line.[23] There was a Saint-Simonian flavor to the Mobiliario's projects. Rothschild was no doctrinaire, and he was much more cautious. One of his policies in Spain was to try to raise local capital rather than to pour French money into the Spanish economy.[24] This caution was reaffirmed after extended contact with the Spanish world of politics and business. It is obvious from their reports to shareholders that the managers of the Sociedad Española did not like the way business was conducted in Spain, and liked even less the legal framework, and the continuous tampering by and incompetence of the government.

The third of the large French credit companies founded under the auspices of the 1858 law was the Compañía General de Crédito en España (General Credit Company in Spain). Its authorized capital was 99.75 million pesetas (399 million reales, or 105 million francs) but no more than a third of this figure was ever fully paid in. It was legally constituted on May 14, 1856. Its founders were a group of French financiers whose leader was Adolphe Prost, the director of the French Compagnie Générale des Caisses d'Escompte— an efficient network of provincial and local discount banks—who was

23. Crédito Mobiliario Español, Shareholders report, 31 May 1858.
24. The Sociedad Española soon circulated a pamphlet in Madrid advertising its current account deposit facilities: Sociedad Española Mercantil e Industrial, *Cuentas corrientes*, 24 November 1856 (BNM). See also advertisement in *GCH*, I, p. 522 (7 December 1856).

extending his banking activities into other European countries. Its board included the brothers Louis and Numa Guilhou, who immediately became the actual managers of the enterprise, and whose control increased after Prost went bankrupt early in 1858.

The General de Crédito soon undertook a very ambitious campaign of railroad, industry, and credit promotion. In the years following its foundation it opened branches in Cadiz, Havana, and Paris, and it established a network of agencies throughout Spain (Barcelona, Valencia, Cartagena, Badajoz, and other towns). In the Prost tradition, the General de Crédito simultaneously practiced commercial banking and company promotion, and it made some use of the authorization to issue short-term bonds. Credit operations during its first seven months totaled 43 million pesetas, of which the largest share (24 million) was a credit to the government.

Although not as impressive as those of its rivals, the railway undertakings of the General de Crédito were considerable. It secured the Cadiz–Seville line (thus shattering the Mobiliario's ambitions to the complete Bayonne–Madrid–Cadiz network) and founded the Seville–Jerez–Cadiz railway company in 1857. It also took a part in the Tarragona–Reus–Montblanch railroad in Catalonia. The General de Crédito also invested outside the field of railways. It brought about the merger of two insurance companies, and subscribed most of the stock of the company resulting from the merger. The General de Crédito also undertook ventures in the fields of mining, gasworks, and banking. After one and a half years of operations, the distribution of its assets was as shown in Table IV.4.

TABLE IV.4

Compañía General de Crédito: Percentage Distribution of Assets,
December 31, 1857

1.	Cash	6.5
2.	Commercial portfolio	7.5
3.	Public debt	11.1
4.	Branches and agencies	12.9
5.	Industrial portfolio (shares)	17.6
6.	Seville–Cadiz Railroad	25.4
7.	General Mining Co.	12.9
8.	Gasworks	2.5
9.	Furniture, etc.	3.6
10.	Total (million pesetas)	27.9

Source: Calculated from General de Crédito, Shareholders report, May 31, 1858.

Table IV.4 shows that promotional activity (industrial portfolio plus direct advances to its companies, i.e. items 4, 5, 6, 7, and 8) made up three-fifths of the General de Crédito's total assets. Railway investments might very easily have been one-third of total assets, since the advances to the Seville–Jerez–Cadiz were already over one-fourth and it is fair to assume that around half of item 5 were Tarragona–Reus–Montblanch shares plus those of other railway companies.

One can safely conclude, therefore, that two years after they were founded the three French credit companies in Madrid had the largest proportion of their assets sunk in railway construction. The General de Crédito, whose interests were the most widespread of the three, probably devoted around one-third of its total assets, or over one-half of its investments, to railways. The Crédito Mobiliario had about three-fifths of its advances made to the Norte railway alone. The total proportion devoted to railways must have been even larger, since the Crédito also had an interest in the Cordoba–Seville railway. After consolidation of their balance sheets, the railway investments of these were about two-fifths of total assets and some three-fifths of total investments. Public debt made about one-tenth of total assets.

Unfortunately, data on the Sociedad Española for these earlier years are lacking, but, as the reports to shareholders make abundantly clear, the only affairs it undertook during these years (aside from occasional loans to the government) were the building and management of the MZA lines. Therefore one can confidently say that more than three-fifths, possibly three-fourths, of the investments made by the three French credit companies was devoted to railways in the years immediately following their foundation.

The Mediterranean ports of Barcelona and Valencia were the cradles of the first credit companies based on domestic capital. Barcelona had already had the first provincial bank, established in 1844, and in 1856 the first provincial credit society, the Sociedad Catalana General de Crédito (General Catalan Credit Company), capitalized at 30 million pesetas, was established there. The Catalana's avowed aim was to be an industrial bank and to devote only surplus funds to commercial banking and to government loans. In fact it became a railroad bank, as can be ascertained from the distribution of its assets by the end of 1858 (Table IV.5).

Table IV.5 shows that almost half of the Catalana's assets were invested in railroads (Item 3a, plus item 4). The Catalana had acquired large packages of bonds and shares of the Barcelona–Saragossa and Barcelona–France railways, the two largest railways built in Catalonia. It also became the building contractor of the Barcelona–France railway company. The remainder of the "bonds and shares" item was made up of public debt, Catalana's own shares, and some small holdings in insurance companies, a mining concern, and the Suez canal company. The Catalana did not own a

TABLE IV.5

Sociedad Catalana General de Crédito: Percentage Distribution of Assets, December 31, 1858

1. Cash	16.0
2. Loans and bills	21.9
3. Bonds and shares	42.5
a. Railroads	(32.4)
b. Other	(10.1)
4. Advances to railroads	14.2
5. Other debtors	4.5
6. Real estate	0.9
7. Total (million pesetas)	21.9

Sources: Calculated from Archivo Histórico Nacional, Madrid (hereafter cited as AHN), Hacienda, Leg. 429; Catalana, Shareholders report, February 23, 1859.

single share of manufacturing firms, in spite of the fact that Barcelona was then the leading industrial center of the country.[25]

The Catalana was by far the most important non-issuing credit institution in Barcelona during those years, comparable only to the Bank of Barcelona. It was undoubtedly the main—and in a strict sense the only—business bank in Barcelona, although there were four other non-issuing incorporated banks in Barcelona at the time. These were the Crédito Mobiliario Barcelonés (unrelated to the Pereires) and the Unión Comercial, which were credit societies, and the Caja Barcelonesa de Préstamos y Descuentos (Barcelona Loan and Discount Office) and the Caja Catalana Mercantil e Industrial (Catalan Mercantile and Industrial Office), which were incorporated commercial banks. None of these banks had any sizable investment portfolio. The Catalana's assets were almost one and a half times as large as those of the other two credit companies combined. By the end of 1858 the only bank in Barcelona with a real investment portfolio was the Catalana, and over three-quarters of its portfolio was railway equity. The other two credit companies (much smaller in terms of capital and assets) had invested not only outside Barcelona, but outside Catalonia as well (the Mobiliario Barcelonés, in an improbable woodcutting venture in Asturias; the Unión Comercial, in canals in Valencia and Aragon). Summing up, we can say that in Barcelona, as in Madrid, the credit companies leaned heavily toward railways, while manufacturing was largely neglected.

25. A very detailed insight into the affairs of the Barcelona credit companies at this time can be gained from AHN, Hacienda, Leg. 429.

The Sociedad Valenciana de Fomento (Valencia Development Company) had been founded in 1846. Of modest size (paid-in capital was 1.6 million pesetas in 1856), it mixed commercial and investment banking. It had undertaken the water works in Valencia, financed the Valencia–Játiva railway, was building the Játiva–Almansa line which would link Valencia to the Madrid–Alicante railway, and was negotiating with the Catalana General de Crédito to join it in undertaking the Valencia–Tarragona railway. By the end of 1856 railway investments made about one-fifth of the Valenciana's total assets, and over one-third of its long-term investments. The remainder of these investments consisted of the Valencia water works plus an operation in real estate development in the outskirts of Valencia. There was no investment in manufactures. The year 1858 saw the end of the Valenciana's monopoly of corporate credit in Valencia. Competition appeared in the form of a credit company and a branch of the Bank of Spain. Consequently, the Valenciana was forced to specialize as a business bank. It finally obtained a credit company charter, augmented its paid-in capital, and oriented itself more openly toward promotional credit.[26]

Seven new banks of issue were founded in Spain in the two years after the new banking laws were enacted.[27] The repercussions of the international financial crisis of 1857 undoubtedly contributed to put a stop to this first promotional wave. The newly founded banks, however, were instrumental in moderating the effects of the crisis, and thus helped preserve the developing banking structure. The additions to the money supply the new banks effected by means of their bank note circulation more than compensated for the tightening of the money markets caused by the crisis. The new banks were founded in industrial and/or commercial centers, most of them port cities (Málaga, Seville, Valladolid, Saragossa, Santander, Bilbao and Corunna, in chronological order).

The resources, business methods, and careers of these new banks of issue varied widely. Most of them ended ingloriously, less than a decade later. Two of them (Bilbao and Santander) are still very prosperous firms today. Most often these institutions acted as commercial banks, devoting the largest share of their assets to discounting bills and making short-term loans, while deposits and note issue formed the largest items on the liability side of their balance sheet. In most cases it is difficult or impossible to ascertain which economic sectors were being most favored by the local banks of issue, if any. But in other cases there are some hints of the way in which some assets were distributed or, at least, what allocative priorities were likely, and these hints point toward the railway companies. The director of the Bank of

26. Reports to shareholders, especially that of 31 December 1856.
27. Basic sources on Spanish banks of issue are cited in Table 1.

Málaga from 1856 to 1873, for instance, was also the promoter of the Cordoba–Málaga railway. The first board of directors of the Bank of Bilbao included exactly the same persons as that of the Tudela–Bilbao railway company, which was established at about the same date. The clearest numerical evidence supporting the presumption that railroads made a more extensive use of the credit facilities of banks of issue than manufacturing corporations did is that of the Bank of Barcelona, and will be examined in detail later. Suffice it to say here that collateral loans on railroad bonds and shares by the Bank of Barcelona in 1858–59 were 3.9 times as large as those on bonds and shares of manufacturing corporations.

It seems safe to conclude, therefore, that the newly created banking system was immediately geared toward financing the construction of railroads. This was the direction the political framework seemed to be indicating to the banking system, and it obediently followed the designated path.

Another area worth investigating is the origins of the capital and entrepreneurial initiative for the banking system. In the case of credit companies as well as in that of banks of issue, the charters were granted to merchants in the vast majority of cases and to industrialists in the minority. Aristocrats and landowners were almost never involved (except on the boards of the big French credit companies, where the Spanish nobility and political elite often enjoyed honorary positions). Generally speaking, the capital invested in the new banks came from trade and from industry (very often the capital invested in industry seems to have originated from profits accumulated in trade), but not from savings accumulated in the agricultural sector.

After the pause caused by the 1857–59 recession, the Spanish banking system resumed the process of growth initiated in the mid-1850's. Table IV.1 shows the large increase in the numbers of banks between 1860 and 1864. By the end of 1864 there were 60 banking companies in Spain (including two banks which had suspended payments three months before and whose future was still unclear, plus the Bank of Spain's branches in Valencia and Alicante), with a combined paid-in capital of 360.3 million pesetas, or an approximate average of 6 million pesetas per bank, though this is a figure of little significance due to the large deviations around the mean which then existed. Banks of issue had a combined capital of 76.6 million (slightly over one-fifth of the total), while in numbers they made up over one-third of the existing firms. Their average capital was 3.6 million; if the Bank of Spain is excluded, average capital is reduced to 1.8 million. The capital of the Bank of Spain was larger than the combined capitals of all the other banks of issue.

The combined capital of all the non-issuing banks was 283.7 million (about four-fifths of the total, while their numerical strength was just under two-thirds), with an average capital of 7.7 million pesetas, more than twice that of the banks of issue, even when the Bank of Spain is included. Nevertheless, the deviations were also very large, since the Crédito Mobiliario Español by itself represented over two-fifths of the total capital, and the six largest credit companies (Crédito Mobiliario Español, Compañía General de Crédito en España, Sociedad Española Mercantil e Industrial, Crédito Mobiliario Barcelonés, Crédito Castellano, and Catalana General de Crédito) represented almost two-thirds of the combined capital. If we exclude the Mobiliario, the average capital of the remaining non-issuing banks goes down to 4.7 million.

The growth in numbers did not modify the investment pattern which had been laid down in the very first years of the banking system. The largest investment banks remained tied to railways and to public debts as a subsidiary outlet for their funds. Some slight changes took place in the emphasis and distribution of assets. The general trend was towards less direct involvement in railways and more emphasis on portfolio investment and asset diversification. But these changes were quantitatively small. Thus, for instance, the Crédito Mobiliario organized the Norte Railway Company in 1859, thereby transforming its own direct outlays in the construction of the railway line into the much more manageable form of a package of shares ready to be unloaded on the financial markets of Europe. After 1862 an effort was made by the Mobiliario to act as a partner to the French Crédit Mobilier in numerous promotions of international firms and foreign government loans. It also acquired real estate in Madrid, founded an insurance company, incorporated the Madrid Gasworks, helped organize a development bank in Valladolid. But its foremost endeavor remained the Norte railway, whose main shareholder and banker the Crédito remained during the period. The future of the Crédito was linked to the Norte in more than one way. Not only did the Norte make up a large share of its assets, but also many other businesses of the Crédito Mobiliario were dependent on the railway line. This was notably the case with the coal mines, the Madrid gasworks, the Valladolid investment bank, and a series of projected iron and briquette factories which were to be built along the railway tracks. This was a logical consequence of the organic vision which presided over the Pereires' affairs in Spain: they were dreaming of an integrated industrial empire in northern Spain, and the Norte was essential to that empire. The Crédito had other investments, such as the Cordoba–Seville railway, the Fénix Insurance Company, and the Madrid real estate. Some were good, some were rather mediocre, but the future of the Crédito did not depend on them. It depended on the Norte in a large measure.

The Sociedad Española Mercantil e Industrial also stuck to its previous investment policy of giving preference to railways, and also tended to substitute portfolio management for direct promotion activities. Thus it terminated the building contract with MZA in 1860, and returned one-third of its paid-in capital to the shareholders. From then on it devoted its energies to the management of its portfolio, which was largely made up of railway bonds and shares, and public debt, a large portion of this debt in turn being railroad subsidy bonds. Table IV.6 shows how its assets were distributed in 1859 and 1861.

TABLE IV.6

Sociedad Española Mercantil e Industrial: Percentage
Distribution of Assets, 1859 and 1861

	1859	1861
1. Cash	11.5	5.8
2. Commercial paper	9.6	2.1
3. Public debt	3.7	11.6
a. Ordinary	(0.0)	(1.0)
b. Railroad subsidies	(0.6)	(8.4)
c. Other public works	(3.1)	(2.2)
4. Railroad bonds & shares	57.0	58.9
a. Isabel II	(21.9)	(30.0)
b. MZA	(35.6)	(28.9)
5. MZA account	13.6	13.2
6. Other	4.7	8.4
7. Total (million pesetas)	32.3	19.0

Sources: Calculated from Shareholders report, April 22, 1860; *Gaceta de Madrid*, June 5, 1862.

The Compañía General de Crédito, whose activities were more diversified than those of the Mercantil e Industrial, nevertheless got progressively entangled in its efforts to improve the economic performance of the Seville–Jerez–Cadiz railway by adding new lines to it. The consequence was a progressive liquidity squeeze which forced it to suspend payments in 1864. Its concerns were liquidated and it was officially dissolved in 1866.

The Catalana General de Crédito restrained its early enthusiasm for railway investment, and it tried to orient itself more toward commercial banking during the early 1860's. Its managers decided to "limit the circle of . . . business for the time being and . . . only take part in those of short maturity."[28] The result of this decision was that they abandoned any manufacturing investment they might have had in mind; they also divested themselves of some railway paper, but of course not fast enough to avoid being caught in the 1866 panic.

28. Shareholders report, 26 February 1862.

The other two large credit companies mentioned above, the Crédito Mobiliario Barcelonés and the Crédito Castellano, were less significant than the Catalana in spite of the fact that their paid-in capitals were larger. The Mobiliario Barcelonés persisted in its faith in the Asturias woodcutting venture, and its enlarged paid-in capital only reflects this dogged conviction. After several years of fruitless or, at best, mediocre pursuits, it wound up its affairs in 1867 with a loss of 50 per cent of its capital. The Crédito Castellano started operations in 1862. It was based in Valladolid, and its most important business was to act as the building contractor for the Isabel II (Santander–Alar del Rey) railroad, although it had also undertaken other public works, such as improvements in the Bilbao harbor, as well as lending recklessly to its own officers. In 1864, taking advantage of the fact that some of its directors also sat on the Bank of Valladolid's board, the Crédito sold the Bank a large part of its portfolio, a deal which was practically equivalent to robbing the Bank of its specie reserve. This was the end of both institutions, and a contribution to the personal fortunes of the officers of the Crédito Castellano; litigation lasted for several years, but without practical results for the victims.[29] The unedifying history of the Crédito Castellano was not exceptional in Spanish business circles of that time.

If we turn from the largest credit companies to those of middle size, we find a similar picture. The Compañia General Bilbaína de Crédito, which started operations in 1862 and had a paid-in capital of 3.75 million pesetas by 1864, was an outgrowth of the Bank of Bilbao. It was set up to manage the Bank's interests in the Tudela–Bilbao railroad, and it suspended payments in 1866, after the railroad company did. In Valencia, the Sociedad Valenciana, after becoming a credit company, concentrated more and more on investment finance and, within this category, on railways. In December, 1865, nearly three-fifths of its assets were bound to railways, almost exclusively to the Tarragona–Valencia–Almansa.

All this indicates that the largest non-issuing banks, making up about 70 per cent of the combined capital of all non-issuing banks, were clearly concentrated in the railway sector as a field of investment. Their second field was government loans, and for those which had a third field, public works, real estate, or mining were more frequently chosen than manufactures. The briquette factories of the Crédito Mobiliario and the General de Crédito's gasworks are exceptions to a very general rule.

The smaller credit companies dealt almost exclusively in commercial credit, making use of the short-term bonds approved by the 1856 law. Their capital was too small for them to even think of entering the promotion and investment business. They usually competed with the local bank of issue where

---

29. *Verdaderas causas que produgeron la crisis de Valladolid* (Valladolid, 1869), *passim*.

there was one, or became *de facto* issuing banks in towns where there was none. They probably would not have been able to help industry even if they had tried, for the simple reason that no industry existed (except for local crafts) where most of them were.

As for the banks of issue, they mainly extended commercial credit in the form of short-term loans and discounts. Who their customers were is difficult to ascertain, since they rarely made this kind of information public in their reports to shareholders or elsewhere. Fortunately, some light can be thrown upon the activities of the two largest ones, the Bank of Spain and the Bank of Barcelona.

TABLE IV.7

Bank of Spain: Sectorized and Consolidated Balance Sheets, 1857–1866
(December 31, million pesetas)

	1857	1858	1859	1860	1861	1862
1. Specie	27.1	30.8	30.9	28.3	23.6	29.0
2. Foreign	0.0	−0.8	2.6	1.5	−1.5	5.8
3. Public	67.8	71.6	97.9	73.3	65.0	49.4
4. Private	9.3	21.9	19.8	31.4	31.7	59.0
5. Real estate	2.3	0.9	1.4	1.4	1.4	1.4
6. Capital	−35.0	−36.0	−38.5	−38.8	−41.3	−37.9
7. Deposits	−33.8	−45.1	−57.4	−43.3	−35.7	−54.6
8. Banknotes	−45.8	−52.0	−66.9	−63.5	−44.9	−52.1
9. Other	8.1	8.7	10.2	9.7	1.7	0.0

	1863	1864	1865	1866
1. Specie	31.1	19.2	27.3	21.6
2. Foreign	5.2	−31.0	−13.7	−8.6
3. Public	83.9	140.9	106.2	95.2
4. Private	41.2	10.8	18.8	11.1
5. Real estate	1.4	1.4	1.3	1.4
6. Capital	−37.6	−47.5	−56.6	−59.0
7. Deposits	−56.8	−22.1	−22.3	−18.0
8. Banknotes	−68.3	−71.8	−61.9	−44.6
9. Other	0.1	−0.1	0.9	0.9

Source: Calculated from Shareholders reports and ledger books of the Bank, in ABE.

Table IV.7 shows the credit-debit situation of the Bank of Spain in three sectors, the government, the private sector, and the foreign sector. The other items are real assets (1 and 5), main sources of funds (6, 7, 8), and a balancing account (9). This table shows that the Bank of Spain's policy toward the private sector was a mere by-product of the needs of the government: after 1863, when the government started to feel the consequences of the depression, the Bank of Spain obtained a series of loans from foreign bankers and sharply reduced its credit to the private sector. It loaned the government almost four times as much as it did the private sector during the decade 1857–66. The Bank, of course, was not making any long-term loans to the private sector, since most of its credit was through the discounting of bills, and probably mostly rediscounting. This means, therefore, that it made very little contribution to capital formation in private industry.

The information we have about the Bank of Barcelona concerns one important item on its portfolio, the loans on collateral (Table IV.8).

TABLE IV.8

Bank of Barcelona: Percentage Distribution of Collateral Loans, 1858–1867

Year (end of month)	(1) On Rr. bonds & shares	(2) On indl. shares	(3) On pub. debt	(4) On other assets	(5) Total (million pesetas)
1858 (Dec.)	43.3	14.9	29.9	11.9	6.7
1859 (Dec.)	58.9	10.7	30.4	0.0	5.6
1860 (Dec.)	13.6	11.4	70.5	4.5	4.4
1861 (Dec.)	20.0	11.4	60.0	8.6	3.5
1862 (Dec.)	29.4	8.8	58.8	2.9	3.4
1863 (Dec.)	45.9	8.1	43.2	2.7	3.7
1864 (Dec.)	31.0	3.4	62.1	3.4	2.9
1865 (Dec.)	22.0	2.0	74.0	2.0	5.0
1866 (Dec.)	6.0	3.0	87.9	0.1	3.3
1867 (Nov.)	7.1	0.0	90.5	2.4	4.2
Mean	29.7	8.0	57.8	4.5	4.3

Source: Calculated from AHN, Hacienda, Legs. 428, 429, 430, 431, 432, 433, 434, 436, 438, 439.

The meaning of these figures is clear. On the average, the Bank of Barcelona loaned almost four times more on railroad bonds and shares as it did on industrial shares (no loans were made on industrial bonds), and almost twice as much on public debt as it did on railroad bonds and shares. That those proportions applied in the most (in strict terms, the only) industrial city in Spain speaks eloquently about the help industry was receiving from the banking system.

It seems clear that those banking institutions making direct contributions to capital formation, i.e. the large and middle-sized credit companies, showed a marked preference for railway investment and very rarely invested in manufacturing. As to shorter term commercial credit, the evidence is elusive, but according to what we know about the two largest banks of issue, public debt and railway companies were much more favored than manufacturing.

YEARS OF CRISIS

In view of all this it is not surprising to find that the capital available to railways was several times larger than that available to the whole manufacturing sector. For example, Table IV.9 shows the results of the tremendous

TABLE IV.9
Railways and Industry: Sources of Funds
Compared, 1859–1866 (million pesetas)

Year	(1) Industry[a] Paid-in Capital	(2) Railroads: Paid-in Capital	(3) Railroads: Cash from Bonds	(4) Railroads: Government Subsidies
1859	99.8	343.9[b]	c	c
1861	96.0	517.4	c	c
1864	98.4	654.8	658.2	240.2
1866	66.5	698.9	710.5	316.5

a Includes (in decreasing order of quantitative importance): textiles, mining, gas, metallurgy, navigation, tanning, waterworks, building, and others.
b Nominal capital.
c Data not available.
Source: *Anuario Estadístico de España*, eds. of 1858, 1860–61, 1862–65, 1866–67.

advantage railroads enjoyed. By the end of 1864 railroad companies had accumulated a total of 1,553.2 million pesetas of long-term capital at their disposal (capital plus bonds plus subsidies). The comparable figure for manufacturing corporations could not have exceeded 100 million by much, since their combined capital for that year was 98.4 million, the circulation of their bonds (if any) was very restricted, and they received no subsidies. This means that the volume of long-term capital available to railroads up to the end of 1864 was between fifteen and sixteen times larger than that available to all other manufacturing and industrial corporations put together, even without counting the direct advances from the credit companies to the railways during the construction period.

With the help of these massive injections of capital the construction of the railroad network proceeded swiftly in the late 1850's and early 1860's: the length of track increased tenfold from 1856 to 1866. But as the length of the network expanded and the work in the main concessions was concluded, the companies found themselves confronted with a hard but inescapable fact: revenues from operation were extremely low, so low, in fact, that they hardly covered operating expenses, and they were frequently insufficient to pay interest on bonds, let alone pay the principal of their debts or distribute profit on shares.

The reason for this disappointing performance of the railways was not circumstantial, but structural. Although transportation was a bottleneck in the Spanish economy, Spain was not developed enough to support railway traffic in amounts sufficient to cover the high fixed and variable costs (probably also inflated by corruption and inefficiency) involved in building and operating railroads on its rugged terrain.[30] Railway construction itself had been an obstacle to economic development: it had absorbed investible funds which might otherwise have gone to the manufacturing sector. Adequate investment in textiles and metallurgy might have created the needed demand for railway transportation, as well as providing the Spanish economy with two possible leading sectors for economic development. Since all railway equipment was imported, the stimulative effects railroad building might have had on Spanish manufactures were lost.

The consequences of the railroad fiasco did not take long to make themselves felt throughout the economy in ever-growing concentric circles which eventually reached the political sphere. The first area to feel the impact was, naturally, the banking sector. The price of railroad stocks and bonds declined on domestic and foreign financial markets, and this put a tremendous strain on the large credit companies, whose portfolio was, as we have seen, dangerously unbalanced on the side of railroads. The General de Crédito fell in 1864 due to its desperate attempts to save the Seville–Jerez–Cadiz railroad. For two agonizing years the whole banking system tottered on the verge of bankruptcy until, in 1866, the crisis burst wide open in Barcelona, where, on May 12, the Catalana and the Crédito Mobiliario Barcelonés suspended payments amid general panic. A chain reaction of failures shook the city. The stock exchange closed, and all other Barcelona banks, except for the Bank of Barcelona, suspended activities. In order to prevent imminent threats to public order, the Barcelona military authorities enforced circulation of inconvertible paper money and promissory notes issued by the local banks. Fearful of a revolt by the workers, they further decreed that industrialists had

30. This is shown by the fact that, as the railroad network spread, revenues per kilometer declined. I have collected evidence on this decline for the main lines (about 80 percent of the track in service by 1864), which cannot be reproduced here for lack of space.

preference in the settlement of their credits in specie by the banks, so they
might be able to pay their laborers' wages.[31]

Revolution was averted in Barcelona, but the crisis could not be prevented
from spreading throughout Spain. After all, this was no momentary psycho-
logical phenomenon, but the consequence of a nation-wide economic mis-
calculation. Foreign and domestic savings had been committed to railways
on a massive scale. The companies could not repay their debts as expected,
and there was no quick solution to that kind of problem. The wave of banking
failures spread throughout the country and the feeling of panic and crisis
accompanied it. An atmosphere of chaos prevailed in the Spanish economy
while the banking system fell apart like a house of cards. A glance at Table
IV.1 tells us that 24 banks went out of business between 1864 and 1869, over
two-fifths of the pre-existing banking system in terms of numbers. But these
are officially dissolved banks; the real figure, that including banks whose
dissolution was not reflected in the official record, was undoubtedly much
higher.

The effects of the crisis went beyond the economic sphere. In September
1868, after two years of virtual military dictatorship, a liberal revolution
overthrew the Bourbon monarchy and its government. The immediate task
of the revolution was to change the economic legislation toward a more
liberal framework. A monetary reform, a tariff reform, and the abolition of
the 1848 Corporation Law were decreed. The Caja de Depósitos was shorn
of its power to attract deposits. A law in 1869 established free incorporation
for all industrial, commercial, and banking firms. These measures, however,
came too late, or were not radical enough. The economic situation continued
to deteriorate in the early 1870's, along with the political situation.

The liberal provisional government opted for a constitutional monarchy
and began its long search for a suitable monarch; at the beginning of 1871 it
finally found one, in a younger son of the House of Savoy, but that prince
abdicated after little more than two years, thoroughly frustrated by the
political intrigue and financial chaos in which he found himself. Meanwhile
General Prim, strong man of the revolution, had been assassinated, and
France entered—and lost—the Franco-Prussian war, thereby cutting off
Spain from the French capital market. Upon the abdication of Amadeo I in
1873, the radical majority of the Cortes proclaimed a republic, but it soon
faced three armed rebellions: anarchists and Carlists on the Peninsula,
separatists in Cuba. In 1874, in its extremity, the republican government again
overhauled the banking system; in return for a new loan of 125 million pesetas
the government authorized a doubling of the capital of the Bank of Spain (to
100 million pesetas), gave it a monopoly of note issue throughout the

31. Nicolás Sánchez-Albornoz, *España hace un siglo; una economía dual* (Barcelona,
1968), Ch. V.

country, and offered advantageous conditions for the provincial banks of issue to become branches of the Bank of Spain. The three strongest provincial banks (Barcelona, Bilbao, and Santander), plus one smaller one, refused to merge with the Bank of Spain, but all the other issuing banks did. Such was the banking structure in Spain when the army overthrew the republic and restored the Bourbon monarchy in 1875.

CONCLUSION

The conclusion is, of course, that during the crucial decade of 1856–65 Spanish banks chose the line of least resistance and followed the guidelines marked by the government. Due to the social and legal framework, promoting railways seemed to be the easy way of doing business, and they followed it blindly without analyzing the economic soundness of their behavior. From one standpoint we might say that they were behaving in a competitive way, and following the indicators of the marketplace. But the rules of that marketplace happened to be biased by outside forces. They, of course, did nothing to circumvent these rules—to see, as is commonly said, the broad picture. As a collective body, they behaved as the docile instruments of a misguided policy.

CHAPTER V

Serbia 1878–1912

JOHN R. LAMPE*

Serbia's final prewar decades do not at first glance appear capable of telling us much about the dynamics of industrial development among the late-comers. Here, after all, was a backward Balkan economy, free of Ottoman rule for less than a hundred years and threatened with Habsburg domination after full political independence was won in 1878. By the start of the Balkan Wars in 1912, the small, landlocked country was from several standpoints still a classic case of underdevelopment.

Industry was no more than a minor part of the economy in 1911, its last peacetime year. Serbian industrial production, generously defined by the Serbian Chamber of Industry to include mining and unmechanized enterprises of the smallest size, if not household industry, amounted to perhaps 25 per cent of purely agricultural output and 15 per cent of the very rough, though best, estimate available for gross national product. Total industrial horse-power fell short of 25,000, and the 16,000 workers employed made up less than 2 per cent of the country's labor force. Although quick to develop political awareness, domestic factory labor lacked the technical training to replace the 1000 workers from the Czech and other Habsburg lands who are included in this latter total. These foreign workers were imported at con-siderable expense and made up half the supply of skilled labor.[1]

* The author was enabled to prepare this chapter in Belgrade during 1969–70, as part of wider doctoral research, under grants from the Foreign Area Fellowship Program and the International Research and Exchanges Board. Working through the Serbian Academy of Sciences and Arts and with its late director, Dr. Jurjo Tadić, the author was accorded the full cooperation of the Yugoslav academic community and access to all relevant archival material. A special debt is owed to Dr. Danica Milić of the Historical Institute of the Serbian Academy and Professor Nikola Vučo of the Economics Faculty of Belgrade University.

1. The Serbian Chamber of Industry, in Industrijska Komora Kr. Srbije, *Izveštaj*, 1911, 67, estimates industrial output for 1911 at about 125 million dinars (equivalent to

Nor had the major demographic changes commonly associated with industrialization begun to occur. Although total population rose steadily during the period 1878–1912 from 1.8 to 3 millions, the urban and non-peasant populations increased proportionally for only the first few years and thereafter remained steady at a mere 13 per cent of the total.[2] The agricultural sector consisted overwhelmingly of small, individually owned holdings. The peasantry was 85 per cent illiterate and two-thirds of their households did not own an iron plow. While there are some indications of more concentrated holdings and higher grade yields after 1895, 80 per cent of cultivated land was split up into series of scattered plots totaling under 10 hectares (about 25 acres), and 55 per cent were under 5 hectares.[3] Rising rural density suggests the advent of overpopulation. One peasant in ten was landless by the turn of the century, but little urban or external migration ensued. Considerable household production of necessary goods still survived. The structure of this predominant peasant sector limited domestic demand and the potential supply of industrial labor.

One important structural change had nonetheless occurred in the Serbian economy. This was the growth of a sizable financial framework. By the end of 1911 the country had 176 commercial banks, including 4 foreign affiliates, plus a large central and mortgage bank. Together they had accumulated over 700 million dinars (equivalent to French francs) in assets. Both the number of these financial institutions compared to population and the size of their assets compared to what idea we have of gross national product yield ratios close to those of nineteenth- and early twentieth-century economies in the process of industrialization.[4] Serbia seems an exception to such a correlation

---

French francs) in current prices. The only systematic, itemized calculation of prewar gross national product is the estimate prepared by a committee of Serbian scholars in Geneva for the Versailles Peace Conference. Their calculation for 1911, of 1.3 billion dinars (Srpski Centralni Komitet, *Srbija pre prvog svetskog rata*, 58–65), reduces to roughly 900 million dinars, when, in the crudest fashion, we take into account the facts that the committee used prices of 1913–14 for livestock—double their 1911 level—and reckoned the total harvest in terms of arable rather than actually cultivated acreage.

The Chamber's estimates for industrial horsepower and labor supply apply to 1910 rather than 1911. Industrijska Komora Kr. Srbije, *Izveštaj*, 1910, Tables 1 and 10.

2. *Državopis Srbije*, vol. XVI, p. XIX; *Statistički godišnjak Kr. Srbije*, 1905, X, 34; *Prethodni rezultati popisa stanovništva, Dec. 31, 1910*, 74–6. The last cited indicates that even in 1910 the 13 per cent of the population in urban areas included residents of 25 towns under 1000 and 16 more than 2000.

3. *Statistički godišnjak Kr. Srbije*, 1893, I, 91, also 1894–95, II, 182–3, and 1898–99, IV, 202–4. For the less than conclusive evidence of rising wheat and corn yields per hectare in the last prewar decades, see Archives Nationales, F 30, 1170, Rapport sur la Serbie, 6–7.

4. Cameron, *Banking in the Early Stages of Industrialization*, 296–99, multiplies the number of commercial bank offices by 10,000 and divides the result by total population to obtain an admittedly crude index of banking density. The Serbian ratio of 0.6 in 1911

if we judge industrial capacity as it was in 1911. But before turning ourselves over too hastily to weighing weaknesses in the Serbian financial structure and economy in order to make sense of this apparent exception, more needs to be said about the state of industry.

SERBIAN INDUSTRIAL STIRRINGS

The modest prewar level of Serbian industrial activity becomes much more significant when it is measured against its virtual absence, at least in the sense of any mechanically powered, factory-centered production, two decades earlier. Private industrial output in 1893 consisted primarily of flour from small-scale local mills, and at that it barely matched the production of the single, state-owned tobacco factory. Table V.1 makes it clear that the main advance in total output occurred after 1905. It is also evident that flour mills, which in 1905 numbered over 200 but included just 15 to 20 of some size, and state industry made only a small contribution to that surge. The addition to mining output consisted of copper and other non-ferrous ores, smelted and shipped from the country by foreign interests. While this activity accounted for 10 per cent of total exports by 1911, and thus increased import capacity, it was not otherwise connected to the rest of the economy. Both in terms of output and number of enterprises, domestic growth took place mainly in private industry other than milling and brewing. Table V.2 indicates that this other industry was also the center for the more mechanized, larger-scale operations we have come to call factory production.[5]

---

represents a "moderate" density that England did not surpass until 1800 and Russia did not even approach before 1914. As for the relative size of bank resources, Goldsmith, *Financial Structure and Development*, 208–11, cites an average 46 per cent ratio of financial assets to GNP for less developed European countries and 138 per cent for the developed ones in 1913. The approximate Serbian ratio of nearly 80 per cent in 1911 places the small Balkan nation about a third of the way between the two and virtually equal to the ratio for the developed European states in 1880.

5. Any definition of what constitutes a factory is arbitrary, but the accepted practice in the pre-1914 Balkan states of including any manufacturer with a minimum of 15 or 20 employees gives no indication of the replacement of human with mechanical power that is the essence of modern industrial growth. (For a summary of the sources of the various definitions of factory production in the prewar Balkans, see Spulber, *The State and Economic Development in Eastern Europe*, 65–66.) Official Serbian statistics claimed a minimum standard of 15 workers employed with some horsepower and 25 workers with none (K. und K. Handelsministerium, *Serbien, Wirtschaftsverhältnisse*, 1911, 27) but in practice firms listing less than this minimum were included. A standard of at least 15 workers and 15 horsepower seems a useful modification. And on this basis, we consistently capture about 85 per cent of private industrial production, milling and brewing excluded, after 1900 and observe in Table V.2 the same sharp increase after 1905 as in Table V.1 for output, if not as much for number of firms.

TABLE V.1

Real Output of Serbian Industry, 1893–1911
Million Dinars in 1898 Prices
(number of enterprises)

Year	Flour Milling[a]	Brewing[b]	Other Private Industry[c]	State Industry[d]	Mining[e]	Total[f]
1893	7 (105)	2 (10)	2 (26)	9 (1)	1 (14)	21 (156)
1898	8 (181)	3 (10)	4 (27)	10 (3)	1 (22)	26 (243)
1899	8 (192)	3 (10)	5 (29)	10 (3)	2 (22)	28 (256)
1900	10 (181)	3 (9)	10 (44)	11 (3)	2 (31)	36 (268)
1901	11 (187)	3 (9)	11 (50)	11 (3)	2 (31)	39 (282)
1902	11 (181)	3 (9)	14 (65)	11 (3)	2 (34)	41 (292)
1903	13 (200)	3 (9)	13 (104)	11 (3)	2 (34)	42 (350)
1904	14 (222)	3 (9)	9 (92)	11 (3)	3 (34)	40 (360)
1905	14 (244)	3 (9)	13 (93)	11 (3)	2 (34)	43 (383)
1906	16 (215)	4 (9)	14 (109)	11 (3)	5 (39)	50 (375)
1907	20 (237)	4 (9)	19 (125)	12 (3)	6 (42)	61 (416)
1908	20 (239)	5 (9)	23 (155)	12 (3)	9 (42)	69 (448)
1910	18 (229)	6 (9)	25 (168)	12 (3)	10 (55)	71 (464)
1911	20 (250)	7 (9)	51 (n.a.)	13 (3)	14 (n.a.)	105 (n.a.)

a Since Serbian statistical yearbooks through 1908 record only value added for flour, total output has been derived by adding this sum to the result obtained by multiplying the total quantity of grain inputs times the average price of wheat from 1893 to 1905, a figure from which there is little deviation after 1898. Values after 1905 reflect not only the use of this price index, but also recognize the appearance of sizable amounts of lower priced corn flour and bran, thus reducing substantially a wheat-based increase varying from 50 to 100 per cent over the 1905 figure. The totals for 1906–1911 are confirmed by unofficial estimates of gross output value.

b Beer output is based on a largely undeviating average price from 1893 to 1903 and has been adjusted upward in value on this basis to reflect a roughly 30 per cent drop in beer prices during the period 1904–8.

c In the absence of any semblance of running price data, the admittedly imprecise expedient has been adopted of assuming, along with assorted secondary sources, that there was no significant change before the Tariff War. Subsequent figures have been adjusted downward on the basis of scattered evidence of price increases in the major branches of private industry, milling and brewing excluded, that averaged 30 per cent over-all. The convention of the Serbian statistical yearbooks in excluding the household activities of plum-drying and brandy-distilling from proper industrial production has been observed.

d Of the state monopolies, only those for tobacco and matches are considered as industrial production. Those for salt, oil, and cigarette paper consisted largely of marketing an imported good. The output of the state tobacco factory, comprising over 90 per cent of the values noted above, has been deflated for a 30 per cent price increase in 1899–1900 and again in 1904–5. Also included above is the production of the small state silk factory, whose output rose slowly toward a million dinars a year by 1911; not included is the entirely military output of the state arsenal.

e Mining output after 1905 has been revised slightly downward to reflect the fact that coal, while fading to one-quarter of total value with the rise of copper mining, nonetheless doubled in price between 1905 and 1911.

f These value totals for real industrial output are useful in showing a relative fivefold increase between 1893 and 1911 plus the predominant role played by "other private industry" in that increase. As absolute values, they are open to charges of some limited double counting, particularly between mining and the other sectors. But since a sizable fraction of the output of coal, the only mining for domestic consumption, and constant in real terms at 2 to 3 million dinars throughout the period, went to the state railways and the military arsenal, the overlap with the sectors noted in the table was not more than 1 to 2 million dinars. In any case, the sum of these few million double-counted dinars was roughly constant after 1898 and therefore does not offset the increase recorded.

Through 1905, the nominal value of total industrial output exceeded the real amounts recorded for each year only by the 2 to 4 million dinars' worth of price increases in state industry. During the Tariff War, from 1906 to 1911, nominal value exceeded the real totals by 13 to 14 million dinars at the start and rose steadily to a 19 million dinar difference by the end. Because of rising real output, however, the nominal figure was nearly 25 per cent over the real one in 1906 but less than 20 per cent in excess by 1910–11.

The Tariff War with Austria-Hungary

The figures for certain sectors in Table V.2 represent more than their meager proportion of the total would suggest. This was the result of the 1906–11 Tariff War with Austria-Hungary, which was initiated on a veterinary pretext by the Ballplatz to smother an increasing Serbian independence and to satisfy Hungarian livestock interests.[6] The dispute occasioned a protective but not prohibitive set of duties, ranging from 40 to 50 per cent ad valorem, for most industrial goods imported into Serbia. Domestic production of sugar, glass, cement, and lumber was able to respond either by eliminating or significantly reducing the percentage of those goods imported.[7] Whatever may be said about the small size of Serbian demand or the relatively higher cost of the domestic article than imports from the Habsburg lands, the fact remains that these sections of industry used largely domestic inputs to produce a large share of what the Serbian market could absorb. The long-run comparative advantage of the nation's economy in all these areas may be inferred from the economic history of Yugoslavia after 1918, if not from the high-cost production of the prewar years.[8] One immediate gain for Serbia was the added potential for economic independence from the Dual Monarchy, not a minor advantage in the context of the times.

The limited amount of meat-packing before 1911 should not, moreover, be traced to lack of capacity. The heavy Austro-Hungarian demand for Serbian livestock exports prior to 1906 had restrained the use of existing facilities for meat-packing, as had high animal prices that cut into profit margins on processed meat. During the so-called Pig War, the Dual Monarchy excluded both live and processed meat exports from Serbia, even for transit.

6. For a comprehensive and well-argued discussion of the causes, course and results of the Tariff War between Serbia and Austria-Hungary, see Djordjević, *Carinski rat Austro-Ugarske i Srbije, 1906–1911.* A good summary in English is found in Vucinich, *Serbia Between East and West, 1903–1908,* 181–205.

7. For comparison with the domestic production recorded in Table V.2, see import data for corresponding goods in *Statistički godišnjak Kr. Srbije,* 1907–8, XII, 220, 537, *Statistike spoljne trgovine Kr. Srbije,* 1909, p. XXI, and 1910, p. XVI.

8. Evidence for this comparative advantage rests in the sizable percentages of Serbian production in the Yugoslav totals for these branches of industry since 1918. And the Serbian shares are consistently higher than those of the neighboring Vojvodina, now part of Yugoslavia but the main producer of such goods imported from the Dual Monarchy before World War I. See relevant sections of *Proizvodne snage NR Srbije.*

Sources: Milling: *Statistički godišnjak Kr. Srbije,* 1893, I, 167, 1901, VI, 321, 1905, X, 365, 1906, XI, 371, 1907–08, XII, 449; Industrijska Komora, *Izveštaj,* 1910, Table 1, 1911, 16. Brewing: *Statistički godišnjak Kr Srbije,* 1907–08, XII, 437; Industrijska Komora, *Izveštaj,* 1910, Table 1, 1911, 16. Other Private Industry. *Statistički godišnjak Kr. Srbije,* 1893, I, 168, 1897, III, 317–9, 1898–99, IV, 331–2, 1900, V, 283–6, 1901, VI, 323–5, 1902, VII, 322–4, 1903, VIII, 346–8, 1904, IX, 374–7, 1905, X, 366–8, 1906, XI, 372–5, 1907–08, XII, 450–9; Industrijska Komora, *Izveštaj,* 1910, Table 1, 1911, 67. State Industry: Sources listed for Other Private Industry plus *Statistički godišnjak Kr. Srbije,* 1907–08, XII, 404, 410 and Samostalna Monopolska Uprava, *Račun izravnjanja,* 1911, 69. Mining: *Statistički godišnjak Kr. Srbije,* 1893, I, 161, 1897, III, 307, 1901, VI, 315, 1905, X, 355, 1906, XI, 361, 1907–08, XII, 431; Archives Nationales, F 30, 1170, b, p. 16.

TABLE V.2

Private Industry Other than Milling and Brewing, Real Factory Output, 1898–1911

Million Dinars in 1898 Prices

(number of factories*)

Industry	1898	1900	1902	1904	1906[a]	1908[a]	1910[a]	1911[a,b]
Meatpacking	0.3 (2)	2.5 (3)	6.3 (5)	3.5 (5)	3.2 (4)	5.8 (2)	4.6 (5)	21
Textiles	1.7 (5)	4.1 (5)	2.2 (5)	1.8 (6)	1.9 (9)	3.0 (10)	4.0 (16)	5
Sugar	—	1.1 (1)	—	—	1.5 (1)	3.1 (1)	4.0 (1)	5
Jam	—	—	0.2 (1)	0.2 (1)	0.2 (1)	0.2 (1)	0.2 (1)	n.a.
Leather	0.5 (1)	0.7 (1)	0.6 (1)	0.4 (1)	0.9 (1)	1.5 (2)	0.9 (2)	n.a.
Lumber	0.1 (1)	0.1 (1)	0.3 (3)	0.8 (4)	0.9 (4)	0.7 (8)	1.5 (8)	2
Cement	0.1 (1)	0.1 (2)	0.1 (2)	0.1 (2)	0.2 (3)	0.4 (2)	0.4 (2)	1
Bricks	—	—	0.6 (2)	1.3 (2)	1.4 (4)	2.9 (4)	1.1 (4)	n.a.
Glass	—	—	—	—	—	0.4 (1)	0.6 (2)	1
Chemicals	—	—	0.1 (1)	0.1 (1)	0.1 (1)	0.2 (1)	0.2 (1)	n.a.
Energy	0.3 (1)	0.3 (1)	0.6 (1)	0.3 (1)	0.5 (1)	0.7 (1)	4.0 (6)	5
Machinery	—	0.1 (1)	—	0.2 (1)	0.4 (2)	1.0 (2)	1.4 (3)	n.a.
Other	0.1 (2)	0.1 (1)	0.3 (5)	0.3 (4)	0.3 (3)	0.2 (1)	0.2 (1)	5
Total output	3.1	9.1	11.3	9.0	11.5	20.0	23.0	45
Total no. factories	(13)	(16)	(28)	(28)	(33)	(36)	(52)	n.a.

* A factory is defined here as any industrial enterprise employing at least 15 workers and 15 mechanical horsepower. See footnote 5 for a defense of this definition.
[a] Once the Serbian general tariff of 1904 (*Zbornik zakona Kr. Srbije*, 1904, 59, 342–54) had been applied to imports from Austria-Hungary, beginning in 1906, producers of domestic substitutes unfailingly passed on the amount of the duty to their customers. These tariff rates plus scattered but consistent evidence in the contemporary Serbian press are the basis for the following value deflations during the period 1906–11; textiles, 25 per cent; sugar, 33 per cent; lumber and cement, 40 per cent. As in the previous table, an assortment of secondary evidence justifies the assumption that prices of these industrial goods did not change significantly between 1898 and 1904.
[b] Number of factories not available for 1911.

Sources: Same as cited for Other Private Industry in Table V.1.

The difficulties encountered in exporting livestock to distant markets prompted still more capacity to slaughter and process meat, but few foreign takers could be found other than the French army. It was Austria-Hungary, after the agreement ending the Tariff War, that finally provided a large market. Relatively low annual quotas were placed on Serbian livestock imported into the Dual Monarchy. Their transit was still not allowed. As a result, the production of slaughtered and processed meat rose fivefold in 1911, and it soon accounted for one-half of private factory production and nearly 20 per cent of total exports.

This kind of export expansion was, of course, crucial to whatever industrial progress an independent Serbia might have made. The country lacked the resources to develop any extensive production of its own machinery or metallurgy. There were no iron deposits. The available coal was of low quality and insufficient even for the needs of existing industry. Thus Alexander Gerschenkron's argument that neighboring Bulgaria "missed an opportunity" in the same period to develop its heavy industry cannot be applied to Serbia.[9] It is true that the expansion of a textile industry relying quite heavily on imported inputs, which he rightly discounts in the Bulgarian experience, also occurred in Serbia. But this was plainly overshadowed by the faster advance of the several domestically supplied substitutes for imports as well as the growth of industrial exports.

THE FINANCIAL STRUCTURE AND ITS EVOLUTION

The set of European-style financial institutions that served the brief Serbian industrial advance had their origins in a much longer process. This was the spread of commercial exchange and money payment that encompassed most of the nineteenth century and represented a major structural change itself.[10] During the first half of the century these capitalistic practices, along with increased civil order, were largely responsible for beginning the dissolution of the self-sufficient *zadruga*, or communal properties, that had previously characterized Serbian peasant farming, into individual smallholdings oriented to the market. Thereafter, the capital accumulated, and the credit demanded in this new agrarian order joined with the state's growing fiscal needs to generate an extensive financial framework.

The Engine of Foreign Trade

Stimulated by the example of Ottoman commerce passing through Belgrade, a few Serbian peasants began exporting their own pigs to the Habsburg lands

9. Gerschenkron, "Some Aspects of Industrialization in Bulgaria, 1878–1939," in *Economic Backwardness in Historical Perspective*, 233.

10. Tomasevich, *Peasants, Politics and Economic Change in Yugoslavia*, 165.

in the late eighteenth century. The internal autonomy achieved in 1830–33 put most of the import business in Serbian hands as well. Limitations on the number of peasants in the export trade were removed when Prince Miloš's reign ended less than a decade later.[11] After 1845 and again after 1865, the value of Serbia's livestock exports northward rose rapidly to account for most of the two sharp increases noted in Table V.3.

TABLE V.3
Serbian Foreign Trade, 1835–1875
(million post-1873 dinars)

Years (Annual Average)	Exports	Habsburg %	Imports	Habsburg %
1835–1838	4.8	n.a.	2.4	n.a.
1843–1845	6.9	84.3	7.2	59.4
1846–1850	12.7	78.7	8.7	50.0
1851–1855	13.6	83.1	10.6	46.2
1856–1860	14.3	70.0	13.0	59.7
1861–1865	16.4	80.4	15.7	69.7
1866–1870	29.2	80.2	26.6	79.3
1871–1875	32.5	85.8	29.4	78.1

Sources: Milenković, *Ekonomska istorija Beograda*, 47; Milošević, *Spoljna trgovina Srbije, 1843–1875*, 34–5, 38–9, 46–7.

The few alternate uses for these export earnings encouraged the growth of imports. Some income went into high interest loans to other peasants. There was some initial investment in land purchases, but the Serbian heritage of smallholdings, plus legislation dating from 1836, hampered the more successful peasant traders in buying up the holdings of others in their debt. In any event, this emerging merchant class, eager for European ways, soon made Austrian manufactures the largest import. These goods were sold in an expanding network of retail shops and cut heavily into the livelihood of artisans in the traditional crafts.[12]

The assortment, if not the amount, of foreign manufactures continued to expand in the first decades after 1878. Austrian sugar became an established

11. Milić, *Trgovina Srbije, 1815–1839*, 12–17, 33, 171–3.
12. Andrić, Antić, Veselinović, and Djurić-Zamolo, *Beograd u XIX veku*, 62–4, summarizes the spread of European manufactures at the expense of the traditional crafts. The definitive work on the demise of Serbian crafts and guilds is Vučo, *Raspadanje esnafa u Srbiji*, 2 vols. It is also worth pointing out that the Serbian craft production did not have a wider Ottoman market to lose, as the Bulgarian did, and the bulk of Serbian exports already flowed to the main source of European imports, Austria-Hungary.

consumer good, and construction materials were essential for the Belgrade building boom and the railway south toward Constantinople and Salonika. Despite a commercial agreement with Serbia in 1881 that made imports from Austria-Hungary virtually duty free, the Dual Monarchy quickly lost one-third of its 90 per cent share in the Serbian market, principally to Germany and Great Britain.

Table V.4 shows that the heavy Serbian dependence on the Habsburg lands as an export market continued until the Tariff War. This did not prevent a 75 per cent jump in Serbian exports during the period 1895–1905, primarily in increased grain sales.[13] A series of export surpluses then emerged that, even after adjustment for the under-valuing of imports noted in Table V.4, reduced the net drain of the foreign debt annuity on the balance of payments to about 5 million dinars a year until the Tariff War.

The increased domestic savings that these export earnings imply are confirmed from other quarters. A survey conducted in 1910 with the help of Serbian agricultural authorities examined the consumption pattern of individual peasant households according to the size of their holdings.[14] The discretionary income earned on holdings exceeding 5 hectares, about 45 per cent of the half-million peasant households before 1900 and probably a bit higher proportion by 1910, averaged 100 to 200 dinars per unit. Such a surplus would have added 25 to 50 million dinars a year to potential savings, without counting the contribution of the purely commercial sector. In 1918 Serbian scholars, assembled at Geneva to calculate prewar national product and any war losses, estimated that total domestic consumption still left 300 million dinars available as an annual increment to savings.[15] Although this figure is probably exaggerated, along with the rest of the Geneva esti-mates for the Versailles conference, it nonetheless reinforces the conclusion that the Serbian economy was heavily involved in profitable commerce and operated significantly above the subsistence level. In the midst of a backward

13. Starting from nothing in the 1860's, wheat and corn exports together matched those of livestock by the early 1890's. On the basis of doctoral research currently being undertaken by M. R. Palairet of Edinburgh University, it appears that the integration of Serbian grain production into the international market was closely correlated with completion of rail access from the center of the country to Belgrade in 1888. The cultivation of wheat and corn, in a ratio of about 5 to 3, had in any event been spreading rapidly in Serbia at this time. As described in Tomasevich, *Peasants, Politics and Economic Change in Yugoslavia*, 157–64, this reflected a density of rural population that tripled during the last half of the nineteenth century and could no longer support itself solely on livestock trade. About one-fifth of the wheat crop was exported after 1890 and almost the same fraction for corn after 1900. Revived livestock and dried plum, i.e., prune, exports from 1896 combined to exceed grain sales until the Tariff War. Then wheat, and especially corn, both buoyed by a 50 per cent price rise since 1900, took up the slack in meat exports through 1910.

14. Avramović, *Naše seljačko gazdinstvo*, 35.

15. Srpski Centralni Komitet, *Srbija pre prvog svetskog rata*, 15, 72.

TABLE V.4
Serbian Foreign Trade and Foreign Debt, 1879–1911
(million dinars)

| | PERIOD | | | | | |
	1879–83	1884–88	1889–93	1894–98	1899–1903	1904–5
Annual Av. Exports	39.0	38.7	45.6	51.2	66.0	67.1
Annual Av. Imports[a]	45.8	45.0	38.7	36.6	49.5	58.3
Foreign Debt Annuity[b]	3[c]	12[c]	15[c]	17.5	18.6	20.2
% Exported to Austria–Hungary	78.3	86.4	87.5	88.8	83.7	90.0
% Imported from Austria–Hungary	90.2	71.2	60.7	57.5	55.4	58.3

| | YEAR | | | | | |
	1906	1907	1908	1909	1910	1911
Annual Exports	71.6	81.5	77.8	93.0	98.4	116.9
Annual Imports[a]	44.3	70.6	75.6	73.5	87.7	115.4
Foreign Debt Annuity[b]	20.2	23.4	25.1	25.1	30.8	32.4
% Exported to Austria–Hungary	42.0	15.9	27.7	31.3	18.1	41.4
% Imported from Austria–Hungary	50.1	36.3	42.5	24.3	19.1	38.3

[a] On the basis of Austro-Hungarian trade figures for 1901–10, in *Statistik des auswärtigen Handels*, 1905, III, 16, and 1910, III, 484–6, it appears that the annual undervaluation of imports in official Serbian statistics of 5 to 6 million dinars a decade before in Royaume de Belgique, *Receuil Consulaire*, 1891, LXXII, 283, had been reduced to 3 to 4 million dinars per year after 1900. Serbian export data continued to match up with the statistics kept by the Dual Monarchy.

[b] These figures do not include a floating foreign debt that drained off an indeterminate few million dinars a year in interest until 1903.

[c] Approximate figure.

Sources: *Statistike spoljne trgovine Kr. Srbije*, 1910, pp. VIII–XII, 1911, pp. XII–XVII; *Završni račun Kr. Srbije*, 1911, p. XXXVII.

---

agrarian economy then, the export trade had created potential capital for industrial development, just as imports had already built up demand for manufactured goods.

The Role of State Finance

The Serbian state absorbed an increasing amount of potential savings into its annual budget. State expenditures already amounted to the equivalent of 10 million dinars in the 1860's, and after independence they rose rapidly to

66 million dinars in 1895 and to 140 million by 1911. At the start, taxes needed to meet such spending helped to monetize the economy by drawing the peasantry into market sales. But the bulk of these expenses were directed to military and administrative ends; another large proportion went to pay the foreign debt annuity, although this fraction gradually declined from one-third to less than one-quarter of budget expenses during the period 1895–1911.[16] State industry consisted almost entirely of an arsenal run by the army, a single coal mine, and the tobacco and match factories whose income was mortgaged to help repay the foreign debt.[17]

The sum of state investment in private industry was even more modest. It consisted of a 200,000-dinar subsidy for meat-packing in 1906 and an annual allocation of 300,000 to 400,000 dinars from the state lottery that was in part diverted to other uses once the Tariff War had begun.[18] Moreover, these few contributions must be balanced against an indirect tax burden that reached 17 million dinars by 1911 and increased the price of sugar, beer, and all construction materials by about one-fifth.

Infrastructure received more attention, but it took a distant second place to military spending. Public works, excluding railway construction, received about one million dinars of annual budget expenses until it climbed to 7 million dinars for 1910 and 1911. The War Ministry took close to 20 million dinars a year before the Tariff War and 40 to 60 million dinars annually after the annexation of Bosnia-Herzegovina by the Dual Monarchy in 1908.

16. *Završni račun Kr. Srbije*, 1911, pp. XXXVII–VIII.

17. The state arsenal represented a fixed investment and an annual output of about 5 million dinars by the Tariff War. Yet it produced only bullets, did not afford any engineering experience to civilians, and had not precipitated the appearance of any noticeable private metallurgy. *Proizvodne snage NR Srbije*, 386; *Statistički godišnjak Kr. Srbije*, 1907–08, XII, 455.

The single state coal mine did account for a large fraction of the limited domestic production, but the needs of the railway and government ministries regularly left none of its output for industry. The price of coal was left to double during the Tariff War. Royaume de Belgique, *Receuil consulaire*, 1912, vol. 155, p. 261, and Archives Nationales, F 30, 1170, b, p. 16.

The tobacco and match factories, taken over as state monopolies about 1890, plus a scarcely mechanized silk factory, were the only other government-owned industry. The first two enterprises were slow to expand operations (see Table V.1) and although they used domestic inputs they were subject to cautious foreign control through the French and German representatives that held half the seats on the commission for administering the state monopolies. Set up in 1895 to guarantee the repayment of a 355 million dinar debt conversion loan, the commission used the net yearly income of the tobacco factory to provide consistently over 60 per cent of the annuity for debt repayment. (The rest came from the other state monopolies.) Such a procedure at least freed the economy from heavy taxation to repay the foreign debt, but it left a sizable part of the state budget under European supervision.

18. Ministarstvo Narodne Privrede, *Izveštaji*, 1907, 28, 78; and 1908–9, 6, 67–8.

After the initial railway obligations of the 1880's and the debt conversion loan of 1895 had built up a half billion dinars in foreign debt, subsequent borrowing favored debt adjustment and the military.[19] The 60 million dinar loan of 1902 was devoted entirely to eliminating the state's floating foreign debt and putting government finances in order. Almost half of the 25 million dinars intended for railway construction from the 90 million dinar loan of 1906 were diverted to the army during the Annexation Crisis. The financing for most of the 365 miles of track completed between 1908 and 1912, which doubled the country's total trackage, came from the third of the 150 million dinar loan of 1909 allocated to rail extension. Perhaps more important, this state-owned railway continued to endure a shortage of freight cars that hindered all domestic producers. Purchases of new cars in 1907 and 1910 added to the supply of rolling stock by 60 per cent but failed to eliminate the costly delays that the longer distance transport of agricultural exports during the Tariff War imposed on already limited facilities.[20]

The state also supported a Serbian shipping company that took some small but undetermined portion of the Danube traffic away from Austro-Hungarian firms. Other than some competitive pressure on foreign freight rates, however, this venture favored economic independence without adding to the net sum of facilities available to industry.

Still the Serbian government professed to favor the rapid industrial development of the country, and it passed some encouraging, if inexpensive, legislation to that end. While the National Assembly had granted exemptions from direct taxes and import duties for favored firms since 1873, these limited concessions had attracted only a dozen proper industrial projects by 1895.[21] But new laws, one passed in 1896, recognizing joint-stock incorporation, and another in 1898 expanding privileges for approved projects to exemption from indirect taxes and full rail freight rates, prompted the granting of 54 industrial concessions during the period 1898–1905. Support for these new laws materialized in the National Assembly after Hungarian livestock interests had used veterinary pretexts to force the closing of their border to

19. French banks furnished about 80 per cent of the funds for the prewar total of Serbian government loans, 71 per cent until 1903 and 86 per cent afterwards. The rest was mainly German capital, as Austria-Hungary contributed none after 1903. By the start of the Balkan Wars in 1912, total borrowing reached 750 million dinars in the effective amount of less than 600 million dinars. For the history of the state's foreign borrowing through 1903, see Nedeljković, *Istorija srpskih državnih dugova*. The subsequent loans are taken up in Aleksić-Pejković, *Odnosi Srbije ca Francuskom i Engleskom, 1903–1914*, 106, 229–63, 812.

20. Djordjević, *Carinski rat Austro-Ugarske i Srbije, 1906–1911*, 354, 447, 631; *Trgovinski glasnik*, August 13, 1911, 1; Državni Arhiv SR Srbije, MNP, T, 1907, 38/11.

21. *Zbornik zakona Kr. Srbije*, 1879–97, vols. 34–50, *passim*; Royaume de Belgique, *Receuil consulaire*, 1883, XLV, 27; Archives des Affaires Étrangères, CC, 1890–96, vol. 8, pp. 259–60.

Serbian stock periodically from 1891 to 1896. The Hungarian action in-
advertently called attention to the advantages of exporting processed meats;
the Serbian Ministry of National Economy also wished to emulate similar
Hungarian, Romanian, and Bulgarian legislation aimed at replacing industrial imports with domestic goods.[22] During the Tariff War the pace of
parliamentary concessions doubled, to reach about 20 a year. Yet the
privileges were not expanded to include direct subsidies, as they were in
Hungary, and the process of obtaining concessions through the National
Assembly remained a slow one, often delayed by political rivalries.[23]

Entrepreneurs, Domestic and Foreign

The success of such passive state encouragement depended in any case on
the availability of investors to take up industrial projects. The entrepreneurs
in most of the early industrial ventures had been immigrants from Czech or
German areas, undoubtedly a net gain for the country since many stayed to
become full citizens and an important part of Serbian society.[24] Although
ethnically Serbian names predominated in the enlarged lists of concessions
granted after 1898, the shortage of entrepreneurial initiative was by all
accounts a major handicap for Serbian industry. Technical training was
available only outside the country, and those few who could take advantage
of it tended to stay in western Europe or to return to government posts.
There do not appear to have been any important number of livestock and
grain traders who transferred their energies to industrial promotion. Only
merchants seeking to produce what they had previously traded made the
transition in noticeable measure. They established several new sawmills, set
up the textile firms branching out from Leskovac (in the southern region,
annexed in 1878), and established the modern glass factory.[25] Nor had the
practice of joint-stock issue by industrial firms spread successfully enough to
attract much agricultural capital in that fashion.[26]

22. Royaume de Belgique, *Receuil consulaire*, 1897, LXXVII, No. 4, pp. 301–3; *Stenografske beleške Narodne Skupštine Srbije*, 1897, 885–6, Proceedings of July 14, 1898.

23. For a description of the heavy subsidies offered industry after 1906 in Hungary, the
main model for Serbia's legislation on industrial concessions, see Berend and Ranki, "The
Development of the Manufacturing Industry in Hungary, 1900–1944," *Studia Historica*,
19 (1960), 11–12. On the status of Serbian industrial concessions during the Tariff War, see
Ministarstvo Narodne Privrede, *Izveštaji*, 1907, 22, 28, 78, and 1908–9, 6, 67–8, also
Djordjević, *Carinski rat Austro-Ugarske i Srbije, 1906–1911*, 643.

24. Grgašević, *Industrija Srbije i Crne Gore*, 61; Royaume de Belgique, *Receuil consulaire*,
1883, XLV, 23, and 1891, LXV, 11.

25. *Srpske novine*, March 25, 1907, 8; Royaume de Belgique, *Receuil consulaire*, 1912,
vol. 155, p. 262; Dimitrijević, *Gradska privreda starog Leskovca*, 86.

26. Of the 172 industrial enterprises (milling and brewing excluded) listed for 1910 by
the Serbian Chamber of Industry, only 22 were incorporated and the majority were not even
partnerships. Industrijska Komora Kr. Srbije, *Izveštaj*, 1910, Table 3.

Within industry itself, the Leskovac textile interests sent the second generation to western Europe for technical training and expanded their operations to include most of Serbian production by 1911. The descendants of the immigrant entrepreneurs, on the other hand, turned increasingly to investment in foreign-run projects for mining copper and other non-ferrous ores. These were mainly French and some English operations, while coal mining, along with the Belgrade street railway system, was basically in Belgian hands. Neither French nor Belgian nationals successfully entered manufacturing. A variety of English schemes fell through, save a textile mill, which was absorbed by the Leskovac interests in 1910, and a small meat-packing operation. A German joint-stock company did put about 3 million dinars into reopening a defunct sugar factory near Belgrade in 1905, but after that date foreign entrepreneurs did not complete any significant new industrial projects.[27] The risk of war intensified following the Annexation Crisis in 1908, and that risk was an obvious deterrent to any foreign investment in fixed Serbian assets.

The limited assistance of government concessions to these relatively few private entrepreneurs does not explain even the brief industrial advance made in the Serbian economy. Hence the logic of looking for an explanation in the behavior of private financial institutions, both domestic and foreign. It should also prove instructive to measure how much failings in these financial institutions account for the lack of further industrial growth and how much non-financial barriers worked to deny banks a role in such industrialization. The available evidence is a mosaic of material, found scattered among foreign diplomatic reports and the contemporary Serbian press as well as in more usual primary sources. General conclusions must therefore be approached gingerly.

The Demand for Commercial Banking Before 1878

One part of the process of monetization in the Serbian economy during the nineteenth century was the credit shortage which had soon accompanied the increasing export of livestock. Adding to the dependence of the many small-scale traders on high interest loans from merchants in Belgrade or the Habsburg lands was the absence of a domestic money supply. Goods were exchanged in the midst of what one French visitor called "a terrible money anarchy"; over 40 varieties of gold, silver, and copper coin circulated in autonomous Serbia, and most were of Habsburg or Ottoman origin.[28] From

---

27. *Berichte der K. und K. Konsularämter*, II, 1905, XVII, 2, p. 31, and II, 1906–12, XVII, *passim*.

28. Andrić, Antić, Veselinović and Djurić-Zamolo, *Beograd u XIX veku*, 67; Vučo, *Privredna istorija Srbije*, 234.

the eighteenth century on an imaginary unit of account, on the pattern of medieval "ghost money," had been employed to afford some order to commercial dealings. After 1826, however, this unit could not keep up with the continuing depreciation of Ottoman coin, and the relatively more stable Austrian denominations became the only ones acceptable where trade with the Habsburg lands was concerned.

This growing dependence on Austrian coin—and credit as well—roused the larger Serbian traders to their first interest in founding a domestic bank. The occasion was, not surprisingly, the spread of the European monetary crisis of 1845 to Vienna.[29] After failing to win state participation the domestic bank collapsed. Yet Belgrade commercial interests began to collect capital among themselves for another such bank when the European money market contracted again in 1857. Sufficient stock was not subscribed until 1866, and then no agreement could be reached on a set of statutes. This lack of urgency can be traced in part to the continuing absence of trade deficits (see Table V.3). In addition, the government set up an administration in 1862 to make mortgage loans from the various funds held by the state treasury. This Uprava Fondova, a department of the Finance Ministry, gave a majority of these loans to Belgrade traders and officials, thereby reducing their demand for credit, or at least for long-term credit.[30]

The founding in 1869 of what was correctly called the First Serbian Bank was therefore left partly to foreign capital and entirely to the ambitious aims of western European banking practice during this boom period. By that time several Serbian traders in Belgrade had despaired of a domestic bank, and they had joined the Franco-Hungarian Bank of Budapest as equal stockholders in forming a "universal bank" on the French model.[31] Its far-ranging statutes, although affording no issue of currency, led the new bank to sink two-thirds of its paid-in capital into a Croatian railway scheme and a Hungarian ship consortium. The European crash of 1873 took these two ventures with it. The Serbian stockholders were left to declare bankruptcy after the Franco-Hungarian Bank, their own partner, or any other foreign bank, refused to make up the losses.[32] In the process, the Serbians suffered a severe blow to their confidence in financial institutions, particularly foreign ones and those inclined to any operations other than secure, short-term loans.

29. Cvijetić, "Pokušaji osnivanja prvih banaka u Srbije," *Finansija*, 1–2 (1965), 120.

30. Glomazić, *Istorija državne hipotekarne banke, 1862–1932*, 79–81; Kukla, *Razvitak kreditne organizacije u Srbije*, 64–8.

31. The government had previously refused offers of foreign financing for a domestic bank from Hungarian, French, English and Belgian interests in that order, as Belgrade traders continued their efforts to found a purely Serbian bank. Ugričić, *Novčani sistem Jugoslavije*, 56; Cvijetić, "Pokušaji osnivanja prvih banaka u Srbiji," *Finansija*, 1–2 (1965), 123.

32. Cvijetić, "Prva Srpska Banka," *Istorijski glasnik*, 2–3 (1964), 120–1.

The several small savings banks that had been set up before the crash survived, but they granted credit only in the smallest of slices.

A Central Bank and a Domestic Money Supply

Interest in founding a bank of issue did not revive until war and the Congress of Berlin had brought the country full independence in 1878. A money crisis quickly mounted. The state treasury had already issued over 10 million dinars in silver coin and just minted 10 million gold dinars with the help of a Paris bank.[33] Many of the new dinars, however, were converted to Austrian coin as soon as they entered circulation.[34] The paper currency in use then was largely the Austrian silver note, and it was suffering speculative depreciation in the face of rising gold prices. Serbian traders felt both the need for a more stable money supply and greater access to credit acutely. Besides the fact that there was much currency speculation, deficits in the state budget and deficits in the balance of payments—the latter arising from the import surpluses noted in Table V.4 and foreign debt repayment—also put pressure on the supply of loanable funds.[35]

When the Srpska Kreditna Banka, set up in Belgrade in 1881 by the Länderbank of Vienna with help from the Comptoir d'Escompte of Paris, failed to accumulate more than a million dinars in paid-in capital, the Serbian government approved the founding of a purely domestic bank of issue, the Narodna Banka. Although it was a private joint-stock institution, this bank was accorded powers of lending to other banks and exclusive currency issue usually associated with a central bank. By early 1884 Serbian investors had subscribed the 2.5 million dinars deemed necessary to begin operations. An equal amount in gold-backed 100 dinar notes was printed at the Belgian National Bank and immediately put into circulation.

The first reaction of peasants and Belgrade traders alike to the new issue seemed to justify the prediction of a French diplomat that, like the Turkish population served by the Ottoman Bank, Serbians would not prove "civilized

33. The Serbian government had introduced its own copper coins in 1868 and silver ones in 1873. These were dinars tied to the value of the French gold franc under the terms of the Latin Monetary Union, but the total issue of 6 million dinars was just a small fraction of the foreign coin and paper currency circulating in the country; there was no domestic paper currency, partly for fear the peasantry would not accept it. Ugričić, *Novčani sistem Jugoslavije*, 57–60; Bajkitch, *Monnaies, banques et bourses en Serbie*, 43.

34. Royaume de Belgique, *Receuil consulaire*, 1883, XLV, 347.

35. A sharp rise in Serbian government spending and imports were largely responsible for both of these imbalances. New taxes were sufficient to cover added military and administrative expenses but not the 8 million dinars in annual debt repayment that had appeared, from the ill-fated Bontoux railway loan of 1881 in the main. Although the loan was quickly renegotiated with a Paris bank after the fall of the French financier, Serbian access to further foreign lending disappeared for several years.

enough" to accept domestic paper money.[36] Loans in the new notes were fast exchanged for metallic gold, even by government offices, and the amount outstanding in gold notes fell below one million dinars by the end of the year. But the simple expedient of issuing 10 dinar silver notes, a small denomination far more convenient for trade and not directly convertible into gold, allowed paper money outstanding to surpass the original 2.5 million dinar issue by the end of 1886 and to climb steadily by about 4 million dinars a year until 1892 (see Table V.6).

The presence of the Narodna Banka and the existence of a redeemable domestic currency encouraged the founding of 54 new banks in the period 1884–93. After its issue of silver notes doubled in 1886, the Narodna Banka was able to offer other banks a one point reduction in its regular interest rate of 6 per cent, and it quickly took their business away from the Austrian-run Srpska Kreditna Banka. By the end of 1893, other banks received almost half the 9.5 million dinars in private credit outstanding from the Narodna Banka, usually in the form of short-term current account loans.[37] Foreign trade took about the same, always in the form of 90-day discounting for bills of exchange. Another stimulus to the founding of new banks was the failure of the Narodna Banka to open branches throughout the country.[38]

The Rise of Small Savings Banks

The number of new banks in the first years after the founding of the Narodna Banka should not be exaggerated in importance. The new entries were small savings banks and credit associations. They did not hesitate to perform the functions of commercial banks, but generally relied on untrained employees and held 100,000 dinars or less in paid-in capital. All were located in the interior of the country. The only domestic institutions with capital approaching that of the Narodna Banka were two Belgrade banks, one a credit association established in 1871 and the other the Beogradska Zadruga, founded with some trepidation in 1882 in the face of recent prison sentences meted out to officials of the First Serbian Bank.[39]

36. Archives Nationales, F 30, 346, Rapport of July 3, 1881.

37. *Narodna Banka, 1884–1934*, 20–21, 23, 291.

38. *Ibid.*, 28. Although the law of 1883 fixing the bank's statutes had made specific provision for branches, the Narodna Banka consistently refused to establish them. Bank officials argued that branches in the interior would bring large losses. They would agree only to commercial agencies, on the pattern of the Belgian National Bank, but these never aroused much enthusiasm in Serbia.

39. The Beogradska Zadruga was set up as an association of small artisan savers seeking relief from high interest rates. Incorporated in 1883, the bank prospered after the creation of the Narodna Banka. A number of larger Belgrade merchants then moved to take over a majority of the stock. Although several large loans were made for public works, the main

Despite their limitations, by the early 1890's the Serbian banks had accomplished several tasks that are relevant to this analysis. The aggregate of paid-in capital had mounted from 3.2 to 15.5 million dinars during the decade after 1883, and annual profits of 10 to 12 per cent were being returned on that capital (see Table V.5). Discounting bills of exchange had been

TABLE V.5

Number, Paid-in Capital, and Profit Ratios
of Serbian Banks, 1884–1898

Year	Number of Banks	Paid-in Capital (million dinars)	Net Profit as % of Paid-in Capital
1884	7	3.2	n.a.
1888	37	8.9	10.4
1889	40	9.8	9.4
1890	43	10.6	11.2
1891	45	11.6	11.0
1892	47	12.0	13.0
1893	61	13.5	12.1
1894	62	14.6	11.1
1895	66	15.2	12.1
1896	69	17.9	10.5
1897	69	18.9	10.5
1898	76	20.5	11.2

Sources: *Statistički godišnjak Kr. Srbije*, 1903, VIII, 487; Kukla, *Razvitak kreditne organizacije u Srbiji*, 22.

established as a safe and profitable piece of business, interest rates had fallen generally to about 9 to 12 per cent (they were to fall little more before the Balkan Wars), and Serbian bankers had already won a reputation for commercial honesty.[40]

The Belgrade Joint-stock Banks

The next stage in the evolution of the Serbian banking system, and the most important for our purposes, was the appearance during the mid-1890's of

business of the bank became discounting bills of exchange for agricultural traders and small interior banks. *25 godišnica Beogradske Zadruge, 1882–1907*, 3; Državni Arhiv SFR Jugoslavije, Annex, *godišnji izveštaj Beogradske Zadruge*, 1891, 17.

40. *Narodna Banka, 1884–1934*, 57; Bajkitch, *Monnaies, banques et bourses en Serbie*, 45–46; Mirosavljević, *Naši novčani zavodi*, 42–45. Two brief declines, noted below in footnotes 59 and 62, brought down the discount rates of the large Belgrade banks from 8–10 per cent to 7–9 per cent in 1904–5 and again in 1910–11.

several more Belgrade banks, professionally staffed and based on plans for at least a million dinars in paid-in capital. Their origins were hardly auspicious. These were years of falling agricultural prices and recurring monetary crises throughout Europe. Serbian deficits in an ever-expanding government budget and in the balance of payments joined with these international pressures to create an acute shortage of credit. The inability of the government to meet its obligations on time and the requirement that all foreign debt repayment be made in gold bank notes put a speculative premium on gold that approached 20 per cent of nominal value by 1894.[41] In order to prevent the Narodna Banka from holding much of the scarce gold coin as reserves for note issue, the government passed a law to reduce the supply of silver notes, the main means of payment in the country, from 28 to 10 million dinars within five years. After several protests and a demonstration of the kind of credit reduction that would have been required to implement this policy, officials of the Narodna Banka won legislation by 1896 for a 25 million dinar maximum on silver note issue.[42]

In the meantime, the first new Belgrade banks to be established in more than a decade were expected to offer some relief to traders from these restrictions. Two were founded with the intention of affording credit to members of the minority Liberal party, setting a precedent for political affiliation that would in the future divide all Serbian banks. A third was set up specifically to relieve the shortage of secured loans. All three proceeded very cautiously in their operations to credit only the most reliable and established clients in a time of commercial uncertainty.[43]

Perhaps the major achievement of the Serbian banks during these several years was that they themselves survived, avoided falling under foreign control, and even added to their numbers. Total bank capital rose from 13.5 to 20 million dinars during the brief period 1894–98, and net profits stayed around 12 per cent of paid-in capital.

Yet the concentration of Serbian resources in the banking system remained small. As late as 1896 total bank assets were barely 80 million dinars, or 40 per cent of agricultural output (livestock sales and harvested crops) and

41. Jovanović, *Vlada Aleksandra Obrenovića*, II, 316–18; *Narodna Banka, 1884–1934*, 157–8, 308–9; Archives Nationales, F 30, 346, Rapport of June 1, 1904, 23.

42. Its annual reports suggest that the Narodna Banka remained dissatisfied even with the 25 million dinar maximum on silver note issue. The bank was still forced by this limit to suspend its discounting operations for several months at the height of the export season. *Godišnji izveštaj Narodne Banke*, 1894, p. X, 1895, p. XIII, 1896, p. XI.

43. The two Liberal-backed banks were the Vračarska Zadruga and the Beogradska Trgovačka Banka. Concerning the circumstances surrounding the founding of the latter, see Državni Arhiv SFR Jugoslavije, Annex, *godišnji izveštaj Beogradske Trgovačke Banke*, 1895 and 1896; concerning the establishment of the Prometna Banka, see "Prometna Banka," *Narodno blagostanje*, I, no. 27 (1929), pp. 440–1.

therefore still less of gross national product.[44] For the same year, the five largest domestic banks (save the Narodna Banka) held only a third of paid-in capital; the rest was scattered among 62 credit associations and savings banks, all but a few in small interior towns.[45] Although these lesser institutions often issued their own stock and did not hesitate to enter fully into discounting and other commercial banking operations, they were, all the same, unsupported by any branch affiliations and heavily dependent on uncertain lines of credit from the Narodna Banka. By the end of the nineteenth century a banking system had evolved that could offer short-term credit to foreign trade. It struggled to do so under restrictions imposed by government arrears and foreign debt obligations. These were also the limits of its capacity when Serbian industry began to stir, at about the same time.

Central and Mortgage Banking After 1898

During the decade after 1898 the level of currency issue by the Narodna Banka remained unchanged, while, in the same period, there was significant growth in the Serbian economy. In the absence of reliable estimates of gross national product, the doubling of exports and government spending during this period may be taken as some measure of the general increase in economic activity. The legal limit on silver note issue had been increased from 25 to 30 million dinars in 1898. It was not raised again until 1908, despite a rise in combined gold and silver reserves well past the required 40 per cent ratio. Table V.6 indicates that from 1898 to 1905 silver notes outstanding were in fact allowed to exceed 30 million dinars somewhat, the addition largely representing the sum of state debts to the Narodna Banka. The maximum still forced the bank to suspend its discounting services at the height of every export season until the Tariff War.[46]

The government continued to fear that currency speculation would endanger the country's metal reserves if the maximum were increased. There was also the fact that many of these on the administrative and governing boards of the Narodna Banka were members of the minority and vaguely Austrophile Progressive party. The predominant and anti-Austrian Radicals did not favor attacking the chronic shortage of credit through such a bank and they threw their decisive support behind a separate export bank. The Izvozna Banka was accordingly set up in 1901 with paid-in capital equal to that of the Narodna Banka but without powers of note issue.

44. *Statistički godišnjak Kr. Srbije*, 1896–97, III, 210, and 1901, VI, 368, 403; "Novčani zavodi u Kr. Srbiji," *Delo*, no. 11 (1896), p. 117.

45. *Statistički godišnjak Kr. Srbije*, 1896–97, III, 457–61.

46. *Berichte der K. und K. Konsularämter*, II, 1900, XVIII, no. 5, p. 40, II, 1901, no. 1, p. 64, and II, 1907, XIX, no. 3, *passim*; *Narodna Banka, 1884–1934*, 111–15.

TABLE V.6
Note Issue and Ratios of Metallic Reserves
for the Narodna Banka, 1884–1911
(thousand dinars)

Year (Dec. 31)	Gold Notes	Silver Notes	Total	Metallic Reserves as % of Total[a]
1884	782	—	782	168.5
1886	438	5,301	5,739	53.3
1888	141	13,937	14,078	56.5
1890	82	23,393	23,475	54.2
1892	160	28,714	28,874	46.6
1894	548	24,516	25,064	45.4
1896	659	23,802	24,461	52.4
1898	364	32,780	33,145	44.5
1900	849	35,029	35,879	46.4
1902	2,124	34,690	36,813	58.3
1904	3,142	34,875	38,017	62.2
1906	2,279	27,952	30,231	74.0
1908	3,374	47,038	50,412	58.5
1910	7,037	42,617	49,848	74.4
1911	13,981	51,842	65,823	77.1

a Reserve coverage of gold and silver notes combined was legally fixed at a minimum of 40 per cent throughout this period. There is unfortunately no precise record of the amount of specie in circulation, as opposed to the gold and silver coin collected as central bank reserves. Scattered evidence does suggest that coin in circulation declined from 15 to 20 million dinars throughout the 1880's to 10 to 15 million by 1911.

Source: *Narodna Banka, 1884–1934*, 291.

In 1908, the government's financial needs during the Annexation Crisis allowed the Narodna Banka to use the legislation for renewing its twenty-five-year charter to win an easier standard for silver note issue: five times a paid-in capital that was simultaneously increased from 5 million to 7.5 million dinars. The new silver quota of 37.5 million dinars, plus provisions for an excess issue of 10 per cent and an unlimited gold note issue to the government in return for metal reserves from the state treasury, account for the doubling of the supply of paper money during the last years of the Tariff War.[47]

The reorganization of the government's Uprava Fondava in 1898 into a semi-independent mortgage bank, the Hipotekarna Banka, completed the

47. Archives Nationales, F 30, 346, Rapport sur la Serbie, 141.

set of European-style financial institutions in prewar Serbia. This last step did not add much to the nation's facilities for financing industrial development. The new bank sharply trimmed the uncollected debts that had paralyzed the previous mortgage operations, and it attracted increased deposits of private savings. But its failure to place more than a fraction of a large bond issue or to attract other long-term capital left almost half of new loans based on short-term liabilities.[48] Annual lending rose to about 15 million dinars until an unfavorable German bank loan in 1905, and the Annexation Crisis in 1908 cut deeply into its supply of loanable funds. A 30 million dinar loan from a French bank in 1910 was used mainly to repay accumulated debts; less than 5 million dinars went into new loans.[49] Over half of the bank's loans were taken on residential or official buildings in Belgrade and thus helped provide demand for construction materials. None apparently went to industrial installations.[50] Since other Serbian banks rarely gave such loans, industry remained essentially without access to mortgage credit throughout this entire period.

SERBIAN COMMERCIAL BANKING AND INDUSTRY AFTER 1906

Like the money supply, the resources of domestic commercial banks made unprecedented advances after the start of the Tariff War. Total assets of Serbian banks, it is true, increased at no faster pace after 1906 than before. They had risen from less than 80 million dinars in 1896 to about 300 million dinars in 1905, and they approached 650 million dinars by the end of 1911, even after subtracting interbank loans. The shares of the Narodna and Hipotekarna Banka in these assets stayed disproportionally large, increasing from 175 million dinars in 1905 to 365 million dinars in 1911.[51] If the assets of these two banks are removed, the probable ratio of domestic bank assets to gross national product is an unremarkable 30 per cent. Yet the other Serbian banks, with their 300 million dinars, had acquired a more solid structure of liabilities on which to base their operations. These other banks accounted for all but 2.5 million dinars in the 23 million dinar jump in paid-in

48. Glomazić, *Istorija državne hipotekarne banke, 1862–1932*, 79–81, 88–92.
49. Aleksić-Pejković, *Odnosi Srbije ca Francuskom i Engleskom, 1903–1914*, 315.
50. *Politika*, May 12, 1909, 1, and December 6, 1910, 1.
51. "Novčani zavodi u Kr. Srbije," *Delo*, no. 11 (1896), p. 117; *Srpske novine*, Feb.–June 1906, *passim*, and Feb.–June, 1912, *passim*; *Trgovinski glasnik*, Feb.–June, 1906, *passim*, and Feb.–June, 1912, *passim*. Goldsmith, *Financial Structure and Development*, 217, 257, 279, finds the combined percentage of central and mortgage bank assets in total financial assets much smaller, less than 20 per cent, for other countries during the period 1880–1913, but about the same proportion for interbank loans, around 6 per cent, as in Serbia.

TABLE V.7

Number, Paid-in Capital, Profit Ratios, and Savings Deposits
of Serbian Banks, 1899–1911

(capital and savings in million dinars)

Year (Dec. 31)	Number of Banks[a]	Paid-in Capital[a]	Net Profit as % of Paid-in Capital	Savings Deposits[b]
1899	77	20.8	11.5	n.a.
1900	82	21.6	11.1	n.a.
1901	93	23.2	11.3	27.7
1902	106	24.8	11.4	27.4
1903	106	26.1	12.6	30.4
1904	112	27.8	12.0	34.3
1905	115	29.4	8.3	39.3
1906	120	29.0	12.6	44.9
1907	130	33.0	11.4	53.5
1908	147	39.8	10.0	48.4
1909	151	40.9	7.0	59.1
1910	163	46.7	6.7	n.a.
1911	174	52.7	6.5	74.5

a Includes Narodna and Hipotekarna Banka and all other domestic banks save a few small state savings banks. The Hipotekarna Banka did not hold any paid-in capital as such and is therefore not included in the two middle columns above.

b The Hipotekarna Banka held savings deposits of 6–8 million dinars before 1906, up to 15 million dinars at the start of the Tariff War, but again only 8 million dinars by the end of 1911.

Sources: *Statistički godišnjak Kr. Srbije*, 1903, VIII, 487, 1905, X, 522, 1906, XI, 510, 517, 1907–08, XII, 646, 658, 667–74; *Završni Račun Kr. Srbije*, 1911, p. XXX.

capital from 1905 to 1911, and for the entire 35 million dinar increase in savings deposits.

In addition, these resources were more concentrated in larger banks than they had previously been. Although the number of small savings institutions continued to rise, the number of banks holding assets over a million dinars increased from 19 to 51. The latter's proportion of total bank assets, excluding the Narodna and Hipotekarna Banka, advanced during the Tariff War from under 60 to over 80 per cent. The 42 Belgrade banks, all but a half-dozen of which fell into this million dinar category, increased their share of paid-in capital from less than half to two-thirds and of savings deposits from one-third to almost one-half, again excepting the central and mortgage banks.[52]

Merchant capital was the primary source of these added funds. Traders made up 60 per cent of membership on bank boards (no other group had as

52. Stanarević, *Beogradske banke u 1911 g.*, 24, 30.

much as 10 per cent, and industrialists were less than 3 per cent), and they seem to have been still more dominant a proportion on stockholders' lists.[53] The burden of the Tariff War on livestock exports in all likelihood diverted a sizable part of the funds noted above from this crippled trade to placement in domestic banks. There was also the desire of the ruling Radical party to repair its relative lack of affiliated banks. Traders tied to this party founded twenty of the thirty-two new banks established between 1906 and 1908.[54] Among them were two large Belgrade banks whose assets quickly surpassed 10 million dinars. This made the Radicals' share of such size banks three out of eight.

It would be misleading to suggest that this transfer of merchant capital to the Serbian banks could have permitted the country a spurt leading to full-scale industrialization, i.e. mobilizing enough of the country's resources to convert a large fraction of national product into industrial goods. If as much as one-half of the 350 million dinars of new bank assets during the Tariff War could have been directed to industry, any kind of minimum capital output ratio, say 2 to 1, would have kept the annual addition to industrial output around 1 per cent of the 900 million dinars that is our rough approximation of gross national product for 1911, the last year before the outbreak of the Balkan Wars.

Such a massive diversion was out of the question. For a start, half of the new assets were largely immobilized in the Narodna and Hipotekarna Banka. And the increased concentration of capital in the other Belgrade banks did not lead to mergers, systems of branch banks in the interior, or a lessening of the political rivalries that divided them. Serbia's precarious position in international diplomacy left domestic banks, which generally carried a ready cash reserve of less than 5 per cent of liabilities, vulnerable to serious runs on savings and other deposits. The Annexation Crisis of 1908 forced most Belgrade banks to suspend payment and turn to the Narodna Banka for extra funds to weather withdrawals.[55]

On the other hand, if we consider the capital and credit actually accumulated in industrial firms, the potential contribution of commercial banking was considerable. The 23 million dinars added to the paid-in capital of Serbian banks from 1905 to 1911 was almost one-half the probable increment

53. *Bankarski glasnik*, no. 5 (May, 1912), p. 140, provides a complete survey of the occupations of all bank board members for 1910. Državni Arhiv SR Srbije, MNP, T, 1906, XVII, no. 1, and XX, no. 4, afford a number of occupational lists of bank stockholders.

54. Djordjević, *Carinski rat Austro-Ugarske i Srbije, 1906–1911*, 360.

55. Archives des Affaires Étrangères, CP, NS 26, 1908–12, V, 22; Državni Archiv SFR Jugoslavije, Annex, *godišnji izveštaj Beogradske Trgovačke Banke*, 1908, 9. Although originally published documents, the annual reports (*godišnji izveštaji*) of this and other banks located in the New Belgrade Annex of the Yugoslav State Archives are generally not to be found elsewhere and have therefore been cited as archival holdings.

in short- and long-term industrial investment, mining excluded, over nearly the same period (Table V.8).

Short-term Credit from the Narodna Banka

The main commercial banking functions of the Narodna Banka were still the discounting of bills of exchange and the granting of current account loans, both for no longer than 92 days.[56] The bank began discounting industrial

TABLE V.8
Fixed Investment and Working Capital in Serbian Industry,
1906 and 1910
(December 31, million dinars)

Fixed Investment	1906			1910		
	Domestic	Foreign	Total	Domestic	Foreign	Total
Milling	9.5	—	9.5	15.5	—	15.5
Brewing	4.0	—	4.0	3.5	—	3.5
Other Private Ind.	8.5	4.3	12.8	24.0	6.0	30.0
Mining	—	11.2	11.2	—	17.0	17.0
Total	22.0	15.5	37.5	43.0	23.0	66.0

Working Capital	1906			1910		
	Domestic	Foreign	Total	Domestic	Foreign	Total
Milling	1.8	0.5	2.3	3.0	1.0	4.0
Brewing	0.8	0.2	1.0	3.0	1.0	4.0
Other Private Ind.	7.5	2.5	10.0	30.0	5.0	35.0
Mining	—	14.0	14.0	—	15.0	15.0
Total	10.1	17.2	27.3	36.0	22.0	58.0

Sources: Stojanović, *Govori i rasprave*, III, 213–14, provides figures collected by the Ministry of National Economy for 1906; Industrijska Komora, *Izveštaj*, 1910, Table 4, K. und K. Handelsministerium, *Serbien Wirtschaftsverhältnisse*, 1909, 17–9, 1910, 21–2, afford admittedly less precise data for 1910. Neither of the two sources for the 1910 data, the Serbian Chamber of Industry and the Austro-Hungarian Consulate in Belgrade, could legally require such information from firms, as the Ministry of National Economy had been able to do in 1906.

56. Although forbidden by statute from issuing longer loans during the 1890's, the bank had nonetheless used the format of current account credit to grant several ten-year loans, totaling 3.5 million dinars, for construction of Belgrade's water system, harbor facilities, and a railway spur for the new Belgrade slaughterhouse. This practice was criticized in the National Assembly, however, and it was discontinued until 1908, when two loans totaling 350,000 dinars were granted. *Narodna Banka, 1884–1909*, 136–41; *Godišnji izveštaj Narodne Banke*, 1908, p. XIII.

bills of exchange in 1900, but the year-end amount stayed under a million
dinars until 1906. The figures in Table V.9 reveal that first a rise in discounting and then the appearance of current account lending (only on the basis of
deposited bills of exchange) pushed total short-term credit from the Narodna
Banka to industry past 5 million dinars by the end of 1911.

TABLE V.9

Direction of Discounting and Current Account Loans
from the Narodna Banka, December 31, 1905–1911
(thousand dinars)

	DISCOUNTING OF BILLS OF EXCHANGE					
Year	Other Banks	Industry	Exports	Imports	Other	Total
1905	594	971	1,733	2,145	691	6,134
1906	732	1,092	1,705	1,630	723	5,882
1907	1,078	2,158	1,790	2,292	473	7,791
1908	1,729	2,963	2,194	3,030	689	10,585
1909	1,262	2,752	2,206	2,437	606	9,264
1910	880	2,166	2,372	2,372	547	8,337
1911	1,200	1,514	1,878	915	588	6,096

	LOANS ON CURRENT ACCOUNT			
Year	Other Banks	Industry	Other	Total
1905	6,794	—	—	6,794
1906	8,146	—	—	8,146
1907	8,317	681	153	9,151
1908	11,094	9	776	11,879
1909	9,559	229	1,021	10,809
1910	10,282	1,339	1,579	13,199
1911	16,489	3,366	1,335	21,189

Source: *Godišnji izveštaj Narodne Banke*, 1912.

This was credit available to joint-stock industrial enterprises in sums up to
half the firm's paid-in capital at the Narodna Banka's regular interest rate of
6 per cent. Virtually constant at that level since 1886, the rate was 3 to 4
points below the short-term credit offered industry by other banks, domestic
or foreign. Even so, the 2.5 million dinar increase in industrial credit from the
Narodna Banka between 1906 and 1910 was less than 10 per cent of the
increment to working capital noted in Table V.8. And the Narodna Banka
continued to do more business on better terms with other banks than it did

with industry. Other Serbian banks generally received loans at 1 per cent under the normal interest rate, with the right to renew them automatically for a full year.[57] If the receiving bank dealt primarily with industry or exports, it received a 2 per cent reduction in interest. Thus the bulk of short-term credit provided by the Narodna Banka was only indirectly available to Serbian industry, through other banks.

Short-term Credit from Other Banks

The rest of the Serbian commercial banks had come into being to discount bills of exchange for agricultural trade. This practice continued to earn these banks high returns on paid-in capital throughout the first years of the economy's industrial stirrings. Yet the figures in Table V.7 reflect an interruption in such handsome profits even before the Tariff War cut into the livestock trade. Although the issue of new currency was still restricted, the Serbian credit market had nonetheless eased temporarily in 1904 and 1905, when the government was finally able to meet its own financial obligations.[58] By 1905, the falling level of European interest rates also began to be felt in Serbia. Austrian diplomatic reports noted that the Serbian banks were anxious to turn away from accustomed operations to new ventures, seeking both higher returns and less risk of delayed repayment. These same reports record roughly a one or two point decline in the discount rate for the major Belgrade banks to a range of 7–9 per cent, the first noticeable decline in the general rate since the late 1880's. Such a fall is consistent with the drop of one-third, between 1903 and 1905, in the ratio of net profits to total bank assets that is the only other indicator available for the behavior of Serbian interest rates over time.[59]

On the side of short-term credit, the Serbian banks increasingly favored current account loans (Table V.10). The Belgrade banks came to account for about 80 per cent of the current account total, the ten largest banks providing one-half of that amount. The current account deposits on which such lending

57. *Narodna Banka, 1884–1909*, 119.

58. The elimination of the state's floating debt in 1903, along with an accounting reform and a heavy surtax the following year, finally ended the chronic deficits in the state budget. The credit squeeze attending these government shortages had helped Serbian banks not only to charge 9 to 12 per cent interest on their discounting operations, but also to speculate on the indirect exchange of the predominant silver-backed currency for gold at 10 to 12 per cent average profit. *Berichte der K. und K. Konsularämter*, II, 1902, XVI, 9–10.

59. *Ibid.*, II, 1904, XVIII, no. 5, p. 85, and II, 1905, XVIII, no. 2, p. 105; *Srpske novine*, Feb.–June, 1903–6, *passim*; *Trgovinski glasnik*, Feb.–June, 1903–6, *passim*. The interest rates that Serbian banks published in their annual reports or released to the state statistical yearbook were generally confined to ranges of several points that were broad enough, for instance, to conceal the decline in 1904–5 suggested by the sources cited above.

could be based also rose fourfold over the same interval, to more than 60 million dinars. This increment exceeded the combined increase, from 30 million to 66 million dinars between the end of 1906 and 1911 according to Table V.6, in the Narodna Banka's outstanding issue of gold and silver dinar notes. These new current account deposits may likewise be regarded as a major addition to the Serbian money supply during the Tariff War.

The sum of the evidence, which has, regrettably, been scattered, is that the easy adoption of this type of loan to industrial credit (without the guaranteeing signatures and sometimes goods in transit required by the bill of exchange) did not occur in Serbia as it had throughout central Europe. Instead, the great majority of these loans apparently were accorded to wholesale importers in Belgrade, who were able to offer bills of exchange drawn on interior traders as security. A survey for 1910, admittedly incomplete, shows that only 17 of 251 of the reporting firms owed debts on current account, while 54 had borrowed by discounting bills of exchange.[60] Many Serbian banks favored stockholders in granting loans, and the proportion of bank shares held by industrial owners was probably small. The evidence given by contemporary observers suggests that total short-term credit for industry from other banks never even matched the amount provided by the Narodna Banka.[61]

Unless a bank held some direct interest in the firm, few loans were given. And those few required the deposit of an equivalent sum in bills of exchange as security and exacted an interest rate 1 to 2 per cent above the normal Belgrade level of 7 to 9 per cent.[62] Industry was thus exempted from the tendency toward a single rate for all customers that had developed among Serbian banks since 1900. Defaults on a number of the current account loans that were granted to industry did not encourage banks to support firms over which they had no control, particularly as their own profits declined throughout the Tariff War (see Table V.7). By 1911 the Serbian Chamber of Industry, a private association of industrial owners, was asking the government to seek a foreign loan so that a large bank could be established exclusively for industrial credit.[63] Part of the reason for the demand, however, was the association's

60. Industrijska Komora Kr. Srbije, *Izveštaj*, 1910, Table 6.

61. *Politika*, Dec. 6, 1910, 1; Stojanović, *Govori i rasprave*, II, 109.

62. Državni Arhiv SR Srbije, MNP, T, 1910, 10901; Report of Sept. 22, 1910; *Bankarski glasnik*, no. 3 (March 1914), p. 51; Državni Arhiv SFR Jugoslavije, Annex, *zapisnici upravnog odbora Beogradske Zadruge*, 1911–12. The interest rate on discounts and current account loans from the major Belgrade banks had risen perhaps a point during the first years of the Tariff War from the 7–9 per cent level first touched in 1904–5. Belgrade rates again declined to that level by late 1909. Evidence for such behavior is unfortunately limited to scattered rate changes for a few important banks and a renewed decline in the ratio of net profits to total bank assets after 1908. *Srpske novine*, Feb.–June, 1903–12, *passim*; *Trgovinski glasnik*, Feb.–June, 1903–12, *passim*.

63. Industrijska Komora Kr. Srbije, *Izveštaj*, 1912–13, 78; Milenković, *Ekonomska istorija Beograda*, 124.

TABLE V.10

Selected Assets of Serbian Banks,* December 31, 1905 and 1911
(million dinars)

Year	Bills of Exchange	Current Account Loans	Secured Loans	Reserves
1905	45.7	22.3	7.0	4.3
1911	81.3	79.0	14.5	14.8

* Central and Mortgage Banks (Narodna and Hipotekarna Banka) excluded.

Sources: Ministarstvo Narodne Privrede, *Izveštaji*, 1906, Table V; Bajkitch, *Monnaies, banques et bourses Serbie*, 43.

concern that too many firms were being drawn into virtual partnerships with certain banks. The difficulties of incorporation or of placing any stock subsequently issued with Serbian investors left industrial enterprises with little recourse for external financing other than the banks.

Direct Bank Investment

Partnerships between banking and industry were not common until the last years of the Tariff War. The obvious explanation is that during the first part of the dispute the domestic banks were waiting for a speedy resumption of normal livestock trade with Austria-Hungary. This seems to be only part of the truth. The banks' restlessness before 1906 to find other business than discounting bills of exchange has already been noted. At the outbreak of the Tariff War, the two largest Belgrade banks (in terms of capital and assets) turned quickly to expediting agricultural trade through the alternate routes of the Aegean and the Black seas. First the Izvozna Banka, or export bank, and then the Beogradska Zadruga handled the majority of this trade, mainly through Salonika.[64] Other Belgrade banks joined these two in running a series of commercial agencies for the government throughout this area and western Europe. The entire operation proved unprofitable, and the agencies were soon handed back to the government. Italy came to be the only large customer for Salonika exports of livestock, and its own merchants took charge of most deliveries. By 1908 bad debts in the dealings of the Izvozna Banka surpassed a million dinars and forced the bank to reduce its paid-in capital;

64. Državni Arhiv SFR Jugoslavije, Annex, *godišnji izveštaj Izvozne Banke*, 1908, 6; Trgovačka Komora Kr. Srbije, *Izveštaj*, 1911, 14–15.

the Beogradska Zadruga recorded no net gain for its efforts as a commercial agent.[65]

The latter bank's lack of success coincided with its decision to enter an industrial venture in 1910, when it purchased three-quarters of the shares in a struggling new glass factory for 300,000 dinars.[66] The firm's output almost doubled the following year, reaching half a million dinars, or one-fourth of domestic demand.

Before the last years of the Tariff War there had been only two cases of direct bank investment in industry. In both of them it was the bank that furnished the entrepreneurial initiative in actually founding the firm. The Beogradska Trgovačka Banka had faced declining profits since 1903 on operations strongly weighted toward discounting. But after 1906 the bank received heavy savings and other deposits from Belgrade traders who had formerly dealt with Austrian or Hungarian creditors. Assets doubled in 1907, when they approached 20 million dinars, exceeding those of the Beogradska Zadruga and the Izvozna Banka. The virtual monopoly on alternate trade routes seized by the latter two banks left industry as the only other investment opportunity for the new resources of the Trgovačka Banka. In 1907, this bank founded the country's fourth cement plant. Its investment in the firm soon amounted to one million dinars. The plant had three times the combined horsepower and a larger capacity than any of the other Serbian plants, plus an output that exceeded total cement imports.

The other early investor, Belgrade's Prometna Banka, had also sought to repair sagging profits, but without comparable financial resources. All the same, that bank commanded technical competence and entrepreneurial daring that no other Serbian bank could match. Its advantage stemmed largely from one stockholder and official, Miloš Savčić, who reportedly was the only European-trained Serbian civil engineer who was not working for the army.[67] Savčić persuaded the bank's administrative board to let him construct Belgrade's first steam-powered sawmill with bank funds, albeit at his own risk in case of failure. The operation quickly furnished half of Serbian lumber production, pioneered timber shipments from the distant state forests to Belgrade, and helped cut Austrian imports from two-thirds to one-quarter of domestic sales during the Tariff War.

The main surge of direct investment by the Belgrade banks sprang from no such individuals or initiatives. Instead the pattern was that set by the

65. *Politika*, March 1, 1910, 1; Državni Arhiv SFR Jugoslavije, Annex, *godišnji izveštaj Izvozne Banke*, 1907, 15–16; Djordjević, *Carinski rat Austro-Ugarske i Srbije, 1906–1911*, 490–92.

66. Državni Arhiv SFR Jugoslavije, Annex, *zapisnici upravnog odbora Beogradske Zadruge*, 1911–12, Meetings of Jan. 11, 1911, and July 12, 1912; *Politika*, Feb. 10, 1911, 1.

67. Prometna Banka, *50 godina rada Inžinjera Miloša Savčića, 1889–1939*, 31, "Prometna Banka," *Narodno blagostanje*, I, no. 27 (1929), p. 441.

Beogradska Zadruga. The spread of support for existing industrial enterprises began in 1909, and it brought the direct investment of the Belgrade banks to more than 10 million dinars by 1910 and to over 14 million dinars by 1911.[68] Ten of the larger banks took part. Several ceramic brick factories, some textile plants, a button factory, a small slaughterhouse, and another sawmill had obtained several hundred thousand dinars apiece by the end of 1910. Only a small hemp factory and the sawmill were bank-founded firms. During 1911, the sawmill and construction investment of the Prometna Banka rose to 1.7 million dinars, while the Beogradska Zadruga increased its commitment to the new glass factory to 1.4 million dinars.

The large new investments for 1911 went to meat-packing, thus bringing the first bank capital to export expansion only when the resumption of normal trade with Austria-Hungary was imminent. These ventures were the 1.7 million dinars put into a plant for the further processing of meat by the Beogradska Trgovačka Banka and another bank's 500,000 dinar purchase of the majority of stock in the main Belgrade slaughterhouse, long held by the state lottery.[69] The production of the firm receiving the larger bank investment was insignificant, though, when compared with that of the slaughterhouse, which furnished almost one-fifth of Serbian export value in 1911.

Outside of Belgrade, only a couple of banks made a noteworthy contribution. The statutes of small town banks often included promises of industrial projects, but usually nothing came of them. In 1910, however, in the south Serbian rail junction of Niš, one bank promoted the founding of a leather factory. It accounted for all but 50,000 of the firm's 780,000 dinars in liabilities.[70] The following year, a Niš savings bank provided about the same amount and proportion of funds to build the country's only mechanically powered mill for spinning cotton.[71] Although they were in fact long-term investments, both of these sums appeared in the banks' accounts as short-term credit on current account.

The few company records available for Serbian industry do not make it clear how much this practice extended to the Belgrade banks. The Prometna Banka, for one, advanced 850,000 dinars to a newly established window glass factory on this basis. Whatever policy the other Belgrade banks pursued, they appear to have offered discounting or current account loans to those industrial enterprises in which they held a direct interest. Short-term credit was typically 30 to 50 per cent of such firms' liabilities; enterprises in which

68. Stanarević, *Beogradske banke u 1911 g.*, 23.

69. Državni Arhiv SFR Jugoslavije, Annex, *godišnji izveštaj Beogradske Trgovačke Banke*, 1911; Državni Arhiv SR Srbije, MNP, T, 1912, 4258, Stockholders meeting of Klanično Društvo, main Belgrade slaughterhouse, March 10, 1912.

70. Državni Arhiv SR Srbije, MNP, T, 1912, 2386 and 7827.

71. Državni Arhiv SFR Jugoslavije, MTI, no. 137, *godišnji izveštaj Niške Akcionarske Štedionice*, 1912, 24–25.

no bank held an interest based at most 10 to 20 per cent of their liabilities on external credit.[72] This disparity suggests that a major portion of the 4 million dinars in short-term credit made available to bank-affiliated firms in 1911 came from those financial institutions and not from the Narodna Banka. In any case, the shortage of working capital reported for Serbian industry in general was by all appearances less acute for firms tied to a particular bank.

Serbian banks made several indirect contributions to industrial development after 1906 that also deserve mention. The Prometna Banka and a few other banks in Belgrade and Niš established construction departments that included dredging operations for sand and gravel. Perhaps a million dinars was invested in all of them.[73] A number of banks invested an undetermined amount in 30 to 40 miles of railway construction, admittedly a small part of the 365 miles built from 1908 to 1912. The Beogradska Zadruga had successfully reorganized its insurance department after a scandal there in 1903, and it became the largest such agency in Belgrade by the time of the Tariff War. The department held assets of 5 million dinars, issued extensive fire insurance to industry, and, from 1910, issued accident insurance for industrial labor. Moreover, it was this department's steadily rising income that provided the funds for the bank so that it could raise its capital from 1 to 2.5 million dinars and begin industrial investment in 1910.[74] Several Belgrade banks, most prominently the Trgovačka Banka, set up so-called technical departments that specialized in importing agricultural and industrial machinery.

Obstacles to Direct Bank Investment

Any appraisal of direct bank investment in Serbian industry should recognize the political and economic obstacles facing domestic financial institutions.

Despite a few charges in the contemporary Serbian press of a government run by "bankokratija," and an occasional case of a bank using political influence to its own ends, the Serbian banks seem in the main to have been the weaker partners in their dealings with the state. A majority of the larger Belgrade banks were not allied to the ruling Radical party. The dominance of members from other political parties on their governing boards exposed them to parliamentary delay in receiving industrial concessions and discouraged any government assistance during the withdrawals prompted by the Annexation Crisis of 1908.

72. *Srpske novine*, Feb.–June, 1909–11, *passim*.

73. Stanarević, *Beogradske banke u 1911 g.*, 23; Prometna Banka, *50 godina rada Inžinjera Miloša Savčića, 1889–1939*, 85–6; Državni Arhiv SFR Jugoslavije, Annex, *godišnji izveštaj Srpske Centralne Banke*, 1911.

74. "Beogradska Zadruga," *Bankarstvo*, I, no. 8 (July, 1924), p. 379; Državni Arhiv SFR Jugoslavije, Annex, *godišnji izveštaj Beogradske Zadruge*, 1910, 9–10.

The Radical-affiliated banks were also open to parliamentary pressure, since the party did not have a workable majority in the National Assembly. In addition, the activities of the Radical banks were sometimes diverted to party or government purposes. The large Zemaljska Banka of Belgrade gave a percentage of its profits to the party press. Its energies during the Tariff War were largely, if vainly, devoted to merging with the Izvozna Banka in order to float another loan for the state in Paris.[75] The Radical ties of the Beogradska Zadruga undoubtedly helped draw that bank deeply into the partly unsuccessful and entirely unprofitable effort to redirect a large share of Serbian exports to the Mediterranean countries.

More widespread in its impact was the economic risk of undertaking a domestic industrial venture. Bank-supported enterprises were hardly immune to the difficulties facing all Serbian industry. Lack of sufficient urban demand hampered the cement factory of the Trgovačka Banka and the sawmill of the Prometna Banka. The annual reports of these and other banks speak constantly of the shortage of skilled domestic labor and railway transport, and the high cost of coal. The transport of timber to Belgrade proved to be an expensive proposition for the Prometna Banka's sawmill, an added cost that the firm did not hesitate to pass on to its customers.[76]

Of all the bank-supported firms, it was only this sawmill and the Belgrade slaughterhouse that showed a profit during this period, and then scarcely 10 per cent. It can be argued that most of these firms were in their first years of operation and could not expect significant gain. This was not the expectation of the investing banks, however, as the easy optimism of their annual reports makes plain.[77] This investment was undertaken with short-term profit in mind. We can only wonder whether the Serbian banks would have kept their funds in industry in the absence of increased profits, had the war not intervened. Indeed, the Trgovačka Bank sold its cement interests in 1913.

Yet, while it lasted, the interests of the Belgrade and Niš banks were crucial to the Serbian supply of fixed industrial capital during the Tariff War. They provided over two-thirds of the roughly 15 million dinars in new long-term domestic investment, milling and mining excluded, from 1906 through 1910. Although the total increment to domestic industry for 1911 is not available, the almost 4 million dinars added by Serbian banks was in all probability a large fraction of it. Among the various branches of industry,

75. Kukla, *Razvitak kreditne organizacije u Srbiji*, 70; Staatsarchiv, AR, 70 F 23, Serbien 3, September 22, 1910.

76. Prometna Banka, *50 godina rada Inžinjera Miloša Savčića, 1889–1939*, 75–6; Državni Arhiv SR Srbije, MNP, T, 1907, 38/35, August 11, 1907; *Trgovinski glasnik*, Jan. 4, 1908, 1.

77. The annual reports of the Beogradska Zadruga and the Beogradska Trgovačka Banka, for instance, reflect full confidence of immediate significant profits in their respective glass and cement investments. Državni Arhiv SFR Jugoslavije, Annex, *godišnji izveštaj Beogradske Zagruge*, 1910, and *godišnji izveštaj Beogradske Trgovačke Banke*, 1908.

the banks' support was clearly decisive only in construction materials. Yet these were important as the only import substitutes which used domestic materials and which furnished inputs for the rest of industry, Serbian banks had afforded their manufacturers virtually all existing investment capital, and a good portion of their short-term credit as well. For export expansion, on the other hand, the belated bank investment of little more than 2 million dinars in meat-packing cannot be called decisive. At least twice that sum had already been invested in that branch of industry by 1911.[78]

THE RELUCTANT IMPERIALISM OF FOREIGN BANKS

Foreign financial institutions furnished very little industrial capital and credit before 1911, and even during that year they probably failed to surpass the increment provided by the Serbian banks. This was not for lack of resources for individual banks. While total assets of foreign banks in Belgrade in that year were just 70 million dinars, compared with 650 million for domestic banking, there were just four of these foreign banks, and their assets ranged from 10 to 40 million dinars apiece. But only the smallest of them, and that a Czech bank acting without the support of European financial centers, made a measurable contribution to industry. With one exception, again of a Czech bank, there was virtually no buying into Serbian financial institutions.

Some of the mythology surrounding the nature of European imperialism suffers from this evidence. Austrian and Hungarian banks could have obtained a controlling interest in Serbian industry, banking, and the economy in general. But they failed to use the Dual Monarchy's political influence over the dynasty ruling Serbia until 1903, and they did not use the Monarchy's overwhelming hold on Serbian exports through 1905. Neither did the great banks of the Entente Powers seize the occasion of the Tariff War to support the industrial independence of their opponent's former enclave, even though Serbia had become a potential ally and a field for their own exploitation. The large German banks committed almost no funds to Serbian industry, for the same considerations of commercial risk that had restrained their activities in Bulgaria and the Ottoman Empire.[79]

The Austrian and Hungarian Banks

In the first years after 1878 it had appeared that a powerful Habsburg presence would enter Serbia, in the form of the Viennese Länderbank.

78. Industrijska Komora Kr. Srbije, *Izveštaj*, 1910, Table 4.

79. German economic activity in Serbia is summarized in Milić, "Nemački kapital u Srbiji do 1918 g.", *Istorijski časopis*, XII–XIII (1963), 319–40. For Bulgaria, see Flaningam, "German Economic Controls in Bulgaria, 1894–1914," *American and East European Review*, XX (Feb. 1961), 99–108, and for the Ottoman Empire, Trumpener, *Germany and the Ottoman Empire, 1914–1918*, 6–12.

Founded in 1880 on the initiative of Eugène Bontoux, the French financier and former director of the Austrian state railways, the Länderbank enjoyed close ties with the Finance Minister of the Dual Monarchy and had taken a 30 per cent share in the Serbian railway concession won by Bontoux's ambitious Société de l'Union Générale. In 1881 the bank joined Bontoux in proposing that they set up the long-discussed Serbian central bank as their private institution, empowered to negotiate all state loans and to issue stock for industrial or commercial ventures. The fall of the Société in the following year brought the Länderbank into the conservative mainstream of Viennese banking.[80] The bank renegotiated the 90 million dinar railway loan, but it confined its stockholdings to a small fraction of the shares outstanding. Its only other undertaking was the purchase of part ownership in the Serbian tobacco monopoly and the financing of its new factory in 1886. When the Serbian government nationalized the tobacco monopoly in 1889, and the railways in 1890, the Länderbank retired from direct investment.

The Srpska Kreditna Banka, the Länderbank's Belgrade branch from 1883, did not have much impact on the structure of the Serbian economy either. The bank earned a reputation for very cautious dealings in short-term credit for agricultural trade. Its paid-in capital never surpassed the original 1.2 million dinars, nor did its total assets go over 10 million dinars. The latter figure was half that of the total assets of the largest domestic banks at the start of the Tariff War. Its only ventures outside trade were the loan in 1902 of 3 million dinars to an ill-fated German project, headed by a Länderbank official, to establish a sugar factory, and the purchase in 1904 of some stock in a lesser Belgrade slaughterhouse.[81] The bank made no effort to buy into the main Belgrade slaughterhouse, which had been set up in 1897 and took over most of the country's meat-packing after 1906. While the bank reduced—but never eliminated—its credits to Serbia's unprocessed agricultural exports during the course of the Tariff War, it participated in no industrial projects until late in 1911. This was just the reverse of what the diplomats on the Ballplatz desired, i.e. the cessation of all credit for livestock or grain exports and the penetration of existing Serbian industry. For the Habsburg government had belatedly recognized that it was in its national interest to obtain some leverage in Serbia's emerging industrial sector. The Austrian consul in Belgrade noted regretfully that the glass factory, which had opened in 1908, had first sought help from the Srpska Kreditna Banka before turning to the domestic Beogradska Zadruga. "The industrialization

80. Länderbank, *Ordentliche Generalversammlung*, 1882, I, 9, 1883, II, 13, and 1887, VII; März, *Österreichische Industrie- und Bankpolitik in der Zeit Franz Josephs I*, 222–24; Royaume de Belgique, *Receuil consulaire*, 1883, XLV, 271–72.

81. Opened in 1899, the sugar factory was in fact forced to close in 1902 because of competition from lower-priced Austrian imports. It reopened again in late 1905, but under new management. Archives des Affaires Étrangères, CP, NS 26, 1908–12, V, 188.

of this country will not stop," he commented, "so at least it should go forward without too much damage for us."[82]

The one Belgrade affiliate of a Budapest bank was hardly any more help than the Srpska Kreditna Banka in penetrating Serbian industry in the Habsburg interest. After the Congress of Berlin in 1878, the Pester Ungarische Kommercialbank had sent a representative to survey prospects in the newly constituted Balkan states. This first appraisal of the Serbian economy did not much encourage the Budapest bank, and it was not until 1889 that a partnership was concluded with the existing Andrejević bank in Belgrade. During the same year, in Bucharest, the Kommercialbank also opened the renowned Marmarosch Bank, an institution that played a large part in Romanian industrial development.[83] But these two new banks did not follow the same policy. The new Belgrade branch turned instead to several forward loans for the Serbian government in order to establish its position in the country. Andrejević and Co. thereafter became the semiofficial bank for transactions in foreign currency, coined issues of silver dinars for the government, and furnished most of the short-term credit for Serbian traders dealing with the Budapest market. The advent of the Tariff War did not prompt the bank to reduce agricultural credit sharply until 1908, nor did the conflict persuade the bank to divert any of its 10 million dinars in total assets to invest in or to credit Serbian industrial enterprises. Plans to support an existing sodium plant and a new asphalt works were studied in 1907–8, but they were dropped.

After 1908, moreover, the Andrejević bank was scarcely in a position to offer support to Serbian industry. During the Annexation Crisis of that year the bank had infuriated Belgrade commercial circles by rushing all of its reserves to a town on Hungarian territory and by withdrawing lines of credit from even its most solvent customers. As a result, Andrejević and Co. subsequently faced blocked access to its dinar deposits at the Narodna Banka, loss of government accounts, opposition from the Ministry of National Economy, and a shortage of new customers. It lacked the political connections with the leading Serbian parties (the Radicals and the Independent Radicals) to undo this damage, despite the effort it made to improve its standing through an incorporation joined by the prestigious Berliner Handelsgesellschaft as equal partner. The bank also appealed several times to the Austro-Hungarian and German governments for their diplomatic intervention, but it was consistently refused.[84] The bank's business turnover continued to fall, dropping by one-half from 1910 to 1911.

82. Staatsarchiv, AR, 70 F 23, Serbien 3, Sept. 22, 1910.

83. *Hundert Jahre Pester Ungarische Kommercialbank, 1841–1941*, 131. On the role of the Marmarosch Bank in Romanian Industry, see Spulber, *The State and Economic Development in Eastern Europe*, 97.

84. Staatsarchiv, AR, 70 F 23, Serbien 3, Sept. 22, 1910, Sept. 28, 1911, and March 9, 1912.

La Banque Franco-Serbe et les Affaires Plus Grandes

The decline of the Hungarian bank left a gap in the network of Serbian financial institutions, and it is not surprising that it was the French interests who filled that opening.[85] Before the Tariff War, the large German banks had regarded any Serbian investment as too risky. Their continuing lack of interest in founding a specifically German bank has been called the best explanation for the decision to place funds instead in the existing Andrejević operation.[86] At the same time, the German banks refused the requests of several domestic Serbian banks for German credit. Plans for an Anglo-Serbian Bank had been drawn up in 1906, but, like the Russian Petersburger Bank's plans to found a Belgrade branch, they never materialized. Opposition from Serbian exporters, already fearful of an Italian monopoly in handling their Salonika trade, prevented the creation of an Italo-Serbian Bank in 1910.[87]

The French desire to found a separate bank had several origins. Their large copper-mining investment, 7 million dinars by 1910, depended on the Austrian and Hungarian banks in Belgrade for short-term credit. More important, Paris banks held 70 per cent of the Serbian public debt. The Quai d'Orsay saw the chance to consolidate this advantage, at the expense of the Hungarian Andrejević bank, into a French-backed financial institution that would serve to influence the policies of the Serbian government. All the same, the initiative for the project belonged to the Serbian side. After the merger of two large Belgrade banks, the Zemaljska and the Izvozna, had fallen through in 1909, members of the Serbian government seeking access to further foreign loans approached the Ottoman Bank, the Bardak concern, and several other Paris houses about a merger between certain Serbian and French banks. Only internal political rivalries in Serbia prevented the participation of one of the Paris banks. A small 60,000 franc subsidy from the French government, and a stock issue of one million francs, taken up by the Ottoman Bank and several other Paris houses, allowed the Banque Franco-Serbe to open in mid-1910.[88]

Its first order of business was to court customers away from Andrejević

85. For a description of the tendency of French finance to exploit such foreign opportunities, often for political rather than economic reasons, see Cameron, *France and the Economic Development of Europe, 1800–1914*, 494–501.

86. Staatsarchiv, AR, 70 F 23, Serbien 11, May 29, 1912. Active interest by German financial circles in founding their own Serbian bank appeared only in 1912, a few months before the outbreak of the First Balkan War, and then was aimed at undercutting the Andrejević bank, as noted in Aleksić-Pejković, *Odnosi Srbije ca Francuskom i Engleskom, 1903–1914*, 306.

87. Staatsarchiv, AR, 70 F 23, Serbien 7, Jan. 22, 1911.

88. *Ibid.*, 70 F 23, Serbien 3, Sept. 22, 1910; Archives Nationales, F 30, 349, Sept. 6, 1910; Archives des Affaires Étrangères, CP, NS 26, 1908–12, V, July 6, 1909.

and Co. The new bank located its Belgrade office directly across the hall from the Hungarian affiliate, and it put 4 million dinars of short-term credit into circulation during its first month of operation, at 1 per cent under the Andrejević rate. In addition to former Andrejević clients, the bank favored the domestic banks associated with the Radical party, which were generally small interior savings institutions or the newer, less well-endowed Belgrade banks. Although industry was charged an interest rate about 4 per cent higher than other clients, it was included in this flow of current account loans.[89]

The bank's attitude toward long-term investment, however, gave no support to domestic industry at all. Its management was from the start concerned only with what one French diplomatic report called "les affaires plus grandes," that is, such investments as railway construction or public loans that could win political influence and serve the interests of the bank's supporters in the Serbian government.[90] But in spite of the flood of rumored projects the bank made no agreement on railway construction until two months before the Balkan Wars began, in 1912, and it made only a single public loan, one of 30 million dinars.[91] This loan was advanced to the city of Belgrade for the construction of public buildings. By 1912 the Serbian Minister of Finance was disparaging the bank's continued reluctance to participate in industrial or fixed investment projects. The Quai d'Orsay dismissed the Serbian anxiety as "impatient ardor"; the director of the Banque Franco-Serbe minimized the need for French industrial investment in the absence of significant Austro-Hungarian penetration.[92]

The Contribution of the Czech and Croatian Banks

Political calculation played no decisive part in the decisions of the several foreign banks that did make a direct contribution to Serbian industrial stirrings. These were banks from the Dual Monarchy's Czech and Croatian lands, areas which obviously lacked the Great Power rationale for the role sought by the Banque Franco-Serbe. Admittedly, French diplomatic reports

89. *Bankarski glasnik*, no. 3 (March, 1914), p. 51; Staatsarchiv, AR, 70 F 23, Serbien 3, Sept. 22, 1910; Archives Nationales, F 30, 349, Nov. 16, 1910. The total of 24.5 million dinars in current account loans outstanding for the bank by the end of 1911 approached half the probable amount of working capital in Serbian industrial enterprises at the start of the year (see Table V.8). Archives Nationales, 65 AQ, A-165, *godišnji izveštaj Banque Franco-Serbe*, 1911–12.

90. Archives Nationales, F 30, 349, Nov. 16, 1910.

91. The bank did make a potential contribution to the Serbian economy by furnishing a French expert to reform the state's bookkeeping system. His efforts were well received by the Serbian government, and they led to the adoption of a centralized system of accounting that included most state agencies by mid-1911. Archives des Affaires Étrangères, CP, NS 26, 1908–12, V, Aug. 16, 1911.

92. *Ibid.*, Oct. 21, 1911, and July 20, 1912.

viewed such support as a Habsburg plan to penetrate the Serbian economy under Slavic guise, while some of the Serbian and Czech press suggested that these activities were an effort toward Slavic co-operation in the face of Austro-German domination.[93] The latter argument may be partly true, but there is no doubt that these banks were led in the main by a desire to use their funds as profitably as they could.

As Richard Rudolph has demonstrated elsewhere, the expanding Czech banks of this period found themselves barred from widespread industrial investment in their own lands by the predominance of the large Vienna banks and, after 1907, by a general economic recession.[94] Several were attracted to Serbia, which had a freer field for investment and an 8 to 10 per cent range of interest rates that was several points above the Czech level.

In 1910, after a couple of unsuccessful industrial investments at home, Prague's Uverena Banka opened a Belgrade branch. It soon became the center of the parent bank's operations. Although total assets never exceeded the 10 million dinar level of the Andrejević bank and the Länderbank branch, the Prague affiliate operated in a far more ambitious fashion than either. It immediately assembled a group of Czech technicians to prepare plans for putting 3 million dinars into a new sugar factory, the second in Serbia.[95] Arrangements were also made for a purely Serbian supply of sugar beets. By 1911 the factory was completed, and it matched the capacity of the first sugar factory. In the following year the bank put over 2 million dinars into modernizing a brewery south of Belgrade.

Another Czech bank, the Prague Sporobanka, provided most of the funds that allowed the domestic Beogradska Trgovačka Banka to raise its paid-in capital from 1 to 2 million dinars in 1910 and to avoid liquidation of its industrial investments. The Prague Sporobanka sent one of its own officials to help supervise the operations of its Belgrade partner, invested in setting up a technical department to sell Czech machinery, and provided a mortgage loan of 600,000 dinars for building a rail connection to the cement plant of the Trgovačka Banka.[96] These Czech advances allowed the Serbian bank to expand its facilities for short-term credit.

The largest Prague bank, the Živnostenska Banka, bought a 25 per cent share in the Länderbank's Belgrade branch in 1911. The influence of the Živnostenska finally pushed the cautious Srpska Kreditna Banka into

93. *Ibid.*, Feb. 20, 1912; Archives Nationales, F 30, 349, Feb. 11, 1911, *Odjek*, January 22, 1911, 1.

94. Rudolph, *The Role of Financial Institutions in the Czech Lands, 1880–1914*, 227–31, 291.

95. Staatsarchiv, AR, 70 F 23, Serbien 3, Sept. 22, 1910.

96. *Ibid.*; Državni Arhiv SFR Jugoslavije, Annex, *godišnji izveštaj Beogradske Trgovačke Banke*, 1910–11; *Politika*, March 1, 1912, 1.

investing 600,000 dinars in a Belgrade leather factory later in the year, after the Tariff War had ended.[97]

What amount of short-term credit these several Czech banks furnished Serbian industry is not clear. Serbian complaints indicate, however, that there was no departure from the Banque Franco-Serbe's practice of charging industrial enterprises 4 per cent above the normal rate of interest.[98]

The Srpska Banka u Zagrebu, a Zagreb institution formed by Serbs in the Croatian lands of the Dual Monarchy, also diverted some of its funds to projects in Serbia. Among them were a long-term credit of 1 million dinars, given in conjunction with some Hungarian investors, to the major Serbian textile complex, and a number of mortgage loans for industrial construction.[99] While an obvious ethnic and perhaps political bond was at work here, by 1908 the Srpska Banka u Zagrebu found itself with larger capital and savings deposits on which to base its lending than any bank in Serbia. Yet the Zagreb institution was located in the same stagnating economy, dominated by the Vienna and Budapest banks, as the Czechs were.[100] Moreover, any economic initiative in the Croatian lands was suppressed by the restrictive atmosphere in this Hungarian half of the Monarchy.

One parallel emerges between the activities of foreign and domestic banks in prewar Serbia. It was limited or reduced opportunities for earnings in existing banking operations that turned certain financial institutions toward industry, essentially for short-run profits. Plans for long-term economic development or the desire for political influence were at most marginal interests.

SUMMARY AND CONCLUSIONS

Industry remained a minor part of Serbia's backward, agrarian economy on the eve of the Balkan Wars, but rapid growth of private manufacturing based on mechanically powered factory production was nonetheless under way. The Tariff War with Austria-Hungary from 1906 to 1911 undoubtedly afforded the occasion for most of the mini-spurt. This should not obscure the fact that the unexpected Serbian ability to respond to the exigencies of the dispute derived from the nation's financial structure. Fresh from the long Ottoman domination, Serbia had experienced no other structural changes sufficient to explain any semblance of industrial advance.

97. Archives Nationales, F. 30, 349, Feb. 7, 1911; Länderbank, *Ordentliche Generalversammlung*, 1911, XXX.

98. Kukla, *Srbské peněžnictví a česky kapital*, 34; *Bankarski glasnik*, no. 3, (March 1914), p. 51.

99. Staatsarchiv, AR, 70 F 23, Serbien 3, Sept. 22, 1910.

100. Šidek, Gross, Karaman, and Šepić, *Povijest hrvatskog naroda, 1860–1914*, 260–5, describes the difficulties of the Croatian economy in the last prewar decade.

Well before Serbia's full political independence in 1878, the export of livestock to the Habsburg lands had begun to accumulate capital in the hands of a trading class rising from peasant ranks. Demand for industrial goods grew as an increasing amount of this income found its way into imports of Austrian manufactures and construction materials. The tax needs of the Serbian state accelerated the monetization process begun by foreign trade. After 1878, however, rising government revenues and a series of large foreign loans were largely applied either to military and administrative purposes or to debt repayment. Aside from a certain amount of railway construction, Serbian industry received little more than tax and tariff exemptions from the state.

Some of the European-style financial institutions that evolved during these later decades proved flexible enough by the time of the Tariff War to transcend their early experience and to provide industry with a sizable part of its long-term capital plus a much smaller amount of initiative and short-term credit. Even this limited transition was not an easy one. The first Serbian brush with aggressive investment banking had ended disastrously in the European economic crisis of 1873. The merchants who founded a Serbian central bank, the Narodna Banka, a decade later sought only to afford short-term export credit in a time of recurring trade deficits and to assure themselves and the government a stable supply of domestic money in the face of a depreciating Austrian currency and a mounting foreign debt. The preference of the Narodna Banka, which was the sole bank of issue, for crediting other banks, rather than establishing its own branches, quickly spawned a network of small savings institutions outside Belgrade, but these were capable only of discounting bills of exchange. It remained for the credit shortage of the early 1890's, occasioned by interruptions of livestock exports to Austria-Hungary and the government's efforts to reduce or at least restrict the supply of silver-backed currency because of rising gold speculation, to prompt the founding of several larger joint-stock banks in Belgrade. Still, these were unit banks, and they were even further divided politically. They were heavily dependent on short-term liabilities, and they were regularly denied discounting facilities by the central bank when the government's inflexible maximum for note issue was reached.

During the Tariff War there was an increased if not overwhelming concentration of paid-in capital and savings deposits in the main Belgrade banks, apparently a diversion of merchant funds from the crippled livestock trade. This process gave a number of banks enough longer-term liabilities to permit the large dispensations sought by young industrial ventures. The response of these financial institutions was, all the same, generally slow and invariably geared to the considerations of short-term profit that had brought them into being. They continued to expand their proportions of current account loans at the expense of discounting bills of exchange, but directed them mainly to imports and not, as had been the case throughout central Europe, to industry. The central bank alone gave industrial firms short-term credit that may have matched that of all other domestic banks, but those banks, in any case, charged industry a higher than normal interest rate. Together with the central bank they furnished probably less than half the working capital added to industrial resources during the Tariff War. Already prodded before 1906 by declining profit margins for agricultural trade, the Belgrade banks turned first to expediting unprocessed exports over alternate routes during the initial years of the dispute. Only at its conclusion did they contribute any substantial direct investment to meat-packing, which was the leading industrial export, and then they put just a fraction of their existing capital in this activity.

In addition to these lesser and hesitant responses, the Serbian banks made the decisive contribution to the growth of import substitutes which were based on domestic materials and which provided inputs for the rest of industry. These institutions furnished about two-thirds of all fixed industrial investment from 1906 through 1910, and most of it went into the manufacture of construction materials previously imported from Austria-Hungary. The partnership arrangements binding together bank and enterprise were sometimes a substitute for the firm's incorporation (successful issues of industrial stock were rare in Serbia). They were usually a guarantee of much larger access to short-term loans than other industrial undertakings enjoyed. With only two exceptions, however, this activity occurred toward the end of the Tariff War, and it involved assistance to already established firms.

Yet when measured against the context in which they operated, the ability of the Serbian banks to offer even this rather spotty response to the opportunities of the Tariff War becomes meaningful. The major political parties and the powerful state bureaucracy were preoccupied with large foreign loans mainly for military purposes. They did far more to draw the banks into these schemes than to promote the industrialization of which they sometimes vaguely spoke. Political divisions among the Serbian banks grew rather than diminished, as the ruling Radical party sought to repair its lack of influence in the larger financial institutions. New unit banks continually appeared and there were no mergers of existing ones. Bank officials with a bent for industrial entreperneurship were rare. Over half of the impressive aggregate of bank assets was located in the central bank and the mortgage banks, the former devoting less than 2 per cent of its assets to industrial purposes and the latter none. In any case, there was limited domestic demand, and supplies of coal and transport were inadequate, and, what was more fundamental, the economy faced a serious shortage of trained managers and skilled workers. All these deficiencies, joined with international uncertainty following the Habsburg annexation of Bosnia-Herzegovina in 1908, made Serbian industrial investment a chancy business.

The reluctance of the Great Power banks to participate in industry is partly a testimony of these hazards. But it is also evidence of the fact that a concern with political rather than economic influence directed the policies of European governments in the age of imperialism. The concept of political influence through industrial penetration was very slow to develop. When it did, the existence of domestic financial institutions and their industrial activities denied the Dual Monarchy, the small nation's chief antagonist, the high ground in the Serbian economy that it belatedly contemplated at the end of the Tariff War. And in successfully promoting the development of some domestic substitutes for imports from Austria-Hungary, the Serbian banks served the political independence that was, after all, the country's most urgent priority before World War I. At the same time, these financial institutions probably served the long-run process of economic modernization better than either the country's cautious trading class, tied to the practice of traditional commerce, or its preoccupied national government, caught up in the crosscurrents of international rivalry.

BIBLIOGRAPHY*

A. Manuscript Collections

Archives des Affaires Étrangères, Paris. Both the *correspondence politique* (CP) and the *correspondence consulaire* (CC) between the French foreign ministry and its representatives in Serbia are informative about Serbian state borrowing and its connection to the Paris banks.

Archives Nationales, Paris. Under series F 30 are materials collected for the French Ministry of Finance that cover the inception of the Banque Franco-Serbe as well as the general outline of Serbian economic history.

Državni Arhiv SFR Jugoslavije, Annex, Belgrade. Contains largely complete series of annual reports (*godišnji izveštaji*) and some minutes of administrative board meetings (*zapisnici upravnog odbora*) from a number of the major domestic banks in Belgrade.

Državni Arhiv SR Srbije, Belgrade. Affords a variety of reports submitted to the Serbian Ministry of National Economy, or *Ministarstvo Narodne Privrede* (MNP), by domestic industrial firms and banks.

Haus, Hof und Staatsarchiv, Vienna. The *Administrative Registratur* (AR) contains Habsburg diplomatic correspondence emanating from Vienna and Belgrade that provides the most continuous and comprehensive account of Serbian financial and economic developments available for the period after 1898.

---

* Since Serbian economic history is virgin territory to most western scholars, the editor requested Professor Lampe to provide an introductory bibliography on the subject. [Ed. note.]

B. Official Publications

Berichte der K. und K. österreichische-ungarische Konsularämter, 1900–1912, vol. II, Vienna, 1906–14.

Državopis Srbije (*State Records of Serbia*), vols I–XX, Belgrade, 1855–94.

Godišnji izveštaj Narodne Banke (*Annual Report of the National Bank*), Belgrade, 1885–1914.

Industrijska Komora Kr. Srbije (Chamber of Industry of the Kingdom of Serbia), *Izveštaj o radu i stanju industrije* (*Report on the Work and Status of Industry*), 1910, 1911 and 1912–13, Belgrade, 1911–14.

K. und K. österreichische Handelsministerium, *Serbien, Wirtschaftsverhältnisse*, 1909–11, Vienna, 1912.

———, *Statistik des auswärtigen Handels des österreichische-ungarische Zollgebietes*, Vienna, 1906–1914.

Ministarstvo Narodne Privrede, *Izveštaji podneceni Ministarstvu Narodne Privrede* (*Reports Submitted to the Ministry of National Economy*), 1906, 1907, and 1908–9, Belgrade, 1907–10.

Narodna Banka (National Bank), *Narodna Banka, 1884–1909*, Belgrade, 1909.

———, *Narodna Banka, 1884–1934*, Belgrade, 1934.

Prethodni rezultati popisa stanovništva i domaće stoke, Dec. 31, 1910 (*Preliminary Results of the Census of Population and Domestic Livestock, Dec. 31, 1910*), Belgrade, 1911.

Royaume de Belgique, *Receuil consulaire*, vols. XLV–155, Brussels, 1883–1912.

Samostalna Monopolska Uprava, *Račun izravnjanja* (*Balance Sheet of the Independent Monopoly Administration*), Belgrade, 1896–1914.

Srpski Centralni Komitet, *Srbija u imovnom pogledu pre, za vreme i posle svetskog rata* (*Serbian Wealth Before, During and After the World War*), Geneva, 1918.

Statistički godišnjak Kr. Srbije (*Statistical Yearbook of the Kingdom of Serbia*), 1893–1908, vols. I–XII, Belgrade, 1895–1913.

Statistike spoljne trgovine Kr. Srbije (*Foreign Trade Statistics of the Kingdom of Serbia*), 1909–11, Belgrade, 1910–12.

Stenografske beleške Narodne Skupštine Srbije (*Stenographic Reports of the National Assembly of Serbia*), Belgrade, 1879–1914.

Trgovačka Komora Kr. Srbije (Chamber of Commerce of the Kingdom of Serbia), *Izveštaj za god, 1911* (*Report for 1911*), Belgrade, 1912.

Završni račun državnih prihoda i rashoda Kr. Srbije (*Closed Accounts of State Income and Expenses*), 1900–1912, Belgrade, 1901–13.

Zbornik zakona i uredaba Kr. Srbije (*Register of Laws and Regulations of the Kingdom of Serbia*), vols. 1–63, Belgrade, 1840–1910.

C. Newspapers, Periodicals, Collective Works

Odjek (Belgrade)

Politika (Belgrade)

Srpske novine (Belgrade)

Trgovinski glasnik (Belgrade)

Bankarski glasnik (Belgrade), 1912–14.

Bankarstvo (Zagreb), "Beogradska Zadruga," I, no. 8 (July 1924).

Delo (Belgrade), "Novčani zavodi u Srbiji" ("Financial Institutions in Serbia"), no. 11 (1896).

Narodno blagostanje (Belgrade), "Prometna Banka," I, no. 27 (1929).

25 godišnica Beogradske Zadruge, 1882–1907 (*25 Years of the Beogradska Zadruga, 1882–1907*), Belgrade, 1908.

Hundert Jahre Pester Ungarische Kommercialbank, Budapest, 1941.

Prometna Banka, *50 godina rada Inžinjera Miloša Savčića, 1889–1939* (*50 Years Work of Engineer Miloš Savčić, 1889–1939*), Belgrade, 1939.

Proizvodne snage NR Srbije (*Productive Forces of the PR Serbia*), Belgrade, 1953.

D. Other Works Cited

Aleksić-Pejković, Ljiljana, *Odnosi Srbije ca Francuskom i Engleskom, 1903–1914* (*The Relations of Serbia with France and England 1903–1914*), Belgrade, 1965.

Andrić, N., Antić, R., Veselinović, R., and Djurić-Zamolo, D., *Beograd u XIX veku* (*Belgrade in the 19th Century*), Belgrade, 1967.

Avramović, Mihailo, *Naše seljačko gazdinstvo* (*Our Peasant Farming*), Belgrade, 1927.

Bajkitch, Velimir, *Monnaies, banques et bourses en Serbie*, Paris, 1919.

Berend, I. T., and Ranki, Gy., "The Development of the Manufacturing Industry in Hungary, 1900–1944," *Studia Historica* (Budapest), no. 19 (1960).

Cameron, Rondo, *Banking in the Early Stages of Industrialization*, New York: Oxford University Press, 1967.

————, *France and the Economic Development of Europe, 1800–1914*. Princeton: Princeton University Press, 1961.

Cvijetić, Leposava, "Prva Srpska Banka" ("The First Serbian Bank"), *Istorijski glasnik* (Belgrade), 2–3 (1964), 97–121.

————, "Pokušaji osnivanja prvih srpskih banaka" ("Attempts to Found the First Serbian Banks"), *Finansija* (Belgrade) 1–2 (1965), 119–23.

Dimitrijević, Sergej, *Gradska privreda starog Leskovca* (*The Town Economy of Old Leskovac*), Leskovac, 1952.

Djordjević, Dimitrije, *Carinski rat Austro-Ugarske i Srbije, 1906–1911* (*The Tariff War Between Austria-Hungary and Serbia, 1906–1911*), Belgrade, 1962.

Feis, Herbert, *Europe, The World's Banker, 1870–1914*, New Haven: Yale University Press, 1930. Citation from subsequent edition, New York: W. W. Norton and Co., 1965.

Flaningam, M. L., "German Economic Controls in Bulgaria, 1894–1914," *American and East European Review*, XX (Feb. 1961), 99–108.

Gerschenkron, Alexander, "Some Aspects of Industrialization in Bulgaria, 1878–1939," in his *Economic Backwardness in Historical Perspective*, New York: Praeger, 1965, 198–234.

Glomazić, Momir, *Istorija državne hipotekarne banke, 1862–1932* (*The History of the State Mortgage Bank, 1862–1932*), Belgrade, 1933.

Goldsmith, Raymond, *Financial Structure and Development*, New Haven: Yale

University Press, 1969.

Grgašević, Jaša, *Industrija Srbije i Crne Gore* (*The Industry of Serbia and Montenegro*), Zagreb, 1924.

Jovanović, Slobodan, *Vlada Aleksandra Obrenovića* (*The Regime of Alexander Obrenović*), vol. II, Belgrade, 1935.

Kukla, Stanislav, *Razvitak kreditne organizacije u Srbiji* (*The Development of Credit Organization in Serbia*), Zagreb, 1924.

——, *Srbské peněžnictvi a česky kapital*, Prague, 1912.

März, Eduard, *Österreichische Industrie- und Bankpolitik in der Zeit Franz Josephs I*, Vienna: Europa Verlag, 1968.

Milenković, Vladislav, *Ekonomska istorija Beograda* (*The Economic History of Belgrade*), Belgrade, 1932.

Milić, Danica, *Trgovina Srbije, 1815–1839* (*The Commerce of Serbia, 1815–1839*), Belgrade, 1959.

——, "Nemački kapital u Srbiji do 1918 g." ("German Capital in Serbia Until 1918"), *Istorijski časopis* (Belgrade), XII–XIII (1963).

Milošević, S. B., *Spoljna trgovina Srbije, 1843–1875* (*The Foreign Trade of Serbia, 1843–1875*), Belgrade, 1902.

Mirosavljević, J., *Naši novčani zavodi* (*Our Financial Institutions*), Šabac, 1888.

Nedeljković, Milorad, *Istorija srpskih državnih dugova* (*The History of the Serbian State Debts*), Belgrade, 1909.

Rudolph, Richard, *The Role of Financial Institutions in the Industrialization of the Czech Lands, 1880–1914*, Unpublished Ph.D. dissertation, University of Wisconsin, 1968.

Šidek, J., Gross, M., Karaman, I., Šepić, D., *Povijest hrvatskog naroda, 1860–1914* (*The History of the Croatian People, 1860–1914*), Zagreb, 1968.

Spulber, Nicholas, *The State and Economic Development in Eastern Europe*, New York: Random House, 1966.

Stanarević, Nikola, *Beogradske banke u 1911 g.* (*The Belgrade Banks in 1911*), Belgrade, 1912.

Stojanović, Kosta, *Govori i rasprave* (*Speeches and Debates*), 3 vols., Belgrade, 1910–14.

Tomasevich, Jozo, *Peasants, Politics and Economic Change in Yugoslavia*, Palo Alto: Stanford University Press, 1955.

Trumpener, Ulrich, *Germany and the Ottoman Empire, 1914–1918*, Princeton: Princeton University Press, 1968.

Ugričić, Miodrag, *Novčani sistem Jugoslavije* (*The Monetary System of Yugoslavia*), Belgrade, 1968.

Vucinich, Wayne, *Serbia Between East and West, 1903–1908*, Palo Alto: Stanford University Press, 1954.

Vučo, Nikola, *Raspadanje esnafa u Srbije* (*The Collapse of the Guilds in Serbia*), 2 vols., Belgrade, 1954–55.

——, *Privredna istorija Srbije do prvog svetskog rata* (*The Economic History of Serbia Until the First World War*), Belgrade, 1958.

CHAPTER VI

Japan 1868–1930:
A Revised View

KOZO YAMAMURA

When one examines the available literature in Japanese and other languages on the role played by the banking system during Japan's industrialization, an apparent consensus emerges: the modern banking system, strongly encouraged by the government, was extremely important in providing the necessary industrial capital and, often, entrepreneurial guidance to rapidly growing industrial firms during the Meiji years (1868–1911).[1] One often encounters observations that the Japanese case was very much like the German case, in which one finds close bank-firm relationships, extensive investment banking, and strong governmental intervention and assistance.[2] This consensus, however, rests on extremely sketchy quantitative evidence and on the general observations of Japanese scholars who were not, as a rule, interested in examining the subject in an international perspective. In short, the generalization that the Japanese case was akin to the German case has never been examined closely.[3]

1. Of the numerous Japanese sources expressing this view, Toshihiko Katō's *Ginkō-shiron* (An Historical Treatise on Japanese Banking) (Tokyo, 1957) is perhaps best. In English, G. C. Allen's *A Short Economic History of Modern Japan* (London, 1946) expresses this view succinctly.

2. For example, compare passages by Gerschenkron and Clapham on the role of German banks in industrialization and bank-firm relationships with what Japanese economic historians, especially Marxists, had to say on Japanese banks. Their fortuitous similarity is evident. John H. Clapham, *The Economic Development of France and Germany* (Cambridge, 1966), p. 390. A. Gerschenkron, *Economic Backwardness in Historical Perspective* (New York, 1965), p. 13.

3. The following observation made by Gerschenkron on Germany could have come easily from any one of a number of Japanese writers on Japan: "The difference between banks of the crédit-mobilier type and commercial banks in the advanced industrial country of the time [England] was absolute. Between the English bank essentially designed to

From my preliminary review of the evidence that is now available on the financing of early industrial firms I have reached two tentative conclusions. First, we can no longer accept the present consensus on Japanese industrial financing without an even more thorough re-examination than I have been able to carry out. Second, the existing evidence suggests that the Japanese experience was in some respects much closer to England's than to Germany's, in spite of the lateness of Japan's industrialization. These complementary conclusions may evolve, with further evidence and research, into the now heretical view that the Japanese case was a variant of the English case and was dissimilar in important respects from the German case.

For the sake of convenience, I shall separate my discussion into three parts. The first deals with the "transition" period, which lasted from 1868 to the mid-1880's. The second treats the period of the "spurt," from the late 1880's to 1905, when the "initial modern economic growth" phase ended.[4] This period, as is well known, was marked by large industrial investments, mostly in the cotton spinning industry and railroads. The data from these periods will provide evidence to establish the first of my two tentative conclusions. In the last part, which covers the period to the end of the 1920's, I will present evidence for my second tentative conclusion.

THE TRANSITION PERIOD: 1868–1885

When the Meiji government came to power, and for nearly two decades thereafter, it took various measures to obtain adequate revenues and to establish a sound currency and a modern banking system. Progress was slow, as the new government had to conquer its huge deficits and had to solve problems created by over-issued paper notes, the fumbling beginnings of the national banking system, and the less than successful government pilot plants. It took the Matsukata deflation of 1881–85, which was carried out in the face of strong political opposition and serious economic dislocation, to ready the economy for modern growth.[5]

---

serve as a source of short-term capital and a bank designed to finance the long-run investment needs of the economy there was a complete gulf. The German banks, which may be taken as a paragon of the type of the universal bank, successfully combined the basic idea of the crédit-mobilier with short-term activities of commercial banks." Gerschenkron, *Economic Backwardness*, p. 13.

4. The terms "transition" and "initial modern economic growth" and the periodization were originated by Professors Rosovsky and Ohkawa. H. Rosovsky and K. Ohkawa, "A Century of Japanese Economic Growth" in W. W. Lockwood, ed., *The State and Economic Enterprise in Japan* (Princeton, 1965), pp. 77–83. On the "transition" period, Rosovsky's article "Japan's Transition to Modern Economic Growth, 1868–1885" in H. Rosovsky, ed., *Industrialization in Two Systems* (New York, 1965) is excellent.

5. For a detailed discussion of the deflation, see Rosovsky, *Industrialization*, pp. 132–39.

Professor Hugh Patrick's observations on the years prior to rapid industrialization can be considered, in my opinion, an accurate summary of the period: "In general, . . . national and private bank purchases of government bonds and private (equity) securities were considerably less important than their lending activities. Most of their funds tended to flow to the traditional sectors of agriculture and commerce, although the financing of production for export was a new use."[6] Furthermore, "it is clear that until the late 1880's most bank loans financed domestic and foreign trade, small-scale units of production in agriculture and processing industries, and, to some extent, the consumption of poor samurai and poor farmers (who, respectively, used pension bonds and land as collateral)."[7] Available aggregate data and recent studies on the activities of early Meiji banks support Patrick's view.

If the consensus on Japanese industrial financing is correct, not only must we accept Patrick's observation, that there were no significant loans to industrial firms by banks before the first industrial spurt, but we must also have evidence that the banks were actively and significantly involved in industrial financing at about the time that the industrial spurt began to take place. But even if we assume for the moment that the latter as well as the former is true, there is still an important aspect of Japanese industrialization which must be considered: there were important industrial firms, in significant numbers, which began the initial phase of their activities without the aid of bank funds and without the entrepreneurial guidance of bankers. It is important to realize this, especially in the case of Japan, because the literature on the subject has too often emphasized the importance of bank capital and bankers as entrepreneurs and has neglected those entrepreneurial activities that preceded the spurt.

A few examples will be helpful in demonstrating the importance of the entrepreneurial activities that took place before the 1890's. These examples are, I must emphasize, only a fraction of the cases that can be compiled from numerous available company histories and biographies of business leaders of the early Meiji era. The first is that of Denhichi Itō. During the years 1875–80, before the large investment boom in the cotton textile industry began, Denhichi Itō was already actively attempting to set up a cotton textile mill.[8] His capital came from his *sake* business, his own savings, and the savings of his relatives. Not until 1886 did it become possible for him to float shares and benefit indirectly from emerging banks. Itō, who founded what was to

---

6. Hugh T. Patrick, "Japan, 1868–1914," in Rondo Cameron *et al.*, *Banking in the Early Stages of Industrialization* (Oxford, 1967), p. 263.

7. *Ibid.*, p. 279.

8. The major sources on Itō are: Taichi Kinukawa, ed., *Itō Denhichi Ō* (The Venerable Denhichi Itō) (Tokyo, 1963) and Tōyō Bōseki Kabushiki Kaisha, *Tōyō Bōseki: 70-nen-shi* (A History of the 70 Years of Tōyō Textile Company) (Tokyo, 1953).

become one of the largest firms in Japan, was an industrial pioneer who suffered innumerable trials in financing a new industrial firm.

No less interesting is the long personal struggle, determination, and tenacity of Tōzaburo Suzuki, who began the first successful modern sugar refining firm in Japan.[9] Suzuki's case reflects the initial hardship common during this period. Venturing into an industry in which even the government had been unsuccessful, Suzuki in the late 1870's built the foundation of his company on personal loans, plowed-back profits, and heroic self-denial. By 1890 his company was a profitable one, though it was still in need of capital for expansion.

Examples of pioneering can even be found in shipbuilding. Tomiji Hirano's success was achieved before the Daiichi Ginkō (the First National Bank) decided that the firm was sound enough to make it a small loan.[10] As early as 1879 Hirano headed a large shipyard capitalized at 40,000 yen, and the first loan from the bank came only after the firm, in 1880, showed a profit of over 30 per cent on its equity. Hirano's road to success was also a long one. First a ship's engineer, Hirano became an exceptionally talented administrator who helped to build a government shipyard and revitalized an unsuccessful type-foundry. It was these activities which yielded him his initial capital. His shipyard was extremely successful. The capital was doubled in 1883, and during the following six years he built 68 ships, a surprising number in Meiji Japan. In examining the company history and Hirano's biography, it becomes clear that capital followed his success, and that banks lent their financial strength only after the initial and most difficult hurdles had been overcome.

The Tokyo Electric Light Company was established because eight wealthy merchants and former *daimyo* (feudal lords) were persuaded by a physics student at the University of Tokyo of the merit of having electric light in Japan.[11] The eight initiators were not as persuasive as the student, however. They had great difficulty in selling the shares of the company, which amounted

9. The sources used for this section are: Gorō Suzuki, *Suzuki Tōsaburo-Den: Kindai Nihon Sangyō no Senku* (A Biography of Tōsaburo Suzuki: A Pioneer of the Modern Japanese Industries) (Tokyo, 1956); and Gorō Suzuki, *Reimei Nihon no Ichi Kaitakusha— Chichi Suzuki Tōsaburo no Isshō* (A Pioneer of Japan's Dawn—The Life of My Father Tōsaburo Suzuki) (Tokyo, 1939).

10. See: Kōkichi Mitani, *Motoki Shōzō to Hirano Tomiji no Shōden* (Detailed Biographies of Shōzō Motoki and Tomiji Hirano) (Tokyo, 1933); Gensui Arai, *Tokyo Ishikawajima Zōsenjo 50-nenshi* (A 50-Year History of the Tokyo Ishikawajima Shipyard) (Tokyo, 1930); and the Ishikawajima Heavy Industry Company, *Ishikawajima Jūkogyō Kabushiki Kaisha 108-nenshi* (A 108-Year History of the Ishikawajima Heavy Industry Company) (Tokyo, 1961).

11. See: Muneo Nitta, *Tokyo Dentō Kabushiki Kaisha Kaigyō 50-nenshi* (The First 50 Years of the Tokyo Electric Light Company) (Tokyo, 1936), and the company's *Tokyo Dentō Kabushiki Kaisha Shi* (A History of Tokyo Electric Company) (Tokyo, 1956).

to 200,000 yen. Though a charter was granted in 1882, it was not until July 1886 that 64 individuals overcame their suspicions of the novel venture and bought shares. Shareholdings ranged from 230 shares held by one of the initiators to 2 shares held by the smallest shareholder. Once the company was established, the public showed such an enthusiastic response that in 1887 the firm decided to increase its capital. The nominal capitalization was increased to 500,000 yen, of which 300,000 were paid in. During this period the firm borrowed only once, a sum of 20,546 yen, in 1888, presumably from a bank. Even if we take into account the natural tendency for company histories to stress their problems in obtaining capital, it is obvious that this company faced unusual difficulties, but it is perhaps understandable that Japanese bankers who had never seen *Erekutorishiti* were reluctant to advance their funds.

My reading of company histories and biographies of early Meiji business leaders has convinced me that there is an unwritten chapter in the economic history of Japan, one that should be seriously considered. For those early Meiji entrepreneurs who began their limited version of industrialization with their own meager resources and abundant optimism and energy were important to the economy. The four examples I have given are neither isolated nor insignificant cases. Of the eighty industrial firms whose histories I investigated, a large percentage had to depend on self-financing, and space alone prevents me from detailing their difficulties.

To summarize thus far, the impression one frequently gains from the literature on Japan, that banks and bankers somehow fundamentally ignited Japan's industrial spurt, needs a thorough re-examination.[12] In spite of Japan's late entry into industrialization, any evidence showing that industry benefited from "special institutional factors designed to increase the supply of capital," and that it availed itself of "less decentralized and better informed entrepreneurial guidance"[13] during Japan's period of transition to industrialization, is far from complete. And such evidence, taken alone, may lead us to wrong conclusions.

12. For a fuller discussion on this point, see my paper "The Role of the Merchant Class as Entrepreneurs and Capitalists in Meiji Japan," presented at the Fourth Congress of the International Economic History Association, September 9–14, 1968, Bloomington, Indiana. For my research de-emphasizing the importance of the role of the government in providing entrepreneurial leadership during the early phase of Japanese industrialization, "The Role of the Samurai in the Development of Modern Banking in Japan," *The Journal of Economic History*, XXVII (June 1967) No. 2; "The Founding of Mitsubishi: A Case Study in Japanese Business History," *The Business History Review*, XLI, Summer 1967, No. 2; and "A Re-examination of Entrepreneurship in Meiji Japan, 1868–1912," *The Economic History Review*, Second Series, XXI, 1968, No. 1.

13. These quotes are from A. Gerschenkron, "The Early Phases of Industrialization in Russia: Afterthoughts and Counterthoughts," in W. W. Rostow, ed., *The Economics of Take-Off into Sustained Growth* (New York, 1965), p. 152.

THE MID-1880's TO THE RUSSO-JAPANESE WAR

During the last fifteen years of the nineteenth century, the Japanese economy experienced its first great wave of industrial investment. Ohkawa and Rosovsky called it the phase of "initial modern economic growth." It is the most important period for evaluating the validity of the long-maintained consensus on Japan's industrial financing. Can we show that bank loans, especially long-term loans, played a significant role in this spurt?

To answer this question, let us examine the often-used data compiled by J. Soyeda in 1896 (see Table VI.1). Patrick, who made use of these data, noted that "it appears that most individual subscriptions to new corporate stock issues were financed to a considerable degree by loans from commercial banks. Table [VI.1] shows that corporate shares constituted the predominant form of collateral for bank loans, and that 40 per cent of bank loans were for a term of more than one year."[14] A closer examination of this table, however, shows that an interpretation of these data is at best extremely difficult.

To begin with, the table shows that 34.8 per cent of total bank loans were made with shares as collateral. We must immediately note, however, that the total paid-in share capital in 1894 was approximately 175 million yen; thus the 43 million yen of bank loans secured by shares amounted to less than 25 per cent of the total share capital paid in. Though Patrick inferred that this amount was used to buy more shares, other problems exist in addition to evaluating the importance of the figure. Obviously, not all of these loans were used to buy shares; moreover, the shares that were bought need not have been industrial shares. In 1894, non-industrial firms accounted for about 50 per cent of shares outstanding.[15]

We note also that approximately one-third, or 33.1 per cent, of total loans were for a period of less than six months, and 81.4 per cent of loans were not renewed at all. The industrial loans might have been a higher percentage of long-term loans than other categories, but it is highly probable that not all of the loans secured by shares were long-term loans. It is equally important to note that, of the various classes of borrowers, "industrial" and "company" borrowers accounted for only 8.3 per cent of total loans, while "agricultural" and "commercial" borrowers accounted for 53.3 per cent, with 40.8 per cent for the "commercial" borrowers alone.[16]

14. Patrick, in Cameron et al., Banking, p. 283.

15. Minoru Hayakawa, ed., Nihon Kinyū Zaiseishi (A History of Japanese Finance) (Tokyo, 1957), p. 57. In 1889 the shares classified as "industrial," including silk-reeling, china, paper products, etc., many of which were produced by traditional methods, accounted for 27.2 per cent of total shares outstanding. This proportion, however, increased over time.

16. M. Lévy-Leboyer wrote in observing this table: "Ils [bank loans] ont été réservés d'abord à l'agriculture at au commerce: en 1894, sur quelque 125 millions de crédits ban-

TABLE VI.1

Distribution of Loans of Ordinary and National Banks
December 31, 1894

A. BY OCCUPATION OF BORROWERS

	Number	Amount (yen)	%
Agricultural	110,673	15,412,960	12.5
Industrial	7,207	1,701,188	1.4
Commercial	74,843	50,407,117	40.8
Local bodies	1,267	10,955,077	8.9
Miscellaneous	25,611	35,527,859	28.7
Companies	2,267	8,484,437	6.9
Unaccounted		1,000,000	0.8
Total	221,868	123,528,640	100.0

B. BY NATURE OF COLLATERAL

	Number	Amount (yen)	%
Government bonds	4,846	3,962,718	3.2
Shares	18,649	42,969,570	34.8
Grain	10,249	5,022,333	4.1
Land	76,620	16,908,562	13.7
Houses	5,201	1,447,203	1.2
Land with houses	16,219	5,696,659	4.6
Fertilizers	993	1,080,385	0.9
Miscellaneous	17,219	11,295,626	9.1
Credit	71,872	35,145,584	28.5

C. BY TERM

	Number	Amount (yen)	%
Within 1 month	7,183	4,060,017	3.3
Above 1 month, but below 3	17,509	11,388,762	9.2
Above 3 months, but below 6	54,704	25,458,417	20.6
Above 6 months, but below 1 year	93,430	32,798,053	26.6
Above 1 year	49,042	49,823,391	40.3

D. BY NUMBER OF RENEWALS

	Number	Amount (yen)	%
Not renewed	179,483	100,512,945	81.4
Renewed once	21,317	11,968,445	9.7
Renewed twice	10,842	6,012,397	4.9
Renewed three times	7,526	3,784,929	3.1
Renewed more than three times	2,700	1,249,924	1.0

Source: Patrick, in Cameron *et al.*, *Banking*, p. 280; from J. Soyeda, "A History of Banking in Japan."

These observations, however, are merely another way of interpreting the data, and they in no way disprove Patrick's interpretation. Although such a situation would be highly unlikely, a farmer could borrow on his land and invest in an industrial firm, and it could be argued that the two-thirds of the total loans which were for a period exceeding six months, and even loans for a shorter term, were important in releasing the borrowing firm's funds for long-range investments.[17]

Are aggregate data on loans and investment by banks for the latter part of the period more helpful in shedding light on the question at hand? If we look at the typical available data—and such data are plentiful—we can find a set of data such as is shown in Table VI.2.

The loans made on shares by all ordinary banks between 1899 and 1902 were in the neighborhood of 25 per cent of total loans in each respective year, and when loans on debentures are added, the figure rises to approximately 30 per cent. The loans made on shares, however, amount to about 22 per cent of the total paid-in share capital in 1899, 18 per cent in 1900, 12 per cent in 1901, and 11 per cent in 1902.[18] The total direct investment in shares and debentures by banks amounted to approximately one-half of total investments in each year. But again the problems are numerous. To list only the obvious ones: (1) it is nearly always impossible to distinguish loans made on industrial shares and debentures from non-industrial shares and debentures; (2) the loans could be long- or short-term; (3) it is not possible to find the percentage of industrial loans made on "other securities and no collateral"; and (4) the impact of the 1900–1901 recession on these data must be weighed. From combing through the data, a judicious conclusion is that it is simply not possible to evaluate in any precise way the importance of direct or indirect industrial loans made by the banks.

If we leave these aggregate data and examine the data for individual banks, do we obtain more useful information for ascertaining the role of banks in industrial financing? Eliminating the aristocratic Fifteenth National Bank (which Patrick uses as an example), on the ground that this bank's extensive involvement with the Japan Railroad Company was unique (as most Japanese economic historians would agree),[19] let us examine the portfolios of three large banks during the period (see Table VI.3).

---

caires, les industriels avaient reçu moins de 2 millions, exactment 1.4 pour cent du total."
This, of course, is an example of misinterpreting the table. M. Lévy-Leboyer, "Le rôle historique de la monnaie de banque," *Annales*, No. 1, XXIII, 1968, p. 5.

17. This point will be elaborated in the next section.

18. The total amount of paid-in capital was taken for each year from Tōkeikyoku (Bureau of Statistics) *Teikoku Tōkei Nenkan* (Annual Report of Imperial Statistics) for the respective year.

19. Patrick, in Cameron *et al.*, *Banking*, p. 283.

TABLE VI.2

Loans and Investment of All Ordinary Banks,
by Collateral & Types, 1899–1902
(in 1,000 yen)

LOANS

Collateral

Year	Total Loans	On government securities	Shares	Bonds and debentures	Other securities & no collateral
1899	311.349	14.670	86.561	1.999	208.119
1900	351.551	19.865	96.052	5.230	230.404
1901	356.757	16.143	93.247	4.295	242.672
1902	376.467	14.226	89.146	5.166	267.929

INVESTMENTS

Invested in

Year	Total Investment	Government securities	Shares	Bonds and debentures
1899	97.119	51.286	37.711	8.121
1900	102.365	50.501	43.112	8.752
1901	108.998	55.765	46.481	6.552
1902	116.494	56.845	51.595	8.053

Source: Tōyō Keizai Shimpō-sha, ed., *Meiji-Taisho Kokusei Sōran* (A Survey of National Economy in Meiji-Taisho periods) (Tokyo, 1924), pp. 12–13 and 36.

One conclusion I reach from examining Table VI.3 is that it is not possible to draw a general conclusion. Of the five largest banks, these three were not only the ones most involved in industrial financing, but also those which became the core of the three largest zaibatsu (literally, "financial cliques"). Also, the data for these three banks were available in the least ambiguous form. Observing the securities (S) to total asset (A) ratios—indicators of banks' involvement in long-term financing—we find that Mitsui's ratio (S/A) is far larger than that of Mitsubishi, but generally smaller than that of Yasuda. For Mitsui and Mitsubishi, the two banks for which data on government bond (G) holdings are available, we note that S/G is significantly smaller for the latter bank. The smallness of S/A for Mitsubishi is surprising, and even the S/A for Yasuda and Mitsui do not indicate a high involvement of these banks in industrial financing since, as will be indicated below, easily

TABLE VI.3
Selected Data on Mitsui, Mitsubishi, and Yasuda Banks, 1893–1905

Year	Mitsui				Mitsubishi				Yasuda*	
	S/G	S/A	l/A	l/s	S/G	S/A	l/A	l/s	S/A	T/A
1893 L	1.58	0.27	0.26	1.39	—	—	—	—	0.35	0.48
1894 F	1.67	0.28	0.22	1.07	—	—	—	—	0.30	0.51
1894 L	1.25	0.23	0.27	1.34	—	—	—	—	0.28	0.51
1895 F	0.97	0.21	0.27	0.72	—	—	—	—	0.32	0.51
1895 L	0.97	0.19	0.30	0.67	0.26	0.02	0.25	0.34	0.31	0.51
1896 F	0.90	0.18	0.24	0.57	0.19	0.02	0.32	0.74	0.70	0.51
1896 L	1.03	0.21	0.18	0.50	0.51	0.05	0.26	0.75	0.28	0.57
1897 F	1.04	0.20	0.16	0.43	0.12	0.02	0.24	0.32	0.28	0.56
1897 L	1.02	0.19	0.13	0.32	0.14	0.02	0.14	0.19	0.28	0.58
1898 F	1.08	0.21	0.12	0.31	0.15	0.02	0.30	0.43	0.31	0.52
1898 L	1.98	0.19	0.12	0.25	0.16	0.02	0.31	0.43	0.31	0.55
1899 F	1.84	0.17	0.05	0.11	0.43	0.04	0.11	0.12	0.33	0.59
1899 L	2.55	0.21	0.03	0.07	0.88	0.07	0.06	0.11	0.27	0.57
1900 F	2.50	0.20	0.03	0.06	0.87	0.07	0.09	0.12	0.29	0.59
1900 L	2.63	0.23	0.02	0.51	0.88	0.08	0.22	0.18	0.23	0.62
1901 F	2.81	0.27	0.04	0.10	0.83	0.08	0.18	0.24	0.25	0.64
1901 L	2.52	0.26	0.12	0.32	0.54	0.07	0.17	0.21	0.25	0.63
1902 F	2.54	0.25	0.14	0.34	0.51	0.06	0.13	0.16	0.25	0.62
1902 L	2.93	0.23	0.15	0.33	0.58	0.06	0.20	0.24	0.22	0.66
1903 F	2.93	0.21	0.20	0.41	0.69	0.05	0.18	0.22	0.24	0.65
1903 L	3.05	0.21	0.21	0.43	1.41	0.10	0.17	0.20	0.21	0.67
1904 F	2.98	0.19	0.21	0.40	1.20	0.09	0.17	0.20	0.24	0.65
1904 L	2.07	0.18	0.24	0.47	0.43	0.08	0.20	0.25	0.20	0.67
1905 F	1.55	0.17	0.24	0.46	0.65	0.07	0.14	0.17	0.20	0.67
1905 L	1.64	0.16	0.21	0.42	0.67	0.07	0.10	0.11	0.22	0.69

* Before 1923, it is not possible to separate the total loans (T) of the Yasuda Bank by term (l or s) but, in view of the bank's relatively high S/A ratios vis-à-vis those of Mitsui, and from the Yasuda Bank's generally conservative loan policy, it is very unlikely that Yasuda's S/A and l/s were higher than those of the Mitsui Bank.

Sources: The Mitsubishi Bank, *Mitsubishi Ginkō-shi* (A History of Mitsubishi Bank) (Tokyo: Mitsubishi Bank, 1954).
The Mitsui Bank, *Mitsui Ginkō 80-nen-shi* (An 80-Year History of the Mitsui Bank) (Tokyo: Mitsui Bank, 1957).
The Yasuda Bank, *Yasuda Ginkō 60-nen-shi* (A 60-Year History of the Yasuda Bank) (Tokyo: Yasuda Bank, 1940).
Notes: F and L following year indicate first and last six months of the year
　　　　S stands for securities (shares and bonds) of firms
　　　　G for government bonds
　　　　A for total assets
　　　　l for long-term loans
　　　　s for short-term loans
　　　　T for total loans
The long-term loans are *kashitsukekin* (literally, "loaned-out money") which are the sums of the loans made against various negotiable instruments (*tegata kashitsuke* and *shōken kashitsuke*).
The total loans include, in addition to long-term loans, bills discounted (*waribiki tegata*), call loans, and overdrafts (*tōza kashikoshi*, literally, "loaned for the moment").
There are various difficulties concerning renewed short-term loans and a small fraction of less than one-year loans made under the heading *tegata kashitsuke*, but adjustments made for these difficulties should not change the ratios observed here by more than a few percentage points. This procedure of separating long- and short-term loans is well accepted by Japanese scholars. See, for example, Shibagaki, *An Analysis of Japanese Financial Capital*, p. 336.

more than a half of those shares and bonds were issued by non-industrial firms. In examining the ratio of l (long-term loans) to s (short-term loans) we discover that Mitsui begins at 1.39 in 1893, sharply drops to 0.06 in 1900, and then returns to a 0.30 to 0.45 level by 1905. For Mitsubishi, this ratio shows two relatively distinct patterns; the ratios before 1899 are distinctively higher than the maximum of 0.25 observed after that date. In evaluating the respective l/A, l/T, and T/A ratios (T stands for total loan), we find that long-term loans were not especially large for any of these three banks.[20]

Beyond these general observations, it is quite unwarranted to draw any clear-cut conclusions. As Shibagaki emphasized recently, the loan policies of the giant banks differed considerably.[21] When we considered this against the fact that the semi-annual reports of nearly two dozen smaller and local banks examined show even more diversity in their loan policies,[22] the conclusion we must reach is that we must refrain from making a general observation from these data on banks' loan policies before a far more complete examination can be made. Here too, discouraging as it may be, I must warn that bank records are too ambiguous, perhaps intentionally, to be helpful in arriving at conclusive observations. For example, in most of the banks' semi-annual reports, industrial loans and other types of loans are not separated, and information on renewals of short-term loans is not as a rule available.

It is only logical, at this point, to turn to the financial records of the industrial firms themselves. How much data are available, and how informative are they? I have been able to examine the semi-annual financial reports of nearly sixty firms, numerous company histories, and the biographies of leading Meiji–Taisho business leaders (which often contain useful data).[23]

20. These ratios are large or small only in relation to equivalent ratios of other periods until we are able to compare these ratios internationally. Comparisons of these ratios are made for the post-1912 period in relation to Table VI.6.

21. Though Shibagaki is committed to the Marxist view and stresses the importance of the bank-firm relationships, his descriptions make it clear that even among the major banks loan policies differed to a degree which cannot be ignored. Kazuo Shibagaki, *Nihon Kinyū-shihon Bunseki* (An Analysis of Japanese Financial Capital) (Tokyo, 1965), pp. 368–69.

22. Enough local and small banks have been analyzed in Japanese publications to present evidence of diversity in their loan policies. A few of these are: Kōkichi Asakura, *Meijizenki Nippon Kinyū Kōzō-shi* (A History of the Financial Structure of Early Meiji Japan) (Tokyo, 1961); Hisaichi Takahashi, *Meijizenki Chihō Kinyū Kikan no Kenkyū* (A Study on Local Financial Institutions in the Early Meiji Period) (Tokyo, 1966); and Kazuo Yamaguchi, ed., *Nihon Sangyō Kinyūshi Kenkyū* (A Study in Japanese Industrial Financing), (Tokyo, 1966).

23. The firms in the sample consist of 59 industrial firms for which the respective financial data are complete except for several missing semi-annual reports and four firms for which only fragmental records are available. These financial reports were originally gathered over

In my judgment, it is highly questionable whether the additional effort and expenditure needed to increase the sample size would be worthwhile. As the sample examined includes most of the better-known, large (or those which became larger over time) firms for which records are known to exist, any additional financial reports obtainable will necessarily be for smaller and/or local firms. It is unlikely that financial data for these latter firms will alter whatever conclusions one can make from these sixty sample firms. Though the details cannot be pursued here, there exist a multitude of major and minor problems in attempting to analyze the financial records of these sample firms.[24]

The data are highly informative for analyzing the financing pattern of each firm. It is an extremely interesting experience to read through these reports and trace each firm's life history. But an attempt to analyze these together as a set of samples and draw a few general conclusions is a most frustrating experience. After a series of unsuccessful attempts to analyze the sample data as a group, I have decided to let the data of five individual firms "represent" what I believe to be five relatively distinguishable patterns of industrial financing. This is a significantly weaker method, as it is based on subjective judgment, but nevertheless I believe it helps to illustrate effectively the basic patterns of industrial financing during the period.

(1) Oji Papers, a firm which was from the beginning closely connected with the Daiichi Bank, and which had the Mitsui as its initiator, shows a high ratio of promissory notes to total assets (P/A) and a relatively high dependency on outside funds as seen in a relatively high ratio of the total of promissory notes, short-term loans, and long-term loans to total assets. These reflected the firm's easy access to bank funds rather than financial weakness.

---

a number of years by Professor Tsunehiko Yui of Meiji University and were published in microfilm by Yūshōdō Microfilms, Ltd., in 1962 as *The Annual Financial Reports of One Thousand Firms: 1868–1945*. In several cases, I contacted firms directly and obtained semi-annual reports which were not included in the microfilms. I shall be happy to make these data and a dozen relevant ratios computed for each firm available for anyone requesting them in computer print-out form. In spite of the problems described in the following footnote, I hope to analyze further these data as a long-range project which will deal with various problems raised throughout this paper.

24. Some of the major problems are: (i) Definitions of accounting concepts which differed by firm and by period; (ii) the gradual absorption of "Western" accounting methods which replaced the traditional methods; (iii) the difficulty in many cases of disaggregating loans by their nature and terms; (iv) constantly varying sample sizes because of various dates of incorporation, mergers, and absorptions; (v) the usual lack of information relating to the collateral for loans made and to specific terms of bonds; (vi) problems, theoretical and practical, of conducting an analysis of the inter-industry and inter-"age of firm" data; (vii) problems of dealing with relatively severe cyclical effects on the data, and they are acute as effects differ by size of firm, bank connection, industry and entrepreneurial reaction, *etc.*

Both the reserves to owners' equity (R/E) and reserves to total assets were relatively high, as the dividend to net profit ratio (D/N) was a low 36.1 per cent. With little need to pay a high dividend to attract public subscription to its shares, this company exemplifies the case of a well-off firm with excellent bank connections.

(2) Tokyo Electric Light, which I described earlier, was one of the most capital-starved of the sample firms. The indicators of financial assistance rendered by banks (P/A), and the ratio of the sum of promissory notes and long- and short-term loans to total assets are the lowest for the five firms. Because of its weak reserve status, which can be seen in cash reserve to owner's equity ratio (R/E) and cash reserve to the total assets (R/A) in Table VI.4, and because of its general financial weakness, the firm floated more shares to raise capital. It undoubtedly would have been difficult for them to sell bonds, had they tried to do so. The high dividend to net profit ratio of 91.9 per cent would appear to show that they were paying high dividend rates in order to sell shares and make it easy for the share-buyers to pay in for the shares. But in reality the dividend rate was a modest 12 per cent of paid-in capital throughout the period.[25] This company typifies the case of a struggling firm which had little access to banks. It also reflects the difficulty of producing and marketing an unknown commodity.

(3) Osaka Shipping was a company which, because of the nature of its capital requirement, depended heavily on all available capital. Well-disposed banks, share capital, and the bond market all had to be fully exploited. The relatively high reserve figures are deceptive, in that these were the reserves earmarked for repairs and insurance for ships owned by the company. Though the dividend to net profit ratio was high, the dividend rate never exceeded 10 per cent of paid-in capital because of large depreciation taken throughout the period. Despite all, when promissory notes, short-term loans, and long-term loans are disaggregated, we find that the firm made only one long-term loan in 1900, a large loan of 1.7 million yen. But this loan was paid back by 1901. Promissory notes and publicly sold bonds, and later, in 1904, the doubling of its capital, were the major sources of its liquidity and capital.

(4) Japan Flour Milling, because of its small size—a nominal capital of 300,000 yen—depended on capital which was paid in over several years. The

25. Patrick's observations that firms paid high dividends so that the shareholders could pay in for their shares and that high dividend rates were declared to cover shareholders' interest costs to banks are difficult to support with the available data. High dividend rates associated with increased paid-in capital are equally observable among the records of sample firms, and the condition necessary for Patrick's second observation that the dividend rate tended to be higher than prevailing interest rates still requires a considerable amount of research before it can be proven. For example, we cannot ignore the fact that the average share prices, which influence shareholders' reactions and expectations, fluctuated widely during the period. Patrick, in Cameron *et al.*, *Banking*, p. 283.

dividend rate, on the average, exceeded 15 per cent, and it went as high as 18 per cent four times during the period. The shareholders—there were thirty-two—appear to have paid in their dividends for their shares. Long-term borrowing was limited to a total of 19,000 yen on three different occasions, and the firm resorted to bonds in 1902 in the amount of 100,000 yen rather than raise its capital. Because of steady good profits, a large amount of depreciation was taken *vis-à-vis* the size of total assets. (It was not unusual for Meiji firms to disregard depreciation when profits were poor.) Liquidity was provided by means of promissory notes. This was a case in which, because of the profit position, the nature of the industry, and the size of the firm, the assistance the firm required was mostly in the form of short-term liquidity. After 1906 the firm grew rapidly, and it became one of the largest flour milling firms in Japan (capitalized at 1.55 million yen in 1909), but it was not until the height of World War I that it made another long-term loan. Because of the small amount of capital, which was paid in slowly, the ratio of owners' equity to total assets for this firm is a low 29 per cent. This should invite our attention to the 50 per cent plus E/A ratios for the other four firms in the sample—as well as to the fact that this ratio for the post-World War II industrial firms in Japan is usually in the 20 to 40 per cent range.

(5) The Kurashiki Cotton Spinning Company represents the general financing pattern of cotton spinning firms, the industry which "led" Japanese industrialization. Because of the importance of this industry, it is perhaps well to point out that I chose this company to represent the industry after examining the semi-annual reports of six firms, fourteen company histories containing useful financial data, and several studies on the industry. The data in Table VI.4 show that, with a modest 7.1 per cent for P/A, the average ratio of long-term plus short-term loans to total assets amounted to 12.4 per cent, or 19.5 minus 7.1 per cent. The ratio ranged between 5.09 and 24.87 per cent, although it exceeded 20 per cent only once during the crucial years of expansion, 1890–1905. The financial records of the company clearly indicate that during the period under examination expansion was financed by increases in paid-in capital and by rapidly increasing internal reserves and publicly sold bonds. For example, by the second half of 1900, the company's paid-in capital had increased from 150,000 yen to 337,500 yen, accumulated reserves had reached 100,000 yen, and outstanding bonds 153,000 yen, while there were no short-term loans, a long-term debt of only 68,000 yen, and an even smaller amount in promissory notes outstanding (only 21,000 yen). (An exception is the Nisshin Cotton Spinning Company, which financed itself almost entirely without bank loans. All through the Meiji years the firm borrowed only twice from a bank—one long-term and one short-term loan—and in both cases the loans were only slightly more than 4 per cent of total assets.)

TABLE VI.4

The Means of Selected Ratios of Financial
Data of Five Sample Firms for
Pre-1905 Period (percentage)[a]

	Oji Papers	Tokyo Electric Light	Osaka Shipping	Japan Flour Milling	Kurashiki Cotton Spinning
P/A	14.5	1.2	5.4	12.1	7.1
$\dfrac{P+s+l}{A}$	25.2	11.5	17.8	12.5	19.5
D/N	36.1	91.9	96.8	67.9	72.9
R/E	28.1	3.8	16.4	14.8	29.4
R/A	13.2	2.0	8.9	4.2	9.5
$\dfrac{B}{B+s+l+P}$	6.5	0	40.4	13.2	27.6
B/A	1.5	0	17.3	4.6	7.8
E/A	54.0	54.2	54.4	29.0	51.9

Notes: P—promissory notes
　　　s—short-term loans
　　　l—long-term loans
　　　A—total assets
　　　D—dividend
　　　N—net profit
　　　R—cash reserve
　　　E—owners' equity (capital paid in)
　　　B—bonds

a The period covered for these firms is from the year indicated for each firm in parentheses below to 1905: Oji Paper (1893), Tokyo Electric Light (1903), Osaka Shipping (1899), Japan Flour Mills (1897), and Kurashiki Cotton Spinning (1890).

Source: Semi-annual reports of these five firms for the respective period.

To get a more general view of this important industry, let us look at F. Yamada's data for the industry as a whole in 1905.[26] At that time the industry's total assets were 51,496,000 yen, with a paid-in capital of 34,332,000 yen, and the total internal reserve stood at 11,598,000 yen. Against this, outside loans of all types amounted to 5,565,000 yen, thus yielding industry-wide ratios of the sum of long- and short-term loans to total assets of 0.11, cash reserves to owners' equity of 0.34, and cash reserves to total assets of 0.23. The internal reserve was nearly double the amount of outside loans.

26. Fumio Yamada, "Capital for Japan's Cotton Textile Industry," *Keizaigaku Ronshū* (Economic Essays), University of Tokyo, VI, No. 2, 1962, p. 147.

All these examples, as well as other evidence not cited here, for lack of space, appear to suggest that the role of banks was not as important as has been described in the literature.[27] Cases such as Oji Paper do exist even in the cotton textile industry,[28] but they are far fewer than one would be led to believe by the existing literature on the subject. After evaluating the quantitative evidence cited here, as well as other data, and after reading numerous company histories, I have yet to be persuaded by Professor Patrick when he says that "by the turn of the century bank loans were clearly the major source" for industrial financing.[29] In making this observation Patrick's only concrete evidence—and I must add in fairness to him, the only available evidence to date—was the Industrial Bank's data, of which the source and coverage are unknown.

According to these data the sources of "a total of 247 million yen in industrial funds supplied to industrial corporations between 1897 and 1913" were bank loans (57.5 per cent), new stock issues (32.4 per cent), corporate debentures (6.5 per cent), and internal reserves (3.6 per cent).[30] I believe these data are small in coverage and heavily biased to over-emphasize bank loans. The new stock issues increased by about 700 million yen during the period 1897–1913. This means that the coverage of the Industrial Bank's data was slightly over 11 per cent in terms of new stock issues, because 32.4 per cent of 247 million is slightly over 80 million yen. It seems evident that the data covered only a small fraction of the total bank loans made to industrial firms. Regardless of the coverage and source, the 3.6 per cent figure attributed to

27. A group of economic historians under the leadership of Professor Genzō Hazama of the Osaka Municipal University has been investigating questions similar to those treated in this paper. Their analyses make extensive use of industry and individual firm data. Avoiding familiar generalizations on the financing patterns of Japanese industrial financing of the Meiji era, they have provisionally advanced a thesis that the financing patterns should be categorized into the following five groups: (i) partnership; (ii) mostly by relatives; (iii) mostly by non-management shareholders; (iv) management and shareholders form two distinct groups, but the number of shareholders is not large; (v) the same as (iv) but the number of shareholders is large. One of their major tentative conclusions is that "though there was a difference in degree, the basic pattern [of financing] approximated the process of development of incorporated firms seen in advanced [Western] nations." Toshimitsu Imuda, "*Meijiki ni okeru kabushiki kaisha no hatten to kabunishi-sō no keisei*" (The Development of Incorporated Firms and the Formation of the Shareholder Class in the Meiji Period) in the Economic Research Institute, the Osaka Municipal University, *Meijiki no keizai hatten to keizai shutai* (Economic Development and Its Main Leading Agents in the Meiji Period) (Osaka, 1968), pp. 89–198. Also see footnote 31.

28. Patrick cites the case of the Osaka Spinning Company which was established by Eiichi Shibusawa, then president of the Daiichi Ginkō, and notes that it benefited from loans from the bank. This firm, established as early as 1882, was unusual in many respects and should not be taken as a typical example. Patrick, in Cameron *et al.*, *Banking*, p. 263.

29. *Ibid.*, pp. 283–84.

30. *Ibid.*, p. 284.

internal reserves is hardly acceptable to anyone who reads through company and industry studies of the period.[31]

Before concluding this section we should ask the question: If the banks were not as important as it has been thought in providing industrial capital during the period of the first industrial spurt, how were their large loanable funds used? It is difficult to obtain precise information to answer this question, but the data available can, nevertheless, suggest what I believe to be the basic patterns of the uses to which these funds were put. First, it is important to note that short-term loans were more important than long-term loans during this period. Table VI.3, for example, shows that, for both the Mitsui Bank and the Mitsubishi Bank, the ratios of long-term loans to total assets were much less than unity. Table VI.1 makes it reasonably clear, despite the problems mentioned above, that nearly 60 per cent of the total loans were for a period of less than one year and that 81.4 per cent of the loans were not renewed in 1894. The Mitsui Bank, for instance, noted that the most visible change observed for the period between 1896 and 1901 were "increases in deposits and paper discounted." During these six years, the amount of paper discounted grew from 2.8 million yen to nearly 8 million yen, while the long-term loans (*kashitsukekin*) declined from 6.4 million yen to 5.1 million yen.[32]

Although the evidence is certainly not complete, company and bank histories inform us that many of the long-term loans made by the largest banks—as will be shown in detail in the next section—went to a small, select group of firms which were closely connected with these banks or to ventures which were originated by the bankers themselves. These were the so-called zaibatsu industrial firms in mining, shipbuilding, and other industries, and they were in many instances firms which were established with the former government plants as their foundation.[33] The firms receiving long-term loans

31. Though it is often ignored in the literature, it is well to note in passing that the total number of shareholders in Japan increased rapidly from 108,296 persons in 1886 to 244,585 persons in 1890, and then rose sharply to 684,070 persons by the end of 1898. When these figures are examined by industry, we find that the average number of shareholders per firm increased rapidly for "modern" industries while it declined visibly for other types of industries. Between 1893 and 1898, the average number of shareholders per firm rose from 136 to 457 in cotton spinning, 714 to 1,040 in railroads, 4 to 124 in shipbuilding, while the same figures declined from 228 to 28 in cocoon raising, from 410 to 45 in foreign trade and 361 to 93 in land development.

This is a kind of evidence which could be added to a recent finding by a group of young economists (at Osaka Municipal University) who, after making painstaking case studies, concluded that by the turn of the century "the base of public capital to the firms had been widened significantly." Imuda, *The Development of Incorporated Firms*, p. 141.

32. The Mitsui Bank, *An 80-Year History of the Mitsui Bank*, p. 145.

33. For a detailed discussion on, and evaluation of the importance of these government plants, see T. C. Smith, *Political Change and Industrial Development in Japan: Government Enterprise, 1868–1880* (Stanford, 1955), pp. 84–95.

were small in number compared to the large number of firms which lamented the lack of long-term credit. The largest banks were, in fact, quite frank in admitting such practices. The Bank of Mitsui noted that "over 7 million yen," or nearly 40 per cent of its total loans, were made to several firms related to the bank. During the 1897–98 recession, the bank "curtailed loans as much as possible to the general borrowers," and large loans were confined to the firms in which Mitsui had a direct interest.[34] The Mitsubishi Bank followed the same practice during the period "by lending only to those firms which are Mitsubishi-related" while "all branch offices sharply reduced loans to general [unrelated] borrowers."[35]

What percentage of the total long-term loans were borrowed by the minority of the zaibatsu firms is difficult to ascertain. One conclusion that can be safely drawn is that it would be extremely difficult to show that a large number of industrial firms enjoyed long-term loans of any appreciable amount. We can be sure of this because we know that the smaller banks were even less willing to make long-term industrial loans than the larger banks were.[36] Anyone combing the available data will find it difficult to demonstrate that the first spurt of industrialization in Japan significantly benefited from the long-term loans supplied by the banking system.

To buttress this view, one can easily show that during this period a large portion of the bank funds were used to buy government bonds. Table VI.2 shows that government securities accounted for nearly 50 per cent of the total investment made by the banks. Table VI.3 indicates that during the 1890's the ratio of shares and bonds to the government bonds held by the Mitsui Bank fluctuated around 1.0, and the ratio for the Mitsubishi Bank for the same period was much lower, indicating the importance of government bonds in bank portfolios.

In interpreting the magnitudes of banks' investments in shares, one must be extremely careful not to consider the amount of shares held by the banks to be synonymous with industrial investment. For all the larger banks examined for the period, one discovers that a large percentage of those shares were either bank shares or shares of commercial firms such as those in trading, export, and other service activities. As late as 1895 the loosely classified industrial shares were outnumbered by the total shares floated by commercial firms and banks by 74.6 million yen to 449.9 million yen, or roughly one to six. For example, of the total shares owned by the Yasuda

34. The Mitsui Bank, *An 80-Year History of the Mitsui Bank*, p. 405.
35. The Mitsubishi Bank, *A History of the Mitsubishi Bank*, p. 90.
36. See case studies found in Hisaichi Takashi, *Chihō kinyū-kikan no kenkyū* (A Study on Local Financial Institutions) (Tokyo, 1967) and other local bank studies cited in my article "The Role of the Samurai in the Development of Modern Banking in Japan," cited in footnote 12.

Bank in 1895, worth 1.33 million yen, 74 per cent was in shares of "banks and insurance companies" while the other 26 per cent was distributed among railroads and "others." [37]

WORLD WAR I TO THE END OF THE 1920's

Data become more reliable with the Taisho (1912–25) and the early Showa years (1926 on). With the addition of these, we can construct a new framework for interpreting the role of banking in Japan's industrialization. More specifically, if the observations and analyses made in this section are accepted, it follows that the consensus on Japanese industrial financing is not correct, and that banking practices of the German type became prevalent only after the end of World War I.

Examining the evidence for the period following the war boom, which made Japan a full-fledged industrial power within the brief span of a decade, we find that banking practices underwent a visible change: The largest banks, which were beginning to be called zaibatsu banks, began to make long-term loans to industrial firms in such capital-using industries as metallurgical, chemical, and utility industries. We note, more importantly, that these new recipients of long-term bank loans were not a small number of firms which were closely zaibatsu-connected, i.e. the firms established partially by zaibatsu capital (such as the Oji Paper) or one of many ventures purchased by the zaibatsu interests from the Meiji government at the beginning of the 1880's. The zaibatsu banks became, during the 1920's, investment banks of the German type.

This transition was possible, I believe, because the once bank-dependent zaibatsu-connected firms, by the end of World War I, had become self-sufficient in terms of financing their own growth, and because the banks themselves, during the 1920's, had become large enough to make the transition. The evidence indicates that these giant banks grew rapidly in strength, absolutely and relatively, through increases in capital and deposits, as well as mergers. It is well known that depositors sought to keep their money in these giant banks after a series of bank runs in the 1920's.

Facts to substantiate these observations can be found in numerous company histories and other sources. Although we will go on to more general observations on the destinations of bank loans later, several samples from the semi-annual financial reports of zaibatsu-connected firms will be useful here in showing the transformation of the financial patterns of these firms or in showing that the rapidly growing zaibatsu banks no longer needed to concern themselves with supplying capital to their "own" firms. These exam-

37. The Yasuda Bank, *A 60-Year History of the Yasuda Bank*, p. 110.

ples are "representative" firms, in that they were selected to reflect the financing patterns of zaibatsu firms during the Taisho and early Showa periods, and they were chosen from 37 major zaibatsu-connected firms for which data are available.[38]

As early as 1907 the Shibaura Seisakusho (Shibaura Machine-Tool Industries) of the Mitsui group had stopped borrowing long-term loans from the Mitsui and other banks, and they did not take a long-term loan again until 1934. Neither does any short-term loan appear on their financial reports after 1908. The firm's capital was increased from 2 million to 5 million yen in 1912, before the investment boom of World War I, and it was increased again to 20 million yen in 1920. A dividend rate in excess of 20 per cent was maintained between 1916 and 1921; thus it was not difficult for the company to sell its shares in order to expand.[39]

The Dai-Nihon Seruroido K. K. (The Greater Japan Celluloid Company), one of the Mitsui group, ceased borrowing at short term in 1921, and long-term loans disappeared from its reports in 1926. The company's long-term loans during the Taisho period never exceeded a small percentage of its total assets. The firm increased the ratio of reserves to owners' equity (paid-in capital) from 5 to 35 per cent during the period between 1921 and 1929. Share capital increased during the same time from 12.5 million yen in 1919 to 100 million yen in 1921.[40]

The Mitsui Kōzan K. K. (Mitsui Mining Company) issued no bonds during the Taisho or early Showa years. Its capital increased from 20 million yen in 1916 to 50 million in 1918, and then to 100 million yen in 1920. This last increase was made to finance the expansion of the boom years. Long-term loans were obtained from Mitsui *Gōmei*[41] until 1918, although the amount was small, in the neighborhood of 0.5 per cent of the total assets. Between

38. Data were obtained from their respective company histories which the writer was able to obtain since 1962 and from the Yūshōdō Microfilms cited earlier. As most Japanese writers agree, there were about 85 firms which were directly controlled by the four zaibatsu holding companies at the end of the 1920's; the sample of 37 covers about 44 per cent of these firms. The zaibatsu affiliates which were controlled by zaibatsu subsidiaries or by the zaibatsu holding companies only to a limited degree are not included in the 85 firms classified as direct subsidiary firms. See Table 5 which shows that, in terms of paid-in capital supplied by zaibatsu, the distinctions between the zaibatsu firms and affiliates are relatively distinct.

39. Data are from the Yūshōdō Microfilms; also see: Yasuichi Kimura, ed., *Shibaura seisakusho 65-nenshi* (A 65-Year History of the Shibaura Machine-Tool Industries) (Tokyo, 1940).

40. Data are from the Yūshōdō Microfilms, and *Dainihon seruroido kaisha-shi* (A History of the Greater Japan Celluloid Company) published by the firm in 1952.

41. A legal entity organized by the Mitsui family, and this owned the Mitsui Bank before 1919. But when a part of the bank shares was sold publicly in 1919, the *Gōmei* was absorbed by the bank.

1919 and 1929 the firm made only six loans from Mitsui Bussan (Trading Company), in the form of extended advances for coal and chemical by-products which the mining company sold to the Bussan. However, these loans from the Bussan did not exceed 1.5 per cent of the total assets of the firm, and the mining company's steadily increasing reserves reached 12 million yen, a large sum, by 1929.[42]

Even the Ōji Seishi K. K. (Oji Paper Company), which had borrowed constantly and rather heavily from the Daiichi and the Mitsui banks, became much more financially independent after the war. Short-term loans disappeared after 1919 and long-term loans amounted to no more than 10 per cent of the total assets with two exceptions; one in 1922, when they came to just over 10 per cent, and another in 1927, when they were 23 per cent. Most outside capital was obtained by means of bonds, which were issued in an amount equivalent to 23 per cent of the total assets in 1916; during most of the 1920's the figure fluctuated within the range of 18 and 26 per cent of total assets. However, the firm's ratio of reserves to total assets was 8 to 14 per cent, compared with a few per cent of total assets during the prewar years. The reserves to owners' equity ratio also increased from 24 to 44 per cent during the period between 1917 and 1929.[43]

Of the Mitsubishi group, the Mitsubishi Zōsen K. K. (Mitsubishi Shipbuilding Company) relied on bond financing to the magnitude of 10 million yen against a paid-in capital of 30 million yen in 1918. The bond obligation was gradually eliminated and it stood at zero in 1927. No short-term loans were made after 1919 and only one long-term loan of 0.5 million yen was made, in 1930, against a reserve which increased from 2 million in 1919 to 5.8 million by 1930.[44] The Mitsubishi Kōgyō K. K. (Mitsubishi Mining Company) was even sounder. In 1918 it was capitalized at 50 million yen, and no bonds were sold and no long-term loans were made after 1919, while reserves rose from 0.3 million yen in 1918 to 3.2 million yen in 1929.[45]

The Nisshin Seifun K. K. (Nisshin Flour Milling Company) stayed clear of long-term borrowing during the Taisho and the early Showa years; it borrowed only between 1922–25 and then in an amount equivalent to 4.2 per cent of total assets. There is no explicit mention in its records of short-term loans. The firm sold no bonds before 1930. Capital steadily increased, from 1.7 million in 1914 to 4 million in 1917 and then to 12.3 million in 1925. Since the dividend rate remained well above the 15 per cent floor after 1916,

42. The Mitsui Bank, *An 80-Year History of the Mitsui Bank*, pp. 210–211.

43. The Yūshōdō Microfilms, and Vol. I of the five-volume *Oji seishi shashi* (A Company History of the Oji Paper) (Tokyo, 1957).

44. The Yūshōdō Microfilms, and *Mitsubishi Zōsen* (The Mitsubishi Shipbuilding Company) (Tokyo, 1958).

45. The Yūshōdō Microfilms, and Saburō Fumoto, *Mitsubishi Iizuka Tankōshi* (A History of the Mitsubishi Iizuka Coal Mines) (Tokyo, 1961).

with an exceptionally high 30 per cent at the height of the war boom, the firm had no difficulty in marketing its own shares for the purpose of acquiring capital for expansion.[46]

It is possible to add many more examples to convey this changing pattern of financing in zaibatsu-connected firms. Suffice it to say that, in addition to these firms, there were many more zaibatsu firms which depended only to a very limited extent on the long-term loans from their respective zaibatsu banks. In fact, of the samples examined, fifteen firms, including the Mitsui Kōzan and the Mitsubishi Zōsen, in the Mitsui, Mitsubishi, Sumitomo, Asano, and Koga groups made no long-term loans at all throughout the 1920's. One can safely conclude from these facts that zaibatsu-related firms were financially secure by the beginning of the 1920's and that they required little long-term capital from their parent banks.[47]

Examination of the bank data confirms the financial independence of zaibatsu firms. If we take the example of the Mitsui Bank, for which useful information is available, we find that by 1930 only 9.8 per cent of its total loans were made to Mitsui-connected firms.[48] Although direct evidence is not available, we can assume that all other major banks followed an essentially similar pattern. For example, for the Sumitomo bank, loans to Sumitomo-related firms were even smaller, because the group's major firms had no long-term loans by the late 1920's.[49]

Throughout the 1920's the basic pattern is that the zaibatsu firms, because of past relationships, enjoyed a high degree of participation from the zaibatsu banks and families, even though these largest firms could easily sell shares to the public. For the subsidiary firms, zaibatsu participation in equity was limited, but these firms, too, were sufficiently sound to be able to float shares of their own and required few or no zaibatsu loans. The share holdings of zaibatsu families, banks, and other zaibatsu firms within the same zaibatsu group in 1928 were as shown in Table VI.5.

That the zaibatsu banks provided an increasing amount of long-term capital to non-zaibatsu firms during the 1920's can be shown easily. First, we must note that bonds were a much more important means of obtaining capital than were long-term loans during that period. Of the 302 largest firms

46. The Yūshōdō Microfilms, and the Company's *Nisshin Seifun Kabushi Keishashi* (A History of the Nisshin Flour Milling Company) (Tokyo, 1965).

47. The firms are the Nihon Cement (Asano), the Koga Mining (Koga), the Mitsui Bussan, the Taiheiyō Coal Mining (Mitsui), the Hokkai Soda (Mitsui), the Mitsubishi Papers, the Nisshin Steamships (Mitsubishi), the Meiji Sugar Refining (Mitsubishi), the Sumitomo Besshi Lead Mining, the Sumitomo Steel Pipes, the Sumitomo Steel Mill, the Fujikura Electric Wires (Sumitomo) and the Sumitomo Electric Wires.

48. Calculated from the data contained in *An 80-Year History of the Mitsui Bank*, pp. 421–22.

49. See footnote 48, and the Sumitomo bank data contained in the Yūshōdō Microfilms.

examined by the Mitsubishi Economic Research Institute, bonds accounted for 21 per cent of the total capital, long-term loans 7 per cent, share capital 56 per cent, and short-term loans 15 per cent. Out of 22 industries examined by the Institute, 13 industries depended more on bonds than on long-term loans.[50]

The total value of bonds sold during the 1920–25 period was in the amount of 2,422 million yen, of which only 18.1 per cent were for zaibatsu-connected firms. The major share of the total, 41.3 per cent, were bonds floated by utility firms (electricity, electric light, etc.), and 20.7 per cent were for railway (*densha*) companies. These were two industries in which the zaibatsu interests were extremely small. By 1930 the total value of bonds floated was 2,927 million yen, of which zaibatsu-connected firms accounted for only 15.2 per cent. The zaibatsu firms floating the bonds were small subsidiaries and affiliates, not major zaibatsu firms.[51]

An important point is that by the end of 1929 the four zaibatsu banks held 27.1 per cent of the total outstanding bonds. If the insurance and credit companies of the zaibatsu groups are added, the bond holdings increase to 29.1 per cent of the total.[52] After the mid-1920's insurance companies' and credit companies' bonds were the most important negotiable papers those banks held. In 1929, among the zaibatsu banks, the ratio of bonds to the total negotiable paper ranged from 46.7 per cent for the Mitsubishi Bank to 37 per cent for the Mitsui Bank.[53]

As I noted earlier, the long-term loans made by the zaibatsu banks increased rapidly during the latter half of the 1920's. Table VI.6 shows that the Mitsui Bank's long-term loans to total assets (l/A) rose from 0.24 in 1912 to 0.44 at the end of 1930. The ratio was somewhat lower during the 1919–24 period, but the rising trend of the ratio is unmistakable. The ratio of l/T (long-term

50. Kazuo Shibagaki, *An Analysis of Japanese Financial Capital*, p. 374.

51. Calculated from the data contained in the Industrial Bank of Japan, *Nihon Kōgyō 50-nenshi* (A 50-Year History of the Industrial Bank) (Tokyo, 1957), pp. 222–23, and Nomura Securities Company of Japan *Koshasai Nenkan* (An Annual Report of Government and Company Bonds) (Tokyo, 1930), the data sections. The zaibatsu firms were identified by referring to Kamekichi Takahashi, *Nihon Zaibatsu no kaibo* (An Anatomy of Japanese Zaibatsu) (Tokyo, 1930), pp. 21–22, 55–60 and 140–41, and Ryūkichi Minobe, *Karuteru, Torasuto, Kontserun* (Cartels, Trusts and Konzern) Vol. 2, (Tokyo, 1931). All through this paper, the expressions "zaibatsu-controlled," "zaibatsu firms," and "zaibatsu groups" are used only for those cases which are clearly identifiable; *i.e.*, connections with zaibatsu families and banks can be readily shown by shareholding, interlocking directorships, or loans made. For the pre-1940 years, such identification is quite straightforward because of evident dependence of zaibatsu subsidiaries and affiliates on the zaibatsu banks and other zaibatsu firms.

52. K. Takahashi, *An Anatomy of Japanese Zaibatsu*, pp. 44–47.

53. From the data contained in the bank history of each bank, and the Yūshōdō Microfilms.

TABLE VI.5
Paid-in Capital Supplied by Zaibatsu
1928 (percentage)

	Mit-sui	Mitsu-bishi	Sumi-tomo	Ya-suda	Okura	Koga	Kawa-saki
SUPPLIED TO ZAIBATSU FIRMS							
*Honsha**	90.2	69.4	79.1	32.0	81.8	73.0	34.4
Zaibatsu Firms	0.4	8.3	1.4	16.0	5.9	16.0	19.4
Total	90.6	77.6	80.5	48.0	87.7	89.0	53.8
SUPPLIED TO ZAIBATSU AFFILIATES							
*Honsha**	21.3	5.0	49.5	36.0	12.1	21.0	21.5
Zaibatsu Firms	8.1	2.7	1.9	3.0	1.5	19.0	6.3
Total	29.4	7.7	51.4	39.0	13.6	40.0	27.8

Note: *Honsha* (head-office) stands for zaibatsu bank that was controlled by a zaibatsu family.

Source: K. Takahashi and J. Aoyama, *Nihon Zaibatsu-Ron* (A Study on the Japanese Zaibatsu) (Tokyo, 1938), p. 162.

loans to total loans) rose steadily, with no visible departure from the trend throughout the 1912–30 period.[54] These data for the Mitsui Bank show that the bank made a clear departure from its previous loan practice during the first spurt period (Table VI.3), but the data for the Mitsubishi Bank show that that bank made an even more distinct change in its loan practices. The ratio of long-term loans to total assets rose sharply during World War I, and, in spite of the gradual decline from the peak of 0.65 in 1917, it remained at a relatively high level throughout the 1920's. The long-term loans to total loans ratio (l/T) jumped distinctly during the war, and it remained at a high level, with no visible sign of declining. It is also noteworthy that the Mitsubishi Bank began to purchase an increasingly large amount of securities (bonds and shares) throughout the 1912–30 period, in clear contrast to the pattern observed in Table VI.3. As the Mitsubishi Bank's holding of the shares of Mitsubishi-connected firms was less than any other zaibatsu bank's holding of the shares of its respective group, the Mitsubishi Bank's S/A and l/T reflect the bank's increased holding of bonds and shares of non-zaibatsu firms.

Since the Yasuda (for which data are shown in Table VI.6), the Sumitomo, and the Daiichi banks also showed similar increases in the importance of

54. See notes for Table VI.3.

long-term loans *vis-à-vis* total assets and total loans, the conclusion that an increasing amount of long-term loans was made by the zaibatsu banks to non-zaibatsu firms during the 1920's appears to be well-established.[55]

To show the increasing dominance of the zaibatsu banks during the 1920's, we need only present a few facts. Table VI.7 clearly shows that there were significant changes in both the absolute and relative positions of the zaibatsu banks between 1919 and 1927. During those eight years the zaibatsu banks increased their relative share of total deposits from 25 to 31 per cent, or

TABLE VI.6
Selected Ratios of Uses of Zaibatsu Bank Funds
1912–1930, end of year

Year	Mitsui		Mitsubishi			Yasuda*	
	1/A	1/T	1/A	1/T	S/A	1/A	1/T
1912	0.24	0.35	0.10	0.14	0.06	—	—
1913	0.25	0.36	0.10	0.13	0.05	—	—
1914	0.21	0.31	0.14	0.16	0.05	—	—
1915	0.23	0.37	0.19	0.23	0.05	—	—
1916	0.26	0.41	0.64	0.82	0.03	—	—
1917	0.25	0.35	0.65	0.83	0.03	—	—
1918	0.28	0.40	0.59	0.79	0.03	—	—
1919	0.20	0.34	0.58	0.89	0.04	—	—
1920	0.17	0.50	0.55	0.81	0.08	—	—
1921	0.23	0.41	0.47	0.84	0.16	—	—
1922	0.19	0.32	0.47	0.83	0.24	—	—
1923	0.19	0.30	0.46	0.83	0.23	0.41	0.67
1924	0.14	0.28	0.47	0.77	0.21	0.42	0.69
1925	0.39	0.76	0.40	0.77	0.28	0.43	0.72
1926	0.43	0.83	0.40	0.73	0.29	0.48	0.74
1927	0.38	0.80	0.36	0.77	0.36	0.50	0.84
1928	0.37	0.81	0.30	0.80	0.44	0.44	0.84
1929	0.43	0.86	0.31	0.86	0.43	0.43	0.90
1930	0.44	0.87	0.36	0.87	0.44	0.43	0.87

Notes: T—total loans.
1—long-term loans.
A—total assets.
S—securities (bonds and shares) held by each bank.
For explanations of loan items, see notes for Table 3.

* The Yasuda bank merged with ten banks in 1923. Thus the earlier data are not comparable with the post-merger data.

Sources: Bank histories and the Yūshōdō Microfilms.

55. The Yūshōdō Microfilms, and the bank histories.

TABLE VI.7

The Expansion of the Big Five,
1919 and 1927
(end of year, 1,000 yen)

	Year	Paid-in Capital	Deposits	Loans
Mitsui	1919	60,000	351,130	318,526
	1927	60,000	560,334	403,512
Mitsubishi	1919	30,000	233,541	208,588
	1927	30,000	470,586	230,308
Yasuda	1919	17,500	128,575	118,535
	1927	92,750	713,276	587,967
Sumitomo	1919	30,000	348,359	345,582
	1927	50,000	552,780	367,497
Daiichi	1919	14,638	374,409	362,532
	1927	50,000	520,883	365,333
Total of Big Five	1919	152,138	1,437,014	1,353,753
	1927	282,750	2,817,860	1,954,617
Total of All Ordinary Banks	1919	717,156	5,744,096	5,666,461
	1927	1,469,708	9,027,897	8,181,695
% of Big Five to Total of all Banks	1919	21.2%	25.0%	24.0%
	1927	19.0%	31.2%	23.9%

Sources: Computed from data in bank histories.

from 5.7 to 9 billion yen in absolute amounts. The market share of loans remained virtually unchanged, but the total amount of loans made by these banks increased from 5.7 to 8.2 billion yen. These developments are especially significant when considered against the fact that the relative share of the paid-in capital of these banks decreased, from 21.2 per cent to 19 per cent. Another way of appraising the financial power of the zaibatsu group is to note that eight zaibatsu groups (banks, insurance companies, credit companies) accounted for 45.7 per cent of the total capital + deposits + reserves of all private banks, insurance companies, and credit companies at the end of 1929.[56]

56. The eight zaibatsu groups are Mitsui, Mitsubishi, Sumitomo, Yasuda, Daiichi (*i.e.* the Big Five involving 29 banks, 4 credit firms, 4 life insurance companies, 19 other types of insurance companies) and the Kawasaki, Yamaguchi, and Kōnoike groups, involving 21 banks, 3 credit firms, 7 life insurance companies, and 6 other types of insurance firms. These three groups are the second group in size to the Big Five. K. Takahashi, *An Anatomy of Japanese Zaibatsu*, p. 39.

A few important factors contributed to this rapid concentration of the financial market. One was the sporadic bank runs which the banking industry experienced after World War I and the nation-wide bank runs of 1927 which resulted from the accumulated ills of the "earthquake bills" and the banks' practice of acting as "organ banks." "Earthquake bills" were those notes which many borrowers were unable to pay because of the earthquake of 1923 and which were guaranteed to banks by the Bank of Japan. These "earthquake bills" forced the Bank of Japan to restrict the scope of freedom which it could adopt with regard to its monetary policy. They also made the portfolios of banks unsound, because the banks had to depend on heel-dragging political decisions for government loans to the banks holding these bills.[57]

"Organ banks" were the Japanese banks of the period which became organs of their specific clients. There were many such banks, and they were often forced into the position of making unsound loans to their clients, mostly industrial firms, who were facing financial difficulties. Since the banks were committed to their clients in the sense that the banks had already made large loans to these firms and their bankruptcy would mean the end of the banks themselves, they were forced to make further unsound loans. Such a practice, as the Bank of Taiwan experienced in its dealings with the Suzuki Shōten, could—and did—lead to a nation-wide bank run.[58]

The instability of the banking industry caused many savers to transfer their deposits to larger and more well-established banks. The zaibatsu banks, which survived these crises with only occasional runs on their branch banks, naturally were the major beneficiaries of these transferred savings. Throughout the period the government was also anxious to stabilize the financial market, and it chose actively to promote mergers and unifications of weaker (small and/or local) banks. Beginning in 1924, the Ministry of Finance engaged in an active program of reducing the number of banks in each prefecture by extending assistance in valuation of assets at the time of a merger, and of helping select the best qualified managers of newly unified banks. This program was carried on throughout the 1920's, and the Ministry's "persuasion" was effective in numerous instances.[59]

No less important in bringing about the highly oligopolistic structure of the banking industry were the aggressive merger and absorption measures adopted by the largest banks themselves. A typical case is that of the Yasuda Bank. In 1923, the Yasuda Bank absorbed ten other banks scattered through-

57. For detailed descriptions, see M. Kajinishi *et al.*, *Nihon shihonshugi no botsuraku I* (The Fall of Japanese Capitalism, Vol. I) (Tokyo, 1960), pp. 185–90.

58. *Ibid.*, pp. 157–61.

59. M. Kajinishi, *Zoku nihon shihonshugi hattatsu-shi* (A Revised History of the Development of Japanese Capitalism) (Tokyo, 1957), pp. 49–50.

out the country, and created a giant bank (See Table VI.7).[60] It was a common practice of the larger city banks to absorb the smaller local banks and make them into branch offices.

How large was the banking industry in which the zaibatsu interest dominated? Table VI.8 may help answer this question. The sum of deposits and paid-in capital of all banks rose from an amount equivalent to 64 per cent of GNP to an excess of 100 per cent by the beginning of the 1920's. The sum of deposits and paid-in capital of commercial banks (excluding the government banks) rose from an amount equivalent to 44.2 per cent of GNP to 80.9 per cent, or nearly doubled, between 1911 and 1926. These high percentages reflect, to some extent, the recession of the period, which caused banks to have excess loanable funds on hand, but there is no doubt that they also reflect the increasing financial power of banks within the economy

TABLE VI.8

Growth of Bank Assets, 1911–1926

(million yen)

Year	All Banks			Commercial Banks		
	Deposits (A)	Paid-in Capital (B)	$\dfrac{(A) + (B)}{GNP}$	Deposits (C)	Paid-in Capital (D)	$\dfrac{(C) + (D)}{GNP}$
1911	1,776	480	64.0	1,256	327	44.2
1912	1,941	534	59.7	1,357	369	41.6
1913	2,110	574	63.2	1,444	392	43.3
1914	2,212	608	71.4	1,520	401	48.7
1915	2,569	622	82.2	1,700	358	53.0
1916	3,464	648	87.2	2,257	374	55.8
1917	5,146	751	95.1	3,234	437	59.2
1918	7,236	888	88.8	4,640	513	56.3
1919	8,734	1,207	73.1	5,744	717	47.5
1920	8,829	1,639	87.5	5,827	964	56.8
1921	9,494	1,747	101.8	6,445	1,045	67.9
1922	9,551	1,875	102.2	7,801	1,450	82.8
1923	9,692	1,929	98.4	7,805	1,491	78.7
1924	10,232	1,953	93.9	8,093	1,508	74.0
1925	10,821	1,918	93.3	8,727	1,501	74.9
1926	11,272	1,924	100.0	9,179	1,497	80.9

Sources: The Bank of Japan, *Hundred-Year Statistics of the Japanese Economy* (Tokyo, 1966), p. 194, and K. Ohkawa, *The Growth Rate of the Japanese Economy Since 1878* (Tokyo, 1957), pp. 170, 247.

60. A detailed description of this merger is found in The Yasuda Bank, *A 60-year History of the Yasuda Bank*, pp. 225–248.

during the Taisho period. These percentages for Taisho Japan were higher than similar percentages calculated by Cameron for West European nations and the United States.[61]

If this evaluation of the facts is accepted, a new interpretation emerges. Generally speaking, in the early stages of industrialization in Japan the role of banks was quite close to that which they had had in England, but during the 1920's the banks began to behave much more like those observed in nineteenth-century Germany. This, in a way, is not a surprising discovery. While the zaibatsu-banks-to-be were still in the process of building their foundations and supplying capital to a limited number of firms which the banks themselves established or in which the banks held major interests, the first industrial spurt was taking place, and this in the cotton industry, which received little industrial capital from the banking system. The cotton industry, as we have seen earlier, depended not on long-term loans from banks, but on their own profits, internal reserves, share capital, and short-term loans.[62]

The cotton textile industry, which accounted for nearly 32 per cent of total gross manufacturing output at the turn of the century, is known for its labor-intensive production and relatively low requirements for fixed capital, unlike the metallurgical, machine, chemical, and utility industries, which developed during and after World War I. For this reason, it was the cotton textile industry which was most vocal and persistent in opposing any legal limitations on work hours, night shifts, and other labor practices which hindered the maximum use of their fixed capital. In 1921, when the first session of the International Labor Organization took up for discussion the night shift in the Japanese cotton textile industry, one industry representative defended it by saying that:

> If night shifts are prohibited ... the equivalent of one-third of the
> cotton textile industry's spindles, i.e. about one million spindles out of

61. Rondo Cameron, "Conclusion," in R. Cameron et al., Banking in the Early Stage of Industrialization, pp. 301–2.

62. We should, however, keep in mind the possible importance of short-term loans, as Cameron emphasized in evaluating the role of banks during the early stages of industrialization. He wrote: "Characteristically, commercial banks grant short-term credit for working capital. Partly for this reason many authorities have asserted that banking has made a negligible contribution to the formation of industrial capital. Apart from overlooking the many instances in which banks departed from the rule of short-term credit, this view fails to take into account the way in which entrepreneurs use short-term credit to free their own resources for fixed investment. In industries with high rates of profit and reinvestment—and these rates are typical of new firms in periods of rapid industrialization—the contribution made in this fashion could be considerable." Rondo Cameron, "Introduction" in Cameron et al., Banking in the Early Stage of Industrialization, p. 11. See also Sydney Pollard, "Fixed Capital in the Industrial Revolution," Journal of Economic History, XXIV (Sept. 1964), pp. 299–314.

3.2 million spindles, will be left idle. To make up for it, the industry would require an additional capital injection of 150 million yen. . . . That the night shift is detrimental to health is beyond question, and it must be eliminated eventually. However, it is not possible to eliminate it now, as has already been done in Europe.[63]

It is a well-known fact that in 1929, when the long-practiced "midnight shift" (*shinyagyō*) was banned, the industry's reaction was to introduce a series of measures, such as shorter lunch periods, more rigidly structured piece-rates, and a finer breakdown of skill levels, which put a premium on speed of work.[64]

By the end of the war boom, however, the situation had changed in many respects. The zaibatsu-connected firms had by then become financially independent and the giant banks were now larger and in a position to supply long-term capital to those industries which, by the nature of the industry, required such capital. The available evidence shows, at least to the satisfaction of this writer, that the often-described German-type banking practices were a phenomenon which appeared during the 1920's, and that they followed the period of the first spurt in which these same banking practices were unimportant.

In historical perspective, one could perhaps argue that the largest banks, especially the zaibatsu banks, were concerned almost exclusively with their own limited industrial ventures, expanding and rebuilding the newly acquired former government plants, buying and trading government bonds, and acting as commercial bankers for the large segment of the economy which included the cotton textile industry. The loans these banks made to their mining, shipbuilding, Western-type paper, and other ventures gave an appearance of banking practices which resembled those in Germany, but, if our earlier observations are correct, these bankers did not in fact become industrial bankers until the 1920's.

CONCLUSIONS

Despite my findings, which appear to show that internal accumulation, share capital, and short-term loans played a much more significant role than has been maintained for the period prior to World War I, and that investment

63. Hiroshi Hazama, *Nihon Rōmu Kanrishi Kenkyū* (A Study of Japanese Labor Management) (Tokyo, 1964), p. 327. Quoted from *Nihon rōdō nenkan* (The Annual Report on Labor), the 1920 volume, p. 669.

64. Hazama *op. cit.*, has a detailed discussion of these changes instituted by the cotton textile industry, pp. 322–39. He noted that "the abolition of the night shift was an extremely hard blow to the entrepreneurs of the cotton textile industry which used low wages and night shifts as the basic source of strength in conquering the international market," p. 326.

banking of the German type developed only during the 1920's, these conclusions are at best tentative.

In an effort to obtain a fuller understanding of the process of industrial
financing, we must not only attempt to make further progress in solving
numerous difficulties involved in using available quantitative evidence, but
we must also be mindful of various special institutional factors which might
have been important in financing Japanese industrialization. The constant
inflationary tendency observed during the spurt,[65] the uniquely Japanese
development of trading companies, as described recently by Nakagawa,[66]
and a set of growth-promoting policies adopted by the Japanese government
are factors which require continued and careful analyses.

It seems to me that this discussion shows the necessity of making a thorough
re-examination of the current consensus on Japanese industrial financing.
Certainly much work yet remains to be done. But it is evident that the
Japanese case fits rather awkwardly within the more accepted mental or
explicitly theorized scheme of the relationships between the patterns of
industrial financing and the time of entry into industrialization. Or, to put it
differently, we must now ask: why did the Japanese case resemble that of
England, the first industrializer, rather than that of Germany or Italy? Was
Japan not "backward" in the Gershenkronian terminology? Was the role of
"historical accident" greater than some logical sequence of events sought
by economic historians?

These questions are only the first step, and they call for continued research,
emphasizing empiricism rather than deductive speculation, with an international perspective which has been sorely lacking, especially in the Japanese
literature. Such research, I believe, can add a significant dimension in
explaining the only "success story" in Asia.

65. This is explicitly stated in Kazushi Ohkawa, *Nihon Keizai Bunseki: Seicho to Kōzō*
(An Analysis of the Japanese Economy: Growth and Structure) (Tokyo, 1962), p. 10.

66. In a recent article, Keiichirō Nakagawa of the University of Tokyo emphasized the
importance of "organized entrepreneurship" in Meiji Japan. According to Nakagawa, the
co-operative attitude among various entrepreneurs was uniquely Japanese. This cooperative entrepreneurship aided rapid growth, "while the government, at no time, played
no more significant role than that of complementing the activities of these organized
entrepreneurs." His typical example is the case of cotton spinning firms and Japanese
shipping lines which helped buy cheaper raw material and increase exports. Keiichirō
Nakagawa, "The Organized Entrepreneurial Activities in the Process of Japanese Industrialization," *Japan Business History Review* (November 1967), II, No. 3, pp. 8–37.

CHAPTER VII

Louisiana 1804–1861

GEORGE D. GREEN

In any study of banking and industrialization among the late-comers, ante-bellum Louisiana might serve as the limiting case, or counter-example. Although both the banking system and the economy experienced substantial growth and achieved high levels of performance by nineteenth-century standards, there was very little industrialization. Manufacturing contributed less than 10 per cent of the state's output. Once we recognize that economic development need not be synonymous with industrialization for every region or even every nation, we may then find much in the Louisiana experience which is comparable with the history of banking and economic development in other areas. After briefly describing the Louisiana economy and its banking system, we will examine the quantitative relationship between banking and the economy, and the impact of the composition or allocation of bank credit.

The economy of antebellum Louisiana developed along two complementary but distinct lines. Like the other Southern states, it grew to be heavily committed to plantation agriculture and slavery for the production of its major cash crops, cotton and sugar. But unlike the rest of the South, Louisiana also developed a prosperous and powerful urban economy in its great commercial center, New Orleans.

At the time of the Louisiana Purchase (1803), a few farms and plantations concentrated along the Mississippi River and the bayous of what is now south-eastern Louisiana produced only about 5000 bales of cotton and 5000 hogs-heads of sugar. The prevailing frontier economy of self-sufficient farming and cattle grazing slowly receded over the next fifty years. In 1812 the State of Louisiana was admitted to the Union. Cotton plantations expanded rapidly after about 1815, and sugar plantations experienced their expansionary surges in 1824–31 and 1842–53. By 1840 cotton production exceeded 400,000 bales, and the greatest antebellum crop, in 1859, yielded nearly 780,000 bales;

sugar production reached a peak of about 450,000 hogsheads in 1853.[1]

By 1803 New Orleans was already a trading city with a population of 10,000, but its greatest era of expansion coincided with the development of the Mississippi valley, especially between 1810 and 1840. By 1840 New Orleans had over 100,000 residents, 29 per cent of the state's population, making Louisiana the most urbanized state in the nation! New Orleans accounted for about 70 per cent of the state's manufacturing, and its commerce contributed about as much to state income as sugar production did. The elite community of merchants, bankers, lawyers, and urban-oriented planters made New Orleans the nerve center of the state's political economy.[2]

Between 1804 and 1836 Louisiana's territorial and state legislatures chartered twenty banks (see Table VII.1). Fourteen of these banks were chartered between 1831 and 1836, raising the state's chartered banking capital from $4.7 million to $36.8 million within six years. During part of this period New Orleans was also served by branches of the federally chartered First and Second Banks of the United States. There were three types of banks in Louisiana during the 1830's: property banks, which invested heavily in agricultural and urban mortgages; improvement banks, which constructed and operated canals, railroads, waterworks, and other projects; and conventional commercial banks. All of the banks were located in New Orleans, but several of them operated branches in small towns across the state; these branches (31 of them in 1840, the peak year) were concentrated in the wealthy sugar and cotton planting areas.[3]

The state government actively promoted and subsidized several of the chartered banks (especially the property banks), either by issuing state bonds in their behalf or by endorsing the bonds of the banks. By 1838 Louisiana had the second largest state debt in the country ($23.7 million), and 95 per cent of this debt was for the benefit of the banks. This bonded debt brought the state to the brink of fiscal crisis in the 1840's, and thus contributed to the reaction against banking.[4]

1. James L. Watkins, *King Cotton: A Historical and Statistical Review, 1790–1908* (New York, 1908); Lewis C. Gray, *History of Agriculture in the Southern United States to 1860* (Washington, D.C., 1933), II, 1033–1034.

2. Edwin A. Davis, *Louisiana: The Pelican State* (Baton Rouge, 1959), p. 139; Richard A. Easterlin, "Interregional Differences in Per Capita Income, Population, and Total Income, 1840–1950," in *Trends in the American Economy in the Nineteenth Century* (New York, 1960), p. 128; *Eighth Census of the United States*, III, "Manufactures," 202–204, 729; Table VII.3 below.

3. *House Documents*, 25 Cong., 3 sess., No. 227, p. 676; *House Documents*, 32 Cong., 1 sess., No. 122, pp. 326–327.

4. *Tenth Census of the United States*, "Valuation, Taxation, and Public Indebtedness," VII, 523, 526. For greater detail on state policy, see my "Banking and Finance in Ante-Bellum Louisiana (1804–1861): Their Impact on the Course of Economic Development" (unpublished Ph.D. dissertation, Stanford University, 1968), chapter VI.

The series of financial crises that began with the panic of 1837 and lasted until 1842 mark the great divide in the banking history of antebellum Louisiana. Of the seventeen banks operating in 1836, eleven went into liquidation, while the survivors contracted severely and limited themselves more strictly to short-term commercial lending. State banking policy shifted from promotion toward strict regulation or even abolition of the banks. The Louisiana Bank Act of 1842 compelled resumption of specie payments, forced liquidation of the weakest banks, and introduced such reforms as the backing of both bank notes and deposits, one-third by specie reserves and two-thirds by short-term commercial loans. The state constitution of 1845 prohibited new bank charters and prohibited the renewal of existing charters. After a decade of shrinking bank facilities, the state constitution of 1852 returned to a more moderate position. Although it still prohibited state debts on behalf of banks, it permitted the revival of the large Citizens Bank and the passage of a "free banking" act (allowing general incorporation of banks according to standardized rules). Six free banks were chartered during the 1850's, bringing Louisiana's banking capital back to 60 per cent of its peak level of 1840. These shifts in state policy toward the banks reveal the dilemma inherent in America's early banking system; it could not consistently achieve the conflicting goals of sound money, based strictly on specie, and easy credit, needed to finance a rapidly growing economy.[5]

THE MONEY SUPPLY AND ECONOMIC GROWTH

What rate of growth of the money supply is appropriate to facilitate economic growth? Economists do not agree on the answer to this question, but most would favor a money supply which grows in such fashion as to maintain roughly stable prices, avoiding both substantial inflation and deflation. The simplest rule of thumb would be to match the growth of money to the growth of real output. But in recent years several arguments have been presented which suggest the need for a rising ratio of money to GNP, money growing faster than output. In terms of the traditional quantity theory of money this is equivalent to arguing that the money supply must outgrow output by enough to offset the declining trend of monetary velocity. Gurley and Shaw have developed one such model in order to explain the long-term growth of the money supply in the United States. They postulated an economy which began with a very primitive financial system, with both the initial stock and rate of issue of primary securities assumed to be near zero. In the early stages of development, money (and debt of all types) grew much more rapidly than income. This rapid monetary growth gradually tapered

5. *Report of the Joint Committee on Banks and Banking* [Louisiana Legislature], 1859, pp. 46–49.

TABLE VII.1

The Chartered Banks of Antebellum Louisiana

	Date	Capital	Amendments, Ultimate Fate
Louisiana Bank	March 12, 1804	$300,000 −2,000,000	into liquidation, 1819; completed 1823
Branch of First Bank of the United States	1805	—	charter expired, 1811
Planters Bank	April 15, 1811	600,000	suspended operations, 1820; charter expired 1826
Bank of Orleans	April 30, 1811 March 26, 1823	500,000 —	scheduled to expire in 1826 charter renewed until 1847, into liquidation, 1842
Branch of Second Bank of the United States	1817	—	charter expired 1836
Louisiana State Bank	March 18, 1818	2 mn.	became State National Bank in 1870; liquidated 1908
Bank of Louisiana	April 7, 1824	4 mn.	into liquidation, 1865
Consolidated Association of the Planters of Louisiana	March 16, 1827	2 mn.	originally chartered to 1842
City Bank of New Orleans	Feb. 19, 1828	2.5 mn.	state bonds issued, capital increased; into liquidation 1843; finally completed, 1883
	March 3, 1831	2 mn.	charter expired, 1850; assets purchased by Louisiana State Bank
Canal Bank	March 5, 1831	4 mn.	originally chartered to 1870; reorganized and survived into 20th century
Union Bank of Louisiana	April 2, 1832	7 mn.	into liquidation, January, 1844
Citizens Bank of Louisiana	April 1, 1833 March 1, 1836	12 mn.	originally chartered to 1884 state guarantee for bank bonds; into liquidation in 1842
	March 10, 1852		legislature revives bank's charter; reorganized and survived into 20th century

TABLE VII.1 (cont).

	Date	Capital	Amendments, Ultimate Fate
Clinton & Port Hudson Railroad Company	1833	500,000	amendment gives mortgage banking powers
Mechanics and Traders Bank	April 1, 1833 March 22, 1850	2 mn.	originally chartered to 1853 authorized to begin liquidation; converted to free bank in 1853; survived past Civil War
Commercial Bank of New Orleans	April 1, 1833	3 mn.	into liquidation, 1843
Atchafalaya Railroad and Banking Company	March 10, 1835	2 mn.	banking operations into liquidation, 1842
New Orleans & Carrollton Railroad and Banking Company	April 1, 1835	3 mn.	banking powers granted to existing railroad company; banking powers surrendered, 1844
New Orleans Gas Light and Banking Company	April 1, 1835	6 mn.	banking powers granted to existing gas light company; banking powers surrendered, March, 1845
Exchange and Banking Company	April 1, 1835	2 mn.	into liquidation, 1842
New Orleans Improvement and Banking Company	Feb. 9, 1836	2 mn.	banking powers granted to existing improvement company; into liquidation, 1842
Merchants Bank of New Orleans	Feb. 25, 1836	1 mn.	into liquidation, 1847
Pontchartrain Railroad and Banking Company	March 12, 1836		banking powers granted to existing railroad company; these powers never exercised
The Bank of New Orleans*	May, 1853	1 mn.	first free bank; capital raised to $2 mn. by 1857
Southern Bank*	1853	1.25 mn.	
Bank of James Robb*	1857	600,000	
Bank of America*	1857	1 mn.	later reorganized as Merchants Bank (1859)
Union Bank*	1857	1.5 mn.	
Crescent City Bank*	1857	1 mn.	

* Free banks.

off as the economy matured. The mature economy has a relatively stable money/income ratio of about 0.3, that is, a money supply equivalent to about 30 per cent of the nation's annual income. Following the Gurley-Shaw approach, Rondo Cameron has elaborated some of the institutional changes which account for this rapid monetary expansion in the early stages of development. When backward sectors of the economy, especially subsistence (frontier) agriculture, are drawn into market-oriented production, the money supply must serve a larger proportion of the total population. As the economy develops, greater specialization and division of labor in production (and consumption) require more monetary transactions between firms at different stages; thus, for a given final output, more money transactions occur.[6]

Did Louisiana's supply of money and banking facilities exist at a level and grow at a rate which was "optimal" for economic development? The first tentative step toward answering this question is to measure the Louisiana experience in terms of the theoretically relevant variables. The resulting estimates may be compared with those of the United States during the same years and with those of other developing nations, past and present.

In *Banking in the Early Stages of Industrialization*, Rondo Cameron and his co-authors developed the concept of "banking density" as a crude index of financial development. This is a measure of bank offices (including branches) per 10,000 of population. From his observations of the experience of several industrializing nations in the past, Cameron defines a "banking density" ratio over 1.0 as "high"; between 0.5 and 1.0 as "moderate"; below 0.5 as "low"; and below 0.1 (one office per 100,000 of population) as "very low."[7] Such data are shown in Table VII.2 for the city of New Orleans, the state of Louisiana, and the United States. New Orleans rates "moderate" on Cameron's scale, reaching the "high" level in 1820 and 1840. Yet this result is quite misleading, because Cameron's index is based on national averages; one would naturally expect a higher "density" of banks in cities. This is confirmed by a very rough comparison of New Orleans with five other United States cities (Boston, New York, Philadelphia, Baltimore, Cincinnati). New Orleans ranked fourth, fourth, and third out of the six cities in 1810, 1820, and 1830, respectively.[8] In comparison with other cities of the day, New Orleans presumably had a "moderate" banking density. The state of

6. John Gurley and E. S. Shaw, "The Growth of Debt and Money in the United States, 1800–1950: A Suggested Interpretation," *Review of Economics and Statistics*, XXXIX (1957), 250–262; Rondo Cameron, "Banking in the Early Stages of Industrialization: A Preliminary Survey," *Scandinavian Economic History Review*, XI (1966), pp. 132–133.

7. Cameron *et al.*, *Banking*, pp. 296–300.

8. The number of banks chartered for each city can be cumulated from J. Van Fenstermaker, *The Development of American Commercial Banking, 1782–1837* (Kent, Ohio, 1964), Appendix A. Interestingly, Boston moved from 3rd to 1st in the group, while New York (6th, 6th, and 4th) and Philadelphia (5th, 5th, 6th) had lower "density."

Louisiana as a whole ranked generally "low" in density, at or below the United States average; the striking exception is 1840, at the end of a decade of rapid bank expansion and proliferation of branch banks across the state.

The "banking density" indicator is admittedly a crude one, mainly because it makes no allowance for variations in bank size or income levels in the economy. Louisiana's banks were much larger than those in other states in the antebellum era. The ratio of bank money to income does consider bank size and income levels and thus overcomes these two disadvantages and gives a sharper picture (where such data are available). According to our previous theoretical discussion, this money/income ratio should show a gradual rising trend during the process of economic development. Gurley and Shaw have concluded, from their study of the historical experience of the United States since 1800 and of about 70 countries since 1945, that the ratio is typically 0.1 or below for the poorest countries, rising to a peak of about 0.30 in the most advanced countries.[9] Table VII.2 shows how antebellum Louisiana compares with these expectations. The level of the ratio is in the moderate range only for the few observations before 1828; after climbing to a remarkable level in the late 1830's it then drops rapidly and levels off at about 0.45 from 1845 to 1860. Both the high level of the ratio and its lack of rising trend require further comment.

To some extent the high level of this ratio is a statistical illusion. The income data used in the denominator are the rough and incomplete estimates from my index of Louisiana output (see Table VII.3). In 1840, the one year for which comparison was possible, my estimate was only 60 per cent of Easterlin's more comprehensive figure. If we boldly assumed the same degree of understatement for all years, we would deflate the money/income series to 60 per cent of its original level. This would lower the 1845–60 data to an average of about 0.27, a more plausible figure than that given in Table VII.2.[10] That the adjusted figures are still relatively high may be partly explained by the historical role of New Orleans as a financial intermediary for the entire Mississippi valley. Since the Louisiana banks were actually supplying money and credit directly or indirectly (e.g. through re-lending by factors) to a larger area, the "true" ratio would reflect the larger regional income in the denominator, and would be correspondingly lower.

The chronology of Louisiana's money/income ratio does not fit our theoretical expectations. There is a gradual rising trend until the early 1830's, but this is followed by a leap to very high levels in 1836–40. Such high levels

9. Gurley and Shaw, "Financial Structure and Economic Development," *Economic Development and Cultural Change*, XV (1967), 261.

10. Easterlin, "Interregional Differences," pp. 73–140. The adjustment would actually involve multiplying each income entry (in the denominator of the ratio) by 1/0.6, which is equivalent to multiplying the ratio itself by 0.6.

TABLE VII.2

Banking Density and Money/Income Ratios

Year	Density[a]			Money/Income	
	New Orleans	Louisiana	U.S.A.	Louisiana	U.S.A.
1810	0.755	0.131	0.141		
1820	1.10	0.195	0.192		0.146
1824				0.14	
1825				0.11	
1826				0.13	
1827				0.16	
1828				0.31	
1829					
1830	0.854	0.185	0.212	0.32	0.157
1831					
1832				0.49	
1833					
1834				0.66	
1835				0.31	
1836				0.72	
1837				0.89	
1838				0.81	
1839				0.69	
1840	1.57	1.33	0.526	0.60	0.125
1841				0.43	
1842				0.57	
1843				0.29	
1844				0.35	
1845				0.44	0.099
1846				0.41	
1847				0.45	
1848				0.40	
1849				0.45	
1850	0.601	0.56	0.353	0.44	0.104
1851				0.30	
1852				0.29	
1853				0.32	
1854				0.47	
1855				0.45	0.107
1856				0.45	
1857				0.53	
1858				0.29	

TABLE VII.2 (cont.)

Year	Density[a]			Money/Income	
	New Orleans	Louisiana	U.S.A.	Louisiana	U.S.A.
1859				0.49	
1860	0.712	0.184	0.496	0.41	0.110

[a] Offices per 10,000 population.

Sources:

George D. Green, "Banking and Finance in Ante-bellum Louisiana (1804–1861): Their Impact on the Course of Economic Development" (Ph.D. Dissertation, Stanford University, 1968), Tables II-1 and VIII-2, pp. 66–70 and 421–23.

Banking offices, Bank money in Louisiana: *House Documents*, 25 Cong., 3 sess., No. 227, p. 676. *Senate Documents*, 52 Cong., 2 sess., No. 38, pp. 102–103.

Banking offices, Bank money in U.S.A.: Joseph Van Fenstermaker, *The Development of American Commercial Banking, 1782–1837* (Kent, Ohio, 1965), p. 111. *Senate Documents*, 52 Cong., 2 sess., No. 38, pp. 69–70.

Louisiana Income: see Table VII.3.

U.S. Income: Robert E. Gallman, "Gross National Product in the United States, 1834–1909," in *Output. Employment and Productivity in the United States after 1800* (New York, 1966), p. 26. The figures for 1820 and 1830 are my own extrapolations, based on data from Paul A. David, "The Growth of Real Product in the United States Before 1840: New Evidence, Controlled Conjectures," *Journal of Economic History*, XXVII (1967), 184.

undoubtedly imply an inflationary excess supply of money during those years, as other price data and qualitative evidence fully confirm. The sharp drop in the money/income ratio after 1840 appears to have moved Louisiana's financial system to a new trend line at a lower level and with slower expansion (if any). The experience of general financial crisis, contraction, and debt default between 1837 and 1843 could account for the downward shift, but it could not account for the slower trend.[11] A full explanation of the statistics will require a broader historical approach.

These several statistical "tests" of monetary theory are crude, I admit, but even so, we should consider them. What do they tell us about financial development in antebellum Louisiana? The state's monetary ratios (even after adjustment) were at relatively high levels, comparable to those of financially sophisticated and moderately prosperous countries, past and present. The ratios were consistently highest and rising fastest in the 1830's, and they were generally somewhat lower and nearly constant after 1845. Unfortunately, these two empirical conclusions do not imply a clear historical interpretation about the *causal* role of finance in economic development. For example, two distinct and nearly opposing hypotheses are both consistent with the above conclusions: (1) The Louisiana banking system was already highly developed by the 1830's; its leveling off thereafter was essentially a sign of financial "maturity." Certainly the system was advanced enough and

11. Gurley and Shaw, "Financial Structures and Economic Development," p. 261.

expansive enough to meet the needs of a growing and prosperous economy. (2) The exceptionally high monetary ratios reflected a brief period of inflationary banking expansion in the 1830's and a continuous tendency for Louisiana banks to finance trade and production outside the state. This seemingly high financial development was abruptly terminated by 1840; premature financial stagnation thereafter retarded economic growth.

Thus, broadly speaking, the high level of finance suggests its adequacy, while the lack of growth of finance suggests its inadequacy. In order to choose between these two hypotheses, more evidence is required. Further statistical evidence on the behavior of prices and output will provide a little help; an examination of particular sectors of the economy and of other historical evidence on the adequacy of finance will shed even more light.

An examination of available data and estimates on Louisiana prices and output (see Table VII.3) appears to support the first hypothesis: that finance permitted (or perhaps encouraged) economic growth. The period of sharp price deflation (1838–42) is balanced not only by the familiar inflation of 1833–38, but also by another period of inflation in the 1850's. Real income data show no clear signs of retardation. In fact, during the decade of the 1840's, presumably the period of most restricted finance, the economy enjoyed more rapid growth than during either the preceding or following decade.[12] The depression of 1839–42 was offset by rapid recovery and expansion after 1842. During the 1850's, on the other hand, aggregate output remained nearly stagnant until after 1857, despite the expansionist free banking movement.

At the aggregate level, at least, there seems to be little indication that lack of financial expansion retarded economic growth. In part this simply reflects the choice of statistics. The emphasis in my index is upon cotton, sugar, and New Orleans trade (which itself included a large amount of cotton and sugar). These are precisely the sectors which were most dependent upon external rather than domestic markets, and they were also the sectors which probably had greatest access to sources of finance outside Louisiana in times of credit restriction. But even if we accept the statistics, and the inferences drawn from them, the causal interpretations are not straightforward or unambiguous. Even these seemingly favorable aggregate statistics can be interpreted in a fashion consistent with the second hypothesis, that of financial retardation. In the first place, if the financial system had been more expansionary, Louisiana's economic growth might have been even greater than it actually was. Second, the economy may have "escaped" some of the restrictive impacts of financial retardation either by financial innovations or by substituting alternative non-financial techniques for mobilizing resources.

12. This result holds regardless of the dating chosen (1830–1840–1850–1860 or 1825–1835–1845–1855, for example), and for similar calculations based on three-year averages for the decadal years.

Finally, inadequate finance may have caused retardation in particular sectors of the state's economy, and this would not be revealed in the aggregate statistics. Evidence of the inadequacy of finance in Louisiana after 1842, given in the following pages, confirms such interpretations.

The most straightforward historical evidence of a restrictive financial system in Louisiana can be found in the record of monetary contraction between 1837 and 1843 and in the explicitly restrictive state policies adopted beginning in 1842. By June 1842 the financial crisis had reduced the supply of bank money (notes and deposits) to only 16 per cent of its previous peak amount (October 1836); the money/income ratio fell by 68 per cent. In response to this disastrous financial collapse, the state shifted its banking policy away from the developmental goal of "easy credit" and toward the goal of "sound money." The Bank Act of 1842 imposed new reserve require-ments, higher and more comprehensive than those of the preceding decades, and initiated procedures for liquidation of several of the banks. The climax of the restrictive movement came in the state constitutional convention of 1845, which voted to prohibit enactment or renewal of any bank charters. This restrictive policy was eventually somewhat relaxed in a new constitution, adopted in 1852, but even after 1852 the concern for sound money signifi-cantly restrained monetary expansion. In an environment of post-crisis uncertainty and strict governmental surveillance, the New Orleans banks cautiously held specie reserves well above the 33 per cent levels required by the Act of 1842; because the banks held these excess reserves they had a correspondingly smaller lending capacity.[13]

Before historical judgment is passed on the restrictive state banking policies of the 1840's, two further questions must be answered. Were these policies effective in achieving their goal of sound money? Was there any alternative policy that might have achieved this goal with less sacrifice of the goal of economic development? The legislators who wrote the constitution of 1845 sought to achieve "sound" *specie* money by gradually closing all of Louisiana's banks and eliminating their notes and checking deposits from the state's money supply. Since this would have required either a further severe deflation or a depression, its "soundness" may be questioned. (In fact, the 1852 constitution reversed the 1845 policy before it could be com-pleted, and before all the bank charters expired.) The effectiveness of the 1845 policy would in any case have been threatened by imports of money from other states and probably by innovation of other "near money" and credit devices. The more sophisticated "reforms" of the Bank Act of 1842

13. The reserve ratio (specie relative to bank notes plus deposits) for all Louisiana banks remained between 70% and 96% during 1843 and 1844, and rose above 60% after the milder crisis of 1857. *Senate Documents*, 52 Cong., 2 sess., No. 38, pp. 102–103; Louisiana Legislature, *Report of the Joint Committee on Banks and Banking*, March, 1855, pp. 5–6; New Orleans *Price Current*, April 9, 1842, p. 3.

TABLE VII.3
An Index of Money and Real Income
(Aggregating total value of sugar and cotton production
and estimated income from New Orleans commerce)

Year	Sugar ($ millions)	Cotton ($ millions)	Cotton and Sugar ($ millions)	Merchant & Trade Income (10% Value of Produce) ($ millions)	Total Money Income (3) + (4) ($ millions)	Cost of Living Index (1850-51 = 100)	Real income (5) ÷ (6) ($ millions)
1821–22				1.51			
1822–23		1.88		1.45			
1823–24	2.14	3.28	5.42	1.51	6.93	91.9	7.54
1824–25	2.00	5.20	7.20	1.90	9.10	95.5	9.53
1825–26	1.91	5.13	7.04	2.04	9.08	94.6	9.60
1826–27	2.04	3.75	5.79	2.17	7.96	88.4	9.00
1827–28	1.91	3.26	5.17	2.29	7.46	86.8	8.59
1828–29	2.87	3.18	6.05	2.08	8.13	95.2	8.54
1829–30	4.97	3.20	8.17	2.21	10.38	83.9	12.37
1830–31	4.51	3.37	7.88	2.60	10.48	87.6	11.96
1831–32	2.64	2.89	5.53	2.18	7.71	92.4	8.34
1832–33	4.38	4.26	8.64	2.82	11.46	94.0	12.19
1833–34	4.41	6.38	10.79	2.98	13.77	97.3	14.15
1834–35	6.00	10.59	16.59	3.76	20.35	109.2	18.64
1835–36	2.70	9.31	12.01	3.92	15.93	126.8	12.56
1836–37	4.20	12.26	16.46	4.35	20.81	124.8	16.67
1837–38	4.06	9.93	13.99	4.56	18.55	116.0	15.99
1838–39	4.38	11.49	15.87	4.23	20.10	143.2	14.04
1839–40	5.75	12.44	18.19	4.98	23.17	116.9	19.82

TABLE VII.3 (cont).

Year	Sugar ($ millions)	Cotton ($ millions)	Cotton and Sugar ($ millions)	Merchant & Trade Income (10% Value of Produce) ($ millions)	Total Money Income (3) + (4) ($ millions)	Cost of Living Index (1850–51 = 100)	Real Income (5) ÷ (6) ($ millions)
1840–41	4.79	12.55	17.34	4.98	22.32	104.6	21.34
1841–42	3.60	9.26	12.86	4.57	17.43	90.5	19.26
1842–43	5.95	10.62	16.57	5.38	21.95	73.5	29.86
1843–44	6.00	11.55	17.55	6.01	23.56	75.8	31.08
1844–45	9.00	9.10	18.10	5.72	23.82	79.3	30.04
1845–46	10.27	12.46	22.73	7.72	30.45	83.0	36.69
1846–47	9.80	12.95	22.75	9.00	31.75	90.2	35.20
1847–48	9.60	13.65	23.25	7.98	31.23	85.2	36.65
1848–49	8.80	11.06	19.86	8.20	28.06	86.7	32.36
1849–50	12.40	8.28	20.68	9.69	30.37	95.5	31.80
1850–51	12.68	12.19	24.87	19.69	44.56	100.0	44.56
1851–52	11.83	13.08	24.91	10.81	35.72	91.4	39.08
1852–53	15.45	17.83	33.28	13.42	46.70	101.0	46.24
1853–54	15.73	12.29	28.02	11.53	39.55	113.9	34.72
1854–55	18.03	11.15	29.18	11.71	40.89	131.4	31.12
1855–56	16.20	18.20	34.40	14.43	48.83	128.4	38.03
1856–57	8.14	18.68	26.82	15.82	42.64	142.8	29.86
1857–58	17.90	19.82	37.72	16.72	54.44	114.8	47.42
1858–59	25.00	27.09	52.09	17.30	69.39	113.5	61.14
1859–60	18.19	39.31	57.50	18.52	76.02	113.4	67.04

Sources: (For fullest details and rationale, see Appendix VII-A, pp. 323–39, of my dissertation, cited in Table VII.2.)
Sugar Production: Lewis C. Gray, *History of Agriculture in the Southern United States to 1860* (Washington, D.C., 1933), II, 1033–34.
Cotton Production: Stuart Bruchey, *Cotton and the Growth of the American Economy, 1790–1860* (New York, 1967).
Value of Produce Received at New Orleans: Guy S. Callender, *Selections from the Economic History of the United States* (Boston, 1909), p. 315.
Cost of Living Index: chaining two indexes of prices of U.S. Products other than Louisiana, at New Orleans, from Arthur H. Cole, *Wholesale Commodity Prices in the United States, 1700–1861* (Cambridge, Mass., 1938), pp. 174, 177.

were also less effective than many contemporaries believed, and, for that matter, less effective than many historians have claimed. Legally required reserves could not be an emergency source of liquidity (money) without simultaneously making the bank deficient in legal reserves and forcing its contraction. Nor did the requirement that bankers back their notes and deposits only with short-term commercial loans automatically guarantee an appropriate and safe money supply. Commercial loans could be the basis for inflationary money creation just as readily as mortgage loans or other "speculative" bank investments could; during financial crises both before and after the Bank Act of 1842 the merchants were often the first to default on their debts, undermining both the liquidity and the solvency of the banks.

But was there any alternative? Certainly the nineteenth-century world, with its international gold standard and widespread domestic circulation of specie as part of the money supply, severely limited the policy options of any single state or nation. Nearly everyone in antebellum America believed in the specie standard, that all bank money or other money must be freely convertible into specie on demand. Yet daily financial practice was less doctrinaire than financial philosophy; ways were found to minimize the conflict between sound money and easy credit, essentially by compromising or suppressing specie convertibility. Banks arranged for regular settlements of their balances and exchanges of their accumulated banknotes with minimal specie transfers. Merchants and other businessmen relied on bills of exchange and other credit instruments. Banks circulated notes of small denomination, which were less likely to be redeemed for specie than large notes were (the state restricted that "unsound" practice, however). Government or private banking cartels (e.g. the Louisiana Board of Presidents) provided insurance on the monetary liabilities held by the public (as in today's FDIC) or served as lenders of last resort to the banks themselves (as in today's Federal Reserve Banks), or acquiesced in temporary suspensions of specie payments.[14] Each of these actions enabled the banks and the public to operate with a lower proportion of specie in the total money supply than would otherwise have been possible, thus permitting a larger supply of money and credit upon a given specie base. A vigorous pursuit of these common practices offered a means of overcoming the restrictive policies which Louisiana had adopted. In effect these practices gave the banks and the public a practical alternative to the doctrine of the specie standard.

It has been shown that the restrictive state policies of the 1840's could not assure sound money, and that alternative policies existed which more effectively reconciled that objective with economic growth. It remains to be shown that the existing restrictive policies actually did retard Louisiana's

14. Louisiana's financial crisis and the policies adopted to deal with it are discussed in chapter VII of my dissertation.

development. The adaptive responses of the economy to such restrictions will also be considered.

Despite the favorable impression conveyed by the statistics of prices and aggregate income, it is clear that restricted financial growth did retard economic growth in antebellum Louisiana. After 1845, as the economy recovered and expanded, it finally outgrew the dying banking system imposed by the constitution of that year; the strain was greatest between 1850 and 1853, after which free banking brought some relief. The constitution of 1845 prohibited (and that of 1852 severely restricted) the state government from external (deficit) financing of internal improvement projects which would have aided growth, and the dismal condition of the state treasury during these years effectively prevented tax-financed improvements as well. Thus government finance could not supplant the restricted private finance.

The evidence of unsatisfied demand for finance takes several forms. Silent testimony came from the exceptionally high profit margins of the banks that survived the financial crises of 1837–42; even when inefficiently run, their monopoly of scarce credit facilities brought returns as high as 30 per cent per year. More eloquent was the evidence of banking business lost to rival cities (see below). There was vocal testimony also: New Orleans businessmen and journalists complained bitterly of the city's economic losses, and they urged amendment of state banking policy.[15]

Further evidence of the impact of restrictive state policy comes from the various financial innovations that were expressly designed to circumvent such restraints. Most notable was the marked expansion of private, unchartered banks. A few chartered banks from other states also established New Orleans agencies to pick up some of the available business. Although direct evidence is lacking, it is also likely that Louisiana businessmen and planters resorted more often to internal or direct finance, and sought more direct financing from businessmen in other states.[16]

The greatest economic impact of restricted finance fell upon the most vulnerable sector of the Louisiana economy—interregional trade through New Orleans. The city did not suffer a decline in its *total* trade; on the contrary, its total receipts continued to grow vigorously right up to the Civil War. But the composition of New Orleans trade was changing—its prosperity was based increasingly on cotton, sugar, and other Southern products, while the relative contribution of the Western trade steadily declined. The city was once the major outlet for trade in Western grain, pork products, lead, and

15. Louisiana Legislature, *Report of the Standing Committees on Banks and Banking*, 1853, p. 2; *House Documents*, 31 Cong., 1 sess., No. 68, pp. 272–273; *DeBow's Review*, X (May, 1851), 587–588.

16. T. P. Thompson, "Early Financing in New Orleans," *Louisiana Historical Society Publications*, VI (1913–14), 44.

dozens of other Western products, but after 1845, and especially during the 1850's, that trade was diverted to other cities. Shrinkage of the New Orleans trading empire occurred even within the South itself, as Kentucky and Tennessee diverted their provisions northward, and Tennessee, Alabama, and northern Mississippi sent more of their cotton eastward to Atlantic ports. The large volume of Western trade that did still come to New Orleans was increasingly destined for Southern consumption rather than for export to Northern or foreign markets; here again arises the indirect dependence of New Orleans commerce upon "King Cotton" and other Southern staples, as Southern planters who specialized in export crops were the major customers for products from the West.[17]

The major reason for the shrinkage of New Orleans' hinterland was, of course, the transportation revolution, which radically altered the American economy during this era. To a large extent the improvements in canal and railroad technology made inevitable the relative decline of New Orleans as a commercial center. No amount of entrepreneurship, railroad building, river and port improvement, or banking expansion in Louisiana could have prevented the ultimate loss of some of the trade of the upper Mississippi and Ohio river valleys. New Orleans had initially received that trade because the Mississippi River provided the only connection between the Western producers and the Eastern or European market. When a more direct and less costly route became available, New Orleans lost the business; geography, now wedded to technology, withdrew her bounty from New Orleans and befriended other cities.[18]

But the argument of ultimate inevitability must not cloud our sense of history. Much of New Orleans' original empire remained within its grasp, even though it had become open to competition with other cities. This was particularly true of the lower Mississippi valley (up to St. Louis, or even to Cincinnati in some cases), and of the interior South, which was once dependent upon the tributaries of the Ohio and Tennessee rivers. Transportation alone does not determine the outcome of such competition. Moreover, the transportation revolution was not instantaneous, nor was it as overwhelming as is often assumed. Throughout the 1850's the still immature railroad network and the river route through New Orleans remained close and evenly

    17. The clearest detailed account of the diversion of New Orleans trade is Alice Porter, "An Economic View of Antebellum New Orleans, 1846–1860" (unpublished M.A. thesis, Tulane, 1942), *passim*. Other useful treatments are Albert Fishlow, *American Railroads and the Transformation of the Ante-Bellum Economy* (Cambridge, Mass., 1965), chapter VII; John G. Clark, *The Grain Trade in the Old Northwest* (Urbana, Ill., 1966), *passim*; John G. Clark, "The Antebellum Grain Trade of New Orleans: Changing Patterns in the Relation of New Orleans with the Old Northwest," *Agricultural History*, XXXVIII (1964), 131–142.

    18. Porter, "An Economic View"; *DeBow's Review*, "The Destiny of New Orleans," X (1851), 440–445.

matched competitors, even for the trade of the Old Northwest. In a good season—in 1857, for example—New Orleans was still able to attract a large flow of Western flour for re-export to the East. As long as, and wherever, the transportation alternatives were nearly even, other factors helped to determine the commercial fate of New Orleans.[19]

Many other factors may have influenced the course of trade—insurance rates (reflecting risks of river accident, spoilage, etc.), winter freezing or summer heat, mercantile commissions and charges, port facilities, frequency of handling and loading en route, and speed of delivery, as well as such indirect factors as the changing location of Western agriculture or the relative expansion of Western, Eastern, and Southern consumer markets.[20] But particularly in the late 1840's and early 1850's, the period of closest competition for trade, many knowledgeable observers placed a large share of the blame for New Orleans' losses on her inadequate credit facilities. Some considered credit as important as transportation:

> Grain is now carried from the Wabash to New York, by the canals, at the same cost of freight as is charged by the way of New Orleans. . . . Last autumn the rich regions of Ohio, Indiana, and Illinois were flooded with the local bank notes of the Eastern states, advanced by New York houses, on produce to be shipped to them, by the way of the canals, in the spring. These moneyed facilities enable the packer, miller, and speculator, to hold onto their produce till the opening of navigation in the spring, and they are no longer obliged, as formerly, to hurry off their shipments during the winter by the way of New Orleans, in order to realize funds by drafts on their shipments. The banking facilities at the East are doing as much to draw trade from us as the canals and railways which Eastern capital is constructing.[21]

The main burden of the argument was that the capital of the Louisiana banks, and hence their capacity to make loans, was too small for even the existing volume of business. While other cities extended their banking capacity even further, New Orleans watched the steady decline of its own facilities as bank charters expired. But an inadequate supply of credit was not the only disadvantage—the credit terms offered by New Orleans banks were not competitive. Banks in New York, Philadelphia, Charleston, and other rival cities made or renewed loans for six to twelve months, at 6 per cent interest. New Orleans banks confined "their discounts, and that to a most limited degree, to thirty, sixty, and ninety days, no matter what amount of

19. Fishlow, *American Railroads*, pp. 290–294.

20. "Routes of Trade up Stream," *DeBow's Review*, XII (1852), 101; Henry Rightor, *Standard History of New Orleans* (Chicago, 1900), pp. 562–564; Porter, "An Economic View," pp. 14–15.

21. New Orleans *Daily Crescent*, July 15, 1851, p. 2. See also the sources cited in footnote 15.

country [i.e. small town merchant's] paper was placed in their hands as collateral security."[22] In part this short maturity of New Orleans loans reflected Forstall's restrictive "fundamental rules" of the Bank Act of 1842, which counted only ninety-day, non-renewable, commercial paper, with local merchants standing ahead of those from out of town. In any case, it seems clear that the small amount and short maturity of New Orleans bank loans contributed substantially to the more rapid and more extensive shrinkage of her trading hinterland between 1845 and 1855.[23]

Restrictive financial conditions retarded economic development in some sectors of the Louisiana economy during the 1840's and early 1850's. Did the more expansive financial conditions of the 1830's and the late 1850's actively aid economic development? It is certainly clear that the chartering of new banks and the expansion of credit facilities between 1827 and 1837 were a direct response to unusually strong demands for external finance. The population of the state increased by about 50 per cent, while that of New Orleans doubled. Cotton production roughly tripled over the decade. The rapid expansion of sugar production after 1827 involved not only investment in preparing the land and acquiring slaves, but also investment in $20,000 worth of sugar refining equipment, which each large plantation required. Edmund Forstall estimated that the formation of new sugar plantations between 1827 and 1830 required a total of $16 million of capital. In the process of expanding their agricultural output Louisianans financed the purchase of nearly $2.5 million of land from the federal government (America's original "absentee landlord," at least in the financial sense). There can be no doubt whatever that expansion of Louisiana's financial system was essential to *permit* this rapid growth in population, output, and productive capital.[24]

The quantitative expansion of banking did more than merely passively permit the growth of the real economy. Financial growth was an independent cause of, and an active contributor to, more rapid real economic growth. This active contribution took three forms: increasing the productivity of existing capital, raising the supply of savings, and improving the allocation of available savings among alternative investments.

22. New Orleans *Daily Crescent*, March 21, 1851, p. 2.

23. Other historians share my view that lack of bank credit severely handicapped New Orleans trade. See Robert E. Roeder, "Merchants of Ante-Bellum New Orleans," *Explorations in Entrepreneurial History* (old series), X (1958), 121; Edwin D. Odom, "Louisiana Railroads, 1830–1880: A Study of State and Local Aid," (unpublished Ph.D. thesis, Tulane, 1961), p. 58; Stephen A. Caldwell, "The New Orleans Trade Area," Louisiana State University *Bulletin*, XXVIII, No. 10 (1936), pp. 6–7.

24. Edmund J. Forstall, *Agricultural Productions of Louisiana* (New Orleans, 1845), pp. 4–7; Merl Reed, "Boom or Bust—Louisiana's Economy During the 1830's," *Louisiana History*, IV (1963), 35–36.

The most significant improvement in the productivity of existing capital was probably the change in the role of specie—gold and silver. When used as a medium of payment, specie had several disadvantages. As a commodity money it was costly to produce and hence costly to import; Louisiana and other states exported their own valuable output in order to purchase specie from other nations (or from California in the 1850's). It was also costly and risky to transport from place to place, or to store away as a form of wealth. But most of all, specie was idle, unproductive capital—it earned no return for its owner or for society. Bank money, by contrast, cost almost nothing to produce, and (through loans) it represented savings put to work. It was active capital. Any development in banking or other financial arrangements which displaced specie thus enhanced the productivity of Louisiana's existing real capital. Specie was sometimes exported in payment for other goods. It was more commonly withdrawn from the private hoards of planters, merchants, or frontiersmen, or from monetary circulation, and transferred to bank vaults to serve more productively as "high-powered" reserves, rather than as low-powered money in circulation. Although the economy became vulnerable to multiple contraction of the money supply (due to external specie flows), at least it made more efficient use of its specie and acquired a less costly form of money in its bank notes and deposits.[25]

Financial expansion also enhanced the productivity of existing physical and human capital on the frontier. By improving access to equipment, slaves, and markets, bank credit enabled a frontiersman to give up subsistence-oriented agriculture, or perhaps cattle-grazing, in favor of more profitable crops, usually cotton or sugar. At a slightly more advanced stage of development, such external finance sometimes permitted a planter to change from the less productive cotton planting to the more productive, but more capital-intensive, sugar planting, or to adopt a more efficient technology (steam powered sugar refining, for example). In each case, the land, slaves, and other capital gained in productivity.

The Louisiana financial system, particularly in the 1830's, also accelerated

25. Hugh Patrick, "Financial Development and Economic Growth in Underdeveloped Countries," *Economic Development and Cultural Change*, XIV (1966), 178–181. At least two contemporary Louisianans argued the unproductivity of idle specie and felt that banks could mobilize it to the advantage of its owners and society. James Lyon, "Enquiry Relative to Banks" (New Orleans, 1804), pp. 35–37. Samuel J. Peters, *An Address to the Legislature of Louisiana, Showing the Importance of the Credit System, on the Prosperity of the United States, and Particularly its Influence on the Agricultural, Commercial, and Manufacturing Interests of Louisiana* (published by the New Orleans Chamber of Commerce, December, 1837), pp. 9–10, Louisiana State Bank Collection, LSU Archives. On the inconvenience of specie, and rural hoarding of it, see Alexander Porter to Dussuau De La Croix, April 27, July 31, 1819; Richard Eastin to Richard Relf, March 1, 1820; Louisiana State Bank, *Letterbook* of St. Martinsville branch, LSU Archives.

economic growth by increasing the supply of savings. Primarily this took the form of foreign savings—capital borrowed from other states or from Europe. A large (but indeterminate) amount of foreign capital entered Louisiana through direct finance, without the help of banks or other financial intermediaries. It sometimes came into the state through immigrant planters or businessmen, but more often it came in the form of trade credit between merchants. To this direct import of capital the banks of Louisiana added another $20.7 million (up to December 1837) by selling their stocks and bonds abroad.[26] It is of course conceivable that in the absence of banks some of the foreign capital would still have come to Louisiana. But foreign lenders had little information about the potential profitability of the individual plantations, urban lands, or improvement projects in which the banks invested their funds. Direct finance from abroad would have been difficult and risky under these circumstances. If foreign capital had been available at all, it would probably have been prohibitively costly to Louisiana borrowers; therefore we must give the banks credit for attracting a full $20 million of developmental capital that otherwise would have been unavailable.

The expansion of Louisiana's financial capacity after 1853, due to the revival of the Citizens Bank and the creation of the free banking system, made a contribution to economic growth, but one more limited in scope than the financial innovations of the 1820's and 1830's. The amount of additional capital was less (about $15 million) and the bulk of it (all but $1.4 million) was raised by selling the bank stocks within the state. This did not represent new savings imported from abroad; it was merely a form (a new financial asset) by which wealth already within the state could be held there. To the extent that the stock, notes, or deposits of the free banks offered Louisiana savers a more attractive liquid financial asset, they may have drawn idle specie out of private hoards into bank reserves, making that specie capital more productive for society. Such attractive financial assets might also have raised the proportion of saving out of current incomes. But in this period the impact on the productivity of existing capital or on the supply of savings was presumably less important than the impact on the allocation of investment.[27] (I will discuss that allocation later.)

A brief historiographical comment may sharpen the significance of the preceding conclusions. Virtually all historians treating this subject have sharply criticized Louisiana's financial expansion of the 1830's as unsound in conception and undesirable in impact. The same negative opinion prevails in most discussions of monetary expansion in the United States as a whole during the same decade. The implicit theory underlying this viewpoint is

26. *Senate Documents*, 25 Cong., 2 sess., No. 471, p. 56.
27. *Ibid.*; *Report of the Joint Committee on Banks and Banking* [Louisiana Legislature], March 4, 1857, Appendix.

often sadly inaccurate. The historian often seems unconsciously to believe that all foreign borrowing is burdensome and unproductive. He may even believe that all "paper money," and all credit and debt, is fundamentally unsound, that only specie represents "true value." Or he may accept the crudest form of the quantity theory of money, believing that any expansion of the money supply is automatically inflationary. Such assumptions are usually disguised in historical descriptions of "wildcat banking" (a much misused epithet), or in vague conclusions that banking was "over-indulged" or "overexpanded." The words of James Winston are typical:

> The credit system was practically universal at this time among the cotton planters of the state, and it was through the instrumentality of the banks of New Orleans that landed property and slaves were converted into circulating notes, with which all kinds of speculative enterprises were forwarded. Much of the capital employed in the various enterprises launched during this decade is said to have been raised in Europe by the sale of mortgages, the whole resulting in an immense turnover of business, but unaccompanied by a corresponding accumulation of real values.[28]

Above all, the historians have been overly preoccupied with the financial crisis of 1837. They condemn the monetary expansion of a decade because it ended in, and (by assumption) presumably caused, that crisis. Accepting a "boom or bust" theory, they discount that decade of real economic growth as "unreal" or "unsound" because it ended in depression.

The conclusions of this study differ almost completely from the popular view. Specie, despite its universal acceptance, was a costly and unproductive form of money and wealth. By partially displacing it and substantially supplementing it, the expanding financial system that Louisiana devised in the 1820's and 1830's both permitted and actively encouraged a decade or more of rapid and genuine economic development. Between 1835 and 1837 the quantity of money and credit was, however, increased "too rapidly" relative to the capacity of the real economy. (I agree with the traditional view, though not with the inferences drawn from the fact of inflation.) The resulting inflation and speculative expectations contributed to, but did not alone cause, the financial crisis and depression after 1837.[29] At this point the full tragedy

28. James E. Winston, "Notes on the Economic History of New Orleans, 1803–1836," *Mississippi Valley Historical Review*, XI (1924), 215. Other examples of the same approach toward Louisiana finance in the 1830's are: Rightor, *Standard History of New Orleans*, p. 595; Reed, "Boom or Bust," pp. 36, 48–49; Caldwell, "The New Orleans Trade Area," pp. 6–7. Even Robert Roeder, who is generally a more sophisticated observer of New Orleans merchants and bankers, adopts the stereotypes of "wildcat banks" and "reckless expansion"; Roeder, "Merchants of Ante-Bellum New Orleans," p. 118.

29. Yet even during these inflationary years of 1835–37 a case might be made for the developmental impact of expanded banking through the effect of "forced saving." See below.

of holding to the specie standard became apparent—it imposed the dilemma of choosing between "sound money" and "easy credit"—choosing between stability and growth. Beginning in 1842 Louisiana abandoned both its practical compromises and the departures from the specie standard it had previously made. A decade of "sound money" retarded financial expansion and hindered real economic growth, particularly in the commerce of New Orleans. After 1853 the financial system once again became expansive, though its quantitative change probably had a smaller active impact on real growth than the expansive system of the 1830's had had. In summary, expansive finance, though operating under the shadow of "sound money" and a specie standard, did accelerate growth, while restrictive finance retarded growth.

THE ALLOCATION OF FINANCE: CONSUMPTION VS. INVESTMENT

Consideration of the allocation of bank credit and other external finance naturally follows any discussion of the available quantity of finance. The expansion or restriction of the total supply of money and credit, and its allocation to particular sectors of the economy, certainly affects their growth. The developmental impact of any given supply of credit obviously depends upon the wisdom and efficiency with which it is allocated. In the particular historical context of antebellum Louisiana, the quantity and quality (allocation) of credit were closely associated matters. Many historians have suggested, for example, that in the 1830's an excessive quantity of finance led to unwise resource allocation, emphasizing "speculative" investments in real estate and certain internal improvement projects. Conversely, the restricted quantity of finance in the 1840's also involved a shift in the composition of bank credit toward short-term, strictly commercial loans. It is obviously necessary to keep in mind the underlying conditions of economy-wide supply and demand for credit when discussing the allocation of such credit to specific sectors or activities.

The natural opening question, from the theoretical viewpoint at least, is: did credit allocation accelerate economic growth by raising the proportion of total output devoted to investment rather than that devoted to consumption? Unfortunately, the available evidence permits only the most impressionistic answer to this broad question. Statistics on rates of saving or investment for the various sectors of the economy are simply not available. The typical institutions of early Louisiana spent their incomes on or borrowed funds for both consumption and investment purposes. Planters and other businessmen did not often separate "business" from "personal" expenses in their bookkeeping. Records of financial institutions contain similar ambiguities, mainly because the descriptions of loans or the collateral behind them do not necessarily reveal how the funds were used by the borrowers.

Despite the lack of quantitative evidence, some educated guesses are possible about the impact of finance on consumption vs. investment in Louisiana. The types of collateral most acceptable for bank loans—mortgages on land, buildings, or slaves, or commodities in the process of production or shipment—were biased in favor of loans for investment. The common practices of modern banks in lending against consumer durables (furniture, automobiles, etc.) or against future income (perhaps without collateral) did not then prevail. Presumably much of the direct finance (borrowing and lending) among family and friends supported consumption, but most of the indirect finance of banks and other intermediaries was at least intended to support investment spending. The clearest exception, a case of frustrated intentions, came during and after the financial crisis of 1837–42, when bankers reluctantly renewed mortgage and commercial loans and thus effectively helped to sustain the consumption of their customers. In this exceptional case access to bank finance favored consumption; but the depression itself was the basic cause of this proportionate decline of investment spending, and the financial system was merely the unwilling means for accomplishing the result.

The banking system probably gave its strongest impetus to investment spending during the decade preceding 1837. Most of the banks chartered during this era were property banks, designed to finance the expansion of cotton or sugar production, or improvement banks, designed to foster particular "social overhead" investment projects. Some of the impetus may have been accomplished through "forced saving," as bank credit financed investment while the inflationary expansion of the money supply deprived consumers of purchasing power. But the argument for a strong developmental impact from "forced saving" is a weak one in the case of antebellum Louisiana. The inflation was concentrated in the second half of the decade, 1835–37. The pattern of investment in those years became somewhat more speculative than before, raising prices of existing capital (especially land) rather than encouraging new capital formation. Several of the new projects begun during those years were interrupted or killed by the subsequent crisis. Had the expansionary period lasted a few years longer, however, it is quite conceivable that "forced saving" would have shown a more lasting contribution.[30]

COMMERCE VS. AGRICULTURE

The banking system can affect development not only by increasing the share

30. A vague suggestion of the "forced saving" idea is contained in Roeder, "Merchants of Ante-bellum New Orleans," p. 120. But Roeder emphasizes the effects on income distribution, benefits to the privileged borrowers at the expense of the mass of consumers, rather than the effects on development.

of investment in total output, but also by encouraging a more productive composition of investment. For Louisianans of that period the most important and controversial issue was the division of financing between city and country, or between commerce and agriculture. There were repeated complaints in newspapers and accusations in the legislature that a few New Orleans factors "monopolized" the credit of the city's banks, to the exclusion of the mass of potential borrowers, and of planters in particular.[31]

Many historians have strongly criticized the chronic indebtedness of planter to factor and banker. Offended primarily by the apparent injustice and inequality of the system, they have also claimed that it helped to retard economic growth in various ways. The high interest rates and other commission charges, and the higher prices charged for supplies purchased on credit rather than with cash, all raised the planter's costs and reduced his income. The planter's indebtedness bound him to his factor in near-servitude and prevented him from seeking the best market for his crops or his purchases, or from diversifying away from the traditional cash crops—cotton and sugar. The factor system concentrated capital in a few large cities (New Orleans alone, in Louisiana) and inhibited the growth of smaller towns and cities which might have offered improved commercial facilities, a larger domestic market, and more industry.[32]

Some of these traditional historical arguments need reconsideration. They misinterpret the causes and significance of the financial relationship between factor and planter. They also misinterpret the effects of that relationship on economic growth, mainly by confusing the welfare of one group (the planters) with that of society as a whole.

From the planter's point of view his indebtedness to the factor or banker was not entirely a misfortune. It enabled him to sustain his living standard even in years of poor crops, for example. But contrary to the usual interpretation, most planters probably did not incur their debts in order to finance "extravagant" consumption. Debts grew most during the good years, and they were merely renewed or extended during the poor years. The debts were originally contracted for productive purposes, such as the purchase of additional land, slaves, or equipment. Even the wealthiest planters often remained voluntarily and continuously in debt to their factors, because they expected to profit from the borrowed funds. Of course these expectations

31. Henry W. Huntington to William N. Mercer, April 4, 1837, Mercer papers, Tulane University; New Orleans *Semi-Weekly Creole*, Jan. 3, 1855, p. 2; New Orleans *Commercial Bulletin*, Feb. 6, 1838, Nov. 27, 1855.

32. Rightor, *Standard History of New Orleans*, p. 568; J. Carlyle Sitterson, *Sugar Country* (Lexington, Ky., 1953), p. 204; Morton Rothstein, "Ante-bellum Wheat and Cotton Exports: A Contrast in Marketing Organization and Economic Development," *Agricultural History*, XL (1966), 94–97; Roeder, "Merchants of Ante-Bellum New Orleans," p. 119.

were not always fulfilled, and planters felt quite free to complain bitterly in hard times about debt "burdens" which they had eagerly assumed a few years earlier. Regardless of the planters' retrospective attitudes, historians should remember that such debts often financed additions to the capital stock of the economy, and that these additions were irreversible.[33]

Granted, the factors charged "high" interest rates and commissions for their services. Such charges reflected a degree of monopoly power, perhaps, although the competition among factors for planter customers limited any such monopoly. Such charges also reflected the scarcity of credit and capital, the uncertainty of future crop yields, and the risks borne by the factor as an intermediary. While these "high" costs did lower the planters' incomes, the lower incomes are not evidence of economic retardation. What the planters paid out became income to the factors, the bankers, the insurance companies, the merchants, or other middlemen. The interest rates and commissions thus determined mainly the distribution of income; they had only secondary impacts on the rate of growth of total income.[34]

Planters did seek to improve their access to credit, both to supplement and to supplant borrowing from their factors. The two major thrusts they made in this direction were the campaigns for property banks and for branch banking.[35]

The property banks were an innovation designed to overcome the concentration of banking in New Orleans by providing planters with direct access to long-term mortgage credit. The first property bank, the Consolidated Association of Planters, did remain under the control of planters, despite the admission in 1836 of city property as collateral for up to one-third of its mortgages. A breakdown of the bank's mortgages in 1847 reveals that of these 23 per cent were on city property, whereas 70 per cent were on sugar plantations and 6 per cent were on cotton plantations. But the other two property banks in New Orleans, the Union and Citizens banks, were from the outset largely urban-oriented in their ownership and lending. Yet even though they were not controlled by planters and did not bypass the New

33. *Tenth Census of the United States*, XIX, p. 254; Lewis Atherton, *The Southern Country Store* (Baton Rouge, 1949), pp. 16–17; Robert M. Davis, *The Southern Planter, the Factor and the Banker* (New Orleans, 1871), *passim.*

34. To the extent that such middlemen were "foreigners" the state's total income was reduced. But in a (hypothetical) world without factors and their "high" charges, the planters might well have imported such services (and lowered state income) in even larger volume.

35. The free banking campaign of the 1850's was supported by many planters, or at least by their rural political spokesmen, partly in the belief that more "competitive" banking would end the factor's "monopoly" of credit. But strong support also came from the New Orleans business community, and in fact no free banks took charters outside of New Orleans.

Orleans factors, the property banks did increase by several million dollars the mortgage credit available to planters, particularly during the crucial decade (1827–37) of rapid expansion and capital formation. The property bank idea became unpopular during the financial crisis of 1837–42, as all three of Louisiana's property banks ended in failure.[36]

Most historians have agreed with Fritz Redlich that the property bank involved an "unfortunate combination of incompatible functions" in its blending of mortgage and commercial banking. Some have accepted the "commercial loan" theory, and they have flatly asserted that a bank which issues note or deposit liabilities is not "sound" if it carries mortgages or other long-maturity assets in its portfolio. Yet the examples of successful mixed banking ventures in Germany, Belgium, and Japan, or those in the modern United States, which has its "full-service" banks, indicate that the condemnation is not generally valid. Rather, the particular circumstances of the antebellum Louisiana economy made mixed banking especially difficult. The mortgage borrowers were concentrated in export-oriented agriculture, giving the banks little opportunity to diversify and thus protect themselves against the risk of unfavorable market conditions. The capital markets for such mortgages, or even for the more liquid commercial paper, were poorly developed, giving the banks little opportunity to sell off their assets. The specie standard, unstable public preferences for bank money vs. specie, and an unregulated money supply increased the risks of a liquidity crisis against which such a "mixed" bank had weak defenses. Despite these handicaps, well-capitalized property banks did provide Louisiana with a much needed mechanism for importing foreign capital and providing long-term credit.[37]

Branch banks were another innovation through which Louisiana's agricultural interests sought to expand their credit facilities. The chartering of each new bank during the 1830's was the occasion for a great tug-of-war in the legislature: each rural representative sought to have a branch in his district and the New Orleans representatives generally tried to restrain the process. As with the property banks, the effort was only a partial success. Of the total of $13.4 million of capital for branches authorized in the various bank charters, only $6,772,500 had actually been allocated by the banks to their branches before the crisis of 1837. By 1846 the failure and liquidation

36. "Descriptions of Properties Mortgaged, 1847," bound volume 68, Consolidated Association of Planters Collection, Tulane University; Roeder, "New Orleans Merchants, 1790–1837," (unpublished Ph.D. dissertation, Harvard University, 1959), chapter 4.

37. Fritz Redlich, *The Molding of American Banking* (New York, 1947), I, 205–209; Roeder, "Merchants of Ante-Bellum New Orleans," p. 120; Cameron *et al.*, *Banking*, pp. 133, 143, chapters VI, VIII.

of many of the New Orleans banks, and the closing of the branches of the surviving Canal Bank, had reduced the available branch capital to about $2 million. Not all of these funds went to planters, however. Roeder estimates that about one-third of branch lending was in mortgages, and some of that went to small-town businessmen who took mortgages on town property. The planters did receive some of the remaining two-thirds, most of it shorter term commercial loans which they used to finance the movement of commodities to market. At its peak, branch banking provided about $7 million of credit to planters and small-town businessmen. If the branch banks had not been established, these planters and businessmen would have tried to get credit through direct finance in New Orleans, through country stores or rural sources, or they would have done without. Probably less than half of the $7 million allocated (and even less in the years before and after 1837) went to finance plantation agriculture.[38]

The makers of banking policy limited the effectiveness of branch banking as a tool for economic development in Louisiana. They were pursuing other, conflicting goals. Again, the tension between "easy credit" and "sound money" overshadowed banking policy. Independent unit banks outside of New Orleans, had they existed, would undoubtedly have provided more local entrepreneurship and a pattern of lending more responsive to the desires of local merchants, planters, and small farmers. The branch banks were consistently restrained in their credit allocation by the parent banks in New Orleans. This restraint protected the liquidity of the New Orleans banks and hence the "soundness" of their monetary liabilities; it also protected the commercial supremacy of "imperial" New Orleans against greater competition from small-town merchants or factors within her domain. Independent commercial banks probably could not have remained liquid enough to survive in the extremely small towns and the one-crop rural economy of antebellum Louisiana (as the lack of small-town free banks in the 1850's confirms). By pooling the illiquid, undiversified rural loans with the more diverse commercial portfolios of the parent banks, branch banking gave the entire state a safer money supply. The branch banks' supply of credit, though less liberal in quantity or allocation than that of independent rural banks might have been, was surely much more liberal than the credit that New Orleans banks would have provided if they had not had these branches. In addition to their contributions toward "monetizing" the rural economy and mobilizing rural savings (largely for re-lending locally) and

---

38. *House Documents*, 26 Cong., 2 sess., No. 111, p. 722; *House Documents*, 29 Cong., 1 sess., No. 226, p. 844; Matthias Purton to Baring Brothers, Jan. 16, 1846, Barings microfilms (frame 59516), Library of Congress, Manuscripts Division; Roeder, "New Orleans Merchants, 1790–1837," p. 306; *Charter, Rules, & c. of the City Bank.*

specie hoards, the branch banks thus accelerated the development of rural Louisiana by serving as a relatively efficient channel for capital inflows from New Orleans.[39]

The allocation of finance between New Orleans and rural Louisiana was as much a question of income distribution between agriculture and the various commercial interests as it was a question of economic development. The expansion of property banks and branch banks did increase the quantity and availability of credit to Louisiana agriculture. Most of this credit apparently went to sugar and cotton planters rather than to smaller farmers, partly because the planters had more political power to influence the location of banks and their lending practices, but also because the small farmers owned little of the valuable land or slaves most suitable for loan collateral. After 1842 the New Orleans bankers and the state legislature, in pursuit of bank liquidity and "sound money," worked to restrain the expansion of rural credit facilities. The New Orleans mercantile community encouraged this restraint in order to protect its own credit supply and to inhibit small-town commercial competitors.[40]

FINANCING INDUSTRY AND SOCIAL OVERHEAD CAPITAL

The allocation of bank credit had developmental significance beyond its impact on the relative growth of New Orleans commerce and plantation agriculture. We must especially examine the allocation of credit to manufacturing, new technology, education, transportation, and other social overheads, since these sectors are usually crucial to the process of economic development.

Louisiana's banks devoted a negligible amount of their resources to the support of manufacturing. Fortunately, there are unusually detailed records for January 1840, and these reveal that four of the banks held $290,000 in stocks, bonds, and loans of two New Orleans steam cotton press companies. There is no evidence of any other such financing, although it is quite possible that other loans to manufacturers may be hidden in the totals of loans on mortgage or personal security.[41]

39. Raleigh A. Suarez, "Bills, Bargains, and Bankruptcies: Business Activity in Rural Antebellum Louisiana," *Louisiana History*, V (1966), p. 193; Cameron *et al.*, *Banking*, pp. 311–313.

40. Raleigh A. Suarez, "Louisiana's Struggling Majority: The Ante-bellum Farmer," *McNeese Review*, XIV (1963), 19–20; Roger W. Shugg, *Origins of Class Struggle in Louisiana* (Baton Rouge, 1939), chapter 5. The small farmers and other less favored borrowers had to rely on their own resources, local direct finance, or such informal financial intermediaries as the country storekeeper.

41. Louisiana Legislature, *Documents, & c., Relative to the Investigation on Banks* (New Orleans, 1840), pp. 106, 127, 144, 156. The Gas Light Bank was also required by a

The banks made their major departure from the financing of commerce and agriculture in order to support the development of canals, railroads, and other public utilities. Of course these projects complemented and strengthened Louisiana's commerce and agriculture, just as the steam cotton presses did. Financial support was provided by direct investment and control through the improvement banks, and also by the more conventional methods of having banks make loans to or purchase the stocks of transportation companies.

The improvement banks of the 1830's combined in one corporate charter the construction of public works projects and the privilege of banking. Usually the construction projects were the primary objective: several of these banks were originally chartered as simple improvement companies and received their banking powers in subsequent amendments. The additional profits expected from banking made the stock of such companies attractive to investors. The bank's issues of notes and deposits could also provide a source of funds to support the project, especially in the early period of heavy construction expenses and incomplete capital subscriptions. During the decade of the 1830's the five improvement banks financed and operated about $4.3 million worth of investments: a canal, a gas lighting system, a waterworks, and two commercial hotels.[42]

The same device was less successful when applied to railroad projects, mainly because their construction was prevented or interrupted by the financial crisis of 1837. In 1840 three railroad banks claimed about $1 million of railroad capital, but little of this had actually been financed through the improvement banking mechanism.[43]

The improvement banks were a partial success as tools of economic development, if they are measured by the improvement projects which they financed, constructed, and managed. But they were quite insecure as banks. One historian has suggested that they exemplified "building America through bankruptcy;" their failure during financial crisis imposed a kind of retroactive "forced saving" on stockholders (many of them outside the state), noteholders, and depositors. Their construction projects loomed large in their total assets, tying up much of their capital and other funds in an

charter amendment of March 14, 1836 (*Acts of Louisiana*, 12 Leg., 2 sess., pp. 182–184) to lend $50,000 for ten years to the Rome Patent Brick Manufacturing Company. But there is no evidence of the loan in the 1840 documents.

42. Louisiana Legislature, *Documents, & c., Relative to the Investigation on Banks*, pp. 46, 123, 129, 144; Rightor, *Standard History of New Orleans*, pp. 588–590; Franz Anton von Gerstner, *Berichte aus den Vereinigten Staaten von Nord America* (Leipzig, 1837), pp. 26–30.

43. Merl Reed, *New Orleans and the Railroads* (Baton Rouge, 1966), pp. 36–40, 50–54; Louisiana Legislature, *Documents, & c., Relative to the Investigation on Banks*, pp. 43, 49, 192; Odom, "Louisiana's Railroads, 1830–1880," p. 19.

extremely illiquid form. In this respect they were much worse off than similar investment banks in other nations, which usually bought stocks or bonds or made long-term loans to investment projects. These foreign banks could increase their liquidity simply by selling a portion of their stocks, bonds, or other financial assets. The Louisiana banks, however, owned their projects directly. To increase liquidity they had to find buyers for a canal, a hotel, or a railroad. In addition, investment banking in Louisiana was less diversified than it was in other countries. Each of the investment banks in Louisiana was committed to only one major project. Despite its illiquid assets, the improvement bank was not an inherently unsound or inflationary institution as many Louisianans of that time believed, just as some historians do today. If such a bank was sufficiently well capitalized, and if it was given time to enlarge its deposits and notes in circulation, it could acquire sufficient liquid assets (such as commercial loans) to balance its portfolio and survive financial pressures, as the success of the Canal Bank clearly demonstrates.[44]

Transportation improvements in the 1830's were not only aided by the direct financial support and entrepreneurial guidance of the improvement banks. Other Louisiana banks helped to finance these projects by purchasing stocks or bonds or by making loans. Six of the banks (the Canal, Citizens, Consolidated Association, Gas Light, Bank of Louisiana, and Union) bought stock in or made loans to the four railroad banks, loans which totaled about $400,000 in 1840. These interbank transactions either provided additional liquid reserves to the railroad banks or enabled them to finance further construction. In this way the risk and illiquidity of these projects were shared and dispersed throughout the larger banking community. In addition to these interbank transactions, there were loans to or stock purchases from ordinary canal and railroad companies; by 1840 railroad companies had accumulated over $300,000 of such bank financing, and canal companies another $192,000. Some of these loans were made under the compulsion of charter requirements imposed by the legislature. But voluntarily or not, the banks provided generous financial support to Louisiana's early improvement projects.[45]

By 1857 the "first generation" of chartered banks no longer provided much financing for improvement projects. All of the original improvement

44. Roeder. "New Orleans Merchants, 1790–1837," pp. 351–361; Reed, "Boom or Bust," pp. 48–50; Reed, "Louisiana's Transportation Revolution: The Railroads, 1830–1850" (unpublished Ph.D. thesis, LSU, 1957), pp. 9–14; Cameron *et al.*, *Banking*, pp. 133–143, chapters VI, VIII.

45. Louisiana Legislature, *Documents, & c., Relative to the Investigation on Banks*, pp. 46, 106, 117, 123, 127, 144, 156, 167, 186. The total of $1.3 million of bank investments in railroads ($1 million of railroad bank property plus $300,000 of financing to other railroads) may be compared to the $3.6 million of total expenditures on railroad construction and equipment prior to 1840. See Reed, *New Orleans and the Railroads*, p. 19.

banks had ceased operations except the Canal Bank, which still owned its canal (valued at $1,080,057). The revived Citizens Bank owned the Improvement Hotel, obtained from the Improvement Bank in 1849 in settlement of debts.[46] The other three surviving banks owned only $39,018 in canal, railroad, and cotton press stocks.[47]

During the 1850's the financial gap left by the withdrawal or failure of the older banks was partly filled by the creation of free banks under the laws of 1853 and 1855. The free bank act of 1853 recognized only government bonds (federal, Louisiana, and New Orleans) as legal reserves for banknotes. The constitution of 1852 had formally divorced the activities of banking and internal improvements by denying banking privileges to all improvement companies. But that divorce was short-lived.[48]

By 1853 New Orleans businessmen had already participated in a series of railroad conventions, and the promotional campaigns for rail links with the Pacific coast and with the North (through Mississippi and Tennessee) were well advanced. James Robb, a prominent banker, merchant, and politician, had led the campaign for both railroads and free banks, and he clearly recognized how the two objectives might be joined. In 1854 the legislature authorized the city of New Orleans to issue $5 million of bonds in order to finance the purchase of an equal amount of stock in the city's three major projects—the New Orleans, Jackson, and Great Northern Railroad; the New Orleans, Opelousas and Great Western Railroad; and the New Orleans and Mobile Railroad.[49]

One short step remained to accomplish the reunion of railroads and banking which Robb advocated, and the legislature took that step. It amended the free banking act in 1855 to permit the banks to count the new bond issues as legal reserves for banknotes. The city could thus act as a financial intermediary between the railroads and the free banks, buying the stock of the former and selling its bonds to the latter. The city actually issued $3,671,000 of bonds in behalf of the railroads in addition to its general debt, which was roughly $3 million. In 1857 the four free banks held over $2 million of city bonds, and the Louisiana State Bank held another $328,750. Even if only

---

46. The hotel was originally valued at $200,000 in 1849; valued at $340,000 in 1857, it was finally sold in 1859 for $200,000. Citizens Bank *Minute Book* #6, pp. 70, 314–315; #8, pp. 217–218, Canal Bank Collection, Tulane University.

47. Louisiana Legislature, *Report of the Joint Committee on Banks and Banking*, 1857, pp. 89, 98, 106, 136. The Consolidated Association, which owned $17,500 of the stock, was in liquidation.

48. *Acts of Louisiana*, 1 Leg., 1 sess. (April 30, 1853), pp. 301–311.

49. Reed, *New Orleans and the Railroads*, Chapters VI and VII; Harry Howard Evans, "James Robb, Banker and Pioneer Railroad Builder of Ante-bellum Louisiana," *Louisiana Historical Quarterly*, XXIII (1940), 181–186, 208; *Acts of Louisiana*, 2 Leg., 1 sess. (March 15, 1854), pp. 69–79.

60 per cent of these bonds represented railroad financing (the rough proportion of railroad bonds to total city bonds), this was still a significant share (say 15 per cent) of the $9 million which Louisiana spent on railroads during the 1850's.[50]

The financing of railroads through the free banks in the 1850's was in several ways "sounder" than similar efforts that had been made by the improvement banks in the 1830's. The improvement banks had directly owned their projects, and often they had provided the total financing. The free banks, on the other hand, were twice removed from the railroads which they helped to finance. They did not own the railroad property itself, nor even the railroad stocks. Instead they held city bonds, and the city bore the risk of participating as a railroad stockholder. Moreover, no free bank held, even indirectly, a large proportion of the financial claims against any one project. The free banks were thus better diversified and more liquid than the earlier improvement banks. Yet despite this advantage, the panic of 1857 revealed the risks of mixing a large proportion of long-term investment banking assets with a large proportion of short-term (deposit and banknote) liabilities. The free banking device diminished the conflict between "sound money" and "easy credit" (especially long-term credit for development), but it did not eliminate that conflict.[51]

In addition to the financial aid that they gave to canals, railroads, and other improvement projects, the Louisiana banks contributed to less tangible forms of social overhead capital. Several of them had stipulations in their charters that required them to pay annual bonuses to support education. In a few cases bank financing may have helped industry to adopt improved technology, as in the application of steam power to sugar refining or to the cotton press. More significantly, the individual banker participated as a promoter or an entrepreneur in a wide variety of developmental activities. When the Pontchartrain Railroad ran short of construction funds in 1831–32, Samuel Peters, a banker, and himself one of the directors of the railroad company, lent his personal credit and also arranged loans from his own bank. Edmund Forstall, in addition to being a banker, a legislator, and a merchant, was the founder of New Orleans' first great sugar refinery (in 1831), and he either promoted or served as a director on a variety of improvement projects. In the 1850's James Robb led the campaign for railroad development, and he

50. Reed, *New Orleans and the Railroads*, pp. 83–84; *Acts of Louisiana*, 2 Leg., 1 sess. (March 16, 1854), pp. 151–152; Rightor, *Standard History of New Orleans*, p. 98; Louisiana Legislature, *Report of the Joint Committee on Banks and Banking*, 1857, pp. 106, 112, 116, 124, 128, 132. For opposition to this indirect blend of banking and railroads see the *Minority Report of the* [Louisiana] *Senate Committee on the General System of Free Banking*, 1854.

51. New Orleans *Daily Delta*, February 28, 1860, p. 2; "The Banking Systems of Louisiana" (anonymous pamphlet, New Orleans, 1860), *passim*.

became the first president of the New Orleans, Jackson and Great Northern. Robb put his personal fortune and the resources of his bank completely behind the project, carrying it almost singlehandedly through the financial crisis of its early years. In the relatively small and tightly knit community of business leaders of antebellum New Orleans the banker was not confined to decisions on strictly financial matters. In his active leadership in the promotion or administration of railroads, public utilities, and various other projects of community service or development the Louisiana banker resembled the present-day influential small-town banker, or the powerful investment banker of J. P. Morgan's day, not the specialized, relatively passive urban banker of today. His general entrepreneurial activities may well have been as important to the state's development as his strictly financial activities were.[52]

The bankers of Louisiana obviously allocated the lion's share of their credit and their entrepreneurial support to the preservation and advancement of the state's commerce and its plantation agriculture. Even their investments in public utilities and transportation supported Louisiana's prevailing economic structure. They did not contemplate large-scale industrialization, the abolition of slavery, land reforms, or other revolutionary changes in their society or economy. As prophets or master-planners of their total economy, Louisiana's bankers failed. But in their more human roles, as entrepreneurs of limited vision and power, facing alternatives within the constraints of the existing economic and social structure, they allocated their financial resources progressively, and reasonably well.

52. Sitterson, *Sugar Country*, pp. 155–156; Pontchartrain Railroad Company, *Minute Book*, pp. 1, 60–67, 155–160, 222, 228, 231, 237, Tulane University; Edmund J. Forstall to Consolidated Association of Planters, March 14, 1836, Consolidated Association of Planters collection, LSU Archives; Evans, "James Robb," pp. 220–243, 248; Reed, *New Orleans and the Railroads*, chapter 7; Odom, "Louisiana's Railroads, 1830–1880," p. 83.

CHAPTER VIII

The United States 1863–1913[*]

RICHARD SYLLA

THE BANKING AND INDUSTRIAL SCENES

On the eve of the Civil War the United States was well on the way toward becoming an industrial economy. Indeed, just prior to that war the nation had experienced such vigorous industrial development that it was probably the second most industrialized country in the world in terms of manufacturing production.[1] It was well ahead of its nearest Continental European rivals, and it was gaining rapidly on the acknowledged industrial leader, Great Britain. It should be clear, therefore, that when we consider the role of banking in postbellum American industrialization we will not be dealing with the usual question of whether banks in some sense initiated or greatly facilitated the country's first industrialization drive: that first drive had already taken place.

There are, nonetheless, a number of reasons why this later period is worthy of attention. The establishment of the National Banking System by Congress in 1863 and 1864 represented a significant banking reform that largely determined the course of American banking development for the

---

[*] Some of the material in this chapter originally appeared in the author's article, "Federal Policy, Banking Market Structure, and Capital Mobilization in the United States, 1863–1913," *The Journal of Economic History*, XXIX (December 1969). The author wishes to thank Professor Robert Gallman, Editor of *The Journal of Economic History*, for permission to use this material here.

1. Comparative data on world industrialization before 1870 are not available, but the following considerations support this relative ranking. The decade of the 1860's in the U.S., largely because of the Civil War, has been recognized in recent years as one of slower industrial growth than the decades immediately preceding and following. Yet by 1870, the U.S.'s share of world manufacturing output was 23.3 per cent, second only to the U.K.'s 31.8 per cent and well ahead of Germany's 13.2 per cent. See League of Nations, *Industrialization and Foreign Trade* (Geneva, 1945), p. 13.

next fifty years. Also, the half-century following this banking reform was marked by sustained high rates of industrial growth and far-reaching innovations in industrial organization which catapulted the United States into the dominant position in the world economy that it has maintained up to the present day. Related to the late nineteenth-century industrial upsurge was a relative, though dramatic, decline of agriculture. In 1859 the value added by agriculture to national output was nearly twice that of the manufacturing sector; 40 years later its value was only two-thirds that of manufacturing.[2] Another reason for taking a new look at postbellum banking is that the direct effects of Civil War banking reforms on later industrial development have so far been neglected by historians. They have instead emphasized the National Banking System's alleged—and real—defects as far as an orderly monetary system is concerned.

Pre-occupation with the monetary deficiencies of the National Banking System has led many economic historians to the view that something was vitally wrong with postbellum banking arrangements, and that nothing short of the great reordering of these arrangements, such as that brought about by the creation of the Federal Reserve System in 1914, could solve the problems of American banking. Recurring financial panics (1873, 1884, 1893, 1907) under the National Banking System constitute the primary sources of evidence for this view. When the National Banking System was established it was thought that if the government provided a uniform currency, controlled in volume and made safe by the backing of United States government bonds, panics would no longer occur. Each of the antebellum financial panics had been marked by a rush on diverse state-chartered banks by holders of banknotes who wanted to convert their holdings into specie. The bond-backed currency of the National Banking System actually did do away with this manifestation of panics; after the Civil War the public did not exhibit doubts about the safety of national banknotes. The postbellum panics were instead marked by rushes of bank depositors to convert their deposits into currency, which included national banknotes and federal government issues as well as specie. The monetary deficiencies of both the antebellum and the postbellum banking systems were clearly ones which would have plagued any fractional reserve banking system that lacked some method of expanding its reserves when the public attempted to change the proportions of its money holdings between bank liabilities and the monetary base.

Even before the passage of the Federal Reserve Act this deficiency of the National Banking System had been in large measure corrected. The Aldrich-Vreeland Act of 1908 in effect allowed groups of national banks that were

2. See U.S. Bureau of the Census, *Historical Statistics of the United States—Colonial Times to 1957* (Washington, 1960), Series F-11 and F-13, p. 139.

threatened by panic runs to increase the quantity of national banknotes to meet depositor demands. A tax on such issues guaranteed that they would be retired once an emergency had passed. On the one occasion when the Act's provisions came into play—in 1914, when World War I broke out and a financial crisis threatened the nation—the Aldrich-Vreeland Act prevented panic liquidation and bank suspensions of cash payments. The Act expired in 1915, and its functions were taken over by the Federal Reserve Banks. Because the Act was designed to stem panics only after they had broken out, it could not prevent them, and for that reason it was an imperfect substitute for a full-fledged central bank. Had it been coupled with a national insurance scheme for bank deposits, however, the Act might have done much to prevent the major cause of panics, namely, the depositors' uneasiness about convertibility of notes, as well as the panics' worst results. In retrospect, the monetary deficiencies of the National Banking System seem to have been well on their way toward being repaired before the creation of the Federal Reserve System.[3]

There remains the question of whether the panics that occurred under the National Banking System actually did much harm to the American economy. Implicit in the views of the system's critics is the notion that the recurring financial crises did in fact promote lasting economic damage. Increasing quantitative knowledge of the economy's performance during this period makes such notions at the least doubtful. The period witnessed some of the highest rates of long-term real economic growth in American history. According to one recent survey of American growth between 1839 and 1959, during the period from 1869 to 1899 the rate of increase of real output per head "at 2.2 per cent per year was the highest one observed during any period of 30 years' or more duration."[4] Nor do we find any lasting effects of financial panics when we consider shorter term movements of industrial production. Selecting well-defined peaks separated by 8 to 11 years (which correspond, roughly, to the peaks of so-called "Juglar cycles," a term popularized by Schumpeter) from Edwin Frickey's index of manufacturing production for 1860–1914, we have computed the continuously compounded peak-to-peak rates of growth shown in Table VIII.1. The over-all rate for 1864–1913 is 4.9 per cent per year, and the data indicate that secular industrial expansion was rather steady in these years. Moreover, the long-term rate of industrial growth was almost certainly the highest of any major industrial

3. An excellent summary of the monetary aspects of the National Banking System is Phillip Cagan's essay, "The First Fifty Years of the National Banking System—An Historical Appraisal," in Deane Carson (ed.), *Banking and Monetary Studies* (Homewood, Illinois, Inc., 1963), pp. 15–42.

4. Raymond W. Goldsmith, "Long Period Growth in Income and Product, 1839–1960," in Ralph Andreano, ed., *New Views on American Economic Development* (Cambridge, Mass., 1965), p. 346.

TABLE VIII.1

Peak-to-peak Rates of Growth of Manufacturing Production
in the United States, 1864–1913

	% per year
1864–1872	6.8
1872–1883	4.3
1883–1892	5.1
1892–1902	4.7
1902–1913	4.3

Source: Computed from Edwin Frickey's index, given in U.S. Bureau of the Census, *Historical Statistics of the United States—Colonial Times to 1957* (Washington, 1960), Series P-13, p. 409.

nation. Even in Germany, the only large country whose industrial development was at all comparable with that of the United States in this period, industrial output declined relative to that of the United States, though its decline was minor when compared with that of Great Britain.[5]

This evidence hardly supports the contention that America's banking arrangements between the Civil War and World War I prevented rapid and sustained industrial progress. But whether those arrangements made a positive contribution to industrial development is a very different question. Even today, when the dimensions of the American achievement in these years are more widely understood, there is still a common view among economic historians that the role of banking in the process was at best passive or permissive.[6]

In the following pages I will subject this view to critical scrutiny. In the next section I will take up the antebellum banking background, the reforms embodied in the Civil War Bank Acts, and their effects on later banking developments. I will then deal with the relations between banking developments, conditions of industrial finance, and trends in industrial development in the period. Finally, I will view the results of the analysis in the framework of comparative economic history, in order to cast some light on the question of how the American experience compares with the banking history of other countries and the contribution of banking to industrialization in those countries.

5. German manufacturing output in 1870 was 57 per cent of that of the U.S.; in 1913 it was 44 per cent. Over the same period the U.K.'s manufacturing output in relation to the U.S.'s fell from 137 per cent to 39 per cent. These percentages are implied by the already cited data on national shares of world manufacturing output from League of Nations, *Industrialization and Foreign Trade*.

6. See, for example, Cameron *et al.*, *Banking*, p. 304.

CIVIL WAR BANKING REFORM: THE NATIONAL BANKING SYSTEM

The significance of the banking reforms of the Civil War era for later American industrialization lay in two basic changes the reforms brought about in the American financial system. The first was the restrictive impact that war-engendered banking laws had on American banking development for the remainder of the nineteenth century. The reforms raised barriers to entry into banking, and these had a differential geographical impact which, when coupled with the increased mobility the National Banking System gave to interbank transfers of funds, worked very much to the advantage of industrial finance. The second change was the tying of national bank organizations and note-issuing operations to the financial policies of the federal government, through the requirement that all national banks invest a portion of their capital in United States government bonds which then could serve as backing for note issues. The first change made the National Banking System a channel through which funds from all over the country were made available to the central money markets where leading industries obtained finance, while the latter change made the national banks into an important accessory of federal budgetary policies that performed a similar fund-concentrating function.

Long-term Banking Trends

Of the American industries that had reached a comparable level of development by the middle of the nineteenth century, few if any matched banking's growth over the next six decades. As the data of Table VIII.2 indicate, between 1850 and 1910 the number of commercial banking enterprises increased some 20 times, while deposits increased about 45 times. Over the same period the population increased about 4 times and GNP, in either current or 1860 prices, about 10 times.[7]

The classification of bank numbers into national, state, and private (i.e. unincorporated) categories in Table VIII.2 emphasizes this important aspect of banking's institutional structure. Another structural characteristic—geographical differences in the distribution of banks, bank deposits, and bank capital both *in toto* and by organizational categories—will be considered below. In each case, however, variations in structural characteristics, both geographically and over time, indicate that no simple or general explanation

---

7. Bureau of the Census, *Historical Statistics*, Series A-2, p. 7; Robert Gallman, "Gross National Product in the United States, 1834–1909," in National Bureau of Economic Research, *Output, Employment, and Productivity in the United States after 1800*, Studies in Income and Wealth, Vol. 30 (New York, 1966), Table A-1, p. 26.

of banking development in the period is possible. Any realistic account must examine the underlying causes of structural changes.

Of all the elements of market structure usually studied by economists the ones most relevant to nineteenth-century American banking are barriers to entry. This is so partly because in banking markets structural elements such as concentration and product differentiation were of limited importance on a national scale, but mostly it is because the legislatures, both state and national, raised barriers to entry. It is not surprising that entry into banking should have been more regulated by law than entry into other industries; this is true nearly everywhere. What is surprising is the extent to which a few trends in banking legislation and specific regulations can account for many of the changes in banking growth and structure in the period in question.

The earliest regulations of any importance were state chartering laws, which permitted free banking, banking only under special charters, or no incorporated banking at all. In the two decades before the Civil War the trend toward free banking laws and away from laws of the other two types was dominant, and both the state-chartered and unincorporated sectors of the banking system grew rapidly. In contrast, the 1863 and 1864 national banking laws, which were nominally free banking measures, contained provisions that, in practice, seriously hindered the responsiveness of the banks to trends in the larger economy. These provisions encompassed national banknote issue restrictions, capital requirements, and types of loans allowed. Nonetheless, the impact of these provisions would not have been nearly as restrictive as it in fact turned out to be had it not been for another federal law, effective in 1866, which made it virtually impossible for state banks to issue banknotes. In some parts of the United States this prohibition had scarcely any effect at all, but in others it was much more restrictive. Since we are dealing in part with a custom, it is difficult to say why, on economic grounds, the note-issue privilege was so important, but it evidently was. In places where people preferred to use currency rather than checks, freedom of issue was often a condition of bank profitability and therefore of bank entry. One result of the restrictions the federal government placed on national banking, and, *de facto*, on state-chartered banking, was that between the Civil War and the early twentieth century the most common type of American bank was the private, unincorporated one that operated under no charter at all.[8]

A convenient way of obtaining a summary measure of the differential geographical impact of the entry barriers that arose out of the national

8. See George E. Barnett, *State Banks and Trust Companies Since the Passage of the National-Bank Act* (Washington, 1911), Tables I and II following p. 248 and Table III following p. 250.

TABLE VIII.2

Number and Deposits of Commercial Banks in the United States, 1850–1910

Year	National	State	Private	Total number	Deposits[a] ($ millions)
1850	—	830	398[b]	1,228	273[c]
1860	—	1,579	1,108	2,687	541[c]
1870	1,612	261	1,903	3,776	925
1880	2,076	1,051	2,318	5,445	1,431
1890	3,484	2,830	4,365	10,679	3,126
1900	3,731	8,696		12,427	5,432
1910	7,138	17,376		24,514	12,286

[a] Excludes interbank and U.S. Treasury deposits.
[b] Estimate for 1853.
[c] Includes note issues of state banks and, for 1850, deposits of private banks as estimated for 1853.

Source: Data are based on the writer's estimations and aggregations from official and unofficial sources, described fully in his unpublished doctoral dissertation, "The American Capital Market, 1846–1914," (Harvard University, 1968), Appendix A. Official sources of underlying data include the following Federal documents: *Report of the Secretary of the Treasury on the Condition of Banks* (House Executive Document series) for 1850 and 1860; *Report of the Commission of Internal Revenue* for 1870; *Annual Report of the Comptroller of the Currency* for 1870, 1880, and 1890; *All Bank Statistics, United States 1896–1955* (Washington: Board of Governors of the Federal Reserve System, 1959) for 1900 and 1910. Unofficial sources include *Banker's Almanac* (New York, 1851) and its later editions: *Merchants' and Bankers' Register* (1860), *Merchants' and Bankers' Almanac* (1870), *Bankers' Almanac* (1880), *Bankers' Almanac and Register* (1890), as well as David I. Fand, "Estimates of Deposits and Vault Cash in the Non-National Banks in the Post Civil War Period in the United States: 1876–1896" (Ph.D. thesis: University of Chicago, 1954).

banking laws is to divide the United States into regions[9] and then ask what percentage of total bank deposits would have had to have been redistributed at given dates in order to make each region's percentage share of deposits equal to its share of population. This can be done by calculating for each region its percentage share of deposits and its percentage share of population, then subtracting the latter from the former, and finally adding up the positive (or negative, since they would be equal to the positive)

9. The six regions selected are: I. New England (Maine, New Hampshire, Vermont, Massachusetts, Rhode Island, and Connecticut); II. Middle Atlantic (New York, New Jersey, Pennsylvania, Delaware, Maryland, and the District of Columbia); III. South (Virginia, West Virginia, North Carolina, South Carolina, Georgia, Florida, Alabama, Mississippi, Kentucky, Tennessee, Arkansas, Louisiana, Texas, and Oklahoma); IV. East North Central (Ohio, Indiana, Illinois, Michigan, and Wisconsin); V. West North Central (Minnesota, Iowa, Missouri, Kansas, Nebraska, South Dakota, and North Dakota); and VI. Mountain-Pacific (Montana, Wyoming, Colorado, New Mexico, Arizona, Utah, Nevada, Idaho, Washington, Oregon, and California).

differences. Table VIII.3 presents the results for decade years from 1850 to 1910.[10]

For 1850 and 1860 the percentages of total deposits that would have had to have been redistributed among the six regions in order to equate regional shares with shares of population are 20.2 and 18.3, respectively. The decline in the percentage indicates that in the 1850's the banking structure was responding to the geographic distribution of population and to shifts therein, and presumably, therefore, to the distribution of demand for banking services. A regional distribution of bank funds equal to the distribution of population is not necessarily indicative of an optimal banking structure, but with regions as large as the ones dealt with here a movement toward greater equality probably does imply that the banking system was responding to the geographical distribution of demand. As a matter of fact, in four of the six decades between 1850 and 1910, there was a movement in this direction, as Table VIII.3 shows, and in one of the two contrary cases (the 1890's) there was almost no change. In spite of this, however, the Civil War decade so

TABLE VIII.3

Equalizing Redistribution of Total U.S. Commercial Bank Deposits*

Year	%
1850	20.2
1860	18.3
1870	40.3
1880	33.8
1890	25.5
1900	25.6
1910	19.5

* For 1850 and 1860, deposits plus note circulation. The data show, for each date, the percentage of total deposits that would have to be redistributed among regions to make each region's percentage equal to its percentage of the total population.

Source: The underlying deposit (and circulation) shares for each region were calculated from data in the sources cited for Table VIII.2; regional population shares calculated from U.S. Bureau of the Census, *Historical Statistics of the United States* (Washington, 1960), Series A 123–180, pp. 12–13. The method of deriving the percentages given in the table is described in the text.

greatly reversed the long-term trend toward greater regional equality that to achieve equality with population distribution in the six regions a larger

10. For 1850 and 1860, the calculation includes deposits and note circulation, while for later dates only deposits. After the Civil War, bank note circulation was almost entirely in the form of national bank notes which were, in effect, liabilities of the federal government rather than of the issuing banks.

percentage of bank deposits would have had to have been redistributed in 1910 than in 1860.

The National Banking System and Entry Barriers

As noted, the one decade of great movement away from equality of deposit distribution with population was the 1860's. In large measure the collapse of banking in the South was responsible for this. In 1860, the South had 32.6 per cent of the country's population and 28.6 per cent of its deposits (including note circulation); in 1870 it had 29.2 per cent of the population and 5.8 per cent of its deposits. But the differences between deposit shares and population shares also increased in both the East North Central and the West North Central regions between 1860 and 1870. The East North Central region would have required a transfer of 8.3 per cent of deposits and circulation in 1860 and 11.8 per cent of deposits in 1870 to equalize its deposit and population shares, while the West North Central region would have required 3.5 per cent in 1860 and 5.1 per cent in 1870.[11] The South was thus the major region, but not the only one, that suffered from the effects of the Civil War on banking.

Two questions are suggested by Table VIII.3. Why did the large shift toward greater regional inequality in the distribution of deposits relative to population occur in the 1860's? And why did the movement back toward the much lower degree of regional inequality of 1860 (and even 1850) take some four decades? The answers to both questions hinge on the banking policies of the federal government.

The federal banking laws of 1863–65 had two major goals, one short-term and the other long-term. The short-term goal of the National Currency Acts of 1863 and 1864 (the latter of which amended the former) was to increase the government's ability to obtain war finance by creating a system of federally chartered banks which could issue notes only by buying federal bonds. The long-term goal was to provide a uniform national currency to replace the great variety of issues made by state banks. A subsidiary goal was the elimination of state banks altogether.[12]

Initially it was thought that all three goals would be achieved simply by the conversion of state banks to nationally chartered banks. When this did not occur, the Congress, in 1865, decided to speed up the process by placing a 10 per cent tax on the amount of state banknotes paid out by any bank. This effectively prohibited such issues, and many state banks soon joined the National System.

11. These calculations have been made from the data underlying Table VIII.3.
12. Statements to this effect were made by Senator John Sherman, sponsor of the National Currency Act of 1863. See Bray Hammond, *Banks and Politics in America, from the Revolution to the Civil War* (Princeton, 1957), pp. 725, 733.

The National Currency Acts of 1863 and 1864 were modeled on the successful New York free banking law of 1838, but in several respects they were far from being free banking laws. Most importantly, there were restrictions, effective until repealed in 1875, on the total amount of national banknote issues to be allowed. (We shall return to this later when we consider the early implementation of the laws.) Other restrictive features, particularly of the 1864 law, which lasted far longer dealt with bank capital requirements and the nature of allowable mortgage loans.

The 1864 law required that a national bank's minimum capital stock be $50,000 in cities under 6,000 in population, $100,000 in cities of from 6,000 to 50,000 in population, and $200,000 in cities with over 50,000 in population. In the late nineteenth century, as population was shifting westward and many new towns were established, these high capital requirements severely restricted the spread of national banking.

The other barrier to national bank entry erected by the Civil War laws was the prohibition of mortgage loans. This prohibition, which remained in effect for over fifty years, naturally had its greatest impact on national bank entry in the predominantly agricultural sections of the country, where most people held land as their major asset. This particular barrier, along with restrictive capital requirements, which were in effect until public outcry forced a change in 1900,[13] directly stimulated the later recovery of state banking in agricultural areas, even though the authors of the Currency Acts had intended to abolish such banks. It also promoted a host of other substitutes, such as mortgage and trust companies, which sometimes shared the same rooms and managements as the national banks.

The restrictive capital requirements and the prohibition of mortgage loans help to explain why in 1900, almost four decades after the national banking laws were passed, the great majority of national banks were concentrated in an area comprising three regions east of the Mississippi and north of the Ohio. As the data in Table VIII.4 show, in 1900 more than 2,300 national banks were in this area, which then contained about one-seventh of the country's territory, while fewer than 1,400 banks were outside of it. In contrast, about five-eighths of the 8,696 non-national banks were in the area consisting of the three Southern and Western regions (see Table VIII.5). It is also significant that in 1900 the country's population was almost evenly divided between the northeastern and southwestern areas. Obviously, the National System was ill-suited to the character of banking needs generated by

13. The Gold Standard Act of March 14, 1900, amended previous legislation to allow the formation of national banks with minimum capitals of $25,000 in towns whose population did not exceed 3,000. In the following decade over 4,600 new national banks were organized and nearly two-thirds of these with capitals less than $50,000, the pre-1900 minimum. See the *Report of the Comptroller of the Currency, 1910*, p. 20.

westward movement. But the restrictive impact was by no means confined to
this aspect of the country's development, for by 1900 the deposits in the non-
national banks were greater than the deposits in the banks of the National

TABLE VIII.4

Regional Distribution of National Banks, 1870–1900
(number of banks)

Region	Year			
	1870	1880	1890	1900
New England	491	548	583	563
Middle Atlantic	589	654	843	1,001
East North Central	353	508	703	777
South	85	177	497	612
West North Central	87	153	630	578
Mountain-Pacific	7	36	228	200
Total	1,612	2,076	3,484	3,731

Source: United States Treasury Department, Comptroller of the Currency, *Annual Report of the Comptroller of the Currency* (Washington, D.C.), for the given years.

TABLE VIII.5

Regional Distribution of Non-National Commercial Banks, 1870–1900
(number of banks)

Region	Year			
	1870	1880	1890	1900
New England	117	114	211	135
Middle Atlantic	600	735	1,021	892
East North Central	629	1,050	1,595	2,283
South	369	498	1,068	1,675
West North Central	334	751	2,789	3,108
Mountain-Pacific	115	221	511	603
Total	2,164	3,369	7,195	8,696

Source: See Table VIII.2, p. 238.

System.[14] And this was the case in every region except New England. The National System, which originally had been intended to replace state and private banks, was declining in relative importance quite generally.

In 1870 and 1880, on the other hand, the banks of the National System far outstripped non-national banks in both capital and deposits. The sectional orientation of the National System in these years was even more pronounced than it was in 1900. In 1870, 1,433 of 1,612 national banks were in the three northeastern regions, and in 1880 this strong sectional difference was but little changed, with 1,710 of 2,076 national banks in the same northeastern area. Capital requirements and loan restrictions undoubtedly account for a part of the concentration of national banks in the more developed Northeast, where agriculture was of lesser relative importance. But the less extreme concentration of 1900, when capital requirements had just been relaxed and the mortgage loan prohibition was still in effect, suggests that these barriers to entry are not the only explanation. Nor can the relatively slow recovery of non-national banking, especially its state-chartered component, be explained by these factors, which, if anything, should have led to the opposite result.

Two additional types of entry barriers appear to account for these aspects of banking development. One is related to the National Currency Laws' provision of ceilings on the total allowable note circulation of national banks—antithetical, of course, to the idea of free banking—and to the early administration of that provision, especially after the privilege of note issue was effectively taken away from state banks. The entry barriers erected by the note issue ceilings of the early history of the national banking led to the System's extreme concentration and have been discussed at length in the literature relating to that history; hence, we shall deal with them but briefly. On the other hand, barriers which impeded the recovery of non-national banking, especially at a time when there was such a great need for it *because* of the restrictions embodied in the National Banking System, have not been so widely discussed, and we will, therefore, go into them in more detail. They, too, were related to the problem of note issue.

The problem created by the limitation of national banknote circulation to $300 million became critical in 1865, after the prohibitive 10 per cent tax was placed on state banknotes, and the state banks rushed to join the National System. Despite a provision of the 1863 Currency Act which called for apportionment of note circulation according to population and economic activity, when the rush came the existing state banks were accommodated with note circulation on a first-come, first-served basis. Thus, by October 1,

14. Data on the regional distribution of bank deposits are given in the writer's unpublished Ph.D. thesis, "The American Capital Market, 1846–1914" (Harvard University, 1968), Appendix A.

1866, when most state banks had converted to national charters and $280 million of the allowable $300 circulation had been issued, the national banks in the New England, Middle Atlantic, and East North Central regions had received $262 million of the total.[15] There were 1,642 national banks at that date, and their numbers remained at about the same level for more than four years.[16] The importance of the note-issue privilege as a condition of bank entry at the time could not be clearer. New national banks could still be formed to engage in every type of allowable banking business except note issuing, but in the absence of note circulation privileges very few new banks were in fact established.

In 1870, an additional $54 million of note circulation was authorized, and preference in its allocation was given to banks in states and territories which had received less than their fair share under earlier legislation. The number of national banks and their circulation began to increase immediately.[17] The Resumption Act of 1875 eliminated all restrictions on the amount of circulation, thus restoring the essential idea of free banking, but by this time freedom of note issue under the national banking laws was a dead letter, because prices of United States government bonds had risen well above par, while national banknotes could be issued only up to 90 per cent of the par value of such bonds. Note circulation thus became unprofitable.

What restrictions on note circulation accomplished was the erection of barriers to national bank entry in places where high capital requirements and loan restrictions would otherwise not have proven prohibitive, and of further barriers in areas where these other restrictive provisions of the laws had already made entry difficult. Together, these barriers account for the extreme concentration of national banks in the northeastern part of the country in 1870 and the slow decline of this concentration between 1870 and 1900.

Since the National Banking System was so unsuited to the banking needs of large parts of the country, why did not the state banking systems respond rapidly to meet their needs? Table VIII.2 shows that as late as 1890 national banks still outnumbered state-chartered banks, and yet, in the decades following the Civil War, state banking laws were generally much less restrictive of entry than were the national laws. State bank capital requirements were lower, real estate loans were allowed, and regulation was either absent or not nearly as strict as the National System was.

The factor that appears to have been responsible for the slow recovery of state banking was the effective prohibition of state banknote issues by the 10 per cent federal tax enacted in 1865 on such issues. This assertion runs

15. Calculated from individual state data for the date cited, as given in *Report of the Comptroller of the Currency, 1913*, Table 62, pp. 343–77.
16. *Report of the Comptroller, 1913*, Table 61, pp. 310–13.
17. *Report of the Comptroller, 1913*, pp. 312 ff.

counter to the opinions of later economic historians, who usually state that by the time of the Civil War note issue was no longer an important banking function, having been superseded by deposit banking and check transfers. That such was not the case can be seen in Table VIII.6, which shows that note issue, while declining in importance relative to deposits in the 1850's, was by no means unimportant on the eve of the war. In every region note circulation was a significant fraction of banks' demand liabilities.

TABLE VIII.6

Note Circulation as a Percentage of Deposits Plus Circulation
of All Banks by Region, 1850 and 1860

Region	1850	1860
New England	64	50
Middle Atlantic	38	26
East North Central	51	36
South	60	54
West North Central	53	46
United States*	48	39

* Calculation includes deposits of Mountain-Pacific Region, where there were no banks of issue at either date.

Source: Calculated from data in the sources cited for Table VIII.2, p. 238.

Table VIII.6 also indicates that the importance of note issue varied considerably from region to region. It was most important in New England, the South, and the West North Central region, and least important in the Middle Atlantic and East North Central States. This sheds some light on the differential impact of the early administration of the national banking laws on these regions. The concentration of national banks and the circulation of their notes in the Northeast was especially favorable to New England, where state banks, relying heavily on the note-issue business, would have been seriously inconvenienced if, after the tax on these issues, they had not been able to put out more than $100 million of national banknotes. The South and the West North Central region were not so lucky; in 1866, when most of the $300 million of allowable circulation had been taken out, these two regions, with close to 40 per cent of the country's population, had been allotted only about $10 million.[18]

State banking was slow to provide a remedy for the deficiencies of national banking in the late nineteenth century largely because an important part of its

18. *Report of the Comptroller, 1913*, Table 62, pp. 343–77.

business, note issue, had been taken away. The habit of writing checks, which seems so simple today, was slow in coming to the rural districts of America in this period, and so, therefore, was pure deposit banking.

Entry Barriers and Bank Behavior

According to the above analysis, bank entry barriers erected with the establishment of the National Banking System had a differential geographical impact in the late nineteenth century. Because of the nature of the barriers and the early implementation of the banking laws, the South and West, where small rural communities predominated, were more affected by federal banking legislation than was the more developed Northeast. If bank entry barriers had the theoretically predicted effect of restricting competition, banks in the South and West should have found themselves operating in less competitive environments than Northeastern banks. Within any one region there should have existed similar differences in competitive environment between country banks and city banks.

Much evidence can be marshaled in favor of the hypothesis that entry barriers did restrict banking competition. A recent paper by Professor Lance Davis which is rich in relevant, regionally classified banking data indicates that in the late nineteenth century national banks in the Southern and Western parts of the United States did in fact charge higher loan interest rates than banks in the Northeast charged.[19] Moreover, country banks within each region charged higher loan rates than city banks. Differences in bank interest charges might, of course, reflect nothing more than differences in bank cost functions, and could, therefore, be unrelated to variations in banking competition. If this had been the case, the banks' *net* returns on earning assets would have been nearly equal between banks of one region and another and between city and country banks. But Professor Davis's data indicate that net returns had virtually the same regional and city–country variations that interest charges did.

More important as a test of the differential effects of entry barriers is the profit experience of country and city banks. For it is possible that in the late nineteenth century the country bankers found it necessary to set higher interest rates and realize greater net returns than the city bankers did in order to make the returns on capital invested in their banks equal to the returns on capital invested in the city banks. For example, because of the minimum capital requirements of national banks, banks formed in smaller communities might not have been able to attract as many dollars of deposits per dollar of equity capital as city banks could; in such circumstances country

19. Lance E. Davis, "The Investment Market, 1870–1914: The Evolution of a National Market," *Journal of Economic History*, 25 (September 1965), 355–99.

banks might have had to charge higher loan rates and earn greater net returns on earning assets merely to earn a rate of return on equity comparable to that earned by city banks. Profit on equity is thus the key consideration relevant to the question of bank entry. If, in addition to charging higher loan rates and earning higher net returns on earnings assets, the country banks earned higher rates of return on their equity capital, then it is evident that entry barriers prevented competition from carrying out its return-equalizing function at the margin.

This supposition is supported by the evidence of national bank net earnings as a percentage of capital plus surplus, given in Table VIII.7. In 33 of 41 region-year comparisons (e.g. New England in 1870) between 1870 and 1900, the country banks of any given region earned greater returns on equity than reserve-city banks in the same region. Bank competition apparently was more effective in the cities. Furthermore, as we move South and West through the regions in given years, profit rates in both reserve-cities and the countryside tend to rise from the levels prevalent in the Northeast, which confirms the regional impact of national bank entry barriers.

The argument that entry barriers associated with the National Banking System led to greater monopoly power for country banks in every region, as well as for all banks in the South and West in comparison with the banks in the Northeast, would appear to be firmly grounded in quantitative evidence. The argument does, however, run counter to a common view of the late nineteenth-century Populists, who saw the National System as a great monopoly and identified it with Eastern bankers—not surprisingly, for because of entry barriers a disproportionate number of national banks and bank assets were concentrated in the Northeast until the twentieth century. According to one observer of the period, the national banking laws were "conceived in infamy and . . . for no other purpose but to rob the many for the benefit of the few." [20] Similarly, in 1887, a North Carolina farm journal noted, "The banks have never done a better or more profitable business, and yet agriculture languishes." [21]

The association of agricultural credit problems with Eastern bankers was, however, a case of mistaken identity. The farmers did in fact pay higher interest rates than borrowers in Eastern cities paid, but this was because their own country bankers were in a position to engage in monopolistic practices. Eastern bankers, especially those in larger cities, were more competitive. The farmers were nonetheless on the right track in identifying a source of their difficulties in the National Banking System and its restriction of banking competition in the countryside.

20. Quoted by John D. Hicks, *The Populist Revolt: A History of the Farmers' Alliance and the People's Party* (Minneapolis, 1931), p. 92.
21. Hicks, *Populist Revolt*, p. 54.

TABLE VIII.7

Average Profit Rates[a] of Reserve-City (RC) and Non-Reserve-City (NRC) National Banks, by Region, 1870–1900

	New England		Middle Atlantic		East N. Central		South		West N. Central		Mountain-Pacific	
	RC	NRC	RC	NRC	RC	NRC	RC	NRC	RC	NRC	RC	NRC
1870	10.3	11.5	10.3	11.3	11.0	13.7	13.3	16.0	17.3	15.5	—	21.1
1875	7.9	9.1	8.7	8.9	12.0	11.4	8.4	9.5	6.4	11.6	17.9	20.1
1880	5.6	7.0	5.9	7.6	11.5	8.5	9.1	7.6	6.5	12.7	7.5	18.7
1885	3.0	5.3	5.9	7.2	7.4	8.1	6.3	9.5	7.3	11.7	5.3	14.3
1890	4.3	6.6	7.4	9.2	9.3	9.9	10.2	11.9	9.7	9.1	9.7	14.2
1895	3.1	4.6	6.0	6.6	6.8	6.4	3.9	7.1	1.9	4.4	8.4	3.4
1900	6.9	7.4	9.9	11.3	10.8	9.0	8.6	12.6	7.7	10.5	12.4	12.6

a Figures are sums of semi-annual unweighted averages of net earnings divided by capital and surplus of national banks in each state and reserve city for the two halves of each year.

Source: Calculated from U.S. Treasury Department, Comptroller of the Currency, *Annual Report of the Comptroller of the Currency* (Washington, D.C.), for the indicated years, except for 1870, where the data have been taken from the 1873 *Report*.

BANKING DEVELOPMENTS AND FUND CONCENTRATION

In the late nineteenth century the National Banking System created difficulties for the nation's farmers by its restrictions on the spread of banking,
but these were counterbalanced by the benefits that the system provided to
industries and commercial activities seeking finance. These benefits were in
part a result of the very restrictions embodied in bank entry barriers. They
were also a result of the accessory role the system and other financial intermediaries played in the federal government's postbellum fiscal and debt
policies.

The National Banking System and the Flow of Funds between Banks

Before the Civil War country bankers frequently deposited a portion of
their funds in the trade centers of their regions, and both country and city
bankers deposited funds in the leading trade centers of the whole country,
particularly in New York City. There were several reasons for this. In the
antebellum era imports were a larger fraction of GNP than they were in
later years, and because there was a flow of goods from the port cities to the
countryside, there had to be a flow of funds in the reverse direction. In
addition, since state banknotes tended to accumulate in the cities, country
banks found it convenient to maintain funds in the cities for redemption of
their notes in order to keep the notes at or near their par values. Finally,
bankers' balances in cities constituted reserves for the depositing banks, and
reserves in this form were especially advantageous to the banks because, as
the balances could be lent out in the cities, the city banker could afford to
pay interest on them. Reserves in the form of banker's balances, unlike cash
reserves in a bank's own vault, thus became earning assets as well as liquid
reserves.[22]

The reserve system enacted in the National Currency Act of 1864 institutionalized these informal antebellum relationships by setting up three classes
of national banks and establishing their reserve requirements. New York
was designated as the central reserve city of the country, and its national
banks were required to maintain lawful money reserves equal to 25 per cent
of their deposits and note circulation.[23] Eighteen other cities were designated
as reserve cities, which meant that, like New York, their banks could hold

22. Margaret G. Myers, *The New York Money Market, Origins and Development* (New
York, 1931), Ch. VI.

23. A. T. Huntington and Robert J. Mawhinney, compilers, *Laws of the United States
Concerning Money, Banking, and Loans, 1778–1909*, National Monetary Commission
publication (Washington, 1910), pp. 345–46. The later Act of June 20, 1874, repealed the
requirement that national banks hold reserves against note circulation. *Ibid.*, p. 418.

reserves of other national banks.[24] The reserve-city banks were also required to maintain 25 per cent reserves, but only half of this amount had to be held in lawful money. The other half could be held as deposits in New York banks. National banks outside of New York and the eighteen reserve cities were required to maintain 15 per cent reserves, of which three-fifths (i.e. 9 per cent) could be held as deposits in reserve cities, including New York.

In this manner the controversial and much criticized reserve pyramid of the National Banking System was established. Because the reserve system allowed several banks to count the same assets as their own reserves, the pyramid in fact was a legalized version of a practice followed by loosely managed antebellum state banks—they often transported a box of specie, or perhaps just a layer of specie atop a keg of nails, from one bank to another just ahead of the state bank examiners.[25] Without question, in the absence of a central bank which could act as a lender of last resort, this system accentuated the severity of post-Civil War money panics. When all the banks attempted to regain their reserve deposits in cash, the amount of cash in the reserve city's banks proved to be less than sufficient to meet these demands without a collapse of values in the security markets, where the bankers' balances had been lent.

The national bank reserve system did, on the other hand, perform a useful mobilizing function. By institutionalizing the flow of interbank deposits, it provided a formal, legally sanctioned mechanism by which funds not employed in one place could be used to meet demands for credit in other places. While the system had its monetary deficiencies, it also increased economic welfare by promoting a more efficient mobilization and allocation of loanable funds.

Under the National Banking System the reserve city banks continued to pay interest on bankers' balances deposited with them by other banks. This institutional practice, coupled with variations in banking competition resulting from the system's entry barriers, produced an important result. The less competitive country banks did not have to hold idle the excess loanable funds generated by monopolistic output restriction. Instead the country banks could send these excess funds off to the cities, where they earned interest and also served as reserves.

In practice, reserve requirements had little effect on the amounts of country bank funds sent off to the cities. Other than providing a minimum below which city balances could not fall, the requirements were more or less irrelevant. A chart in Margaret Myers's *The New York Money Market, Origins and Development*, demonstrates this very clearly. It shows that

24. During the next fifty years Chicago and St. Louis became central reserve cities, and the number of reserve cities increased to 47. See *Report of the Comptroller, 1913*, p. 282.

25. Hammond, *Banks and Politics*, p. 601.

throughout the late nineteenth century country national banks held city balances far in excess of reserve requirements. In reserve cities, where competition was keener, excess reserves were never as large in relation to required reserves as they were in the countryside. New York City banks generally stayed close to their minimum required reserves of 25 per cent in cash, the major exceptions occurring after financial panics.[26]

The magnitude of the country banks' excess reserve balances was in fact far greater than the difference between actual bankers' balances and the 9 per cent required (three-fifths of the total requirement of 15 per cent), because excess cash reserves offset required balances. Miss Myers's chart shows that the country banks always held excess cash in the period. To cite one extreme case, on October 1, 1878, the reserve required for $289.1 million of net deposits held by country national banks was $43.4 million, of which two-fifths had to be held in cash while the other three-fifths could be held in the form of reserve-city balances. But on that date the country banks held $39.1 million in cash and $11 million in a fund for the redemption of their banknotes which also counted toward reserve requirements, so that all of the $56 million the country banks had deposited in reserve-city banks on that date were excess reserves, which could have been recalled had the banks chosen to lend the funds at home.[27] That they did not do so indicates that the banks regarded their city balances as at least as profitable, after taking account of the relative risks involved, as local loans were. This situation was made possible by the lack of competition in country banking, which led to large excess reserves, and by the reserve-city bank practice of paying interest on bankers' balances, which meant that excess reserves could be transformed into earning assets.

The regional incidences of the effects of the bankers' balance transfer mechanism are given in Tables VIII.8, VIII.9, and VIII.10. Table VIII.8 shows the *net* amounts of balances due to country banks from other banks— we can be sure these are from city banks, since amounts due from and due to other country banks would disappear in the netting process—for decade years between 1870 and 1900. The data are given in absolute terms and as a percentage of country bank assets in each region, and, in order to minimize seasonal influences, they are averaged over the five call dates given for each year in the *Annual Report of the Comptroller of the Currency*. They are thus indicative of the average net amounts of funds the country banks transferred to the cities. The absolute amounts rise throughout, and the percentage figures are generally highest at the end of the period, in 1900. The regional effects caused by the differential impact of entry barriers on banking competition are apparent; the percentage of assets transferred out of the countryside rises as we move West. However, country banks in the Middle

26. Myers, *New York Money Market, Origins and Development*, p. 236.
27. Data from *Report of the Comptroller of the Currency, 1878*.

TABLE VIII.8

Bankers' Net Balances[a] of Non-Reserve-City National
Banks Due From Other Banks, 1870–1900
($ million)

Year	New England	Middle Atlantic	South	East N. Central	West N. Central	Mountain-Pacific
1870	16.4	17.4	2.3	8.8	2.6	0.6
1880	16.4	29.1	6.8	20.6	5.2	3.9
1890	17.3	35.5	14.1	26.5	12.4	11.3
1900	23.9	69.3	32.8	58.9	23.7	28.0

Balances Due from Other Banks as
Percentages of National Bank Assets[b] in Non-Reserve Cities

Year	New England	Middle Atlantic	South	East N. Central	West N. Central	Mountain-Pacific
1870	6.1	6.7	6.1	6.9	9.0	16.7
1880	5.0	9.4	7.6	10.0	8.7	15.4
1890	5.0	8.4	6.2	9.0	6.7	8.2
1900	5.8	11.2	10.1	13.5	10.9	18.3

[a] The dollar values for each region are the sum of "due from national banks," "due from state banks," and "due from reserve agents," less the sum of "due to national banks," "due to state banks," "due to trust companies," and "due to reserve agents," for each state, summed over the states in the region. In order to reduce seasonal influences, the items in quotation marks were averaged arithmetically over the five call dates reported for each year.

[b] Like the bankers' net balances figures, bank assets are annual averages calculated by taking the arithmetic mean of total assets reported at five call dates for each year.

Source: *Report of the Comptroller of the Currency* for each of the indicated years.

Atlantic and East North Central regions tended to transfer greater percentages of their funds to city banks than did banks in the adjoining South and West North Central regions, probably because there were more reserve cities, and hence more opportunities for sending off funds, in the former two regions.

Tables VIII.9 and VIII.10 show the amounts of funds received by the net recipients under the operation of the transfer mechanism, i.e. by reserve-city and central reserve-city banks. It is apparent that over time the city banks tended to receive an increasing proportion of their funds as net transfers from other banks. Non-national banks, it should be noted, played a role in these trends because they maintained net balances both in reserve cities and in country national banks in their own areas. Such balances counted as reserves in addition to earning interest. The state banks were thus joined to the national bank reserve system, forming another, less formal, layer at the bottom of the reserve pyramid. At the apex of the pyramid were the central reserve-city banks of New York, and later those of Chicago and St. Louis.

TABLE VIII.9

Bankers' Net Balances[a] of Reserve-City National Banks Due to Other Banks, 1870–1900
($ million)

Year	New England	Middle Atlantic	South	East N. Central	West N. Central	Mountain-Pacific
1870	4.4	0.5	−0.2	2.8	−0.2	—
1880	8.1	4.2	1.2	11.5	3.9	0.3
1890	11.7	5.5	2.9	4.1	8.2	0.5
1900	27.5	38.7	1.9	13.1	21.3	1.7

Balances Due to Other Banks as
Percentages of National Bank Assets in Reserve Cities

Year	New England	Middle Atlantic	South	East N. Central	West N. Central	Mountain-Pacific
1870	3.1	0.3	−2.6	4.2	1.0	—
1880	4.3	2.1	4.7	11.1	2.6	7.3
1890	5.4	2.0	6.9	3.9	13.4	6.3
1900	10.2	7.7	3.0	6.0	15.1	3.8

[a] See notes to Table VIII.8. Unlike the dollar amounts reported in Table VIII.8, the figures of this Table and Table VIII.10 are derived by subtracting the "due from . . ." items from the "due to . . ." items.

Source: *Report of the Comptroller of the Currency* for each of the indicated years.

By 1900, as Table VIII.10 shows, these banks received from one-quarter to one-third of their total assets as net transfers from other banks, i.e. after amounts due from other banks were deducted from the bankers' deposits they held.

The net amounts of funds transferred out of the countryside under the National Banking System were by no means inconsequential, whether we measure them in absolute values or as a percentage of assets. Assuming a typical loan-asset ratio of 0.5, country banks which transferred 5 to 10 per cent of their assets to the cities could have increased their local loans by 10 to 20 per cent if the funds had not been transferred. Not all of the funds, of course, could have been called back, for reserve requirements and the normal course of money flows would have continued to require the holding of some city balances. But observers of that period were well aware that the amounts of bankers' balances actually held were far in excess of these needs; to some they represented "funds not needed by business" in the countryside, while to others they were funds "taken away from legitimate business."[28] Questions

28. See B. H. Beckhart and James G. Smith, *The New York Money Market, Sources and Movements of Funds* (New York, 1932), p. 184.

TABLE VIII.10

Bankers' Net Balances[a] of Central Reserve-City
Banks Due to Other Banks, 1870–1900
($ million)

Year	New York	Chicago	St. Louis
1870	65.9		
1880	101.8		
1890	140.6	28.5	6.6
1900	339.3	60.0	21.2
	Balances Due to Other Banks as Percentages of National Bank Assets in Central Reserve Cities		
1870	16.4		
1880	22.1		
1890	27.1	22.3	16.9
1900	33.7	24.1	23.0

[a] See notes to Tables VIII.8 and VIII.9.

Source: *Report of the Comptroller of the Currency* for each of the indicated years.

of legitimacy aside, what these transfers represented was the movement of funds out of agriculture and into industrial and commercial activities.

The Banks and Government Financial Policies

Wartime borrowing had made the federal government the predominant factor in the American capital market, but this role did not end with the conclusion of the Civil War. It could not, because at the war's end the federal debt was nearly $3 billion and the Treasury contained less than $100 million in cash. A large part of the debt had to be funded and then refunded in the postwar years in order to make it manageable. These operations lasted some sixteen years. The weight of public opinion, furthermore, favored retiring the debt as rapidly as government revenues would allow.[29] While this was not new in American public debt policy, the sheer magnitude of the postwar debt and the enlarged sources of federal revenue created during the war and generally retained thereafter gave the popular feeling increased significance.

From the end of the Civil War until 1893, the federal budget was in surplus every year. The surpluses were used to reduce the interest-bearing national

29. Robert T. Patterson, *Federal Debt Management Policies, 1865–1879* (Durham, North Carolina, 1954), pp. 51–58.

debt, which fell from more than $2,300 million in 1866 to less than $600 million in 1892–93.[30] Two aspects of the government's policy served to make the real impact of these transfers of public revenues to private uses greater than these nominal values suggest. First, the government sold bonds during the Civil War for currency which had depreciated substantially in terms of gold, but after the war interest and principal payments on the debt were made in gold, which was appreciating in value as general price levels in terms of gold fell. Second, after 1887, when the Treasury had called all of its callable bonds, it continued the policy of debt retirement by purchasing its bonds on the open market at premiums well above par.[31]

Thus for more than a quarter-century following the Civil War, annual budget surpluses were fed by the Treasury into the capital market. In length of operation alone this was a classic example of a growth-inducing, tight fiscal, easy monetary policy favoring capital formation. Since government revenues were derived almost entirely from customs duties and internal excise taxes on alcoholic beverages and tobacco products which had a heavy incidence on consumption, it is almost certain that the policy transferred resources out of consumption and into investment.

The country's growing financial intermediaries, and particularly the national banks, played an important role in maximizing the beneficial effects of the government's debt-reduction policy on the borrowers' side of the capital market. National banks had to purchase government bonds both as a condition of their existence and in order to issue banknote currency. Other intermediaries demanded government bonds because, as liquid secondary reserves, they had a more attractive yield than cash, and because these bonds were prominent on the legal investment lists maintained by supervisory authorities. In both cases, substantial non-price incentives entered into the institutional component of the demand for government bonds.

The growing institutional demand for government bonds, coupled with the Treasury's policy of reducing the supply of those bonds, created a very strong upward pressure on bond prices. During the Civil War, when investors were uncertain about the government's credit, its bonds were sold at yields greater than 16 per cent in gold; by the late 1880's these yields had fallen to 2 to 2.5 per cent.[32] Non-institutional investors, therefore, were strongly induced to switch funds out of government bonds and into private securities. These substitutions operated to reduce the whole structure of asset yields and to improve the terms on which borrowers could tap the capital markets in late nineteenth-century America. In this process national banks and other

30. U.S. Bureau of the Census, *Historical Statistics*, Series Y-256, p. 711; Series Y-372, p. 721.

31. Joseph G. Martin, *A Century of Finance* (Boston, 1898), p. 180.

32. Edward Atkinson, *The Industrial Progress of the Nation* (New York, 1890), p. 74.

financial intermediaries were important accessories of federal debt policy, which resulted in the fostering of private capital formation, although this was largely unintentional.

FINANCIAL CONDITIONS AND INDUSTRIAL DEVELOPMENT

Through the channels above described, the National Banking System provided a very favorable financial climate for American industrialization after the Civil War. The operations of the national bank reserve system and of federal debt retirement, in both of which the banks were involved, served to gather funds from every part of the economy and to concentrate those funds in leading financial centers. Towering above other centers was the New York money market, where the balances of thousands of scattered banks found a continuing employment in call loans at the money post of the stock exchange. In this manner, funds nominally available for only the shortest of times helped to finance the long-term capital needs of industry and transportation.

The power of the growing capital market as an engine of economic development in its own right did not go unnoticed at the time. As one observer, describing and interpreting an episode hardly unique in the annals of post-bellum Wall Street, put it:

> The power to manufacture securities, and to make artificial prices for them, as an inevitable consequence led to the building of railroads without regard to public needs. In ordinary times, securities are offered to the end that railroads may be built. But in 1881, railroads were built to the end that securities might be offered. Thus, over-production of railroads resulted from the unnatural facilities for the manufacture of securities, and the prices of securities.[33]

This comment testifies to the ease with which long-term capital funds could be obtained in the late nineteenth century. Indeed, evidences of this ease are still present; in the New York bond market today the issues having the most favorable terms to the original borrowers date back to this period.[34]

The highly capital-intensive railroads, as major security issuers, were direct beneficiaries of postbellum financial conditions, but there can be little doubt that manufacturing industry also was favored. The movement of funds through the banking system from the countryside to the cities and from the

33. William M. Grosvenor, *American Securities* (New York, 1885), p. 226.
34. Examples are the West Shore Railroad 4 per cent bonds issued in 1885 and due in A.D. 2361, and the Northern Pacific Railway 3 per cent bonds issued in 1896 and due in A.D. 2047.

agricultural to the industrial areas points in this direction. Manufacturing activity was concentrated in urban areas of the northeastern part of the country, the primary recipients of interbank fund flows under the National Banking System. In terms of manufacturing value added, the states of the Middle Atlantic, East North Central, and New England regions, containing about one-seventh of the country's land area, accounted for 84 per cent of the national total in 1869, and 76 per cent in 1909.[35] With agriculture increasingly located outside of the Northeast, and yet returning funds to the industrial sector through the operation of the banking system, the stage was set for a dramatic reversal of the relative positions of the two sectors. In just fifteen years, between 1879 and 1894, the agricultural share in commodity output shrank from 49 to 32 per cent, while that of manufacturing grew from 37 to 53 per cent.[36]

Industrial development in the period was, however, more than just a case of simple expansion at relatively high rates. From about 1880 on there was a growing tendency for industrial enterprises to consolidate and integrate their operations, both vertically and horizontally.[37] The peak period of consolidation activity took place during the years around the turn of the century, when a number of giant industrial corporations were formed by merger. These mergers marked the birth of large-scale business enterprises, national in scope, that have dominated American industrial life in the twentieth century.

The reasons for this great merger movement have been the subject of vigorous debate among historians and economists. Ralph L. Nelson, the author of the most complete quantitative study of the merger wave, found, after testing a number of hypotheses, that the prior existence of a highly organized capital market capable of absorbing the multimillion dollar security issues generated by the consolidations provided the best explanation.[38] Non-financially oriented hypotheses concerning the stimulus toward consolidation, such as the assumption that industrial growth was retarded, or that a national market was formed through completion of the railroad

---

35. Calculated from data for individual states as presented by Richard A. Easterlin in Simon Kuznets, A. R. Miller, and R. A. Easterlin, *Population Redistribution and Economic Growth—United States 1870–1950*, Vol. II: *Analysis of Economic Change* (Philadelphia, 1960), Table A3.1, p. 125.

36. The underlying data are in terms of value added in 1879 prices. Robert Gallman, "Commodity Output, 1839–1899," in National Bureau of Economic Research, *Trends in the American Economy in the Nineteenth Century*, Studies in Income and Wealth, Vol. 24 (Princeton, 1960), Table 4, p. 26.

37. See Alfred D. Chandler, Jr., "The Beginnings of 'Big Business' in American Industry," *Business History Review*, 33 (Spring 1959), 1–31.

38. Ralph L. Nelson, *Merger Movements in American Industry, 1895–1956* (Princeton, 1959), especially Chap. 4.

network, proved insufficient when rigorously formulated and tested. Nelson's conclusion on the importance of the capital market in the great merger wave is obviously consistent with the arguments made here concerning financial conditions in the late nineteenth century.

The question left more or less open by Nelson's analysis of the merger movement around 1900 is whether a developed capital market was a cause of the consolidations, or whether it was an effect of them.[39] The fact that a concentration of bank funds in financial centers and the development of modern methods of marketing securities began much earlier than the process of consolidation supports the former view. The concentration of bank funds was one result of the National Banking System, while large-scale security marketing techniques received a powerful stimulus from government borrowing and debt management. Consequently, the development of an efficient capital market was more a result, or a legacy, of the Civil War than it was of the industrial merger movement. The fact that large-scale railroad financing took place between the Civil War and the wave of industrial mergers tends to strengthen this interpretation.

Thus, in the decades after the Civil War, American banking, with the National Banking System as its core, performed a great service to the industrial sector of the economy. The process of bank fund mobilization was a harsh one as far as the nation's farmers were concerned, for it resulted in part from constraints on the spread of banking in rural areas. Likewise, when the concentration of funds engendered by the National System's pyramiding of bank reserves compounded the ill effects of financial panics the result was general distress throughout the economy. But the history of modern economic growth is one of the declining relative importance of agriculture and the rising importance of industry; in the United States, banking developments merely hastened these trends. Furthermore, the effects of fund concentration on industrial investment during the years between the panics far outweighed the effects of the crises themselves in their historical significance, for the crises were short-term, while the fund concentration was long-term. If there was a defect in the postbellum American banking system it was not that it hindered long-term economic development, but that it promoted industrial investment and growth with a ruthless efficiency, restricting banking growth in some areas, economic as well as geographical, and producing banking advantages in other areas.

THE COMPARATIVE FRAMEWORK

The development of banking in America between 1863 and 1913 has a number of parallels with the development of banking in other countries. As

39. This question is explored by Ralph Andreano in Andreano, ed., *New Views on American Economic Development*, pp. 15–19.

is usually the case in historical developments separated in time and space, the parallels are far from exact, but they are similar enough to be worth commenting on here, even though we must recognize that their deviations from one another may eventually prove to be as illuminating as their similarities.

One feature of the postbellum American banking experience that appears to have been significant in other contexts is the importance of freedom of note issue as a condition of bank entry. One need not go so far as Fritz Redlich does when he states that "Conditions in the South and West were then still approximating those in Europe in medieval times when the available amount of a circulating medium had determined the borderlines of economic activity," and that banking in these areas ". . . was still identical with note issue as it once had been throughout the land," [40] in order to sense the entry problems that would-be bankers faced when there were no national bank-notes for them to issue and when they could not, because of a federal tax, make any profit by issuing their own. In actuality, the South and West were, in note issue, on a par with a good part of the world at that time.

For example, in a recent comparative study of banking systems of seven countries (the United States was not included), Cameron reported that, in nineteenth-century Scotland, "Freedom of issue was evidently a greater inducement to enter banking than the privilege of incorporation, for no new banks were set up in Scotland after 1845, when incorporation remained a simple matter of registry but new note issues were prohibited." Cameron concluded that:

> . . . for a country in which the banking system is but little developed, the right or privilege of note issue is one of the most effective means both of eliciting a rapid growth in the number of banks and of habituating the public to the utilization of financial intermediaries.[41]

Much of this is reminiscent of the rapid growth of state banking in the United States during the 1850's, when free banking was making its inroads, and the example of Scotland is paralleled by the slow growth of both national and state banking in America immediately after the Civil War. In the latter period, national bank entry was first limited by ceilings on total circulation when note issue was profitable, and then entry continued to be restricted after the ceilings were removed because of the rise of United States government bond prices, which reduced the profitability of issue. State bank entry was limited by the 10 per cent federal tax on state banknote issues, effective in 1866, which destroyed the profitability of this banking function.

40. Fritz Redlich, *The Molding of American Banking, Men and Ideas* (New York: Part I, 1947; Part II, 1951), Part II, p. 118.
41. Cameron *et al.*, *Banking*, pp. 293, 295.

Turning from the importance of note-issuing privileges as a condition of rapid banking growth in historical development (which is confirmed by the American experience) to the more general question of the role of banking in industrialization, it is useful to have a fairly comprehensive historical framework with which we may draw comparisons. Professor Gerschenkron's approach to European industrialization, which has been commented on elsewhere in this volume, is well suited for this purpose because of its emphasis on the sources of industrial finance.[42] Gerschenkron looks for banks to substitute for deficiencies in the "original" accumulation of liquid wealth in moderately backward economies. Germany's nineteenth-century industrialization furnishes the chief example. In advanced countries, such as England, Gerschenkron considers original accumulations and plowed back profits to be the prime sources of industrial finance, while in very backward countries, such as Russia in the 1880's and 1890's, he looks to the state to assume the dominant role in industrial finance that original accumulations or banks played in less backward countries.

Since Gerschenkron's approach is primarily concerned with sources of finance during the initial industrialization drives of various European countries, one would not expect its insights to be directly applicable to the United States after the Civil War. But his approach does venture to go beyond initial industrial upsurges in noting that, once these drives have been accomplished, the relative economic backwardness of the successful countries is reduced and techniques of industrial finance appropriate to less backward situations come into play. Thus, in Germany after 1900, industrial profits more and more assumed the role that bank funds had played in earlier decades, while in Russia at roughly the same time banks took up some of the industrial financing functions that had been performed earlier by the Ministry of Finance.

Does the American experience, as described above, appear to follow any of the European patterns delineated by Gerschenkron? The answer would seem to be that it does not, and yet there are certain parallels. In part the answer to such a question rests on the relative emphasis given to sources of finance. For example, even though original accumulations and plowed back profits may have played the major role in English industrial finance in the first industrial revolution, the part played by banks was by no means unimportant. As Pressnell notes in his study of English country banking between 1750 and 1844, elaborate systems of correspondent relationships that developed between country and London banks effected an efficient system of fund transfer from surplus areas, which were primarily rural, to deficit areas,

42. Alexander Gerschenkron, *Economic Backwardness in Historical Perspective* (Cambridge, Mass., 1962), especially Chap. 1, pp. 5–30, and Postscript, pp. 353–64.

which were primarily industrial.[43] In this manner, the connections of country bankers with the London money market helped to finance England's industrial revolution. There is an obvious parallel between this English development and the operation of the national bank reserve system in the United States after the Civil War. In this sense, the United States fits the English pattern, as a Gerschenkronian might expect, given the similar levels of economic advancement in the two countries.

But this does not exhaust the similarities between American and European financial developments. The manner in which American bankers of the late nineteenth century, who were stationed at the pivotal points where the banking system and the capital markets were connected, employed financial resources to rearrange the structure of American industry is paralleled, in Continental developments, by the entrepreneurial activities of German and German-style mixed banks. In addition, the behavior of post-Civil War American administrations and Congresses in subsidizing railroad building through land grants and bond issues, in aiding industries through tariff protection, and in channeling funds into the capital market through budget surpluses and debt retirement is similar in many ways to industrialization policies followed by late nineteenth-century Russian governments.

Why did these European patterns, virtually superimposed upon one another, emerge in the United States after the Civil War? Gerschenkron's explanations of the European patterns most certainly do not apply. In the first place, the near simultaneity of their appearance implies that innovations which increased the importance of banks and the government in American industrial finance cannot be regarded as substitutions dictated by an inability to rely on techniques appropriate to more advanced levels of development. The United States at the time of the Civil War could not be regarded as a relatively backward country in the Gerschenkronian sense. Furthermore, the United States was not at that time beginning to industrialize; it had already made notable industrial achievements. Why, then, was so much of English and Continental financial experience compressed into the postbellum period?

The answer that suggests itself to this writer is the impingement of overriding political considerations on the American financial system as a result of the Civil War. Gerschenkron's explanations of European financial patterns are economic in content, being organized around the idea of differing degrees of economic backwardness. But such economic explanations do not apply to the American experience. Postbellum tariff and debt policies were alike conditioned by the remnants of war finance rather than by economic backwardness. The financial power concentrated in the hands of a relatively small

---

43. L. S. Pressnell, *Country Banking in the Industrial Revolution* (Oxford, 1956).

number of late nineteenth-century bankers was also to a great extent the consequence of a wartime creation, the National Banking System. This concentration, according to J. P. Morgan and Company in 1913, was

> ... not due to the purposes and activities of men, but primarily to the operation of our antiquated banking system which automatically compels interior banks to "concentrate" in New York hundreds of millions of dollars of reserve funds. . . .[44]

While comparative analysis thus serves to bring out the diverse nature of postbellum American finance, it also assigns an important role to the banking system as a source of funds for the period's remarkable industrial development. Within a country already quite advanced industrially by the time of the Civil War, the National Banking System assumed functions that the Gerschenkronian approach would look for banking to take on in an economically more backward context. Undoubtedly, this was of major importance in making America's late nineteenth-century industrial growth resemble that of Germany more than it did that of England.

44. Cited by Redlich, *The Molding of American Banking*, Part II, p. 189.

Index